Praise for *More than Parcels*

"*More Than Parcels* brings together highly accomplished scholars to illuminate the neglected subject of humanitarian relief during the Holocaust. Through concise and valuable case studies, Láníček and Lambertz supply convincing evidence that sending relief into ghettos and camps was a form of rescue, involving many individuals, private organizations, and, occasionally, government agencies."

—Richard Breitman, Distinguished Professor Emeritus, American University, and author of *The Berlin Mission: The American Who Resisted Nazi Germany from Within*

"This collection, a first of its kind, explores the help that was possible as the Nazis ghettoized, incarcerated, and starved Jews. In painful detail, the essays also describe the myriad obstacles that prevented sufficient aid and the organizations, families, and individuals who mailed packages of food, sending love and solidarity."

—Marion Kaplan, author of *Hitler's Jewish Refugees: Hope and Anxiety in Portugal, 1940–1945*

"This is a remarkable collection of brilliantly researched and subtle chapters on the various forms of relief for the persecuted Jews during the Holocaust. Superbly organized and edited, this is the first sustained treatment of the subject providing a wide range of case studies that help to reinterpret well-known bodies such as the Red Cross and bring into focus little-known but important smaller organizations. While it is impossible to know how many Jewish lives were saved by food parcels, this book shows the huge effort that was put into such work by Jewish and non-Jewish organizations and individuals and that, on an emotional level, they made a huge difference to the victims."

—Tony Kushner, professor at The Parkes Institute, University of Southampton

"A fascinating book. Demonstrating considerable skill in navigating the archives, the contributors reveal the remarkable extent of aid to ghetto and concentration camp inmates. How these programs operated, why the Nazis permitted them, and what difference they made to the recipients are all investigated. This is a much-needed book, tackling issues that are often observed but rarely addressed by historians."

—Dan Stone, professor of modern history and
director of the Holocaust Research Institute at
Royal Holloway, University of London

"This is an excellent, innovative, and important collection that provides striking evidence of Jewish and non-Jewish humanitarian agency and communication across the Nazi empire—though even the most courageous and determined interventions could hope to alleviate the thrust of Nazi policies only on the margins."

—Mark Roseman, author of *Lives Reclaimed:
A Story of Rescue and Resistance in Nazi Germany*

MORE THAN PARCELS

MORE THAN PARCELS

Wartime Aid for Jews in Nazi-Era Camps and Ghettos

EDITED BY JAN LÁNÍČEK
AND JAN LAMBERTZ

WAYNE STATE UNIVERSITY PRESS
DETROIT

ISBN 978-0-8143-4922-9 (paperback)
ISBN 978-0-8143-4923-6 (hardcover)
ISBN 978-0-8143-4924-3 (e-book)

Library of Congress Control Number: 2021951023

On cover: A line of people at the entrance to the post office in the Łódź (Litzmannstadt) ghetto. Photo by Mendel Grosman, circa 1940–43. Courtesy of Beit Lohamei Haghetaot (Ghetto Fighters' House Museum).

Wayne State University Press rests on Waawiyaataanong, also referred to as Detroit, the ancestral and contemporary homeland of the Three Fires Confederacy. These sovereign lands were granted by the Ojibwe, Odawa, Potawatomi, and Wyandot Nations, in 1807, through the Treaty of Detroit. Wayne State University Press affirms Indigenous sovereignty and honors all tribes with a connection to Detroit. With our Native neighbors, the press works to advance educational equity and promote a better future for the earth and all people.

Wayne State University Press
Leonard N. Simons Building
4809 Woodward Avenue
Detroit, Michigan 48201-1309

Visit us online at wsupress.wayne.edu.

Contents

Abbreviations

ACICR	Archives du Comité international de la Croix-Rouge
ADPA	Archives départementales des Pyrénées-Atlantiques
AHEJ	Arbetsutskottet för hjälp åt Europas judar
AHPJ	Arbetsutskottet för hjälp åt Polens judar
AIPN	Archives of the Institute of National Remembrance in Kraków
AJDC	see JDC
AMDR	Archives of the Museum of Danish Resistance
AMZV	Archiv Ministerstva zahraničních věcí, Archives of the Czech Foreign Ministry
ARC	American Red Cross
CDA	Buying Cooperative, Coopérative d'achats
CDJC	Contemporary Jewish Documentation Center, Centre de documentation juive contemporaine
CENTOS	Central Office of the Union of Societies for the Care of Orphans and Abandoned Children, Centrala Związku Towarzystw Opieki nad Sierotami I Dziećmi Opuszczonymi
CH-BAR	Swiss Federal Archive
CKŻP	Central Committee of Jews in Poland, Centralny Komitet Żydów w Polsce
CWC	Polish Central Welfare Council, Polska Rada Główna Opiekuńcza
CZA	Central Zionist Archives
DNA	Danish National Archives
DRK	German Red Cross
FDRL	Franklin Delano Roosevelt Presidential Library and Museum
GKH	Ganzach Kiddush Hashem
HAFIP	Hilfsaktion für die notleidenden Juden in Polen
HIA	Hoover Institution Library & Archives
HKO	Help the Victims of War! (Hjälp Krigets Offer!)

ICRC	International Committee of the Red Cross
JDC, AJDC	Joint Distribution Committee, the Joint, American Jewish Joint Distribution Committee
JDK	Danish Jewish Museum
JFA	Judiska Församlingens Arkiv
JSS, ŻSS	Jewish Social Self-Help, Żydowska Samopomoc Społeczna, Jüdische Soziale Selbsthilfe
JUS	Jewish Aid Agency in the Generalgouvernement, Jüdische Unterstützungsstelle für das Generalgouvernement, Kraków
LMA	London Metropolitan Archives
LOC	Library of Congress Manuscript Division
MEW	British Ministry of Economic Warfare
MFA	Czechoslovak Ministry of Foreign Affairs
MSW	Czechoslovak Ministry of Social Welfare
MSZ	Polish Ministry of Foreign Affairs
NARA	U.S. National Archives and Records Administration, College Park, MD
NKVD	People's Commissariat for Internal Affairs (Soviet internal security forces)
NL	*Nachlass* (estate of)
NRO	Main Welfare Council, Naczelna Rada Opiekuńcza
NSDAP	Nazi Party, Nationsozialistische Deutsche Arbeiter-Partei
ORT	Organization for Rehabilitation and Training, Organisation Reconstruction Travail
OSE	Children's Relief Organization, Œuvre de secours aux enfants
PWRB	Papers of the War Refugee Board
RA	Riksarkivet Arninge
RELICO	Relief Committee for the War-Stricken Jewish Population
RGO	Central Welfare Council, Rada Główna Opiekuńcza
RKKS	German occupation currency, Reichskreditkassenscheine
RPŻ	Council for Aid to Jews, Rada Pomocy Żydom, code name Żegota
SM	Saly Mayer collection
SS	Nazi "protective squadron," Schutzstaffel
TOZ	Society for the Protection of Jewish Health in Poland, Towarzystwo Ochrony Zdrowia Ludności Żydowskiej w Polsce
USHMM	United States Holocaust Memorial Museum
VHA	Visual History Archive, University of Southern California Shoah Foundation

VSIA	Association of Jewish Swiss Welfare Services, Verband Schweizer Israelitischer Armenpflege
WILPF	Women's International League for Peace and Freedom
WJC	World Jewish Congress
WRB	War Refugee Board
YIVO	YIVO Institute for Jewish Research
YUA	Yeshiva University Archives
YVA	Yad Vashem Archives
ŻIH	Żydowski Instytut Historyczny, Warsaw, Jewish Historical Institute
ŻKK	Żydowski Komitet Koordynacyjny, Jewish Coordinating Commission

INTRODUCTION

Relief Parcels in an Era of Nazi Camps and Ghettos

JAN LAMBERTZ

Religious communities, philanthropic and state agencies, relatives, friends, and strangers shipped a stream of relief aid to Jews trapped in Nazi-era camps and ghettos for most of World War II. Remittances of cash and shipments of medicine, clothing, and particularly food parcels played a critical role during the war in maintaining morale and prolonging life for Jews in all corners of the Nazi empire. Recent histories of wartime rescue have marginalized these relief efforts, instead focusing on a handful of activists who hid Jews or led them to safety under perilous conditions, or on the small pool of courageous individuals who worked to secure the release of camp prisoners and precious visas for refugees. These acts were indisputably important. Yet the parallel story of relief shipments is no less important. References to and requests for food parcels permeate wartime correspondence sent from inside Nazi detention sites. Typical was the March 1941 postcard that a Chicago family received from their relatives in the Warsaw ghetto: "We are healthy but we have no means of support. Try to send bigger packages. . . . Send us packages so that we can somehow survive."[1] *More than Parcels: Wartime Aid for Jews in Nazi-Era Camps and Ghettos* brings together insights from a group of historians with wide-ranging expertise on the Nazi-era detention system and its victims, international humanitarian work, and the Holocaust. Drawing on case studies from Europe and beyond, our volume maps out the broad array of parcel relief schemes organized by

---

The views expressed here are my own and do not necessarily reflect those of the United States Holocaust Memorial Museum.

and for Jews during the Holocaust and assesses their impact. It details the aid efforts underwritten not only by the International Red Cross and major Jewish groups but also by thousands upon thousands of individuals on both sides of the Atlantic and deep in the Soviet interior.[2]

The chapters in *More than Parcels* shift the focus away from the gas chambers and "death by bullets"—mass shootings in the forests of eastern Europe—and back to the story of the deliberate, systematic starvation of Jewish civilians confined to Nazi-era ghettos and camps.[3] As Laurie A. Drake, one of the authors in this book, succinctly concludes, "Hunger defined daily life for internees." And in the words of a 1943 publication of the Institute of Jewish Affairs in New York, those targeted by Germany for extermination were receiving rations "which are but death by another name."[4] This volume restores a focus on world awareness of mass killing by starvation under the Nazis and the measures mobilized to prevent it, giving a central place to the hundreds of thousands of food parcels that were shipped to Jewish prisoners in occupied Poland, France, Czechoslovakia, and elsewhere for much of the war. The modest relief parcel, often weighing no more than three or four pounds, could extend the lives and health of prisoners for at least a time. For Jews all over occupied Europe, the "parcel economy" simultaneously provided critical emotional sustenance in the face of grief and peril.

Each of the chapters identifies a long chain of obstacles that tripped up these operations. As Gerald J. Steinacher reminds us in his contribution, the Geneva Conventions applied only to soldiers and POWs. Expansion of such legal protection had in fact been discussed in the decade before the war, and the German government did extend special status to some civilian prisoners from enemy countries. Jews were excluded from such protection and from International Committee of the Red Cross (ICRC) aid for most of the war. Far more intensely than for parcels shipped to POWs in German hands, uncertainty shadowed every stage of organizing relief parcels for Jews trapped in Europe, be it for small individual dispatches or mass shipments. The risk assessments made by their organizers thus varied considerably, often relying on the most fragmentary information on ghettos and camps imaginable. Taken together, we find no overarching timeline that applied equally to all the food parcel projects described here. The authors demonstrate that while these aid shipments remained uneven and were often held up for long months, diverted, or stolen, they continued to be delivered in some form, on some scale, throughout the war. Every shift in war conditions, combatants, and government and border policies demanded new calculations of risks and the restructuring of programs. Even before shipments were assembled, aid activists and volunteers needed to constantly monitor changing export licenses and currency regulations and the perpetually fluctuating availability of foodstuffs, be they from Yugoslavia, Romania, Turkey, Sweden, or Portugal. Even without the limits imposed by the Allied blockade of most of Europe (which permitted only a few humanitarian exemptions), Allied governments proved to be difficult, often intransigent partners for relief initiatives, imposing rigid demands. Once dispatched, the parcels faced new enemies, including the bombing of warehouses and transport routes, delays of many months, spoilage, and poor packing materials. The policies of and pilfering by German and Nazi-allied officials and personnel could further disrupt the parcels' journey to Jewish communities and detention sites. Monitoring the arrival and distribution of the packages on the ground in Europe remained almost impossible, even where trustworthy couriers and partners existed. Aid workers in Allied or neutral countries found themselves in a ghastly bind, caught between the need for discretion, even secrecy, and the need to seek further donors and publicity for their small victories. And as Jan Láníček concludes in his chapter, Allied governments would never have approved parcel shipments had they believed that most of Europe's Jews were no longer alive.

Occupation officials permitted the sending of food parcels into some of the major ghettos until at least early 1941, but then largely halted such shipments into sites such as the Łódź ghetto (even though remittances of money continued on some scale).[5] At the same time, ever more ghettos in occupied Poland were dissolved, with mass deportations of their inhabitants to killing centers. The entry of the United States into the war and the tightening of the Allied blockade during 1941 greatly decreased the flow of civilian relief parcels into Europe as well, with the American Jewish Joint Distribution Committee (JDC), the World Jewish Congress (WJC), and other mainstream aid agencies for the most part complying with limits imposed by British and American authorities. But the flow of packages did not stop entirely; relief organizers such as Abraham Silberschein in Switzerland and his connections in Portugal continued to send food, albeit in smaller quantities. The changing tides of the war and increasing public knowledge outside Europe about the mass killing of Europe's Jewish population may have contributed to further shifts in this picture. The willingness of Allied officials to make exceptions and of Nazi officials and their allies to permit more shipments to proceed appears to have increased in pockets, particularly in late 1942 and early 1943. In her close study of the wartime Allied blockade, Meredith Hindley argues that the Allies made just a few concessions—for instance, to counteract the famine in Greece—either "out of political necessity or when conditions became so inhumane as to demand action."[6] The prospect of an

Allied victory in the last years of the war likewise, if indirectly, persuaded leaders such as Antonescu in Romania to accommodate more humanitarian work on behalf of Jews in Transnistria. And, yet, deteriorating conditions on the ground in the last two years of the war greatly limited how effective the exceptions proved to be. Rebecca Erbelding's account in this volume of one project that emerged in 1944, the U.S. Treasury Department's War Refugee Board, shows that the uncertainties and official hurdles surrounding parcels would persist until the final days of the war.

Related to these policy shifts over the course of the war is the underlying question of why Nazi authorities allowed *any* special relief shipments to the Jews under their control, particularly in the first half of the war. What did these policies signal about these authorities' sharpening of anti-Jewish measures and their eventual pursuit of outright genocide? The story of parcels does not offer one compact answer; the full scope of many officials' calculations and motives remains opaque. In the very limited case of Theresienstadt or the Jewish aid operation working out of Kraków, allowing parcels may have functioned as a kind of decoy measure, masking the depth of cruelty and privation operating in other Nazi camps and detention sites, diverting attention from a road that ended in mass murder. In other instances—until 1941 in Poland and the 1942 deportations from internment camps in Vichy France—parcels may have been tolerated because they alleviated some of the burden of provisioning captive communities, although a purely economic explanation seems unlikely. Late in the war, as suggested above, relief parcel shipments may have again been tolerated for largely opportunistic reasons, even as access to detention sites for Jews (much reduced in number) remained almost wholly blocked.

* * *

Nazi food policy and the resulting mass starvation of civilian populations have been the subject of several important historical works. A handful of studies have also begun the work of assessing relief parcels against this backdrop, above all, Ronald W. Zweig's 1998 article, "Feeding the Camps: Allied Blockade Policy and the Relief of Concentration Camps in Germany, 1944–1945," which Jan Láníček revisits in his chapter. Zweig broke new ground in scrutinizing Allied relief programs for concentration camp prisoners in the latter part of the war, particularly those organized by the ICRC and the War Refugee Board.[7] A more recent book by Sébastien Farré, *Colis de guerre: Secours alimentaire et organisations humanitaires (1914–1947)*, discusses the genesis and evolution of the wartime food parcel over a much longer period. While the author touches on a wide array of relief organizations active in World War II (the JDC only in passing), like Zweig, he focuses most heavily on the policy decisions made by the ICRC in his account of the period and efforts to send parcels to concentration camp prisoners late in the war.[8] A large number of detention sites for Jews and initiatives, formal and informal, thus fall from view. The chapters in our volume, offering multiple new vantage points from across Europe, build on these important studies and work in concert to expand our understanding of state, philanthropic, and Jewish responses to the Nazis' mass internment and incarceration projects. Indeed, placing the modest relief parcel front and center in a history of World War II and the Holocaust challenges a number of long-standing myths and certainties about Nazi rule and Allied responses.

First, the traffic in relief parcels and remittances—some even received by Jewish prisoners—shows that the walls of Nazi detention sites and the wartime borders separating Axis Europe from the outside world were not hermetically sealed but instead proved porous and permeable.[9] Prisoners at many sites continued to receive and send mail into the first war years, both through facilities such as ghetto post offices and through more illicit channels. More research is needed to determine how censorship or close surveillance and intimidation affected the contents of these messages to the outside world.[10] Furthermore, *More than Parcels* concurs with the handful of recent studies that argue that wartime camps and ghettos were deeply embedded in the local economies around them and dependent on them for material necessities. Laurie A. Drake's chapter on Vichy—southern, unoccupied France under Marshal Pétain—argues this most explicitly, and Stefan Cristian Ionescu's case study of Romania reveals similar ways in which Jewish deportees or internees relied upon and also affected local economic structures. Beyond this, the wartime traffic in relief parcels reveals, almost improbably, that a system of somewhat isolated Nazi institutions remained tied into the reduced but still functioning international flow of consumer goods, particularly food. Those pathways of exchange became a hotly contested battleground in themselves. As in World War I, Anglo-American government officials during World War II attempted to cut off German imports of food and other vital goods and raw materials, viewing the blockade as a critical weapon of war. Our volume documents the tense battles fought by organizers of relief parcel programs with Allied officials over the inflexibility of the new wartime blockade and the ethical standoffs it provoked again and again.[11]

Second, our book uses the story of parcels to address a central historical puzzle about these years. How much was known about the events we now call the Holocaust as it unfolded? Historians have answered this question from many different perspectives.[12] We can deduce here that the traffic in relief parcels (and particularly the urgent detainee and prisoner requests for such aid) greatly contributed to the flow of informal information about the lethal nature of Nazi detention sites to the outside world: censored and uncensored, explicit and implicit. Aid requests and parcel receipts—even those returned undelivered "to sender"—became a kind of ad hoc tracing service for missing persons and refugees on the move. Jewish "missing person" tracing or contact services were organized soon after war broke out in Europe and supplemented information gathered by national Red Cross organizations, which played a pivotal role in reaching across the borders of combatants. Pleas for news about Jews last residing in Germany, Austria, France, Belgium, and Poland quickly filled the logbooks of the Board of Deputies of British Jews in London, for instance. In some of these cases, internment camps or even ghettos were listed as the last known address of persons being sought.[13] Letters routed through neutral countries (Sweden and Switzerland) or countries that entered the war late (the United States) had some chance of getting through, but these options proved increasingly fragile and unworkable.[14] The World Jewish Congress embarked on a sustained commitment to tracing work after moving its headquarters across the Atlantic from Geneva to New York in July 1940. Parallel initiatives sprang up everywhere: by late August 1943, the Jewish Agency and various Zionist organizations had set up a relatives' search agency in Jerusalem. Dr. Jacob Hellman in Buenos Aires and Hilel Storch in Stockholm created similar offices.[15] The WJC's search department in London, just one of several initiatives operating in wartime Britain, opened its doors on March 1, 1945. On the other side of the Atlantic, a group of major relief agencies, both Jewish and non-Jewish, joined forces to form their own Central Location Index, Inc. in Manhattan in August 1944.[16] The JDC, one of its partners, maintained a whole network of location offices alongside its relief operations in European capitals after the war ended, if not earlier.[17] The success of these offices in obtaining information on missing relatives and friends became ever more rare in the second half of the war. Package receipts thus became one of the few vehicles for transmitting clues about the location, living conditions, and fate of Jewish prisoners to families, humanitarians, and Jewish advocacy groups scattered across the globe.[18] While flawed and partial, some of the information that relief activists took seriously and acted upon defies our latter-day expectations. Three of the authors in this volume find evidence that aid organizations attempted to send relief packages to Auschwitz-Birkenau during or around 1943. Survivors of the camp later reported that some even arrived.[19]

Third, a related set of questions concerns the visibility of Jewish suffering in an era when many other European and colonial populations were facing famine and extreme food insecurity. How much awareness existed about the discriminatory sanctions and "racial" hierarchies that cut access of Jewish civilians in Europe to adequate food ration levels and did so even more acutely when they became prisoners? Jan Láníček asks us to think about whether Jewish suffering ever became a central reference point in wartime Allied publicity around "starvation in Europe." A growing number of historical works have in the past few decades documented the drastic human consequences of Nazi wartime agricultural policies, including Reich Minister of Food (later, Minister of Agriculture) Herbert Backe's "Hunger Plan" and the "Generalplan Ost."[20] Many regional studies have now also detailed extensive famine and mass starvation in non-Jewish European populations living under Nazi occupation.[21] Famine and death by starvation were pervasive in virtually all the areas affected by World War II, with an estimated twenty million or more people dying from this and related causes.[22] However, many of the new general histories of food policy during World War II rarely feature the particular plight of Jewish civilians in any depth, with Alice Weinreb's 2017 study of food and power in Germany a notable exception.[23] Our contributors invite readers to consider the ways in which the histories of Jews have been either embedded or passed over in the story of the wartime occupation and humanitarian aid campaigns for civilians.

Fourth, the diverse stories in *More than Parcels* reveal some of the little-known but deep fissures that opened within Jewish organizations and communities themselves around food aid. Several contributors to this volume chronicle painful internecine tensions over how the relief parcels should be organized and to which camps or ghettos they should be sent. Some groups at least initially balked at sending any food aid into territories under Nazi rule; like many Allied government officials, they worried that the shipments would simply be hijacked and serve the enemy. Among officials of even the major international Jewish advocacy organizations, such as the WJC, some favored continued diplomatic pressure and legal interventions for Europe's Jews, while others pushed ahead with risky mass parcel shipments sent by any means possible, their delivery far from guaranteed. Firm confirmations that shipments were successfully delivered to their intended recipients were few and far between. The percentage of losses—through theft by Nazi officials or corrupt couriers—that parcel and remittance organizers were willing to swallow became a continuous source of tension in the ranks of activists. The JDC, a critical funder for many wartime relief projects, appears to have tolerated far greater losses than many parallel organizations.

Jewish activists on the ground in occupied Poland and Transnistria came to view some of their own aid officials very guardedly as well, concerned they were de facto collaborating with the occupiers or skimming off valuable goods for their own enrichment. Not least, Jewish committees within ghettos and camps faced standoffs and competing claims around the scarce goods that came into their captive communities through parcel deliveries, as the discussions of Theresienstadt in this volume emphasize. These disputes became all the more acrimonious as goods for barter such as food and clothing grew more valuable than cash and other forms of currency. A history of wartime relief parcels demonstrates painfully the persistence of social stratification and "privilege" even in Nazi ghettos and camps, often at the cost of physical collapse and starvation.

Finally, our volume delves into a series of difficult methodological problems about how we evaluate the outcomes of these relief initiatives in Nazi-controlled Europe. How can success or failure be measured in this story? How many parcels arrived or were instead confiscated, pillaged, and consumed by a vast network of jailers and corrupt officials along the way or at their final destination? How many were stockpiled in the storerooms of concentration camps and never distributed until after liberation? The quantity of money and medicine sent to Jewish prisoners by clandestine routes and couriers, through unofficial channels, remains even more difficult to judge. The volume of food aid—hundreds of thousands of packages spread out across the whole war—can be partially reconstructed, for the financial records of many international organizations from the period survive intact. That possibility shrinks as we move farther east, as the missing account books of the head of the major Jewish self-help organization in the Generalgouvernement, for instance, suggest. Nonetheless, historians have succeeded in determining the quantity of packages and other forms of mail that entered some of the large ghettos in occupied Poland for a time; that number is at first glance shocking. In the year leading up to March 1941, for instance, the mail service in the Łódź ghetto reportedly handled over 64,000 money transfers from abroad, over 135,000 domestic parcels, and over 14,000 packages from abroad, along with more than a million letters and postcards.[24] The numbers appear to be evidence of vigorous, sustained support for family and friends trapped inside until the first months of 1941, when occupation authorities abruptly curtailed the traffic in parcels. Still, figures for the packages that survived long journeys and were delivered are so fragmentary for most detention sites that they do not tell us much on their own.

Aid activists experimented with a range of methods to obtain confirmation that parcels had arrived where intended, initially using test shipments and package receipt postcards. In the case of Theresienstadt, test remittances were also sent to the ghetto's bank, as Pontus Rudberg shows. If the very handwriting on wartime letters from ghettos in occupied Poland sometimes provided clues about the state of a person's health, then signed, stamped, or initialed receipt cards remained highly ambiguous documents throughout the war: they were difficult to read and difficult to interpret. Incoming receipts at the offices of several Geneva-based philanthropies also make this clear. Still, more than any other tool, the registered parcel receipt became a marker of success for many of the initiatives described in these pages: demonstrating delivery of food parcels became critical "proof" used to persuade Allied and neutral state officials to allow the programs to continue. As insurance that food did not fall into the hands of the enemy, Allied officials long demanded that parcel shipments be supervised on their journey to Nazi camps and that they be sent to identifiable, named prisoners. With few exceptions, these conditions remained impossible to implement, so receipts became an important bargaining chip for food relief organizers. Lack of delivery confirmations could be cause for refusing export licenses, space for parcels on ships and trains, replacement tires for transport trucks, exemptions to the strictures of the blockade, or funds for renewed relief shipments. Receipts in some instances also became a means of tracing known prisoners and their location, and they even generated further names of Jewish prisoners: some receipt cards were returned with multiple (unsolicited) additional names, and contributor Gerald J. Steinacher notes that Jean (Johannes) Schwarzenberg of the ICRC's Joint Relief Commission managed to identify thousands of further prisoners through this avenue.

Anecdotally, many food parcels did arrive and, if actually distributed, extended many Jewish prisoners' lives; we have learned this both from the massive number of wartime letters from occupied territory and the Reich that begged for food parcels and from Holocaust survivor testimonies, as the chapters by several of our contributors so poignantly remind us. The numbers of parcels for Jewish civilian prisoners fell far short of the parallel program of parcels sent to western Allied POWs through the ICRC. Yet the projects described here demonstrate that even a single, one-time parcel provided emotional sustenance and hope, commodities for barter, and nutrition that could improve and prolong the lives of recipients or their families.

Parcels could prolong life but not indefinitely. Some exceptions stand out: the analyses offered here of Jewish deportees from Romania in Transnistria and from Denmark in Theresienstadt make a strong case that parcels and aid initiatives had a marked impact on survival rates in certain locations. A few authors here raise the question of whether stockpiled, undistributed parcels at sites such as liberated concentration camps in 1945 played a significant role in prisoner survival right after liberation, especially when the Allied armies had not fully prepared for the humanitarian crisis that awaited them.[25] Still, the consensus of most of our volume's authors is that even the massive infusion of parcels into a few detention sites and a few Jewish communities could never have halted mass Jewish death under Nazi rule. For many, receipt of food parcels only delayed death for a time. Most parcels arrived too late, after most of Europe's Jews had been deported or already killed. Those that did arrive were, in the words of a historian cited by Jan Láníček, "but a drop of relief in an ocean of agony."[26]

More is clearly at stake in this history than an account of successes and failures and how they were measured by activists at the time. We still possess only a highly fragmented history of relief work—including food packages and cash remittances across borders—during the Nazi occupation of Europe. Who had access to mail and to parcels at ghettos, concentration camps, or the myriad of forced labor camps in the Reich and beyond? What special restrictions applied to Jewish prisoners in camps or ghettos? How did the logistics of sending and receiving packages change over the course of the war and vary from place to place? And what survived of the novel philanthropic projects that emerged during and in the immediate wake of World War I, many revolving around providing large-scale food relief that some historians now call the "new humanitarianism"?[27] The JDC and the even longer-lived ICRC adapted in new ways.[28] But a whole new roster of groups had also formed in response to Nazism.[29] Continuities with the structures and protocols of past relief work remain an open question for future research.

* * *

This volume is divided into three geographical sections, beginning with aid schemes organized from Allied and neutral states. The first section pays special attention to some of the major international philanthropic organizations that mobilized resources for parcel schemes (the International Committee of the Red Cross, the American Jewish Joint Distribution Committee, and the World Jewish Congress) but highlights a number of less remembered and more informal relief initiatives as well. Eliyana R. Adler's "Ties That Bind" tracks the story of Polish Jews who fled into the Soviet Union following the German and Soviet invasion of Poland in 1939. Adler follows the movement of relief packages that refugees both sent and received over constantly shifting wartime borders. Her chapter contains the striking finding that even refugee communities in the USSR under severe economic strain managed for a time to support family and community members who had been forced into ghettos back home in German-occupied

Poland. They likewise marshaled resources for kin and friends who had landed in the Soviet prison system or settlements in the Soviet interior. These refugees in the east maintained family ties and support over remarkably long distances well into the war.

Anne Lepper shifts our focus to the history of the Relief Committee for the War-Stricken Jewish Population (RELICO), an international wartime parcels project created in late 1939 by a Polish Zionist refugee in Geneva, Switzerland. While its founder held a position with the WJC office in the city, the project remained a largely independent operation that relied on a combination of informal couriers and the fragile wartime postal system to deliver goods to Jewish communities and prisoners trapped in Europe's war zones, first in occupied Poland and then in internment camps in Vichy France. The entry of the United States into the war in late 1941, escalating supply shortages in Europe, and mass deportations in occupied Poland would radically curtail the scheme, but during its short run, the organization managed through sponsors across the globe to purchase and route tens of thousands of relief packages into occupied territory.

We next cross the English Channel to a slightly later period, with Jan Láníček's assessment of the humanitarian programs for Jews organized by the London-based Czechoslovak and Polish governments-in-exile together with international Jewish activists and organizations. Between 1942 and 1945 these governments contributed to the shipment of thousands of food parcels—mostly from Lisbon but also from Switzerland, Sweden, and Turkey—to ghettos in occupied Poland and Czechoslovakia, as well as to a range of concentration camps. The chapter scrutinizes the commitments that exile government politicians made to their citizens, including Jews, but also the special deep bonds forged between Allied Jewish communities and Jews suffering persecution in Europe through repeated efforts to send food to Nazi ghettos and camps. How did those officials and activists respond when the obstacles on the ground became increasingly difficult? Lack of information about the fate of dispatched relief packages as well as the Allied economic blockade of continental Europe tested the limits of their commitment and ingenuity. Pontus Rudberg considers the parallel story of Jewish humanitarian aid in Sweden for Jews trapped under Nazi occupation. Central in his account are the main Jewish communities and rabbis in Stockholm, Gothenburg, and Malmö, who organized a formidable quantity of food and medicine for Jews in Poland, internees in France, and concentration camp prisoners. They worked with such partners as RELICO, the Swedish Red Cross, and the officially sanctioned Jewish aid organizations in Kraków, yet like their counterparts in other neutral countries, they struggled with nearly insurmountable difficulties: restrictions on exports, lack of reliable suppliers under deteriorating wartime conditions, declining donations, lack of information about where Jews remained alive in occupied Poland, and the struggle to convince Allied officials that shipments would not simply be confiscated by the Germans. Rudberg demonstrates that bitter disagreements among Jewish organizations about how to proceed led to unexpected results late in the war.

Two final chapters in this section highlight developments in the latter half of the war. We return to Geneva with Gerald J. Steinacher's reassessment of what measures the International Committee of the Red Cross sponsored to aid Jews from 1942 to 1945. Steinacher documents the organization's ties to the World Jewish Congress and particularly the Joint Distribution Committee. The ICRC ultimately did work closely with the latter to organize relief for tens of thousands of civilian prisoners. A few officials within the organization such as Jean (Johannes) Schwarzenberg also began a concerted effort to bring relief to civilians held in concentration camps. A familiar and formidable series of obstacles again stood in the way: the limitations of international law concerning civilian prisoners' rights, uncooperative Nazi authorities, the Allied blockade, anxiety about German military plans, and the hesitation of Red Cross leaders to redirect resources and personnel away from their traditional mandate, assisting POWs. Still, the combined work undertaken between the International Red Cross and the JDC resulted in some of the most significant food relief operations marshaled in the final stages of the war and the immediate postwar months. The section concludes with Rebecca Erbelding's incisive analysis of the War Refugee Board, a U.S. government agency created late in the war to aid European Jews and other Nazi prisoners. After determining that it would be impractical to focus solely on rescue work, WRB officials also launched relief projects, such as organizing shipments of parcels containing food, clothing, and medicine to prisoners in Nazi concentration camps. As with other initiatives explored here, the agency used the distribution channels, experience, and monies of major philanthropic organizations to help assemble and finance its relief program. Erbelding tracks the obstacle-strewn path by which thousands of parcels were finally delivered to a few concentration camps just as rail and other transport possibilities for relief shipments were collapsing all over Europe. Only in the final days prior to and shortly after liberation, with mass starvation of camp prisoners looming, did the prospects for providing help change to some degree.

The second section scrutinizes internment and transit camps for Jews in territories under regimes aligned with Nazi Germany, offering case studies for Vichy France and Transnistria. Laurie A. Drake's chapter recounts the struggle of Jewish individuals and families, many of them foreign nationals or stateless, to secure food aid while trapped in a range of internment camps in southern unoccupied France. Drake argues that these Jewish camp populations faced unique subsistence challenges: detained in often isolated rural settings, they found themselves unable to secure support from their communities and families back home or to tap into help from nearby French Jewish communities, where they even existed. Camp conditions continued to deteriorate through the Allied blockade and implementation of rationing in France. Nonetheless, she demonstrates that both interventions from international philanthropic organizations and a unique set of self-help initiatives helped Jewish camp prisoners stave off mass famine. This work continued right up to the departure of mass transports to Drancy and the killing centers of eastern Europe in the summer and early autumn of 1942.

Stefan Cristian Ionescu's contribution focuses on Romania's wartime Jewish leadership and humanitarian aid for Jewish prisoners deported by the Romanian regime to Transnistria in an occupied area of the southwestern Soviet Union. After the harsh winter of 1941–42, regime authorities increasingly began permitting relief operations on behalf of the tens of thousands of Bessarabian and Bukovinian Jewish deportees and Ukrainian Jews confined to camps and ghettos in the region. The chapter uncovers the networks created by individuals and Romanian Jewish leaders with the help of both national and international aid societies. The goods and funds they brought into Transnistrian ghettos and camps between 1942 and 1944 would have a critical impact on the region's Jewish survival rate. Here Ionescu also illuminates the gradual shift in Jewish policy pursued by the Antonescu regime as the war continued.

The final section examines parcel relief in a small number of the major ghettos and camps in Nazi-occupied Europe, a few revealing cases among thousands. Each case opens new questions about relief, social ties, and resilience in wartime. Katarzyna Person's chapter follows the extensive correspondence of two families divided by World War II and the Nazi occupation to illustrate how aid and news reached the Warsaw ghetto from the world outside. Wartime developments eventually ended those families' ability to communicate long-distance, yet their earlier exchanges demonstrate that contacts were still possible across international borders and the walls of the largest Jewish ghetto in Nazi-occupied Europe long after the occupation began. Despite strict censorship, a ghetto postal service continued to pass letters and tens of thousands of parcels to residents in the year before the mass deportations of residents to Treblinka. The author draws on these examples to reveal how news circulated through families and whole communities during the war and the complexity of interpreting such communications. Person's case study advances our understanding of the long reach of the Holocaust and of family ties, gender roles, and the history of emotions in a time of existential distress. Alicja Jarkowska turns her lens to occupied Kraków and the politics surrounding the Jewish Aid Agency in the Generalgouvernement (JUS), the major Jewish aid agency operating in occupied Poland until the summer of 1944. Like its predecessor under the occupation, the Jewish Social Self-Help (JSS or ŻSS), the JUS furnished food, clothing, and medicine to Jews trapped in dozens of forced labor camps and ghettos near the city, largely supplied by international aid funneled through Portugal and elsewhere. The chapter closely scrutinizes the work of and controversy surrounding Dr. Michał Weichert, head of the two agencies. Because his work entailed extensive and continuous negotiations with German occupation authorities, a number of leading Polish Jewish activists condemned him as a collaborator and traitor. The chapter follows Weichert into the postwar years, when the controversy raged on. Relief work under the conditions of wartime occupation long continued to divide Jewish survivors after 1945, as they revisited questions of resistance and accommodation.

The volume's final contributor, Silvia Goldbaum Tarabini Fracapane, examines the little-known history of parcels earmarked for Jews deported from Denmark to the Theresienstadt ghetto near Prague during the war. Jews residing in wartime Denmark did not initially experience anti-Jewish measures prevailing elsewhere, and most managed to escape or hide successfully before the September 1943 mass roundup. Here Goldbaum Tarabini Fracapane follows the nearly 500 Jews who were arrested and deported; virtually all were sent to Theresienstadt rather than to killing sites lying farther to the east. The chapter follows a highly engaged group of volunteers from diverse professions, both women and men, who through a large-scale and unique collaboration with Denmark's central government, church officials, and the Danish Red Cross began regularly shipping hundreds of food and clothing parcels to the Danish contingent in the ghetto each month for the duration of the war. These unique efforts, the author argues, had a marked impact on the survival rate of Denmark's Jews, both citizens and refugees.

The cases featured in this volume reveal sharp divisions and distrust but also new, unexpected, and often uneasy alliances in the realm of parcel relief work. We find divided and skeptical government officials in the pages of *More than Parcels* partnering with Jewish advocacy groups for the first time, groups that were rarely of one mind about how to proceed. Many of the contributors also underline the ongoing, singularly critical importance of the JDC in financing and even organizing the new food relief projects in Europe. Rebecca Erbelding's chapter makes clear that the organization even provided financial assistance to Allied government agencies. Informal initiatives receive their due here as well, largely invisible in the topography of the "new humanitarianism." Eliyana R. Adler, Laurie A. Drake, and Katarzyna Person all remind us of the centrality of individual ingenuity and generosity in extending Jewish lives during the war. *More than Parcels* has only begun the daunting project of mapping how and where food aid reached Jews in Nazi-controlled Europe. The cases presented here are hardly exhaustive, leaving many questions open about the economies and prisoner life in tens of thousands of smaller Nazi detention sites. They confirm that individuals, Jewish communities, and philanthropic endeavors did make hundreds of thousands of interventions on behalf of Jews trapped in Europe during the war, understanding something of the gravity of what awaited them. If we regard systematic and deliberate starvation of Jewish prisoners as a major feature of the Holocaust, the modest relief parcel packed with sardines, sultanas, and semolina must also count as a vital form of rescue work.

Notes

1 Jonas and Anka Leah Tenebaum in the Warsaw ghetto to Anka's sister and daughter in Chicago. United States Holocaust Memorial Museum Archive (hereafter USHMM), photo 28569A.

2 Reference to and requests for food parcels permeate the correspondence compiled in Reuven Dafni and Yehudit Kleiman, eds., *Final Letters* (London: Weidenfeld and Nicolson, 1991) and other collections of wartime mail from occupied Europe. Cf. Barbara Engelking and Jacek Leociak, *The Warsaw Ghetto: A Guide to the Perished City* (New Haven: Yale University Press, 2009), 375–77. Many packages were privately organized or at least largely paid for by individuals rather than by the organizations that actually filled orders (typically, e.g., tins of sardines from neutral Portugal).

3 Raul Hilberg listed over 800,000 Jewish dead through ghettoization and general privation (out of an estimated 5.1 million total Jewish dead under Nazi rule) in his classic study, finding that "for the German decision makers, the pace [of Jewish death in ghettos] was not fast enough." However, he chose to classify ghettoization in German-occupied eastern Europe and starvation in the ghettos as part of the "concentration" phase of the destruction process, not yet over the "dividing line" into the complete annihilation of Jewish existence in Nazi Europe. See Raul Hilberg, *The Destruction of the European Jews*, 3 vols., 3rd ed. (New Haven: Yale University Press, 2003), 1:274, 276; 3:1320.

4 Boris Shub and Zorach Warhaftig, *Starvation over Europe (Made in Germany): A Documented Record, 1943* (New York: Institute of Jewish Affairs, 1943), 7–8, cited by Jan Láníček, this volume.
5 See Lucjan Dobroszycki, ed., *The Chronicle of the Lodz Ghetto, 1941–1944* (New Haven: Yale University Press, 1984), 25, 284–85, 354.
6 Meredith Hindley, "Blockade before Bread: Allied Relief for Nazi Europe, 1939–1945" (PhD diss., American University, 2007), 462, cf. 459–61.
7 Ronald W. Zweig, "Feeding the Camps: Allied Blockade Policy and the Relief of Concentration Camps in Germany, 1944–1945," *The Historical Journal* 41, no. 3 (1998): 825–51.
8 Sébastien Farré, *Colis de guerre. Secours alimentaire et organisations humanitaires (1914–1947)* (Rennes: Presses Universitaire de Rennes, 2014). For a brief account of a "food draft" remittance program created for Europeans by Herbert Hoover in the wake of World War I, see Mary Elisabeth Cox, *Hunger in War and Peace: Women and Children in Germany, 1914–1924* (Oxford: Oxford University Press, 2019), 275–80.
9 See, e.g., Karola Fings, "The Public Face of the Camps," in *Concentration Camps in Nazi Germany: The New Histories*, ed. Jane Caplan and Nikolaus Wachsmann (New York: Routledge, 2010), 108–26; and numerous examples in Wolfgang Benz and Barbara Distel, eds., *Der Ort des Terrors. Geschichte der nationalsozialistischen Konzentrationslager*, 9 vols. (Munich: C. H. Beck, 2005–8).
10 See, e.g., Karen Taïeb, ed., *Je vous écris du Vél'd'Hiv. Les lettres retrouvées* (Paris: Robert Laffont, 2011) and *Je vous écris d'Auschwitz. Les lettres retrouvées* (Paris: Tallandier, 2021).
11 Meredith Hindley has skillfully analyzed the blockade in her dissertation, "Blockade before Bread." Cf. Zweig, "Feeding the Camps," 834–40, and the earlier study, W. N. Medlicott's two-volume *The Economic Blockade* (London: HMSO, 1952–59). Alice Weinreb declares categorically that British attempts to re-create a hunger (food) blockade in World War II were simply not effective as warfare against Germany; the "terrifying military success of Nazi Germany, as well as its aggressive seizure of foodstuffs across the continent, rendered British attempts at another hunger blockade similarly ineffective." Alice Weinreb, *Modern Hungers: Food and Power in Twentieth-Century Germany* (New York: Oxford University Press, 2017), 89.
12 For recent literature, see Jürgen Matthäus, *Predicting the Holocaust: Jewish Organizations Report from Geneva on the Emergence of the "Final Solution," 1939–1942* (Lanham, MD: Rowman & Littlefield in association

with the USHMM, 2019); Michael Fleming, *Auschwitz, the Allies and Censorship of the Holocaust* (New York: Cambridge University Press, 2014); the five-volume series *Jewish Responses to Persecution, 1933–1946* (Lanham, MD: AltaMira/Rowman & Littlefield in association with the USHMM, 2011–15); Annette Becker, *Messengers of Disaster: Raphael Lemkin, Jan Karski, and Twentieth-Century Genocide* (Madison: University of Wisconsin Press, 2021).

13 "Missing Persons" lists, books 3, 4, 5, Oct. 17 to Nov. 1944, London Metropolitan Archives, Acc/2793/04/04/02–04 (Central British Fund for World Jewish Relief).

14 See, e.g., the exchange of letters between teenagers in Jürgen Matthäus, with Emil Kerenji, Jan Lambertz, and Leah Wolfson, *Jewish Responses to Persecution, Vol. III: 1941–1942* (Lanham, MD: AltaMira Press in association with the USHMM, 2013), 70–82.

15 World Jewish Congress, *Unity in Dispersion: A History of the World Jewish Congress*, rev. 2nd ed. (New York: WJC, 1948), 298.

16 "Index Established Here to Locate War Refugees," *New York Times*, Aug. 10, 1944, 17.

17 On postwar tracing efforts, see Jan Lambertz, "Early Post-war Holocaust Knowledge and the Search for Europe's Missing Jews," *Patterns of Prejudice* 53, no. 1 (2019): 61–73.

18 Marion Kaplan also emphasizes the importance of food parcels in her compelling new study of Jewish refugees in Portugal during the war, *Hitler's Jewish Refugees: Hope and Anxiety in Portugal* (New Haven: Yale University Press, 2020), 197–201.

19 Cf. the correspondence about parcels sent to prisoners in the Auschwitz camp complex in Yad Vashem Archives, RG-0.75, file 167 (1943–44). I thank Joel Nommick for this reference.

20 See the discussions in, e.g., Adam Tooze, *The Wages of Destruction: The Making and Breaking of the Nazi Economy* (London: Allen Lane, 2006); Mechtild Rössler, Sabine Schleiermacher, and Cordula Tollmien, *Der "Generalplan Ost." Hauptlinien der nationalsozialistischen Planungs- und Vernichtungspolitik* (Berlin: Akademie Verlag, 1993).

21 Important early contributions include Christian Gerlach's *Krieg, Ernährung, Völkermord. Forschungen zur deutschen Vernichtungspolitik im Zweiten Weltkrieg*, updated ed. (Zurich: Pendo, 2001), and his *Kalkulierte Morde. Die deutsche Wirtschafts- und Vernichtungspolitik in Weissrussland 1941 bis 1944*, 3rd ed. (Hamburg: Hamburger Edition, 2000), as well as Karel C. Berkhoff's *Harvest of Despair: Life and Death*

in Ukraine under Nazi Rule (Cambridge, MA: Harvard University Press, 2004). For more recent works detailing German agrarian and food policy, mass starvation, and economic planning for the occupied Soviet Union, see Alex J. Kay, "Germany's Staatssekretäre, Mass Starvation and the Meeting of 2 May 1941," *Journal of Contemporary History* 41 (October 2006): 685–700; Gesine Gerhard, "Food and Genocide: Nazi Agrarian Food Policy in the Occupied Territories of the Soviet Union," *Contemporary European History* 18, no. 1 (2009): 45–65. For one of many works on the siege of Leningrad, see Alexis Peri, "Queues, Canteens, and the Politics of Location in Diaries of the Leningrad Blockade, 1941–42," in *Hunger and War: Food Provisioning in the Soviet Union during World War II*, ed. Wendy Z. Goldman and Donald Filtzer (Bloomington: Indiana University Press, 2015). An important study by Christian Streit, *Keine Kameraden: Die Wehrmacht und die sowjetischen Kriegsgefangenen, 1941–1945*, 4th ed. (Bonn: Dietz, 1997), recounts the brutal treatment of Soviet POWs in German captivity, including their massive mortality rate stemming from lack of food, and this research continues. Mass starvation resulting from the German war offensive can be seen in many populations beyond the Eastern Front; see, e.g., Violetta Hionidou, *Famine and Death in Occupied Greece, 1941–1944* (Cambridge: Cambridge University Press, 2006). For a comparatively early English-language account of the Dutch famine in the winter of 1944, see Henri A. van der Zee, *The Hunger Winter: Occupied Holland 1944–1945* (Lincoln: University of Nebraska Press, 1998). An extensive secondary literature on the effects of civilian rationing now exists for the world wars as well as under state socialism in eastern Europe.

22 Lizzie Collingham, *The Taste of War: World War Two and the Battle for Food* (London: Allen Lane, 2011).

23 Weinreb, *Modern Hungers*, 52, 76–80; cf. 106–7.

24 Dobroszycki, ed., *Chronicle of the Lodz Ghetto*, 35. On the quantity of letters, cards, money orders, and parcels arriving in the Warsaw ghetto for part of 1941 and 1942—and the difficulty of interpreting these numbers—see Engelking and Leociak, *Warsaw Ghetto*, 370–71; cf. Katarzyna Person, this volume.

25 Anglo-American wartime policy bodies only partially anticipated this crisis of mass malnutrition on the continent; see, e.g., Melville D. MacKenzie, *Medical Relief in Europe: Questions for Immediate Studies* (London: Royal Institute of International Affairs, 1942).

26 Avraham Milgram, *Portugal, Salazar, and the Jews* (Jerusalem: Yad Vashem, 2012), 204–5.

27 Recent histories focus on the more secular philanthropic enterprises arising in particular in the wake of World War I and their contribution to an emerging "human rights" discourse; some major works in this field include Bruno Cabanes, *The Great War and the Origins of Humanitarianism, 1918–1924* (Cambridge: Cambridge University Press, 2014), and Stephen R. Porter, *Benevolent Empire: U.S. Power, Humanitarianism, and the World's Dispossessed* (Philadelphia: University of Pennsylvania Press, 2017). Cabanes has called Herbert Hoover's work for starving Belgian, German, Polish, and Soviet citizens the most important humanitarian operation of the early twentieth century (Cabanes, *Great War*, 241). Farré's *Colis de guerre* works to bridge the history of food relief in Europe across the two world wars.

28 On the long-term and shifting activities of such organizations as the ICRC and the JDC, see Gerald Steinacher's *Humanitarians at War: The Red Cross in the Shadow of the Holocaust* (London: Oxford University Press, 2017); Avinoam Patt et al., eds., *The JDC at 100* (Detroit: Wayne State University Press, 2019). This new volume on the JDC revisits the organization's wartime activities and Yehuda Bauer's earlier conclusions in *American Jewry and the Holocaust: The American Jewish Joint Distribution Committee, 1939–1945* (Detroit: Wayne State University Press, 1981), 333–34.

29 Britain's Famine Relief Committees, including the branch in Oxford that became Oxfam, emerged during the war and quickly grew to 149 local branches, in part advocating food relief for occupied Greece and Belgium. See Ruth Jachertz and Alexander Nützenadel, "Coping with Hunger? Visions of a Global Food System, 1930–1960," *Journal of Global History* 6 (2011): 106; cf. Maggie Black, *A Cause for Our Times: Oxfam, the First 50 Years* (Oxford: Oxford University Press, 1992), chap. 1. She mentions that a Jewish refugee was among the founders of the group but does not provide details beyond his name (Dr. Leo Liepmann). Liepmann spent time in a British internment camp in Ramsey, Isle of Man.

I

RELIEF FROM THE ALLIES AND NEUTRAL STATES

1

TIES THAT BIND

Transnational Support and Solidarity for Polish Jews in the USSR during World War II

ELIYANA R. ADLER

In 1942, Salomea L. recorded a testimony for the clandestine Oyneg Shabes Archive in the Warsaw ghetto. She had recently returned from spending over a year in Soviet-controlled Polish territory, now under German occupation, and described her experiences there. As an aside, she mentioned that the Polish Jews living in the newly incorporated Soviet areas after 1939 were sending packages both east and west. They aided friends and relatives who had been deported east by the Soviets, as well as those in the German-held territories to the west.[1] In doing so, they not only provided much needed sustenance to suffering members of their communities but also let them know that they were not alone. Additionally, they served as a conduit, passing information about life-cycle events and tribulations from the ghettos to the Gulag and back again.

It is well known that war leads to separation, dislocation, and death and that World War II decimated the Polish Jewish population. This is undeniable. Polish Jews on either side of the new border established by the German and Soviet occupiers in September 1939 had limited and diminishing resources. Occasional packages were not capable of turning the tide of the war or saving them. Thus, the prevalence and prominence of aid packages in testimonies about these years require explanation. This chapter will explore both the routes and the impacts of parcels sent and received by Polish Jews in the USSR during the war. It will argue that the psychological significance, especially of packages

---

I would like to thank the editors of this volume and Marion Kaplan for thoughtful comments on drafts of this chapter.

sent by friends and family, was ultimately greater than any demonstrable physical effects.

The chapter looks primarily to the written and oral testimonies of Polish Jews in order to assess the meaning and the memory of material aid. Archival documents provide statistical information about the quantity of goods collected and sent, but they rarely extend to listing individual recipients and their responses to the aid. Reflections from the time period and afterward tell an emotional story and provide a window on the efforts expended in preparing a parcel for posting or the supreme joy of receiving one. Furthermore, these sources also grant the reader a greater sense of the vast distances crossed by people and packages. Packages provided a bridge between Jews under Nazi occupation, in the USSR, and around the world, thereby demonstrating ongoing networks of association, despite the war.

Understanding how Salomea L. and others found themselves in the unenviable and unexpected situation of providing material aid to their friends and relatives in both German-occupied Poland and the Soviet interior requires some historical background. As a result of the division of Poland between Germany and the Soviet Union in September 1939, several hundred thousand Jews fled from the western, German-held Polish territories to those soon to be annexed by the Soviets.[2] In many cases, families chose to split up, believing that men or younger family members would be safer and have more opportunities in the USSR.[3] Relatively good relations between the two occupiers, as well as continual border crossing in both directions by Polish Jews, meant that ongoing contact remained fairly easy until the German invasion of the Soviet Union in June 1941. Before that point, both the regular postal service and personal deliveries allowed letters and packages to pass back and forth.

Packages from German-Held Poland to Soviet-Annexed Poland

The Polish Jews who fled their homes under German occupation in the fall of 1939 frequently arrived in Soviet territory almost penniless. Even those fortunate enough to pack carefully before they left often had to abandon possessions or pay hefty bribes and fees along the way. Some had relatives or friends to stay with, at least temporarily, on the other side of the Bug or San Rivers. Those who did not found the new Soviet republics of Western Belarus and Western Ukraine overrun with new arrivals. Homeless refugees filled public buildings while Soviet officials from the east arrived and took over the better housing stock. Eventually most of the refugees managed to find work and places to stay, but their existence remained precarious. Goods from home made a real difference for them. They also kept in close touch with relatives left behind, as they constantly reevaluated their decision to flee and whether to return or bring family members to join them.[4]

The unsettled quality of refugee life, as well as the pushes and pulls of the two occupation zones, is evident in the testimony of Roza Buchman. She lived a comfortable life with her husband and two children in Radom before the war. In September 1939, the family fled the German invasion to Białystok. Yet, as the Soviets established control there, her husband, a well-known industrialist, feared arrest. Roza traveled back across the demarcation line to her parents in Warsaw to see if it was safe to return to the Nazi-occupied areas, but after suffering an assault on the street, she decided that it was not. Back in Soviet Bialystok, she tried to caution her husband, but he elected to go back to their home in Radom. For the next few months, they exchanged letters about the situation on both sides of the new border. Then in June 1940, Roza and the two children, as refugees who had not accepted Soviet citizenship, were deported to a special settlement in the Soviet interior. The labor there proved taxing, with pay and nutrition lacking. They survived on packages sent from Radom. Buchman, writing in 1943 before she knew about the genocide unfolding back in Poland, noted that the hardest part about the German invasion of the Soviet Union in 1941 was the ruptured contact with her husband. It was at this point that the children began to go hungry.[5]

Younger men had often been the first to flee the Germans, believing only they would be targeted, so the Buchmans' choice proved somewhat unusual. In his Yiddish memoir from the 1950s, Avraham Zak, for example, recalls receiving packages of cash and messages from his wife in Warsaw while he lived in newly Sovietized Grodno.[6] In both cases, what is noteworthy is that these families chose to separate physically but also managed to retain contact and support through packages. When people think of families separated by war, they imagine people torn apart without any agency. Such cases certainly existed, but in the period after the German invasion of Poland and before the German invasion of the Soviet Union, families also made tactical decisions to separate, while remaining intimately linked and in frequent contact.

Packages from Soviet Poland to German Poland

Aid did not flow just in one direction. As family members in Soviet territory gradually found their footing—and those under Nazi occupation were increasingly displaced and dispossessed—packages began to move from east to west. After Mike Weinreich and his father crossed the border to Bialystok in 1939, they kept in close touch with Weinreich's mother, still living in their home with his sister in Grójec, a town southwest of Warsaw. Later the women were forced to move into the Warsaw ghetto, but the men were still able to send them packages from Kletsk, a city farther from the border where they had moved after accepting Soviet citizenship.[7]

The Davidson family moved in stages from their home in Łódź, across the new border to Soviet Bialystok, and then to Vitebsk, a city in the Belarusian Soviet Socialist Republic before 1939, after registering for work in the Soviet interior. After the wife and children caught up with the father, Simon, who had fled earlier, they were able to build a relatively stable life together in the USSR. Both Simon Davidson and his daughter Hannah Davidson Pankowsky write of receiving disturbing news from the other side of the border and sending a package to their cousin Marie in the Warsaw ghetto.[8] Peretz Opoczynski, who served as a mail carrier in the Warsaw ghetto and wrote for the underground Oyneg Shabes Archive, described the anticipation surrounding the arrival of such parcels:

> Of course the sender of these packages from Russia would always alert the recipient with a letter stating that goods were on the way, usually arriving some time before the package itself. People therefore treated a letter from Russia as something much more than writing on a scrap of paper: it was greeted as if it were a living messenger of good news still to come. With trembling fingers elderly mothers would caress a letter sent by their sons that told them a package was on the way.[9]

Barbara Engelking's research reveals that in the second half of July 1941, the Warsaw Judenrat's postal service delivered 54,192 packages, 36,906 of them large and 17,286 small.[10] According to historian Ruta Sakowska, before the summer of 1941, 84 percent of the packages reaching the Warsaw ghetto from abroad came from the USSR.[11] In the Łódź ghetto, it proved closer to half of all packages, according to an entry in the ghetto chronicle lamenting the end of such deliveries after the start of the German-Soviet war.[12] Opoczynski, the postman in Warsaw, noted this change as well:

> As the nightmare of Jewish Warsaw darkens, hope is gradually extinguished: no more letters from Russia, no more packages, just walls—drab, red, and cold ghetto walls, like the walls of so many cheerless prisons. Who cares about the Jewish post office or the swollen feet of the Jewish letter carrier now?[13]

Packages Sent to Polish Jewish Prisoners in the USSR

Many of the initial family separations triggered by the war were voluntary, although, of course, they were meant to be temporary. Over time, however, more and more families underwent forced separations. In the Soviet territories, these were a result of the growing presence of the security state in the form of the NKVD (Soviet internal security forces). The first prisoners were captured Polish soldiers. Soon afterward, even as many refugees continued to stream across the border into Soviet territory, back to German territory, and into the independent Baltic states, Soviet border guards arrested others as alleged spies. The web of arrests spread to so-called speculators (large and small players in the black market), political leaders, and other suspect groups in Polish society. While all Polish citizens had a difficult time adjusting to Soviet norms and what was often a lower economic and social status, prisoners suffered from real hunger, deprivation, overcrowding, disease, and even torture. Occasional opportunities to receive packages and visits were thus particularly crucial.

Avraham Steinberg, a child in these years, fled with his family from Jarosław to his grandparents' home in what became Peremyshliany, Western Ukraine. They were able to settle in there and send regular packages to his uncle, Baruch Steinberg, chief rabbi of the Polish Army, who was imprisoned and later executed along with other Polish officers in the Smolensk area.[14] When Shimon Dzigan, a beloved prewar entertainer, felt himself growing weak from conditions in a transit camp between prisons, he asked one of the local people working in the camp to tell the Polish Jews in the area about his situation. He was deeply touched to receive milk the very next day and a package soon afterward.[15]

In his memoir of imprisonment in the USSR, Menachem Begin, future prime minister of Israel, arrested for his political activism, described the dual role of packages in tending to basic needs and also in passing along information: "Clothing parcels continued to arrive and warm our hearts. I sensed that it was my wife who was sending the parcels, but I knew that my friends were providing them. My wife had no money." As each package arrived, he searched for hidden messages. At last he found the letters O-L-A embroidered on a handkerchief. It took him several days and the help of a friend to figure out that his wife was subtly signaling her new status as an *olah hadashah* (new immigrant to the Land of Israel). She was moving from newly Sovietized Lithuania to Palestine.[16] Later, after she had already left, Begin received a visit from a friend who pretended to be his wife in order to bring a package. Speaking in Polish, the woman informed him in the presence of his guards that the products she had brought were from his dear aunt *iggeret besabon* (Hebrew: letter in soap), alerting Begin to the presence of a letter from his wife embedded in the bar of soap.[17]

Both communication and aid were vitally important to the recipients of the packages. Of course, their relative weight differed according to circumstances and interpretation. For example, writing from the relative comfort of the State of Israel in the midst of the Cold War, Begin enjoyed emphasizing the ways he and his friends and family had outsmarted the Soviets. In his memoir about being the child of refugees, Joseph Berger quotes his mother's anguished description of visiting her brother, who had been imprisoned for speculation:

> That prison was some scene. There was a long line of prisoners and a long line of Russian mothers and wives. The prisoners were all waiting for their packages. Believe me, they wanted these packages as much as seeing their mothers and girlfriends. Breads filled with cabbages, potatoes, meat. I brought Simcha dark bread, which I had to steal from my nine-hundred-gram ration. I dried it in the oven so it wouldn't get molds. When I gave it to my brother he ripped open my package like he never saw food before. But he didn't seem so satisfied with what he saw.[18]

For Berger's mother, the pain of having lost her brother to the Soviet prison system and of not having been able to provide him with what he needed was still raw decades later.

Packages to Siberia

Packages to prisoners clearly made an important difference in their lives, and this was also true for those who were deported. In the late fall of 1939, and more intensely in the spring of 1940, the Soviets began deporting potentially disloyal groups from the Polish population. In June 1940, after taking away political leaders, religious leaders, municipal staff, police officers, and wives and families of soldiers, the NKVD swept up the refugees from western Poland who had refused Soviet citizenship.[19] They were picked up in the middle of the night, often without enough time to pack their belongings. Yet the package deliveries already began at the train stations.

Menahem Ben-Moshe, writing in the Sanok memorial book, claims that after the arrest of his family and hundreds of others on Friday night, June 30, 1940, "every Jew in Galicia heard about our plight and so the train yards filled with people bringing us food and other items."[20] This development was particularly fortuitous for Rabbi Yisrael Orlansky, who voluntarily joined his father on the deportation train. Neither had been at home during the roundup, and so they had nothing with them at all. Fortunately, while the train waited at the station, Orlansky's brother and sisters brought them useful items from home.[21]

After a long and difficult journey, the Polish Jewish refugees finally reached the camps, farms, or special settlements in the Urals, the Arctic, northern Kazakhstan, or Siberia, where they had to work in order to eat. The labor was punishing and the conditions terrible. Yosef Weidenfeld's religious father would not allow the family to eat the soup served in the cafeteria. He describes the arrival of each package from his grandfather in the Soviet-annexed Polish territories as a "miracle." Weidenfeld's mother cried when she discovered a box of butter in one.[22] Moshe Bunem Gliksberg titled one chapter of his testimony recorded for the Polish government-in-exile in Palestine in 1943, "The Sister as Savior." Gliksberg's sister, who is not named in the testimony, had been out of town trading the family's goods for products that could be sold when the rest of them were deported from Ive (Belarus). Although they begged the NKVD commander to wait for her return, they were forced to leave her behind. Providentially, after their departure she was able to get a position as a bookkeeper in an *artel* (cooperative workshop) for 400 rubles per month. Once the family sent her a telegram with their whereabouts, she commenced sending them regular shipments of cash and goods. For Pesach of 1941, Gliksberg's sister sent thirty kilos of matza, raisins for wine, and *schmaltz* (rendered chicken fat). With the addition of the potatoes they were able to gather, they finally had enough to eat. Gliksberg states that he and the younger children wished that the whole year could be Passover. Of course, the packages stopped once Germany invaded the Soviet Union.[23]

Packages passed not only from the relatively better-off, newly annexed Soviet territories but even between camps. Dina Stahl, in her testimony to the Polish government-in-exile in 1943, stated that her immediate family of four would not have survived in their camp in Asino (Tomsk Oblast) had they not received packages from her grandparents in a nearby camp with better access to food.[24] Even more remarkably, some of the deportees were in such dire straits that they relied upon help from their relations under German occupation. Writing in her diary in April 1941 from deep in the Siberian taiga, Pearl Minz complained that while others received packages from home, she had not heard from her daughter back in Warsaw.[25] During that same month, Helena Starkiewicz, who had been arrested and tried for crossing the German-Soviet border over a year before, was moved to a camp in the Mariinski Oblast. From there she was able to reestablish contact with her parents back in Hrubieszów, in the German-held territories, and they soon began sending her packages.[26] Harry Berkelhammer and his brother were pleased to receive warm underwear in Omsk from their parents back in Brzesko, Poland, over 4,000 kilometers away.[27]

As conditions worsened in the Soviet labor camps and Nazi ghettos, some of the Jews in the annexed areas of Western Belarus and Western Ukraine found themselves responsible for relatives who were victims of both regimes. Such was the case with Salomea L., whose story opened this chapter. Tania Fuks, who accepted Soviet citizenship and stayed in Lvov, describes the anxiety of preparing and sending packages in both directions. To collect goods to send to her brother in the ghetto in Łódź and to her friends deported into the Soviet interior, she had to save up her meager teacher's salary to purchase items on the black market. Fuks lived in fear of being arrested for buying or transporting illegal products, until the German invasion put an end to those worries and created a far more dangerous situation for her and all the Jews in the annexed territories.[28]

Polish Government Aid

The massive surprise invasion the Germans launched against the Soviet Union in June 1941 ushered in utter chaos, which was followed soon by genocide for the local Jewish population. The USSR, brought to its knees, was forced to make common cause with the western Allies. In approving what came to be known as the Sikorski-Maiski Pact, on July 30, 1941, Stalin caved in to British and Polish demands regarding Polish citizens in the USSR.[29] While many Poles at the time, including conservatives in his own cabinet, disparaged General Władysław Sikorski, the prime minister of the Polish government-in-exile, for not wresting a guarantee regarding future borders out of Stalin, he nonetheless succeeded in securing an agreement for the creation of a Polish army, a general amnesty, and relief work.

In the succeeding months, most of the efforts and attention of the Polish leadership were on the recruitment, training, administration, equipping, feeding, and evacuation of the Polish forces. Yet they also made a valiant attempt to locate and map the far-flung Polish citizens deported into the interior, assess their needs, and establish and stock aid centers. Indeed, the two programs were related. In his memoir, *The Inhuman Land*, Polish officer Joseph Czapski describes his efforts to find missing Polish POWs and how these intersected with other complementary goals of the men who reached the recruiting stations. "We spent our days drawing up lists of names, recording statements of the men who had come straight from the labour-camps, and entering the addresses of their relations," Czapski explains, adding, "We displayed the first lists we were able to compile on the outside wall of our shanty. No matter what the state of the weather, there was always a long queue waiting to decipher the rain-soaked information, each man hoping to find the names of his nearest and dearest."[30]

This information was then passed on to the Polish civilian leadership in the USSR, which was meeting in Kuibyshev (now Samara, Russia, where the Soviet government evacuated in the fall of 1941). In addition to the piecemeal collection of the names and locations of their charges, the Polish representatives faced enormous challenges. First, displaced Polish citizens took to the road following their amnesty—leaving camps, collective farms, and special settlements in the north for more temperate climates in Central Asia. Second, the exiled Polish government in London had no source of income. It had to rely on aid from friendly governments and philanthropic organizations to feed and clothe its people. Beyond this, even after gathering funds and goods, transporting them into the Soviet Union in the midst of the war proved perilous. In March 1942, a large transport of flour for matza was torpedoed by U-boats long before reaching its destination.[31]

From the start, tensions existed between the various cooperating bodies. The Poles and the Soviets, already jockeying for control over postwar Poland behind the scenes, did not trust one another. Local Soviet authorities often created bureaucratic hurdles for the distribution of goods and mobilization of soldiers, and the higher authorities, especially as the tides of the war turned, had little interest in honoring the terms of their agreement with the London-based Poles. At the same time, some Jews within the exiled Polish community began to complain of discrimination in both military recruitment and aid allocation. As word of these allegations reached the United States and the United Kingdom, the Polish government-in-exile found itself in a difficult situation.[32]

Yet despite the many obstacles, Polish Jews in the far reaches of the Soviet interior did receive some aid from the *delagatura* bureaus that their government established in Soviet regions with the highest concentrations of Polish citizens. These distribution points, staffed by officially chosen delegates as well as other Poles residing in the areas, collected and disbursed funds, household items, clothing, medical supplies, and foodstuffs to the Polish citizens in their geographic reach. In the two years they were allowed to function, the Polish delegates, according to their own records, sent out over two million rubles in remittances and 100,000 packages. They also provided both cash and in-kind relief to individual Poles who came to their depots and supplied considerable amounts of food and other products to the Polish institutions, such as schools and orphanages, they were allowed to establish in the USSR.[33]

Helena Starkiewicz secured winter clothing from the Polish office nearest her communal farm in the Merke (now Merki) district of Kazakhstan. Yet she also complained in her privately published memoir that the pleas of a nearby group of Polish yeshiva students went unanswered.[34] After his release from a labor camp, Shaul Shternfeld worked in a hospital in Berezniki (Perm region), an area with fewer refugees and no local delegate. He was thrilled when a package arrived from the Polish office in Kuibyshev with a coat and shoes. Between those items and his hair growing back, he writes that he finally "had a human look."[35] For Dorothy Zanker Abend, the delight was less in the goods than in the opportunity to reconnect with others in her social group. While waiting in line at the Polish delegate's office in Ashkhabad (Ashgabat, Turkmenistan), she met another Polish Jew who had news of her brother Roman. He had been deported separately, and now she learned that he had joined the Polish forces in Kermine (Navoiy, Uzbekistan).[36] Thus, although she mentions receiving helpful items and especially appreciating reading material in Polish, Abend's trip to the Polish office yielded unexpected and even more welcome results.

This route of relief—with its positive and negative consequences—came to an end by early 1943. As already mentioned, the Soviets had increasingly abrogated the treaty, especially by denying Polish citizens of Jewish, Ukrainian, or Belarusian descent access to the Polish military or aid. With the Germans' grisly discovery in April 1943 of the mass murder of the missing Polish military brass by Soviet forces—the Katyn massacre—the already strained relationship collapsed. The Polish and Soviet governments broke off diplomatic relations, and the aid and other programs came to an abrupt halt. In the coming months, many of the Polish delegates were arrested and their aid stores confiscated, but the work they had done collecting the names and locations of Polish citizens in the USSR did not go to waste.

Jewish Communal Aid

To amass the funding and goods required for their ambitious aid projects, the Polish government-in-exile had relied on help from both governmental and nongovernmental organizations. While the United Kingdom was already stretched thin by its substantial war expenditures, the United States entered the war later and initially less directly and was thus able to provide more support for this relief project. Jewish organizations in the United States and other unoccupied nations were particularly eager to help their coreligionists suffering in the war zone.[37] Indeed, the contributions of Jewish organizations to the Polish effort made the accusations of unfair distribution especially damaging. In his rebuttal to the statement denying discrimination issued by the Polish government-in-exile in June 1942, Dr. Ignacy Schwartzbart, a Jewish member of the Polish National Council in London, pointed this out:

> Jewish institutions the world over are actively participating in the relief work for the refugees from Poland now stranded in Russia without stipulating that their contributions are intended for Jews only. The relief activities for these refugees now conducted by Jewish organizations in America, Canada, Palestine and England are certainly not smaller than those conducted by private Polish relief groups in the United States.[38]

Although many Jewish philanthropies contributed, chief among them was the American Joint Distribution Committee (JDC).

The JDC, also known as the Joint, came into being to help with the massive refugee crisis caused by World War I. Its founders aimed to create an amalgamated agency to expedite the collection and disbursement of aid to Jewish refugees. Unlike many of the other Jewish organizations involved in relief work, the Joint was deliberately meant to be apolitical and impartial in its treatment of all needy Jews. During the interwar period, and especially as antisemitism and poverty in Germany and Poland increased, the Joint provided material aid as well as logistical and financial support for emigration.[39] The start of World War II pushed most Jewish aid organizations out of Europe. The JDC maintained an office in neutral Switzerland throughout the war, continued to operate in Lithuania before its invasion and annexation by the USSR in 1940, and tried to smuggle aid into and people out of occupied countries.[40] On the whole, however, they could do very little for the Jews under Nazi control. Thus, the Joint and other Jewish aid organizations embraced the opportunity to help Jews in the Soviet Union.

By late 1941 the JDC had already begun to use the free shipping supplied by the American government's lend-lease program, which allowed the United States to contribute to the Allied war effort before entering the war at the end of 1941, sending medical supplies and food to the Polish government-in-exile's collection points in Teheran, Iran. While there was no guarantee that their donations would go to the Jews among the Polish recipients, they could at least request that their aid be sent to the areas with the heaviest concentration of Jewish refugees.[41] By the time the Polish delegates were forced to cease their efforts in early 1943, the Joint had contributed over $100,000 to the Polish cause in the Soviet Union.[42]

JDC matza packing in New York, to be sent to the USSR. Courtesy of the JDC Archives, 17788.

Even as they supported Polish aid efforts, the JDC also actively pursued two other avenues for directly reaching the Polish Jews in the USSR. The first of these involved negotiation with Soviet representatives to implement an aid program for Jews displaced by the war. As Mikhail Mitsel has shown, despite some internal dissent, the Joint opened this discussion in early 1942. By the following year, with the breakdown of Soviet-Polish relations, it took on added significance. Working through the Soviet Jewish Anti-Fascist Committee and the Soviet Red Cross, the JDC was eventually able to establish an ad hoc program to take over some of the functions of the Polish aid program. In the next few years, the Joint donated hundreds of thousands of dollars to the USSR. Yet, their generosity notwithstanding, they found it difficult to ascertain information about the distribution of what they sent. Mitsel concludes, "The principal underlying tension in JDC's Soviet program during World War II was the ultimate provision of nonsectarian aid to a struggling nation versus adherence to JDC's specific raison d'être: to serve Jews."[43]

At the same time, however, the JDC also began sending aid packages to individual Polish Jews and their families. Unlike bulk aid, which had to go through the Soviet Red Cross and thus left the JDC entirely out of aid distribution, parcels allowed the JDC to directly help Jews in need. According to Mitsel, the Joint sent 10,000 packages per month from Teheran to Jews in the USSR between 1942 and 1944.[44] A 1944 report on the operation provides a sense of the complexities entailed with warehousing underwear coming from India and South Africa, clothing and shoes from Palestine, and foodstuffs from Egypt and Iran.[45] Although the JDC became the largest player in this market, it was not the first: "Since late 1941, the American Federation of Polish Jews had been sending parcels to Russia through a Polish bank in America. In Palestine, *Landsmannschaftn*, groups of Jews originating from the same town or village in Eastern Europe, collected names and addresses in Russia from postcards that were arriving."[46]

A variety of Jewish organizations in the United States and Palestine in particular, but elsewhere in the world as well, organized to send packages to Polish Jews in the Soviet interior. Indeed, Atina Grossmann has emphasized the transnational aspect of this aid, tracing the collection of funds from across the Jewish diaspora, the purchase of goods from across the Middle East and elsewhere outside the war zone, and the packaging and labeling conducted in Teheran.[47]

An effort of this size and scope required the cooperation of a vast array of organizations. In addition to the work these groups did to raise funds, collect supplies, and transport them across the world, Yehuda Bauer calls attention to the critical importance of gathering addresses. The earlier Polish delegates in the USSR had already started this process, and the addresses they collected in their effort to find their citizens and army officers proved useful to the JDC and other Jewish groups seeking to send individual packages. Jewish organizations obtained other names and addresses from the Jews evacuated to Iran with Anders' Army, the Polish military forces, and even more as Soviet authorities increasingly allowed people to contact relatives abroad. Jewish organizations then shared these addresses with family members and vice versa. The frustrations of providing aid under Soviet auspices meant that sending personal packages became increasingly attractive. Yet the only way to reach even a fraction of the Polish Jews in the Soviet interior was through access to their mailing addresses.

Many of the Polish Jewish refugees moved around during their period of exile, greatly complicating aid efforts. Whether for occupational or educational opportunities, to reunite with friends or family members, or simply in the hopes of finding better conditions elsewhere, mobility was a regular part of their lives. Aid organizations sought to keep track of their whereabouts and share information with one another. To offer just one example, the Consular Legal Department of the Polish government-in-exile received a list from the Jewish Agency, the major group representing the Jews of Palestine in the pre-state period, of Polish Jews who had been granted certificates to immigrate to Palestine in 1942. Among the names was one Rabbi Uszer-Szaja Halpern, listed as residing at Swobody 9 in Bukhara.[48] By July 1943, when Vaad Hatzalah, an American organization dedicated to helping Orthodox Jews, prepared a list of Polish Jews to receive financial subsidies through American Express, Rabbi Halpern's address in Bukhara was Tolstego 29.[49] When the World Jewish Congress (WJC) created a list of rabbis and rabbinical students in the USSR in need of relief in 1944, Rabbi Halpern had apparently taken in some yeshiva students, or was at least collecting mail for them, as he and several others appear at the same address.[50] A version of this same list appears in the files of the Polish government in London from 1945.[51] This accumulation of details demonstrates that aid organizations pooled their information widely in order to amplify their impact.

Yet despite these and other impressive efforts, the Polish Jews in the USSR have had very little to say about the JDC and other institutional aid packages in their memoirs and oral testimonies. Relatively few of the survivors mention aid from the JDC at all, let alone as a factor in their survival. Of those who do, the references are somewhat ambivalent. Frumie Cohen had her first chocolate in a Joint package. Later, a second package arrived with sardines and tuna. She remembers gobbling up her portion, while her more mature sister saved her share for their parents. In the end, Frumie and her parents came down with food poisoning while her sister felt fine.[52] Dina Gabel was pleased to be able to find matza for Passover in 1944. After several years of going without or baking it clandestinely, she discovered boxes of Manischewitz matza that year, courtesy of the Joint, on sale on the black market in Tokushi (Kazakhstan).[53] Far more valuable, in her mind, were the packages she began to receive later that year from Vaad Hatzalah. The American tea in them fetched a high price in flour from the local Kazakhs.[54]

In testimony given long after the end of the war, Avraham Steinberg recalled that his father, a well-respected rabbi in Samarkand during the war, served on a committee charged with dividing up the relief that arrived from the Joint. Steinberg avers that this was a thankless and miserable job and led to complaints and personal attacks but that the aid did make a difference for the refugees.[55] The most positive evaluation comes from Marian Feldman, who was mobilized into the Red Army in 1943. During this period, he was very concerned about his sister, whose boyfriend had already been killed fighting for the Soviet Union, alone on a *kolkhoz* (communal farm). Fortunately, in addition to money he was able to send from his stipend, she received some packages from the Joint during this difficult time, which he says helped her to get by.[56] In his postwar oral testimony, Szymon Gracjar refers in passing to having received goods from the United States, the United Kingdom, and the JDC while trying to survive in Uzbekistan. Yet none of these greatly enhanced his material situation. It was only when Gracjar began working for a Polish organization—most likely the Union of Polish Patriots, a Soviet-sponsored group founded after the break with the London-based Polish government—that he finally had enough to eat and began to "revive."[57]

Jewish organizations around the world solicited donations to be able to contribute aid to the Polish Jewish refugees suffering in the Soviet interior. Of course, Jews across Europe under Nazi occupation had far greater needs, but the obstacles to helping them directly were considerable, as shown by other contributors in this volume. At the same time, the Soviet government's voracious need for material support in the midst of the war, and its willingness to countenance greater openness and communication with the West in order to receive it, led to a temporary opportunity for foreign donations. Jewish organizations, chief among them the JDC, jumped at the chance to help, whether through bulk shipments and cash contributions or through packages. Yet notwithstanding the tremendous efforts made by the Joint and other aid groups, the refugees mention them only in passing in their postwar reminiscences, unlike their recollections about family packages.

Personal Packages

While the Joint and other Jewish aid organizations received relatively short shrift in the memoirs and testimonies of Polish Jewish refugees in the USSR, packages received from friends and family members abroad were remembered very fondly. As we have seen, the same Soviet policies that encouraged the JDC to send aid—and allowed goods into the formerly closed country—also made it possible to send individual packages. In a similar vein, the process of gathering names and addresses started by the Polish delegates and continued by the JDC and other Jewish aid groups enabled family members around the world to locate their relatives and send them packages.

On Sunday, July 11, 1943, amid a horrific wave of news of the genocide across Europe, the Jewish Telegraphic Agency reported an announcement from the WJC that American Jews could "now send food and clothing packages to their refugee relatives and friends in Russia." Those unsure of the proper contact information were urged to contact WJC offices.[58] In addition to the larger organizations such as the WJC and the JDC, American Jews relied on smaller groups, such as those with their religious, political, or geographic commitments, to provide information and send packages. Parallel opportunities existed in Jewish communities around the world.

Only a limited number of packages could be sent monthly from the Yishuv, the Jewish community in Palestine, and the recipients had to pay a tax on them. Larger numbers could be sent without a fee from Teheran, but only through ongoing negotiations with the Iranian, Polish, Soviet, and other authorities. Shlomo Kless notes that many of the senders were members of the same political organizations rather than blood relatives. He adds that in addition to providing logistical support, the Jewish Agency kept a master list of all of the Polish Jewish refugees whose names and addresses could be located.[59]

In the United States and the Yishuv, as well as elsewhere, formal and informal networks allowed Jews around the world to locate and send letters and packages to what in many cases were their only remaining relations in Europe. The packages they sent proved very meaningful for the recipients. As in the earlier period discussed above, this had to do both with the physical contents of the parcels and with what they represented. While still in a special settlement in the Vologda region in northern Russia with her husband and infant, Dorothy Abend Zanker received a package with a can of Crisco and boots for her baby from her parents in the United States. It was, she states in her interview with the Shoah Foundation, a "true treasure." Commenting on the packages that he and his father received from his uncle in Tel Aviv while they were struggling to get

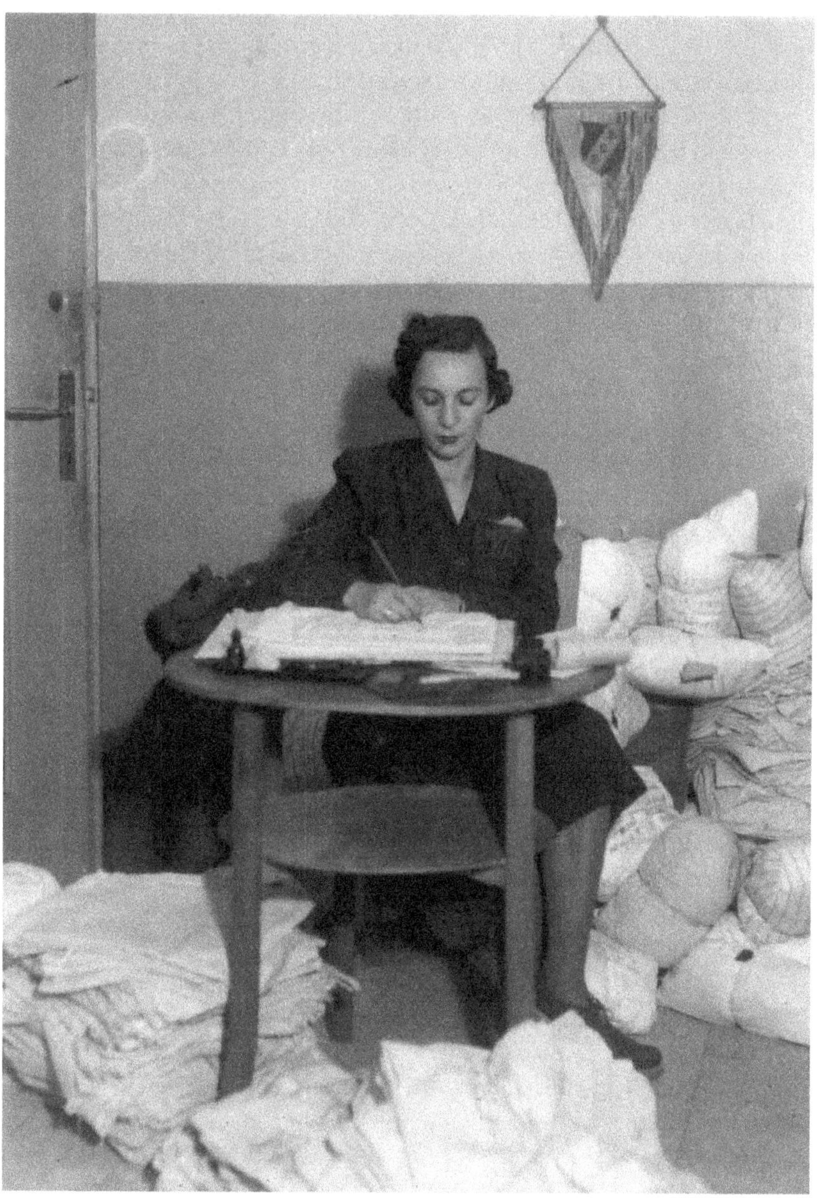

Preparing packages in Tel Aviv for Lithuanian Jewish refugees in Russia. Courtesy of Yad Vashem, Photo Archive, Jerusalem, 7176.

by near Dzambul (now Taraz, Kazakhstan), Mietek Sieradzki wrote, "The arrival of a food parcel, which our family, like many others, received from time to time, was a great event in our lives and a godsent."[60]

Such packages often helped not only the recipients but also their closest friends and relations. In a particularly dramatic case, the Leshem family in Tel Aviv—having reached Palestine from a German-occupied section of Lithuania in October 1940—ended up aiding an evacuated Soviet Jewish family as well as their own relative. Roza Iasvena, a young woman, fled from Vilna on her own. In the Tatar Autonomous Soviet Socialist Republic, she was fortunate to be taken in by Roza Barbanel' and her family, Soviet Jews from the Leningrad region, as well as to reestablish contact with her own relatives in Palestine. After Iasvena was mobilized into the Red Army in June 1942, the Barbanel' family continued to receive packages sent to her and began a correspondence with her relatives in Tel Aviv. Commenting on the arrival of a parcel containing tea, soap, and oil in July 1943, Barbanel' wrote to Yehudit Leshem, "We are very grateful for the package. We wish you good health. If it is possible and not difficult for you, please send another, and we will not let Roza remain alone. She should only be alive and well."[61] In this letter and others, Barbanel' thanked the Leshems warmly and assured them that she and her family were doing what they could to help Iasvena and to save the nonperishable goods for her. At the same time, Barbanel' also alluded to her own difficult situation and requested help from this stranger whose relative she was sheltering.

In addition to letters, some refugees were able to send telegrams to their benefactors. This may have depended on the proximity of the Polish Jews to a city with public access to the technology as well as on their means. In August 1943, Taube Shapiro, at 75 Fourth Avenue in New York, received a telegram from Bronia Shapiro in Fergana (Uzbekistan) that stated simply, "parcel received regards kisses."[62] In October 1944, Yuda Morko wrote from Dzhambul to the company that had sent his package, letting them know that he had received it and asking them to thank his relative.[63] Although many of the former refugees describe correspondence with family and friends outside of Europe in the latter part of the war in their testimonies, they do not mention sending telegrams. It is unlikely that this was a common way of maintaining contact or responding to deliveries.

Some of the small number of Polish Jews fortunate enough to evacuate from the Soviet Union to Iran with the Polish Army were even able to send packages back to those they had left behind. In her oral testimony, Miriam Yehieli stated that although most of the members of her Zionist party were not accepted into the Polish forces, the handful who did join up began to send packages as soon as they reached Teheran. She and the other party members still in the USSR sold the clothing they received for money to sustain them.[64]

Bob Golan, at the time known as Srulik Goldman, fled his hometown of Chełm along with his parents and his younger brother, Moshe, in 1939. After their deportation to a special settlement outside of Asina, Golan writes, only the packages from his aunt back home saved them from starvation. Once the Germans invaded and the family relocated to Krasnovardeysk, their hunger became so severe that Golan's mother took the two boys to a Polish orphanage. From there, he, Moshe, and the other children were evacuated to Pahlevi in Iran and then, after making contact with the Jewish Agency representatives there, to Mikveh Israel in Palestine in February 1943. From there, Golan was able to send both letters and packages to his parents back in Soviet Central Asia. They survived the war and were reunited with their sons in Israel six years later.[65]

Conclusion

Few families were as lucky as the Goldmans. Those separated in 1939 generally lost members in the Holocaust. Even many who escaped to Soviet territory as a unit often saw their numbers diminish due to living conditions, hunger, disease, and lack of access to medical care. A few letters and packages delivered within or from outside Soviet borders were not going to stop the mass killing of the Jews under German occupation or the ravages of epidemic diseases that preyed on the already weakened deported Polish Jews in the Soviet interior. Yet the packages were important to them and cropped up in many of their written and oral recollections. For that reason alone, they demand attention. Many of the voices cited in this chapter come from decades after the war. Even for those composed earlier, amid all of the upheaval they describe, it bears noting that so many of the former refugees refer to personal packages they received. Clearly the receipt of packages while far from home and in difficult straits meant a great deal. At least in the construction of memory, many of the Polish Jews highlight parcels from home as saving them at one juncture or another, either physically or spiritually.

Yehoshua Gilboa underlined this twofold benefit when he described his period of living and working in Shu (Kazakhstan):

> My spiritual world was taken up with my ever-increasing contacts abroad. I wrote letters and received answers although I cannot say what percentage of my communications reached their destination and how many stuck to the probing hands of the NKVD. . . . Every

> bit of information about Palestine was like a breath of fresh air. I also received a number of food packages.[66]

In Gilboa's case, the ability to reconnect with loved ones abroad was paramount. He even quotes some of the letters he sent to his brother in Palestine. His relationships with people and place trumped even the food he received. Gilboa also pointed to the importance of a variety of relationships. The opportunity to reestablish contact with people in Allied countries allowed him to share news with his brother and also with a number of other Zionist activists. As a member of the executive board of ha-Noar ha-Tsiyoni, Gilboa had devoted much of his life to politics. Corresponding with his comrades and hearing news about the situation in Palestine, in coded language in order to get by the Soviet censors, was a source of great comfort to him. From an emotional perspective, political groups could function like families.

The letters—and especially the packages—sent by friends, family, and ideological compatriots thus occupy a central place in postwar narratives of survival in the unoccupied regions of the USSR. Looking back on their time in Soviet exile, Polish Jewish returnees from the Soviet Union frequently recall the experience of receiving a private package, in addition to writing about the adversity they faced as Poles, Jews, and refugees and the relationships they built along the way. Even though receiving a package was a relatively rare occurrence, and their ability to send packages even more limited, both experiences mattered deeply.

Clearly, postwar testimonial sources provide a mediated reconstruction of the past. From the relative comfort of their lives in new countries decades after the events under discussion, the survivors chose what to narrate. Their stories are guided, however unconsciously, by the cultural and historical circumstances at the time of recording.[67] Yet, the diary, letters, and early testimonies collected by the Oyneg Shabes Archive in 1942 and the Polish government-in-exile in 1943 cited in this chapter display a similar enthusiasm. Parcels from home and from those associated with home, including targeted political and philanthropic groups, receive outsized attention.

The larger, more generic Jewish organizations do not seem to have generated the same sorts of feelings. Whereas packages sent by family members or comrades, whatever the period or place, made a deep impression, the refugees described the receipt of goods from the JDC or other aid groups fairly dispassionately. These Jewish organizations, like the Polish government, were another source of necessary goods. They carried out an important service in providing for basic needs. Yet they did not touch the refugees emotionally. Thus, the recollections of them tend to be perfunctory rather than heartfelt.

What the refugees did not know at the time or even afterward was that the preliminary steps of the Polish governmental relief program—and the ongoing efforts of the JDC and other Jewish organizations—enabled families and smaller organizations to send individualized packages. Without their commitment to collecting names and addresses, it would have been nearly impossible to reach the far-flung refugees. Although some of the Polish Jews in the USSR had retained the contact information of their relatives abroad and proactively wrote to them when it became possible to do so, most lacked the knowledge and resources to act on this desire. They became aware of the feasibility of renewed contact with friends and relations abroad only when packages began to arrive from across the world.

In addition to tracing the emotional responses of Polish Jews sending and receiving packages in the USSR during World War II and the ways those differed depending on the source, this chapter has also mapped the widespread and ramified networks of people and organizations committed to helping the Polish Jewish refugees who spent the war in the far reaches of the Soviet Union. Before the German invasion of the USSR, both packages and people passed back and forth across the border established by the German and Soviet occupiers. Within Soviet territory, packages also passed between imprisoned and deported Polish Jews and those who became Soviet citizens and stayed behind in the formerly Polish regions. With the 1941 invasion and the subsequent realignment of international relations, Jewish individuals and organizations in the United States, Canada, Palestine, Australia, South Africa, and South America were able to establish contact with their relatives, friends, and coreligionists in Soviet exile and send them financial and material aid. Testimonies of the widely scattered refugees describe the tremendous reach of philanthropic efforts in the midst of the war, as well as the strength and sustenance they delivered.

Notes

1 Rabbi Shimon Huberband, "Notebook Two," in *Kiddush Hashem: Jewish Religious and Cultural Life in Poland During the Holocaust*, ed. Jeffrey S. Gurock and Robert S. Hirt (Hoboken: Ktav, 1987), 414, 416.

2 On the experiences of these Polish Jews, see Eliyana R. Adler, *Survival on the Margins: Polish Jewish Refugees in the Wartime Soviet Union* (Cambridge, MA: Harvard University Press, 2020). For more on numbers, which are very difficult to determine given the chaotic and ongoing flight, see Mark Edele and Wanda Warlik, "Saved by Stalin? Trajectories and Numbers of Polish Jews in the Soviet Second World War," in *Shelter*

from the Holocaust: Rethinking Jewish Survival in the Soviet Union, ed. Mark Edele, Sheila Fitzpatrick, and Atina Grossmann (Detroit: Wayne State University Press, 2017), 95–102.

3 On these difficult decisions and the role of family in them, see Eliyana R. Adler and Natalia Aleksiun, "Seeking Relative Safety: The Flight of Polish Jews to the East in the Autumn of 1939," *Yad Vashem Studies* 46, no. 1 (2018): esp. 41–53.

4 See, e.g., Eliyana R. Adler, "Hrubieszów at the Crossroads: Polish Jews Navigate the German and Soviet Occupations," *Holocaust and Genocide Studies* 28, no. 1 (spring 2014).

5 Testimony of Roza Buchman, Hoover Institution Library & Archives (HIA), Poland, Ministerstwo Informacji I Dokumentacji, 123–5, protocol 69, 5.

6 Avraham Zak, *Knekht zenen mir geven* [We were slaves], vol. 1 (Buenos Aires: Tsentral-farband fun poylishe yidn in Argentine, 1956), 91.

7 Interview with Mike Weinreich, Visual History Archive, University of Southern California Shoah Foundation (VHA), December 12, 1995, Toronto, 10011, tape 1, minutes 26–28.

8 Simon Davidson, *My War Years, 1939–1945* (San Antonio: University of Texas Press, 1981), 112; and Hanna Davidson Pankowsky, *East of the Storm: Outrunning the Holocaust in Russia* (Lubbock: Texas Tech University Press, 1999), 44.

9 Peretz Opoczynski, "The Jewish Letter Carrier," in *In Those Nightmarish Days: The Ghetto Reportage of Peretz Opoczynski and Josef Zelkowicz*, ed. Samuel D. Kassow (New Haven: Yale University Press, 2015), 37.

10 Barbara Engelking and Jacek Leociak, *The Warsaw Ghetto: A Guide to the Perished City* (New Haven: Yale University Press, 2009), 370.

11 Ibid., 376.

12 Lucjan Dobroszycki, ed., *The Chronicle of the Łódź Ghetto, 1941–1944* (New Haven: Yale University Press, 1984), July 5–12, 1941, 63.

13 Opoczynski, "Jewish Letter Carrier," 53.

14 Interview with Rabbi Avraham Steinberg, Ganzach Kiddush Hashem (GKH), August 29, 2010, disc 1, minutes 42–44.

15 Shimon Dzigan, *Der Koyekh fun Yidishn humor* (Tel Aviv: Orli, 1974), 245–46.

16 Menachem Begin, *White Nights: The Story of a Prisoner in Russia* (New York: Harper & Row, 1979), 131. See the obituary of society columnist Masha Leon for further elaboration of this incident: Sam Roberts, "Masha Leon, Columnist Who Fled Nazis, Dies at 86," *New York Times*, April 10, 2017, sec. D, 8.

17 Begin, *White Nights*, 135.
18 Joseph Berger, *Displaced Persons: Growing Up American After the Holocaust* (New York: Scribner, 2001), 228–29.
19 Exact numbers remain out of reach. Edele and Warlik concluded that over 100,000 Polish Jews were either arrested or deported during this period. See Edele and Warlik, "Saved by Stalin?," table 2, 102.
20 Menahem Ben-Moshe, "Metsukat-gerush, derekh-golim ve-yesure galut," in *Sanok: Sefer zikharon le-kehilat Sanok ve-ha-sevivah*, ed. Elazar Sharvit (Jerusalem: Irgun yotse Sanok ve-ha-sevivah be-Yisrael, c. 1970), 396.
21 Interview with Rabbi Yisrael Orlansky, GKH, July 31, 2008, disc 3, minutes 20–50.
22 Testimony of Yosef Weidenfeld, GKH, Flinker Collection 45714, protocol 123, 2.
23 Testimony of Moshe Bunem Gliksberg, GKH, Flinker Collection 45664, protocol 73, 3–9.
24 Testimony of Dina Stahl in Maciej Siekierski and Feliks Tych, eds., *Widziałem Anioła Śmierci: Losy deportowanych Żydów polskich w ZSRR w latach II wojny światowej* [I saw the angel of death: Experiences of Polish Jews deported to the USSR during World War II] (Warsaw: Rosner I Wspólnicy, 2006), 224.
25 Pearl Minz, *Surviving the Holocaust in Siberia, 1940–1945: The Diary of Pearl Minz* (USA: D. de Frain, 2009), 63.
26 Helena Starkiewicz, *Blades of Grass between the Stones* (Melbourne: private printing, 1998), 82.
27 Interview with Harry Berkelhammer, VHA, 14300, April 16, 1996, Toronto, tape 2, minutes 11–14.
28 Tania Fuks, *A vanderung iber okupirte gebitn* [Wandering through occupied territories] (Buenos Aires: Tsentral-farband fun poylishe yidn in Argentine, 1947), 86–87.
29 General Sikorski Historical Institute, *Documents on Polish-Soviet Relations, 1939–1945* (London: Heinemann, 1961), 1:141.
30 Joseph Czapski, *The Inhuman Land* (London: Polish Cultural Foundation, 1987), 27.
31 Keith Sword, "The Welfare of Polish-Jewish Refugees in the USSR, 1941–43: Relief Supplies and Their Destination," in *Jews in Eastern Poland and the USSR, 1939–46*, ed. Norman Davies and Antony Polonsky (New York: St. Martin's Press, 1991), 151.
32 Ibid., 153–57.

33 "Report on the Relief Accorded to Polish Citizens by the Polish Embassy in the USSR with special reference to Polish Citizens of Jewish Nationality," 1943 Kubyshev, Polish Institute and Sikorski Museum Archive, A.7/307/30, 14–16.
34 Starkiewicz, *Blades of Grass*, 110, 115.
35 Shaul Shternfeld, *Halom ben gederot* [A dream between the fences] (Tel Aviv: Halonot, 1999), 197.
36 Interview with Dorothy Zanker Abend, VHA, 08317, April 11, 1995, Tucson, Arizona, tape 4, minutes 14–19.
37 Sword, "Welfare of Polish-Jewish Refugees," 149–50.
38 As quoted in "Jewish Deputy Takes Exception to Polish Statement," *Jewish Telegraphic Agency Daily News Bulletin* 9, no. 145 (June 24, 1942), 2.
39 On the early decades of the JDC, see Yehuda Bauer, *My Brother's Keeper: A History of the American Jewish Joint Distribution Committee, 1929–1939* (Philadelphia: Jewish Publication Society of America, 1974).
40 For more on the JDC during this period, see Yehuda Bauer, *American Jewry and the Holocaust: The American Jewish Joint Distribution Committee, 1939–1945* (Detroit: Wayne State University Press, 1981).
41 Ibid., 297.
42 Mikhail Mitsel, "American Jewish Joint Distribution Committee Programs in the USSR, 1941–1948: A Complicated Partnership," in *The JDC at 100: A Century of Humanitarianism*, ed. Avinoam Patt et al. (Detroit: Wayne State University Press, 2019), 102.
43 Mitsel, "American Jewish Joint Distribution Committee Programs," 97.
44 Ibid., 102.
45 "J.D.C. Program in the U.S.S.R. 1942–1944" (July 17, 1944), JDC New York Archives, file 1056, 2/3, 2.
46 Bauer, *American Jewry and the Holocaust*, 298.
47 Atina Grossmann, "Remapping Relief and Rescue: Flight, Displacement, and International Aid for Jewish Refugees during World War II," *New German Critique* 39, no. 3 (117) (fall 2012): 69.
48 "List of persons receiving visas for Palestine in Kubyshev," HIA, Polish Ambasada (USSR), Consular Legal Department, folder 15-6.
49 "Thru American Express—July 30, 1943," Yeshiva University Archives (YUA), Vaad Hatzalah Collection, Correspondence Concerning Collection and Distribution of Merchandise Overseas, 1943–49, box 11, folder 4.
50 "Rabbis and Student Refugees in USSR, 1944," United States Holocaust Memorial Museum Archives, RG-67.011M, Records of the New York

Office of the World Jewish Congress Relief and Rescue Department, Series D, 57, 3.

51 "List of Rabbinical Students and Rabbis Refugees in U.S.S.R," Polish Institute and Sikorski Museum, A.11.E/681 Żydzi 1945, VI. Wojsko oraz pokrewne, 12.

52 Interview with Frumie Cohen, VHA, 47312, November 23, 1998, Brooklyn, New York, tape 3, minutes 9–11.

53 Dina Gabel, *Behind the Ice Curtain* (New York: CIS, 1992), 278.

54 Ibid., 398–402.

55 Interview with Rabbi Avraham Steinberg, GKH, August 29, 2010, tape 2, minute 41.

56 Marian Feldman, *From Warsaw, through Luck, Siberia, and Back to Warsaw* (self-pub., Ryszard Feldman with LuLu, 2009), 117.

57 Interview with Szymon Gracjar, VHA, 16434, June 24, 1996, Toronto, tape 4, minutes 17–22.

58 "World Jewish Congress Sends Food-and-Clothing Parcels to Russia," *Jewish Telegraphic Agency Daily News Bulletin*, 10, no. 159 (July 11, 1943), 4, www.jta.org/archive (accessed September 25, 2019).

59 Shlomo Kless, "Pe'ilut tsionit shel pelitim yehudiyim be-Vrit-ha-Mo'atsot be-shanim 1941–1945 ve-kesher ha-Yishuv ha-Yehudi be-Erets Yisrael 'imahem" [Zionist activism among Jewish refugees in the Soviet Union in the years 1941–1945, and the connection between them and the Jewish Yishuv in Palestine] (PhD diss., Hebrew University of Jerusalem, 1985), chap. 6.

60 Mietek Sieradzki, *By a Twist of History: The Three Lives of a Polish Jew* (London: Vallentine Mitchell, 2002), 30.

61 Letter from Roza Barbanel' to Yehudit Leshem, July 17, 1943, Yad Vashem Archive, RG-0.37/70, cited in Arkadi Zeltser, ed., *To Pour Out My Bitter Soul: Letters of Jews from the USSR, 1941–1945* (Jerusalem: Yad Vashem, 2016), 185.

62 Postal Telegraph, August 13, 1943, YUA, Vaad Hatzalah Collection, Telegrams from USSR Concerning Parcels Received, box 11, folder 5.

63 Mackay Radio Radiogram, October 14, 1944, YUA, Vaad Hatzalah Collection, Telegrams from USSR Concerning Parcels Received, box 11, folder 5.

64 Testimony of Miriam Yehieli, Moreshet Archives, A.1488/2 (C.54), Shlomo Kless Collection, January 16, 1980, 12.

65 Bob Golan, *A Long Way Home: The Story of a Jewish Youth, 1939–1949* (Lanham, MD: University Press of America, 2005).

66 Yehoshua A. Gilboa, *Confess! Confess! Eight Years in Soviet Prisons* (Boston: Little, Brown, 1968), 119.

67 Hannah Pollin-Galay's *Ecologies of Witnessing: Language, Place, and Holocaust Testimony* (New Haven: Yale University Press, 2018) demonstrates divergences between testimonies of Lithuanian Jewish survivors of the Holocaust in three different linguistic, national, and cultural settings.

2

"BECAUSE I KNOW WHAT THAT MEANS TO YOU"

The RELICO Parcel Scheme Organized in Geneva during World War II

ANNE LEPPER

In the autumn of 1943, Fritz Ullmann, a representative of the Jewish Agency in Geneva, received a small card containing a few sentences from Siegmund Pergamenter, a prisoner in the Auschwitz-Birkenau killing center. Pergamenter sent greetings to Ullmann and his wife, stating that he and his family had just recently arrived in the camp and were in good health. He also added a short sentence at the very end of the card: "Herzl. Grüsse von uns auch an Reliko" (Our best wishes, also to Relico).[1] Responding at the beginning of November 1943, Ullmann assured Pergamenter that he had conveyed his regards to the Relief Committee for the War-Stricken Jewish Population (RELICO).[2]

This brief exchange hints at the reputation that RELICO attained during the war, reaching all the way behind the barbed wire surrounding the Birkenau camp, where more than a million Jews were murdered. This chapter will lay out some of the immense efforts made by individual Jewish activists and organizations stationed in neutral countries during the war to sustain the Jewish population in the Nazi-controlled and Nazi-allied territories. Headed by Abraham Silberschein, a recent émigré from Poland, the small organization supported thousands of Jewish refugees and prisoners of ghettos and camps,

The quote in the title is taken from A. Silberschein to Nathan Eck, June 18, 1941, Yad Vashem Archive (YVA), Record Group (RG) M.20, file no. 115.

often working against the strategies pursued by other more established Jewish organizations.[3] At a time when the major Allied powers opposed any shipments to the Nazi-held territories, Silberschein, who was well aware of the starvation in the camps and ghettos, developed an extensive chain of relief efforts for saving lives. Hundreds of letters in the archival collections related to the organization testify to the centrality of his efforts for the physical and mental sustenance of Jewish prisoners of the Nazis. He developed the activities against all odds, in an atmosphere that was not conducive to extensive relief efforts, and in opposition not only to the Allied governments but also to some of his closest collaborators in Geneva.

Fallout from the Invasion of Poland

The situation in Poland was marked by extreme chaos during the first weeks after Germany attacked on September 1, 1939. Nobody knew how Poland's looming defeat and a Nazi occupation would affect daily life in the long term. In big cities such as Warsaw, where destruction and disorganization crippled public life, food shortages rapidly became an issue. While the non-Jewish population was in part able to draw on assistance provided by local aid structures and to a limited extent even by German occupation forces, the Jewish population immediately began to experience the harsh fallout of an antisemitic German agenda.[4]

In October 1939, a man regarded as a "respected figure" from Jewish Warsaw was able to travel to Stockholm to report to Jewish organizations in Sweden on the events of the past weeks.[5] He stated:

> Through the food campaign initiated by the National Socialist People's Welfare organization [Nationalsozialistische Volkswohlfahrt] . . . on 16 squares in Warsaw, half a million kilos of bread and one million servings of hot soup are distributed daily free of charge to the Polish population, which lines up by the tens of thousands on the streets waiting for these donations [*Liebesgaben*]. Among them we also find a large number of Jews, who hope to receive something and often have to wait 6 to 8 hours. These Jews still cannot understand that they will be mocked and chased away empty-handed when their turn comes.[6]

After the German attack on Poland, the Jewish population was initially not able to fall back on existing community support networks or establish even remotely adequate new aid structures. Under the German-Soviet Nonaggression Pact, West Prussia and Posen, two border regions, were annexed by the Reich, and a German-occupied entity called the Generalgouvernement was established in central Poland by the end of October. Those Jews under German rule who were able to flee, many of them activists in prewar political and religious Jewish life, tried to either reach Soviet-ruled Galicia or cross into neighboring countries such as Lithuania in the northeast or Slovakia, Hungary, and Romania in the south.

Organizing Help from Abroad: Switzerland as a Hub of International Relief Work

The Jewish population remaining in annexed territory and the Generalgouvernement desperately tried to activate their contacts abroad to solicit support. In Geneva, many of their letters landed on the desk of a man who had just recently arrived in Switzerland from Poland himself. Silberschein (1882–1951) was a socialist-Zionist activist from Galicia. He had grown up in a liberal Jewish family in Lwów and studied law and politics at the Universities of Lwów and Vienna, completing a doctorate in both subjects. After finishing his studies, he began working as a lawyer in his hometown but gradually began to focus more and more on his political and social activities. In doing so, he quickly developed into one of the leading representatives of the Zionist labor movement in Poland. His political influence expanded even further when, at the age of forty, he was elected to the Polish parliament, the Sejm, as a member of the Poale Zion Jewish Workers' Party in November 1922. From then on, he strove to promote socialist and Zionist concerns at the local level and developed strategies for securing basic rights for the Jewish population in Galicia. In his function as a local politician and leading representative of socialist-Zionist circles in Poland, Silberschein was able to establish extensive contacts with Jewish and non-Jewish leaders and organizations within Poland as well as in the United States, Britain, Germany, and Palestine. In August 1939 he traveled to Switzerland in his capacity as one of the leaders of Polish Zionism to attend the Twenty-First Zionist Congress held in Geneva. Following the German attack on Poland, Silberschein—like most members of the Polish delegation—did not return home and instead decided to stay in Switzerland to organize help for destitute Jews in his home country.

Following his decision, he was soon integrated into the ranks of the World Jewish Congress (WJC). The international organization, which had been founded in 1936 in Geneva to serve as "the diplomatic arm" of the Jewish people internationally, had its prewar headquarters in Paris and a liaison office in Switzerland. The office was located in the venerable Palais Wilson, a huge and impressive property next to Lake Geneva built in 1875. The building had previously been used by the League of Nations, and it now housed many international organizations, among them several Jewish advocacy groups such as the Jewish Agency for Palestine and its Palestine Office in Switzerland, the American Jewish Joint Distribution Committee, and the WJC. The WJC Geneva office was headed by one of its founders, Nahum Goldmann, and, from early 1939 on, by the young lawyer Gerhart Riegner, who had left Germany for Paris and then for Switzerland in 1934 and joined the WJC soon after its founding.[7]

A couple of months after the outbreak of the war, in early 1940, the executive board of the WJC decided to move its headquarters to New York, converting its European branches into subdepartments of its main office. From then on, the European offices "would report to headquarters in New York, and the organization's policy would be determined in New York alone. It was clearly stated that any significant activity by the branches in Europe required prior authorization from New York, and that prominent European functionaries would move from Europe to the United States as part of the organizational transformation."[8] One of them was Goldmann himself, who decided to relocate to the United States in the same year. Nevertheless, the Geneva office remained in place as a small outpost close to the war zones, from which it would potentially be easier to obtain and transmit information. Riegner stayed on as general secretary, and Silberschein was appointed as second representative for the office in September 1939, a few weeks after his arrival in Geneva.

The two men diverged sharply on what goals and priorities the organization should set under the new conditions thrown up by the war. Nearly thirty years younger than Silberschein, Riegner had just finished his legal studies at the University of Geneva when he began working for the organization shortly after its founding. He was full of verve and energy and had cultivated many connections in the city through his university. These included, for instance, his former professor Carl Jacob Burckhardt, a high-ranking official of the International Committee of the Red Cross (ICRC), who eventually became its president in January 1945. By September 1939 Riegner had already been working for the Geneva office for several years and was therefore more familiar than Silberschein with the structure and functioning of the organization as well as with politics and society in Switzerland. Silberschein's official status as a "tolerated foreigner" was not quite clear at first, including the question of how to obtain a work permit; remaining in the country brought many new challenges.[9] Despite this, he remained well connected within the Zionist movement and had gained extensive experience in initiating and coordinating large projects through his political work during the 1920s and 1930s.

On one level, the two men complemented each other well due to their divergent backgrounds, experiences, and skills. However, these differences also meant that they often failed to see eye to eye about how to proceed with work for the office. Riegner generally believed that aid and progress had to be achieved mainly on the official, diplomatic level—for instance, by collecting and passing on information about the German atrocities to the Allies. By contrast, Silberschein thought that only more informal, more direct support could really bring relief to Jewish communities under siege. It thus proved difficult at times for him to accept that Riegner, as general secretary and head of the office, was often reluctant to make quick decisions and unwilling to approve relief measures without prior consultation with the head office in New York.

The emissaries in Switzerland were seen as an important source of information, but the New York executive board also expected to be kept well informed about all steps in advance, something that could only be done with great delay under wartime conditions.[10] This arrangement created dependency, especially on a financial level. The New York office paid staff salaries and generally set the agenda for its representatives in Switzerland, a fact that Riegner rarely questioned. Silberschein, by contrast, felt strongly limited in his ability to operate within the set guidelines. This and the fact that the wheels in a large, international organization often turned slowly prompted him to found his own aid committee as early as in October 1939. RELICO was officially created as a subdepartment of the WJC and was meant to be responsible for the organization's future international relief work. Nevertheless, this structural spin-off in fact gave Silberschein a large degree of independence from New York headquarters and from Riegner. To reinforce this stance, he attached great importance to maintaining RELICO's financial autonomy. Although the WJC continued paying his salary and that of his secretary, Silberschein mainly drew funds from international Jewish organizations such as the Association of Galician Jews in the United States, the Palestine Rescue Committee of the Jewish Agency, Agudas Israel, Histadrut, and the Joint, as well as private donors, to finance his new activities, believing this would give him more freedom.[11] But this approach did not endear him to Riegner, who continuously tried to convince Silberschein to keep in line with the organization's official directives. Yet the structural separation between the two institutions also had advantages for the WJC in general and Riegner in particular: it allowed them to support international relief work vicariously—even personally—without being directly associated with it on an official level. It proved particularly beneficial in terms of future international diplomatic efforts, for the WJC could continue to present itself as a strictly diplomatic organization while engaging actively in aid work at the same time.

During the first years of the war this proved helpful in their interactions with government representatives and international organizations such as the ICRC, since they often had no interest in cooperating openly with representatives from activist circles, fearing these contacts would endanger their relations with German officials and their collaborators. Hence, the WJC officially remained an organization that tried to do everything possible to improve the situation of the European Jews on a diplomatic level, while engaging in transnational relief and rescue activities in an unofficial capacity.

RELICO: Approach and Early Activities

For Silberschein, the underlying goal driving RELICO was to provide quick and direct support to all Jews forced into desperate straits by the war, no matter where they were located. In practice, this meant that RELICO tried to intervene wherever the German war machine had rolled in or in locations that had become centers for Jewish refugees. The challenge proved enormous, with the organization attempting to provide aid simultaneously to numerous regions, including Poland, the Baltic countries, Hungary, Romania, Slovakia, Belgium, the Netherlands, France, and Germany itself. Nevertheless, the main focus throughout the war remained on two operational areas, occupied Poland and both occupied and unoccupied France, even though it became increasingly difficult to stay active in the French occupied zone as the war continued. Silberschein had strong professional and emotional ties to Poland, and France afforded relatively good opportunities for exchanging information and providing relief because of its geographical proximity to both Switzerland and Germany.

During the early weeks of its existence, RELICO tried to get some idea of what had actually happened on the ground during this initial phase of the war and what would constitute effective support for the most vulnerable Jewish populations. First and foremost, this meant establishing contact with the remaining Jewish communities within the war zones and mapping out the aid networks that had managed to survive the invasion. The information received by Silberschein from the occupied territories, much of which came from contacts he had cultivated as a Zionist leader and politician in Poland, helped tailor aid imperatives for each area and Jewish population.[12]

Already in the early days of the war, it had proven extremely difficult to contact the Jewish communities in the war zones: the postal system had been brought to a standstill, and telephone lines had become precarious and very expensive to use. One of RELICO's first and most important activities was thus to set up a communication system that used couriers who traveled back and forth across borders. Through their services, RELICO's *shaliach*—the Hebrew word for "courier" or "messenger"—offered a fairly regular exchange of information between the organization in Geneva and Jewish organizations in occupied areas.

The circle of couriers consisted of three main groups. The first entailed business travelers, merchants who were still crossing borders and agreed to deliver messages alongside these activities. The second group consisted of members of the diplomatic corps, whose activities allowed them, at least in some areas, to travel back and forth across borders. They were particularly popular as couriers, since they were able to transport documents in their diplomatic pouches, which remained private and not subject to border controls. Finally, some clergymen offered their help to RELICO, among them the apostolic nuncio in Switzerland, Monsignor Fillipe Bernardini. RELICO as well as other Jewish organizations in Switzerland began to exploit these opportunities almost immediately after the outbreak of the war.

Not until nearly a year later—toward the end of 1940—was a reasonably stable postal connection between Poland and Switzerland gradually restored. However, many letters only arrived after long delays or not at all. Added to this was the problem of censorship. Depending on their destination, letters sometimes had to pass through three sets of censors: German occupation authorities, officials in the borders of the old German Reich, and, finally, the Swiss authorities. This resulted not only in enormous additional delays but also in very constrained communications and the risk of drawing unwanted attention from authorities. The problem of unstable postal connections cropped up repeatedly as the Germans pushed into new territories and eventually surfaced again with renewed force when the Wehrmacht finally began retreating from early 1943 on. For this reason, the courier system remained critical even after functioning postal connections had been gradually reinstated, and it was continuously expanded through the services of new couriers.[13] In addition, various Jewish organizations in Geneva and elsewhere began to "share" their go-betweens. This meant, for example, that if a particular organization was expecting a courier, it would inform representatives of other organizations so that they could prepare documents to send back with that traveler. This arrangement also allowed individual organizations to share the cost. Some of these individuals supported the work of Jewish organizations in Switzerland ideologically, offering their services free or nearly free of charge, while others demanded financial compensation for their help.[14]

When in the course of 1940 it gradually became easier for people in occupied Poland to get into contact with the outside world, more and more desperate letters began arriving in Switzerland.[15] Word about the new relief organization in Geneva spread quickly through the civilian Jewish population, both in the occupied territories and beyond, and a growing number of people now tried to contact RELICO asking for support either for themselves or for their relatives in the war zones. Thus the organization soon began serving in tandem as a transnational tracing service, making its information available to individuals all over the world but also to other organizations such as the International Red Cross, the Joint Distribution Committee, and the Jewish Agency.[16]

The letters arriving in Geneva quickly made it clear that the central issue in the occupied territories was hunger. A Jewish man residing in Warsaw wrote the following letter in February 1940, spelling out the fate of thousands: "Dear Executive Board, Since I have now fled for the third time and lost all my possessions through the outbreak of the war, I would be extremely grateful for some food parcels so that I can feed my family of four. I implore you not to turn your back on me and my family and allow our distress to increase even further. . . . Assistance is greatly needed here."[17]

In the face of these pleas, Silberschein knew that concrete aid in the form of material support had to be organized as quickly as possible. Still, the course of the war and intensifying anti-Jewish persecution had created an opaque situation in which it remained unclear how the infrastructure for such aid could be realized. Uncertainty notwithstanding, Silberschein and representatives of other Jewish aid organizations in Switzerland, such as the Hechalutz, the Hilfsaktion für die notleidenden Juden in Polen (HAFIP), and the Hilfscomité für notleidende Juden, invested a large part of their time and energy in the following months to finding ways to send food, clothing, and medicine to the Jewish population in occupied territories. All conceivable and seemingly inconceivable possibilities for transport routes, cooperating partners, and financing were considered and tested out. Aware of the ever-changing conditions and their own vulnerable positions as immigrants, they often pursued a range of approaches simultaneously, knowing that only some would actually succeed.

Collective Shipments or Private Packages?

Two different approaches for how relief shipments could be sent to the occupied territories on a large scale eventually crystallized within the ranks of the WJC/RELICO in Geneva. The different schemes being initiated and sustained more or less independently of each other strongly mirrored the distinct character of the two men who devised them, Riegner and Silberschein. In line with his legal training and diplomatic contacts, Riegner attempted to organize large collective shipments through official and licensed channels. At the beginning of 1940 he reached out to representatives of the ICRC in Geneva, hoping that the organization would be able to help in overcoming various obstacles connected with the sending of aid shipments. Because Riegner had been sending activity reports to Burckhardt on a regular basis since taking over the WJC office in the spring of 1939, his former professor was well informed about both the WJC's and RELICO's objectives. Even though Burckhardt and several other officials were generally open to the idea of sending large shipments to the Jews in the occupied territories, negotiations proved difficult and protracted from the beginning: representatives of the ICRC were always concerned about endangering their relations with Germany.[18]

In addition, the sending of aid supplies from Switzerland was rapidly becoming more and more difficult as the war began to spread. Swiss state authorities—worried about impending supply shortages and the domestic unrest that those might produce—decided to increasingly restrict the export of goods as a precaution, making it extremely difficult from 1941 on. While it was still possible to send some parcels containing foodstuff in single or collective consignments at least until November 1940, a new regulation on December 8 generally banned the export of single shipments of every description and largely restricted the possibility of sending collective shipments, even through official channels.[19] Further constraints emerged. During these initial months of testing the waters, the Żydowska Samopomoc Społeczna (Jewish Social Self-Help, or JSS), a committee set up in September 1939 for organizing Jewish welfare in the Generalgouvernement, soon became the main partner in Poland to discuss how aid shipments could be sent and distributed among the Jewish population.[20] In May 1940, German authorities designated it as the only official Jewish charity organization within the Generalgouvernement, banning all other existing Jewish charity institutions henceforth.[21]

Around the same time, the German Department of Population Affairs and Welfare (Abteilung für Bevölkerungswesen und Fürsorge) set up an official body called the Naczelna Rada Opiekuńcza (Main Welfare Council, NRO) in the Generalgouvernement. The body was intended as a kind of umbrella organization that would bring together the three initiatives that already existed: the Polish Rada Glówna Opiekuńcza (Central Welfare Council, RGO), the Ukrainian Centralny Ukrainski Komitet (Ukrainian Central Committee), and the Jewish JSS.[22] The NRO would begin to coordinate and allocate all incoming foreign aid shipments among the different local population groups according to a predefined distribution formula. Philanthropic organizations in the "outside world" thus had an opportunity to send aid to the Generalgouvernement, believing that it would be distributed in an orderly manner, provided they found a way to deliver the shipments. Many of the Jewish organizations in Switzerland were ambivalent about the possibility of sending aid shipments to the JSS through the channels of a German-controlled umbrella organization. On the one hand, it seemed to be the easiest and most reliable way to send material help to the Generalgouvernement. On the other hand, it was clear that only a relatively small proportion of the dispatched goods—about one-quarter in 1940—would actually reach Jewish recipients and that the senders were not able to actively influence the distribution process.[23] Moreover, correspondence with the JSS functionaries in Warsaw showed that the share of the total donations intended for the Jewish population had gradually been curtailed. Finally, in the summer of 1941, the JSS informed relief committees in Geneva that although until then they had received 17 percent of all parcels (*Liebesgaben*) arriving from abroad, they did not expect to receive more aid supplies through the channels of the Main Welfare Council at all.[24] Not knowing if and to what extent shipments to the Main Welfare Council should be pursued under these circumstances, the functionaries of the various relief organizations in Geneva feverishly tried to find other channels. Many of them eventually contacted RELICO, for the organization had already made it clear that it did not trust the Main Welfare Council channels months earlier and had tried to find other avenues for aid.

At the same time, the number of incoming requests for material aid rose continuously, and they were no longer limited to Poland. In 1940, the German troops occupied western Europe. In France, the government had already started on September 4, 1939 (one day after the French entry into the war), to detain what they called "unwanted aliens," also including Germans Jews.[25] In October 1940, only a few months after the French surrender on June 22, the Vichy government began to detain all foreign Jews residing in France in internment camps in the so-called free zone in southern France.[26] The occupation authorities in the northern part of the country also started in the fall of the same year to deport Jews who were expelled from the German Reich to the French internment camps.[27] The internees were allowed to communicate with the outside world to a limited extent by writing letters to family members, friends, and organizations outside the camps and abroad.[28] Soon not only their appeals but also hundreds of requests from concerned relatives all over the world began arriving at RELICO offices in Geneva.[29]

RELICO and its partners in the occupied territories urgently tried to find ways to react to these pleas and to adapt their efforts to the reality that most people in the outside world willing to spend money on aid work were actually trying to help specific individuals or communities. The JSS, for instance, tried to find a way for relief organizations to influence the distribution process for consignments by sending along lists stipulating the names of the intended recipients. Yet it would remain completely unclear to Silberschein's staff in Geneva if any of the goods had actually reached those people.[30]

As a result, instead of financially supporting the charity drives that many Jewish organizations in Switzerland kept organizing to raise funds for collective shipments, many people in Switzerland and abroad tried to find ways to send help to individuals.[31] They resorted to ordering packages privately through commercial shipping companies. This, too, carried risks: such parcels were subject to market conditions and wartime prices, and senders often had to pay exorbitantly high postage and related costs. In addition, many of the commercial companies offering services were not familiar with the ever-changing postal connections to and within the countries at war (or occupied) and were also ignorant of the most recent Swiss export regulations. As a result, a large proportion of the packages never reached the addressees or only arrived after several weeks or even months.

Implementing a Parcel Scheme

Silberschein was well aware of all the difficulties of sending collective consignments, on the one hand, and the urgency of the matter for both the victims and their relatives abroad, on the other. He sought ways to establish a direct and efficient scheme that could function without depending on the goodwill of official agencies and on lengthy approval and financing procedures. These goals conflicted to some extent with Riegner's overtures to the ICRC after the outbreak of war.[32] He thus started to investigate how others were dealing with the problem of aid shipments, entering into a lively exchange about shipping routes, costs, purchase opportunities, and financing with other relief committees in Switzerland and other neutral countries.[33] In the process, he eventually realized in November 1940 that Swiss export regulations were extremely stringent compared with those of other countries. He discovered, for instance, that neither the Yugoslavian nor the Portuguese governments had as yet put restrictions on any goods for export. Accordingly, RELICO immediately began to establish contacts with potential Jewish partners as well as with local shipping companies in these countries. Silberschein's office now also worked on creating a transnational scheme under which parcels could be ordered in Switzerland but sent to addressees in Nazi-occupied territories from either Yugoslavia or Portugal. In Yugoslavia his main contact was his own brother, Alexander Silberschein, who was living in Zagreb with his wife and helped him make arrangements with local shipping companies through November and December 1940. Abraham Silberschein soon started to work closely together with Isaak Weissman and his wife, Lilly Weissman, in Portugal as well.[34] The Weissmans had lived in Berlin until 1937, when they fled the Nazis, initially moving to Paris. They eventually escaped to Portugal via Spain in the summer of 1940 after the German attack on France.[35] As another long-standing member of the Zionist movement, Weissman was an old acquaintance and a person Silberschein relied on heavily.[36]

In consultation with his partners on-site, Silberschein selected a range of goods that would be available for shipment. These options mainly came down to food that was likely to be available in sufficient quantity over a considerable period of time and at a reasonable price, especially locally produced products. In both cases, these included some "classic" products such as wheat flour, coffee, cocoa, tea, marmalade, and honey but also some typical local goods, such as canned sardines and tuna fish, dried prunes and figs, assorted nuts, and tomato puree.

Before the scheme could be put into action, however, several logistical problems still had to be solved both in Yugoslavia and in Portugal. On November 26, 1940, Silberschein wrote to fellow Swiss activist Kusiel Stern, head of the small private aid organization Hilfskomitee für die notleidenden Juden in Lucerne, that a general organizational framework had successfully been put in place in Yugoslavia in order to send packages out to different destinations, including the Generalgouvernement and unoccupied France. According to his letter, the only remaining problem concerning the French "free zone" was that a functioning postal service had not been reestablished between Yugoslavia and France yet.[37] However, by early December 1940, RELICO was able to start sending out packages on a regular basis at least to the Generalgouvernement from Yugoslavia (apparently passing through Hungary and Slovakia). To minimize the work required on-site—it mainly had to be done by one person, his brother Alexander—Silberschein decided to compile several "standard packages" that could be purchased for a fixed price, containing a selection of either meat or dairy products.[38]

A few weeks later, in January 1941, the required organizational scaffolding had finally been set up in Portugal as well, and RELICO was able to start sending parcels from there to unoccupied France. A standardized preprinted request form was created and distributed among the Jewish organizations and interested individuals in Switzerland, as well as in other countries such as Italy, the United States, and several Central American countries.[39] The form included spaces for the names and addresses of both the donor and the prospective recipient, as well as a table that listed all the available products with their prices. In contrast to the approach used with the Yugoslavian packages, each parcel sent from Portugal only contained one product. The prices of each product changed over time depending on availability, cost, and shipping charges. In November

1941, for instance, the request form listed nineteen products, with half a kilo of sardines costing 4.50 Swiss francs (CHF); dried figs, 3.00 CHF; wheat flour, 3.25 CHF; and Ovomaltine, even 8.00 CHF, which was a considerable amount at that time. Only two months later, a deterioration in the supply situation in Portugal meant that the same list had to be reduced to thirteen products, with sardines now costing 5.00 CHF and dried figs (still) 3.00 CHF. Other products had been added to offset those missing, such as almonds for 6.75 CHF per half kilo and tomato puree for 3.50 CHF.[40]

Donors could fill in what and how much they wanted to order, using one form for each potential consignee. The RELICO office in Geneva collected the forms until they had accumulated a reasonable number and then sent a collective order to Weissman in Lisbon, who in turn commissioned parcels from the local shipping companies. In the early spring of 1941, only a few weeks after the scheme had finally been put into effect both in Yugoslavia and in Portugal, the situation in the former had deteriorated again. In April 1941, Silberschein wrote to Samuel Scheps at the Palestine Office in Geneva that suddenly "certain difficulties concerning foreign currency regulations had arisen with the Yugoslavian National Bank, which resulted in lengthy negotiations. When these negotiations were satisfactorily concluded, the political events that are familiar to you occurred, and these ultimately made it impossible to send gift parcels from Yugoslavia."[41] The "political events" he mentioned in his letter—the attack, defeat, division, and occupation of the country by the Axis powers—led to an abrupt halt of the RELICO supply chain from that country. Added to Silberschein's concerns about whether and how the parcel scheme could be continued was his concern about his brother and sister-in-law's safety: they were now living under German rule.[42] However, parcels from Portugal could still be sent, and the project gained momentum during the first half of 1941 as more and more people and organizations learned of the Geneva scheme.

Organizing the Scheme: Purchasers and Recipients

Orders were put in motion in three major ways. First, private parties created individual orders for relatives or friends living in the occupied countries, usually a few one-time shipments. It was initially possible to take out a subscription, commissioning a parcel to be sent every week to one particular person. However, this ceased to be an option, as continuously increasing prices and changing export restrictions made every subsequent shipment increasingly difficult. The second way that RELICO organized parcels was through bundled orders from official bodies such as charities, Jewish communities, smaller aid organizations, political parties, or youth organizations, among them, for instance, the Jewish community of the city of Kreuzlingen, Stern's Hilfskomitee für die notleidenden Juden, the Hechalutz, the Jewish Agency, and the WJC.

In these cases, the organizations themselves collected money and names, filled in the order forms, and gave them to RELICO, usually in bulk. Recipients of these packages were mostly members of specific religious or social groups, compatriots from a certain city or political party, but also relatives and friends of the organizations' members. In the early stages of the operation, groups could also decide to send collective shipments containing a larger amount of parcels to be distributed freely among the needy population of a particular town or region. But as the distress within the occupied areas grew ever greater, this approach created the almost impossible task of deciding who most needed a package. As a result, RELICO kept asking the purchasers to earmark their orders for specific individuals or—if they did not have enough names of potential recipients at their disposal—to allow RELICO to provide them with additional names.[43] These names mainly came from individuals and organizations at the destination: from inmates in the camps in France, for instance, or local rabbis, Zionists, Jewish youth organizations, or the offices of the JSS/Jewish Aid Agency. All of them spent time collecting the names of individuals and families in need who did not have relatives or friends abroad. In addition, private individuals in Switzerland who lacked funds to send parcels to all their acquaintances in occupied areas also had the opportunity to forward names to RELICO, which the organization then passed on to potential donors.

A third route for RELICO parcels was the use of so-called *Gratispakete*. In this case, organizations that made substantial contributions to the parcel scheme were allowed to commission a certain number of parcels free of charge. Organizations usually resorted to this possibility if they had already spent their monthly budget but had not been able to send parcels to every person they wished to reach. They also requested these when they heard of people in acute need who were not directly connected to their organization or movement. RELICO itself paid for the *Gratispakete*, using operational funds or general donations.

Organizations were allowed to order their collective consignments at cost, whereas private purchasers had to pay an additional 20 percent.[44] This "tax" was intended to make wealthier individuals automatically cofinance future *Gratispakete* for people without connections abroad. In a letter from August 1942, Silberschein informed Chaim Barlas, representative of the Jewish Agency in Istanbul, how this system worked: "1) Through orders from private parties to relatives, acquaintances, and friends. A supplement of 20% of the cost is charged, which RELICO then uses to send some packages gratis. 2) Orders from communities

81|113 (157)

18/III/42

poste avec 4/4

BESTELLZETTEL

An das
Komitee zur Hilfeleistung für die
Kriegsbetroffene jüdische Bevölkerung
52, rue des Pâquis
Genf

Hiermit bitte ich Sie, an Herrn ~~Frau~~ Franz Israel Berend
(genaue Adresse) Litzmannstadt, Getto
Kranichweg 13, Zimmer Nr. 14

das - die folgende (n) Paket (e) zur Absendung zu bringen (*) :

1	Paket (e) 1/2 Kg Sardinen	à Fr. 5.--	Betrag	5.-- Fr.
....	" 1/2 Kg Thonfisch	à " 5,50	"	"
....	" 1/2 Kg Spinat	à " 3,50	"	"
....	" 1/2 Kg Grüne Bohnen	à " 3,75	"	"
....	" ~~1/2 Kg Spargel~~	à " ~~3,50~~	"	"
....	" 1/2 Kg Tomatenpuree	à " 3,50	"	"
1	" 1/2 Kg Getrocknete Feigen	à " 3,25	"	3.25 "
....	" 1/2 Kg " Kastanien	à " 3,25	"	"
1	" 1/2 Kg " Pflaumen	à " 4,50	"	"
....	" 1/2 Kg Gezuckerte Pflaumen	à " 4,50	"	4.50 "
....	" 1/2 Kg Rosinen	à " 5,25	"	"
....	" 1/2 Kg Mandeln (geschält)	à " 6,75	"	"
....	" 1/2 Kg Haselnüsse (geschält)	à " 6,50	"	"
3	Pakete	Gesamtbetrag		12.75 Fr.
		15%		1.90
				10.85

Ich erkläre mich damit einverstanden, dass Waren, deren Versendung infolge eines in Zukunft eintretenden Ausfuhrverbotes oder aus sonstigen wichtigen Gründen unmöglich geworden ist, durch andere Artikel gleichen Wertes ersetzt werden.

Ich habe heute die Summe von ....Fr. auf Ihr Postscheckkonto Genève I 5092 überwiesen.

Ort : Genève Unterschrift : M. Ed. Berend

Datum : 7. April 42 Genaue Adresse : 21A Avenue de Miramont

(*) Nicht Gewünschtes durchstreichen.

Order form filled out by Ed. (Eduard) Berend on April 7, 1942, for three parcels to be sent to Franz Berend, living in the Litzmannstadt (Łódź) ghetto. Each parcel in the order contained half a kilo of either canned sardines, dried figs, or dried plums. The 15 percent discount indicates that Eduard was a Jewish refugee himself. He lived on the same street in Switzerland as Silberschein (Avenue de Miramont), which might explain how he heard of RELICO's work. Courtesy of Yad Vashem, Photo Archive, Jerusalem, RG-M.7, file no. 451.

(mostly Swiss) and other organizations, according to Chaluz, various aid committees, including non-Jewish and foreign ones, mainly Swedish. Of course no subsidy will be charged for these shipments."[45] This principle of cofinancing *Gratispakete* through additional fees did not, however, apply to individuals who could prove that they were themselves refugees living in Swiss exile. Recognized refugees who wanted to order packages for their loved ones were granted a discount of 20 percent, in fact the same discount that organizations also enjoyed when ordering large consignments. Later, when the financial footing of RELICO became less stable, this discount was reduced to 15 percent.[46]

Many of the purchasers had heard about the efforts of RELICO through representatives of the WJC or other Zionist organizations or through recommendations by relatives, friends, or colleagues. They ordered parcels from Silberschein's office from across the globe and even from inside the German Reich.[47] Many Jews living in the occupied areas also in turn reached out to any contacts they had in the Allied or neutral countries, informing them about RELICO and urging them to order parcels. Because RELICO was able to achieve a quite large coverage within a relatively short period of time, the parcel scheme quickly gained momentum within just a few months and was soon sending out around 1,500 packages weekly.[48] According to a report on activities that the WJC sent to the Hilfsverein für Jüdische Auswanderung in Zurich in December 1941, around 69,500 packages had been sent out of Portugal for the scheme since the outset of the initiative in January 1941. These included around 14,500 packages that had been purchased at cost by organizations and around 44,700 packages commissioned by individuals who were paying the additional fee of 20 percent per order. Moreover, RELICO had sent out about 10,300 *Gratispakete*, financed with the monies accumulated through the "tax."[49]

To determine if and when the outgoing packages were actually arriving at their destination, Silberschein invented a control system by attaching a preprinted postcard to each package that recipients were meant to send back to the RELICO office in Geneva as an acknowledgment of receipt.[50] The postcards already had the address of RELICO printed on the back, so the writers only had to fill in the date and the number of packages that had arrived. These receipts allowed RELICO to generate statistics of the scheme and gave them an idea of where parcels were principally still arriving.[51] This not only helped them to assess the situation and decide whether parcels should still be sent to certain regions. It also enabled them to give out information on the known whereabouts of relatives to donors and assure them that the parcels they had financed had arrived at their destination. Because the average delivery time of a parcel was between four and eight weeks, many concerned purchasers contacted the RELICO office to ask why it was taking so long. Using statistical data from the receipt postcards at hand, RELICO was able to either reassure them or tell them that the packages would most likely not reach their intended recipients.[52] However, Silberschein was also aware that this control system was prone to error; he assumed that many postcards had gotten lost on their way through several warring countries or could have been filled out and sent by third parties instead of the actual addressees.[53] Nevertheless, the postcards sent to RELICO by the recipients of the packages were often the first signs of life of relatives and friends in months or even years; they offered a faint signal to refugees and relatives abroad that their loved ones were still alive.

Increasing Difficulties and the Cessation of Activities

After initial success over the course of 1941, the scheme gradually collapsed by the end of the year. By the beginning of Operation Barbarossa, the Axis invasion of the Soviet Union on June 22, 1941, postal connections to the east had already greatly deteriorated, with the major transportation lines mainly reserved for military causes. While packages typically would be en route for an average of about four weeks until June 1941, they were now usually in

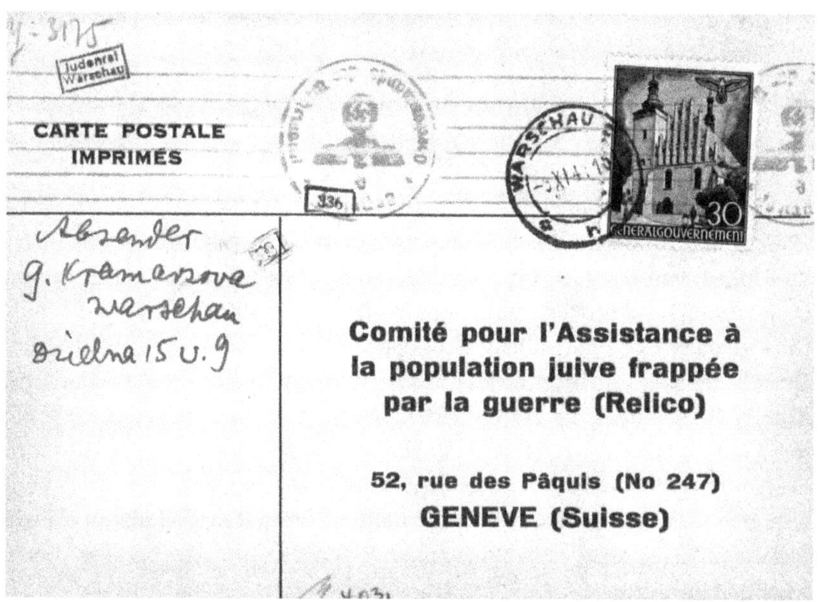
Judenrat Warschau

CARTE POSTALE
IMPRIMÉS

Absender
g. Kramarzova
Warschau
Sielna 15 u. 9

Comité pour l'Assistance à la population juive frappée par la guerre (Relico)

52, rue des Pâquis (No 247)
GENEVE (Suisse)

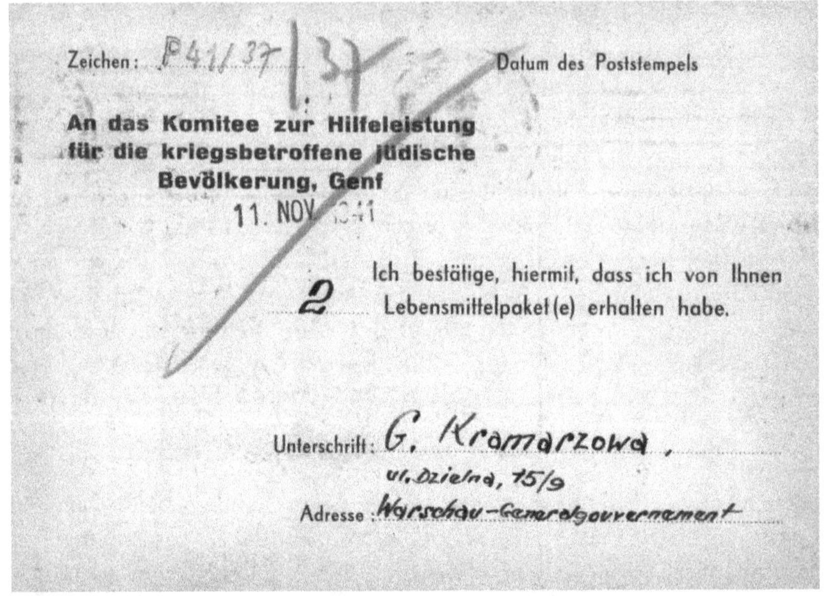
Zeichen: P41/37 37

Datum des Poststempels

An das Komitee zur Hilfeleistung
für die kriegsbetroffene jüdische
Bevölkerung, Genf
11. NOV 1941

2 Ich bestätige, hiermit, dass ich von Ihnen Lebensmittelpaket(e) erhalten habe.

Unterschrift: G. Kramarzowa,
ul. Dzielna, 15/9
Adresse: Warschau-Generalgouvernement

Preprinted receipt postcard sent to RELICO by G. Kramarzowa in the Warsaw ghetto. The Warsaw post office stamped the postcard on November 5, 1941, and it arrived in Switzerland on November 11. Further stamps indicate that the postcard passed through several hands, including the Jewish council in the ghetto (Judenrat), the German authorities, and the Swiss. The sender of the postcard confirmed to RELICO that two parcels had arrived. Courtesy of Yad Vashem, Photo Archive, Jerusalem, RG-M.7, file no. 322.1.

transit for six or even eight weeks. As a result, several receipt postcards arrived in Geneva in which recipients complained that the packages had contained spoiled food.

In addition to these infrastructural difficulties, which escalated after June 1941, another problem was that the purchase orders sharply diminished after the United States entered the war in December 1941. Prohibitions on certain transactions involving foreign-owned property had already increased.[54] As a consequence, many individuals and organizations based in the United States, Great Britain, and other countries became extremely reluctant to order packages from RELICO, including the WJC itself. On June 18, 1941, Silberschein wrote to his old Zionist friend Nathan Eck, who was living in the Warsaw ghetto with his family: "The family [the Socialist-Zionist Poale Zion Party, of which both were members] thinks that one should not send any packages. I disagree. I will make an effort to raise funds here to provide you with packages because I know what that means to you."[55]

While Silberschein feverishly tried to keep RELICO shipments going by putting up large amounts of his own remaining assets, the recurring, gradually worsening supply shortages in Portugal made maintaining the scheme in any systematic way extremely difficult. Every time he altered the order form to reflect current supplies, new export restrictions curtailed the range of products that were available. To still be able to send out parcels, Silberschein decided to add a phrase at the end of each order form by November 1941, giving RELICO the official right to substitute products that had been ordered but were no longer available with others of equal value—and to do so without consulting the purchasers again.[56]

As Silberschein was still struggling to stabilize the scheme again in the first half of 1942—for instance, by focusing on nonperishable, affordable, and nutritious goods—another larger problem gradually came to light. When the mass deportations began in the spring of that year, with thousands of Jewish men, women, and children being transferred to the Operation Reinhard killing centers, many of the parcels RELICO was still sending out could not be delivered: the recipients were no longer at their old registered addresses. The organizers in Switzerland, who had been well informed about what was going on in the war zones up to that point, quickly understood what this meant. By August 1942, Silberschein's colleague Gerhart Riegner had sent a telegram to several officials in the United States and Great Britain, informing them of an apparently systematic plan of the Nazi regime to kill all the Jews of Europe. Information gathered while trying to run the parcel scheme most likely helped Riegner and other Jewish organization officials assess the plausibility of the information arriving in Geneva.

During this highly unsettling time, the receipt postcards that kept arriving intermittently in Switzerland continued serving as an ad hoc tracing service to find out if persons were still living and could be reached under a known address. Because these little signs of life were diminishing rapidly, it became clear in Geneva by mid-1942 that other solutions had to be found to help the Jews to survive. Silberschein and Riegner, who had always held very different opinions on how relief should be provided, could no longer find a way to cooperate. The disagreements between the two became so fundamental that in December 1942 they finally decided to officially split RELICO into two separate organizations: RELICO I, led by Riegner as the relief department of the WJC, and RELICO II, led by Silberschein as a completely independent organization. From then on—until the end of the war—Riegner put much effort into collecting information about Nazi atrocities in order to inform Allied officials about what was going on and to prepare legal cases against the perpetrators.

For his part, Silberschein kept searching for ways to provide relief for the Jews trapped in Europe, without troubling himself too much about the legal framework of his efforts. He eventually started to cooperate with several consuls of Central American countries in Switzerland, who agreed to issue papers that Silberschein could send to Jews still living in the occupied countries, identifying them as citizens of a foreign country. This eventually brought trouble from the Swiss authorities, who strongly disapproved of any relief work that involved illegal or semilegal activities. A house search was conducted in the office of RELICO II in September 1943, and Silberschein spent eight days in police custody. After he was released, the authorities kept him under observation, and his parcels work became extremely difficult to carry on. The shipments, which had already declined massively starting in mid-1942, virtually ceased by the end of 1943. Around the same time, Jewish activists in Switzerland were aware that the majority of Polish Jewry had been annihilated. The situation concerning international relief activities improved a bit again at the beginning of 1944 with the founding of the U.S. War Refugee Board, but by that point Silberschein had seemingly given up hope. In 1951, six years after the war had finally come to an end, he died in Geneva with a broken heart, mourning most of his lost relatives, friends, and colleagues and all of those he had tried to save but who had been killed instead.[57]

In his pain and depression, Silberschein strongly reproached himself and others. Convinced that he had not done enough to help the Jews, he refused to speak or write publicly about his activities during the war. In early 1950, about ten years after the founding of RELICO, he wrote to his old friend and fellow Zionist Jacob Hellman of the WJC office in Buenos Aires:

> Today I am in the process of liquidating RELICO and I know that it would be my duty to write a report on its ten years of work. However, I know very well that I will not do that, not only because of the difficulty of focusing on this topic (I personally lost and suffered too much in this war), but also because I would then have to attack people who today are generally considered very commendable and who are regarded as "rescuers."[58]

As a result of Silberschein's silence and his early death, RELICO and his activities were almost completely forgotten in the following decades.

This chapter has tracked one short-lived but vital aid project emerging from what was essentially a one-man initiative. The project underwent a continual evolution and faced considerable obstacles before its definitive demise starting at the end of 1942 and continuing over the course of 1943. Despite being an emigrant who had just arrived in Switzerland, Silberschein was able to build RELICO into a huge and comprehensive scheme with just two or three staff members and very little outside help. Unaware of the difficulties facing the organization, a man in Brussels wrote to RELICO in March 1942, thanking them for parcels that had been sent to his brothers in the French internment camp Noé: "You have provided great assistance to my brothers. . . . A shipment of your food donation has truly helped to alleviate their suffering, all the more because no other agency has provided such aid for them. I need not tell you how grateful I am to you."[59] Letters like this one arrived in great numbers in Geneva, expressing profound gratitude from the recipients themselves or their relatives and friends abroad, along with their relief at having found at least one remaining ally who was able to help. Gizi Fleischmann, a Zionist activist and member of the Jewish council in Bratislava, even finished one of her letters by stating that "this is a historic deed."[60] She was killed in Auschwitz some months later, as were most of those Silberschein had tried to save.

As this chapter has documented, a small group of Jewish activists in Switzerland, with limited means and against opposition from Allied countries and leaders of some of the major international Jewish organizations, initiated and executed ambitious plans to support Jewish communities in Nazi-controlled Europe. Their position inside continental Europe allowed them to bypass the Allied blockade, as long as they could find groups and individuals willing to cover the expenses associated with the shipment of relief parcels. In contrast to more established Jewish agencies such as the World Jewish Congress, they skirted blockade rules and continued with the shipments even after 1941 and the entry of the United States into the war. Faced with constantly changing rules and many other obstacles such as price spikes and uncertainty about the fate of deliveries, Silberschein and his contacts managed to ship thousands of parcels from Switzerland and other neutral countries to desperate communities in the Nazi ghettos and internment camps. The name RELICO, associated with a small office in Geneva, raised hopes among prisoners and their relatives abroad. At a time when the major Allied powers stubbornly rejected pleas by Jewish agencies in Britain and the United States for intervention, Silberschein and his contacts—risking conflicts with their closest associates and the WJC headquarters in New York—worked tirelessly to send support to starving communities.

Notes

1 Central Zionist Archives (CZA), A320/226, Pergamenter to Ullmann, September 17, 1943.

2 Ibid., Ullmann to Pergamenter, November 4, 1943.

3 Abraham Silberschein was born Adolf Henryk Silberschein. In the late 1930s, he stopped using his first name, usually signing only "A." in letters and other official documents. From 1940 on, he began using the first name Abraham instead of Adolf, which soon became the name most of his colleagues and friends called him. Some contemporary documents refer to him as Alfred, but Silberschein does not appear to have used this name himself.

4 Within the newly established "Generalgouvernement," the Germans introduced some help for the local population using the structure of their National Socialist People's Welfare organization (Nationalsozialistische Volkswohlfahrt). The support, mainly made up of soup kitchens and public food distributions, was meant exclusively for the non-Jewish population, especially the so-called ethnic German *Volksdeutschen*. For an overview, see Herwart Vorländer, "NS-Volkswohlfahrt und Winterhilfswerk des deutschen Volkes," *Vierteljahrshefte für Zeitgeschichte* 34, no. 3 (1986).

5 Report, "Die Deutschen in Warschau. Das Martyrium der jüdischen Bevölkerung," October 19, 1939. Author not identified by name, ETH Zurich/Archiv für Zeitgeschichte (AfZ), RG IB JUNA Archiv, file no. 933. A written protocol of his report was sent to the Jewish news agency JUNA (Jüdische Nachrichten) in Switzerland.

6 "Die Deutschen in Warschau," translated from the German original.

7 Gerhart Riegner, *Niemals verzweifeln. Sechzig Jahre für das Jüdische Volk und die Menschenrechte* (Gerlingen: Bleicher Verlag, 2001).

8 Zohar Segev, *The World Jewish Congress during the Holocaust: Between Activism and Restraint* (Berlin: De Gruyter Oldenbourg, 2014), 5. See also Official Announcement of the Directorate of the World Jewish Congress in New York, August 1, 1940, American Jewish Archives (Cincinnati), 361 A5/2.

9 Silberschein's status remained somewhat uncertain until the end of the war. He held an official work permit that allowed him to work officially for the WJC, but Swiss authorities questioned its validity repeatedly. The authorities also considered detaining him in an internment camp for foreign refugees in Switzerland several times, the last time in the fall

of 1943. See detention order for Silberschein, Swiss Police Department (EJPD), October 28, 1943, in the Swiss Federal Archive (CH-BAR), Dossier E4264#1985/197#514*, Az. N12333, Silberschein, Adolf Henryk, 30.03.1882, 1943–75.

10 For an analysis of knowledge and information coming into Switzerland, see Jürgen Matthäus, *Predicting the Holocaust: Jewish Organizations Report from Geneva on the Emergence of the "Final Solution," 1939–1942* (Lanham, MD: Rowman & Littlefield in association with the USHMM, 2019); Gaston Haas, *"Wenn man gewusst hätte, was sich drüben im Reich abspielte . . .": 1941–1943, was man in der Schweiz von der Judenvernichtung wusste* (Basel: Helbing & Lichtenhahn, 1994); Raya Cohen, "Das Riegner-Telegramm—Text, Kontext und Zwischentext," *Jahrbuch für deutsche Geschichte* (Tel Aviv), no. 23 (1994): 301–24; Raya Cohen, "The Lost Honour of Bystanders? The Case of Jewish Emissaries in Switzerland," in *"Bystanders" to the Holocaust: A Re-evaluation*, ed. David Cesarani and Paul A. Levine (London: Frank Cass, 2002), 146–70.

11 Cf. Nathan Eck, "The Rescue of Jews with the Aid of Passports and Citizenship Papers of Latin American States," *Yad Vashem Studies* 1 (Jerusalem, 1957): 140; and Israel Gutman et al., eds., *Enzyklopädie des Holocaust. Die Verfolgung und Ermordung der europäischen Juden* (Munich: Piper Verlag, 1998), 3:1218.

12 For a detailed account on the activities of RELICO in its first year, see the official report "1 Jahr RELICO. Bericht über die Tätigkeit des Committee for Relief of the war-stricken Jewish population (RELICO), 1939–1940," YVA, RG M.20, file no. 20.

13 However, working with couriers was always problematic. On the one hand, some were arrested during their travels; documents falling into the hands of the authorities remained a constant danger. On the other hand, one could also never know how trustworthy a courier was; every courier could potentially also be an undercover agent for one side or the other. The case of one Mr. Oehri is striking. During the war, he offered his services as a courier between Romania and Switzerland to several Jewish organizations in Switzerland, but he disappeared in the autumn of 1944 after he was suspected of passing on information. Only in September 1945 were Swiss authorities able to determine that he had indeed been a German spy and had defected to Germany. See CH-BAR, Dossier E4320B#1971–78#971.

14 On the costs incurred and the coordination of "shared" couriers, see, e.g., Silberschein to Weissmann (Lisbon), October 23, 1943, YVA, RG M.20,

file no. 28, and Silberschein to Weissmann, November 24, 1943, YVA, RG M.20, file no. 29.

15 In the activity report that RELICO published in October 1940, one year after its establishment, the organization stated that about 300–400 letters were by then arriving each day, containing both inquiries about missing persons and requests for material support in the form of food supplies. Cf. "1 Jahr RELICO. Bericht über die Tätigkeit des Committee for Relief of the war-stricken Jewish population (RELICO), 1939–1940," YVA, RG M.20, file no. 20.

16 For this purpose, RELICO created a special card file containing the names of tens of thousands of Jews still believed to be living in the occupied territories. The names they had been collecting from incoming letters were then regularly passed on in long lists to the ICRC and other interested organizations.

17 Letter from Jacob Isaak Landau to RELICO, February 19, 1940, YVA, RG M.7, file no. 849. The letter was sent to the Jewish community in Lisbon, which then forwarded it to RELICO in Geneva.

18 For an in-depth depiction of the work done by the ICRC in this context during the war, see Gerald J. Steinacher, this volume. See also Meir Dworzecki, "The International Red Cross and Its Policy vis-à-vis the Jews in Ghettos and Concentration Camps in Nazi-Occupied Europe," in *Rescue Attempts during the Holocaust: Proceedings of the Second Yad Vashem International Historical Conference*, ed. Israel Gutman and Efraim Zuroff (Jerusalem: Yad Vashem, 1977), 71–110; Jean-Claude Favez, *Warum schwieg das Rote Kreuz? Eine internationale Organisation und das Dritte Reich* (Munich: DTV, 1994); Gerald Steinacher, *Hakenkreuz und Rotes Kreuz. Eine humanitäre Organisation zwischen Holocaust und Flüchtlingsproblematik* (Innsbruck: Studienverlag, 2013).

19 See letter from the Swiss Federal Department of Economic Affairs, Trade Department (Eidgenössisches Volkswirtschaftsdepartement, Handelsabteilung) to the imports and exports section (Sektion für Ein- und Ausfuhr), December 28, 1940, in CH-BAR, Dossier E7110#1967/32#4789* (Liebesgaben, Internationales Rotes Kreuz).

20 Ghettos were created at more than 1,150 sites in eastern Europe between 1939 and 1944.

21 After this point, all other organizations still operating finally merged into the JSS, making any independent work practically impossible. Cf. letter from the JSS to the Jewish community of Lisbon, December 20, 1940, YVA, RG M.2, file no. 295. The JSS, which the Germans liquidated

in June 1942 and reestablished only four months later as the Jewish Aid Agency (Jüdische Unterstützungsstelle, or JUS), was headed by a board of notable Jewish leaders who had been appointed and recognized by Jewish communities or councils and several important Jewish organizations such as the Joint, the TOZ, ORT, and CENTOS. Michał Weichert served as director of the JSS/JUS. Cf. YVA, RG O.21, file no. 16. See also the contribution by Alicja Jarkowska, this volume.

22 Dworzecki, "International Red Cross," 95. On the RGO, see also Arnon Rubin, *Facts and Fictions about the Rescue of the Polish Jewry during the Holocaust* (Tel Aviv: Tel Aviv University Press, 2003), 2; Favez, *Das Rote Kreuz*, 308.

23 The distribution formula that determined the percentage of the total incoming contributions that the three subcommittees would receive thereby changed over the course of time, gradually diminishing the portion distributed to the JSS from an initial 25 percent to 16 or 17 percent and later to only 10 percent. Cf. M. Weichert (JSS) to the administration of the Generalgouvernement (Regierung des Generalgouvernements, Hauptabteilung Innere Verwaltung, Abteilung Bevölkerungswesen und Fürsorge), April 7, 1942, YVA, RG O.21, file no. 16. See also Favez, *Das Rote Kreuz*, 308ff.

24 Cf. the JSS to B. Tschlenoff (OSE) (copy), June 1941, YVA, RG M.20, file no. 114.

25 Cf. Annette Nogarède, "Deutsche Emigration nach Frankreich 1933–1940," *Lernen aus der Geschichte, Flucht und Migration im Vorfeld und während des Zweiten Weltkrieges* 5 (2015): 14. On the persecution of the Jewish population in France during World War II, see Henry Rousso, *Vichy. Frankreich unter deutscher Besatzung 1940–1944* (Munich: C. H. Beck, 2009); Christian Eggers, *Unerwünschte Ausländer. Juden aus Deutschland und Mitteleuropa in französischen Internierungslagern 1940–1942* (Berlin: Metropol 2002).

26 Most of these internment camps were located in southwestern France in the Pyrenees close to the Spanish-French border, such as Gurs, Noé, Récébédou, Le Vernet, Rivesaltes, St.-Cyprien, and Argelès-sur-Mer.

27 One of the best-known actions in this context was the deportation of more than 6,500 Jews from the Baden and "Saarpfalz" regions of southwest Germany to Gurs in October 1940. The so-called Wagner-Bürckel operation was one of the first systematically planned mass deportations of Jews during the Third Reich.

28 See the chapter on Vichy internment camps by Laurie A. Drake, this volume.

29 See, e.g., YVA, RG M.7, files no. 224, 239, 301.
30 Cf. the JSS to the Hilfsaktion für die notleidenden Juden in Polen (HAFIP), July 25, 1941, YVA, RG O.21, file no. 33. See also YVA, RG M.20, file no. 28.
31 Cf., e.g., the donation appeal circulated among the Swiss Jews by the Schweizerischer Israelitischer Gemeindebund, the umbrella organization of Jewish communities in Switzerland, May 22, 1941, AfZ, RG IB Jüd. Gemeinde Kreuzlingen, file no. 116.
32 While Silberschein tried to find new ways of sending parcels (to private individuals) on a large scale in the coming months, Riegner stuck to his strategy of sending collective shipments. As a result, two largely independent strands of action developed, one led by Riegner and one by Silberschein. Although both continued to be in close contact and exchanged information about postal costs, legal and organizational conditions, and possible partners in Switzerland and abroad, both made it clear that they only wanted to have informal contact with each other's activities. One exception was contacts with New York. While Riegner initially made Silberschein's new parcel scheme appear to be a joint effort in his communications with the WJC's New York headquarters, he increasingly distanced himself from it, and the clearer it became that New York did not support the cause. This development reached its climax with the entry of the United States into the war in December 1941, after which Riegner no longer mentioned Silberschein's scheme in his reports. Cf. Riegner to WJC NY, December 10, 1940, CZA, RG C3, file no. 617.
33 Cf. CZA, RG C3, file nos. 175, 212. See also YVA, RG M.20, file no. 48.
34 In addition, Silberschein also maintained relations with various private shipping companies in both countries, as well as with several other Jewish organizations in Portugal, such as the Refugee Relief Department of the Lisbon Jewish community and the Portuguese commission for assisting Jewish refugees, COMASSIS (Comissão portuguesa de Assistência aos Judeos Refugiados em Portugal). Cf. YVA, RG M.20, file nos. 28, 29, 105. See also Avraham Milgram, *Portugal, Salazar and the Jews* (Jerusalem: Yad Vashem Publications, 2011), 127ff. and 198ff.
35 The couple stayed in Portugal officially as refugees, trying to immigrate to the United States, but eventually gave up this plan after it became increasingly difficult to obtain visas after the United States entered the war in December 1941. See Weissman's postwar autobiographical notes: YVA, RG P.3, file no. 10; Milgram, *Portugal*, 165ff.

36 In 1941 Silberschein therefore appointed Weissman as the official representative of RELICO in Lisbon, and, in addition, the New York headquarters even designated him as the official WJC spokesman in Portugal in 1943. Cf. Weissman to WJC New York, June 28, 1943, YVA, RG M.20, file no. 29.

37 The postal connection had been cut off in the course of the German attack on France. In his letter to Stern, Silberschein wondered whether parcels could be sent first from Yugoslavia to Switzerland, from where they then would be passed on to France. Silberschein to Stern, November 26, 1940, CZA, RG C3, file no. 175.

38 Silberschein to Isaac Feldstein (HAFIP), January 31, 1941, CZA, RG C3, file no. 212. Silberschein placed great significance on sending kosher products, particularly in the early months of the campaign (e.g., he succeeded in sending kosher meat from Yugoslavia). As coordinating shipments became increasingly difficult, the question of whether the products were kosher played less and less of a role. In the later years, Silberschein nonetheless still made efforts to send matzot for Passover. Cf. also Silberschein to Stern, November 26, 1940, CZA, RG C3, file no. 175, and Silberschein to Tartakower (WJC NY), January 16, 1941, CZA, RG C3, file no. 618.

39 See image of order form below. The RELICO collection held at the Yad Vashem Archive today (RG M.7) contains thousands of request forms that had been filled out by organizations and individuals and sent back to RELICO. See YVA, RG M.7, file nos. 451–475.

40 Cf. YVA, RG M.7, file no. 453. Silberschein and his partners on-site always tried to keep up to date on developments concerning the local supply situation and put much effort in keeping track of products that could still be purchased and sent if others were no longer available. Silberschein was also in constant contact with representatives of other Jewish organizations in Switzerland that were ordering packages, explaining the situation to them and RELICO's own experiences. See, e.g., letter from Silberschein to Isaac Feldstein, July 18, 1941, CZA, RG C3, file no. 212.

41 Silberschein to Scheps, 8 April 1941, YVA, RG M.7, file no. 586.

42 After the division of former Yugoslavia, Zagreb became part of the newly established fascist Independent State of Croatia, which almost immediately passed antisemitic laws. Silberschein tried to stay in contact with his brother and sister-in-law and tried to provide them with any means of support. Nevertheless, they lost contact by the end of 1941, when

Alexander and Filomene presumably were deported to the Jasenovac camp. Cf. YVA, RG M.20, file no. 180.10; and CZA, RG C3, file nos. 1168 and 1266.

43 Cf. RELICO to Hilfsverein für jüdische Auswanderung, September 29, 1944, CZA, C3, file no. 211.

44 In addition, organizations had to pay an administrative contribution of 3 percent. Cf. RELICO to Stern, May 8, 1941, CZA, RG C3, file no. 175.

45 Silberschein to Barlas, August 2, 1942, YVA, RG M.20, file no. 35.

46 Cf. RELICO to Emigrantenkolonie Degersheim, May 29, 1941, YVA, RG M.7, file no. 477.

47 On August 31, 1942, e.g., a representative of the Jewish community in Essen, Marianne Strauss, ordered packages to be sent to three members of their community who had been deported to the transit ghetto Izbica in the Generalgouvernement. Her letter was first sent to the Portuguese relief organization for Jewish refugees in Lisbon and subsequently transmitted to RELICO. See letter, Marianne Strauss to the Comissão portuguesa de Assistência aos Judeos Refugiados, August 31, 1942, in CZA, C2, file no. 1481.

48 Cf. Jacques Picard, *Die Schweiz und die Juden 1933–1945*, 2nd ed. (Zurich: Chronos Verlag, 1994), 395.

49 These numbers do not include the packages sent from Yugoslavia. According to the document, these constituted another "several thousand." Cf. WJC (presumably Riegner) to Hilfsverein für Jüdische Auswanderung, December 16, 1941, CZA, RG C3, file no. 211.

50 See preprinted postcard sent to RELICO below.

51 Several thousand receipt postcards, sorted by region, can be found in the archive of RELICO. See YVA, RG M.7, file nos. 322–30.

52 Cf., e.g., RELICO to Anny Kulka (New York City), December 4, 1941, CZA, RG C3, file no. 111. See also CZA, RG C3, file no. 211.

53 Whenever possible, RELICO tried to show the postcards to the original purchasers of the parcels to see if they could identify the recipients' handwriting.

54 See *Administration of the Trading with the Enemy Act. Hearings before the Subcommittee to Investigate the Administration of the Trading with the Enemy Act of the Committee on the Judiciary, United States Senate, Eighty-Third Congress, First Session, Part 1* (Washington, DC: U.S. Government Printing Office, 1954), 421–25, and www.presidency.ucsb.edu/documents/executive-order-8389-protecting-funds-victims-aggression (accessed June 6, 2021).

55 Silberschein to Eck, June 18, 1941, YVA, RG M.20, file no. 115. Eck and his family managed to leave the Warsaw ghetto with the help of foreign passports that Silberschein had sent to them. They were deported to an internment camp for foreign civilians in Vittel. Despite these papers, they were later put on a train to Drancy and subsequently to Auschwitz. Eck survived by jumping off the deportation train, but his wife was killed in Auschwitz. Their daughter was able to survive in hiding with a Catholic family in France. She and Eck later emigrated to Israel, where he became one of the founding members of Yad Vashem.

56 See, e.g., YVA, RG M.7, file no. 232.

57 He never managed to find his brother and sister-in-law, the sole Silberschein relatives known to the author. After the war, he eventually had to come to terms with the fact that they had most likely been killed. See YV, RG M.20, file no. 180.10; CZA, RG C3, file nos. 1168 and 1266.

58 Silberschein to Hellman, February 15, 1950, in YVA, RG M.20, file no. 24. The organization had not been active for some time.

59 Julius Lorch to RELICO, March 3, 1942, in CZA, RG C.2, file no. 1499.

60 Gizi Fleischmann to Silberschein, May 9, 1943, in YVA, RG M.20, file no. 93.

3

HELP FOR THE GHETTOS AND CONCENTRATION CAMPS

Exile Governments, Jewish Agencies, and Humanitarian Aid for Deported Jews during the War

JAN LÁNÍČEK

> *Jewish life in Europe has not yet been snuffed out, and we certainly cannot sit back and ask, "Why should we give money for relief? There is nothing further to be done."*
>
> —Joseph J. Schwartz, 1943[1]

In June 1943, Symcha Gausman, a recent immigrant to Australia, sent a letter from Adelaide to Adolph Brotman, secretary of the Board of Deputies of British Jews in London:

> Dear Sir!
>
> The Honorary Secretary of the Australian Jewish Welfare Society of Melbourne Miss F[rances] Barkman M.A. advised me to apply to you for the help I need. I have a wife Ester Leja Gausman (age 35) "**MAKOW** Süd Ost Priesen Grüner Markt No 13" and two children

---

My research for this chapter was supported by the 2019 Ruth and David Musher/JDC Archives Fellowship. I would like to thank Ruth and David Musher for their generous support and the staff of the JDC Archives for the warm welcome in New York.

> Lejb Gausman age 6 years boy [and] CHANA Gausman age 4 ½ years girl, formerly Poland (near Warsaw). I would like to give them any possible financial help, a food parcel or a clothing parcel. I am in a good position and money does not matter to me if it only can help my family. You can imagine in what conditions a young woman and two little children in Nazi occupied Poland live. From Miss Barkman I got to know that you are the only man that can help my family in Poland. I would be very obliged if you would kindly try to do your best in such desperate moment for my family. I will anxiously await your answer.[2]

With the last immigration routes closing in late 1941 and options for physical rescue in the realm of pure utopia, Gausman's desperate attempt shows one of the few avenues left to those who wanted to support Jews living under the Nazis. Relief food parcels, they hoped, would allow their families and friends to survive until the end of the war. Unknown to Gausman, the ghetto in Maków Mazowiecki had been liquidated seven months earlier, in November 1942, and the surviving Jewish inmates were deported to Auschwitz. His wife and children were most likely no longer alive in June 1943, when he tried to help them.

In Nazi-controlled Europe, hundreds of thousands of both non-Jews and Jews shipped food parcels to their relatives, friends, former neighbors, and even casual acquaintances. Some of them sent only one parcel, while others developed extensive networks that shipped hundreds and even thousands of packages with food, medicine, and clothes.[3] Further help reached the ghettos and camps from outside the Nazi realm. Major international humanitarian and philanthropic organizations initiated extensive schemes for thousands of deportees and incarcerated prisoners. Help reached the Jews in the first years of the war, until mid-1941, when the U.S. Treasury Department tightened the restrictions on remittances of funds to occupied Poland, imposing further restrictions after Germany declared war on the United States in December 1941.[4] It took over a year, until early 1943, before Jewish activists managed to revive any Allied government–approved programs on a very modest scale and carried them forward with varying success until the end of the war. Unfortunately, this was at a time when the majority of Holocaust victims had already perished in overcrowded ghettos, forced labor camps, execution pits of eastern Europe, or the gas chambers.

Relief parcel programs from overseas have been marginalized by historians at the expense of other rescue initiatives. The most detailed account of the American Jewish Joint Distribution Committee (JDC, or the Joint) pays only scant attention to the food distribution programs, especially to those developed after

1941, when the Allies fully enforced the blockade of continental Europe.[5] Only in the last two decades have several historians researched the Allied governments' attitudes toward such relief initiatives. Ronald W. Zweig draws far-reaching conclusions about the nature of the help that relief parcels could offer in wartime, arguing that they "had greater potential for saving lives than the chimerical hopes of any negotiated last-minute reprieve by the Nazi authorities for the concentration camp internees."[6] His contribution also raises the question of when the relief schemes developed. Zweig dates the origins of the shipments from outside of Nazi Germany only to June 1943, when the International Committee of the Red Cross (ICRC) initiated trial shipments to concentration camps in Germany, and traces a real increase in the shipments in June 1944, after the U.S. government joined the programs.[7] Meredith Hindley, in contrast, gives several examples of earlier relief programs, pointing to the role that the "increasingly testy" London-based governments-in-exile played in persuading the British to relax the economic blockade of Europe. However, she also concludes that any humanitarian interventions were, naturally, secondary to military objectives. By late 1942, she remarks, the Allies "knew the Jews had little time," but "they remained reluctant to alter policies engineered to produce the defeat of Nazi Germany."[8]

Searching for the origins of the Allies' reluctance to help civilians, Michael R. Marrus suggests that the early twentieth century saw a "retreat from humanitarian intervention," which "was one of the casualties of the First World War, and had atrophied" before what might have been humanitarianism's greatest test to that point: World War II and the Holocaust. The Great Powers became less willing to intervene purely on humanitarian grounds. In this way, Marrus puts the allegedly inadequate responses of the major Allied powers to Nazi persecution of the Jews into a longer-term perspective.[9] The Allies during World War II simply believed that they had to use the tools of economic warfare to bring Nazi Germany to its knees. This strict enforcement of the blockade could for a long time not be challenged and thus prevented even minor shipments of food parcels to the starving Jewish population. At a theoretical level, the political scientist Joan C. Tronto writes about relations between politics and morality, where ethical issues, especially in international relations, are on the agenda only "when power disputes have been resolved, or when there is a strategic advantage to be gained by appearing to be moral."[10] Her conclusions can help explain Allied attitudes toward the economic blockade during the war. They were willing to allow only small-scale programs, token gestures that could never bring any significant amount of food to the Jews in Nazi Europe.

This chapter looks anew at the topic of the humanitarian aid organized by exiled Allied governments with the help and often at the instigation of international Jewish agencies and activists. Despite the fact that the help from abroad could not bring relief to any substantial number of Jewish prisoners, the programs that developed in Britain, the United States, and especially Portugal, Switzerland, Turkey, and Sweden offer a new perspective on humanitarian intervention during World War II. Those individuals such as Gausman or Brotman who tried to organize relief from the Allied and neutral countries faced formidable obstacles in their efforts to reach Jewish prisoners. Their perseverance in the face of bureaucratic obstacles and the Nazis' brutal persecution of the European Jewry attests to the individual and group feeling of an obligation to care for those who had been sentenced to a slow death in overcrowded ghettos and camps of eastern Europe. Their efforts found willing supporters and advocates but also ran up against many who staunchly opposed the shipment of food to the territories under the Nazi rule.

Food and Starvation in the Nazi Empire

Food planning was one of the cornerstones of Hitler's government policies from 1933 onward. The Nazis felt the need to cut short the rise of dissent and social unrest in the country. Memories of the German Revolution of 1918–19 and the Great Depression were constantly on Hitler's mind, and "the vow to eliminate hunger was one of the NSDAP's first and most important promises, more important for many Germans than ridding the nation of Jews."[11] The war that Hitler unleashed would not have been possible without access to food, but, more fundamentally, one Nazi ideological justification for the war itself was future access to food resources: the acquisition of *Lebensraum*, the grandiose idea about living space in the East, could help secure the existence of the purportedly superior "Aryan" race.[12]

Confiscation of food and other resources became an integral element of German occupation policies in the conquered territories during the war. The occupation armies were fed using brutally acquired local resources, and these policies against local populations reached their peak in the occupied eastern territories. Access to food and the allocation of specific food items were determined by the racial status assigned to a particular group on the Nazi ideological spectrum. The Jews, the perceived archenemies of the "Aryans," were relegated to the very bottom of the imagined hierarchy of the human races and were among the first to be deprived of access to food.

Hunger soon spread across Europe's Jewish population. Its access to basic consumer goods such as meat, dairy products, fruit, and vegetables was gradually restricted in Nazi Germany and then, after the outbreak of war, in all the territories under German rule. Beginning in October 1939, ghettos were set up across eastern Europe. Behind their walls, Jews were increasingly isolated from the local population and were almost entirely dependent on food allocations received from local German administrations. In addition to unsanitary conditions, raging epidemics, and daily instances of physical violence, most Jewish ghetto residents soon suffered from severe malnutrition.[13] Their food allocations were much lower than the daily caloric intake that adults and children alike needed to stay healthy.[14] Science writer Sharman Apt Russell succinctly summarizes the situation: "The official Nazi policy was starvation."[15] According to Chaim Kaplan, chronicler of conditions in the Warsaw ghetto, in May 1942, "As many as sixty per cent [of the Jews of Warsaw] are starving in the full sense of the word. Up to thirty per cent are in a state of terrible deprivation and hunger, even though it is not apparent from without."[16] The situation for the Jews was even worse in concentration and forced labor camps. Jews in Nazi camps, alongside Sinti and Roma and Soviet POWs, resided at the bottom of the hierarchy of prisoners and received among the smallest allocations of food.

Soon hundreds, even thousands, of interned or incarcerated Jews succumbed to hunger or to diseases stemming from severe malnutrition.[17] Miriam Wattenberg, another oft-cited observer in the Warsaw ghetto, noted in her diary on September 19, 1942: "My mother lies on her mattress all day long; she is so starved that she cannot move. Ann is like a shadow, and my father is terribly thin, just skin and bones. I seem to bear the hunger better than the others. I just grit my teeth when the gnawing feeling in my stomach begins."[18] In the industrial city of Łódź (called Litzmannstadt by the Germans), Dawid Sierakowiak wrote that the permanently raging hunger was physically and spiritually breaking down Jewish residents. Sierakowiak's father began to steal food from his wife and children.[19] Starvation could destroy families trapped in ghettos even before prisoners physically succumbed to malnutrition.

In these circumstances, any extra food the Jews were able to obtain on the black market increased their chances for survival for another day or week. Others attempted to get more substantial help from the outside. Already in April 1940, those deported to the Lublin district in eastern Poland sent desperate pleas to their relatives in western Europe: "We are maintained solely by what you sent recently. We are grateful that at least our child is given dinner by some compassionate people. We can never get used to this life. Many good people have ended their suffering."[20] Similarly, Jews in the Warsaw ghetto contacted their friends in Switzerland and Britain, pleading: "Save us from a death by hunger. . . . Our parents have died. Please send me a parcel of food. Love and kisses."[21] But what did potential parcel sponsors and activists actually know about the living and working conditions of the Jews under the Nazis?

The Outside World and Starvation under the Nazis

The deliberate starvation of the Jews under the Nazis was a recognized fact even outside Europe early in the war. Newspapers relayed reliable reports about life in the ghettos, and individual prisoners found ways to contact their relatives or friends in the Allied and neutral countries. Jewish refugees who before 1941 managed to escape from occupied Poland via the Soviet Union provided further details. The flow of information decreased as the war dragged on, but reports and letters still managed to reach relatives abroad. German, Austrian, and Czech Jews deported to the east in 1941–42 sent cards depicting the horrific situation in the ghettos. They used regular postal service where possible or relied on illegal channels. The family of Ida Herrmann managed to smuggle a letter to their friends back in Prague from their exile in the eastern shtetl of Izbica: "We beg you to send us packages as often as possible, mainly sugar, roux, artificial honey, groats, millet. In short, we would be really grateful for everything [not legible] hunger is painful."[22] Similar messages were transmitted through Switzerland, Sweden, and Palestine to the Allied countries. In April 1942, a representative of the Polish Jewry in Palestine appealed to the Polish government-in-exile in London and to the Jewish organizations in Britain and America, describing the "unprecedented hunger . . . raging among the Jews in occupied Poland." He asked them for "immediate action to save hundreds of thousands of starving Jews in the ghettos from extinction." The report was published by the Jewish Telegraphic Agency in New York.[23]

Only a few international humanitarian agencies operated in occupied Poland in the first years of the war, with the Joint leading the Herculean effort to stave off starvation. The JDC office in Warsaw, in cooperation with other organizations in Poland such as the Jewish Social Self-Help under Michał Weichert, distributed tonnes of food delivered from Romania, Yugoslavia, Slovakia, and Lithuania. The JDC designed a particular way to finance their work in occupied Poland to ensure that the Nazis could not directly benefit from the aid. This was in line with the principle adopted by American Jewish organizations and "in conformity with the policies of the United States Government in its effort to lend aid to Great Britain."[24] The Jews who were emigrating from Germany and German-dominated countries deposited local currency with local Jewish philanthropic agencies, who supported less fortunate members of the community. The Joint then paid for the transportation of the refugees once they left German territory. A large part of such funds deposited in Nazi-dominated Europe were—with the consent of the German authorities—used to support Jews in Poland but also in Germany, Austria, the Protectorate of Bohemia and Moravia, and Slovakia.[25]

The JDC used the funds to run soup kitchens in ghettos and to finance relief for children's homes, old-age homes, and hospitals. For the first six months of 1942, the JDC planned to use 72.1 million zloty in Poland, stating that "the percentage of persons applying for assistance in the various communities range[d] from 30% to 70% of the total Jewish population. . . . The program of aid include[d] work conducted through 1,500 institutions in 400 towns."[26] Between 500,000 and 650,000 Polish Jews were dependent on the aid. The committees set up or supported by the Joint at the beginning of the war continued to function even after December 1941, when Germany declared war on the United States. Anticipating that all contacts between the United States and occupied Poland could be severed, the Joint, even before the war, had authorized welfare workers in Poland to "borrow funds locally to carry on emergency relief work" and had promised to repay all debts at the end of the hostilities.[27] Historian Yehuda Bauer believes that it was "in no small part due to JDC's efforts that, early in 1942, a kind of balance was found that might have enabled Polish Jews to survive under ghetto conditions."[28] The Nazis, however, soon dissolved many of the ghettos and turned to shooting or using purpose-built gas chambers to mass murder the Jews remaining in Europe.

Help also reached the Jews directly from Jewish organizations in the United States. Further smaller shipments were posted from Switzerland by the Hilfsaktion für notleidende Juden in Polen, supported by the Federation of Polish Jews in America, and the Relief Committee for the War-Stricken Jewish Population (RELICO), headed by the Polish Jewish émigré Abraham Silberschein. Early in the war, both organizations received funding from the United States. The British government, already at war with Germany, followed these activities with apparent uneasiness. After the successful naval blockade of continental Europe during World War I, the British believed that the enforcement of the blockade could again contribute to the collapse of Germany. They prohibited imports of any items to continental Europe that could be used by Hitler's regime to prolong the conflict, including extra food in the form of relief parcels. The British were concerned, quite rightly, that the Germans could confiscate the packages, but their belief that it was Germans' duty to feed the local population played an equal role. The Nazi systematic policies of starvation of the civil population were beyond the "liberal imagination."[29] Bauer writes about "an almost unbelievable naiveté regarding Nazi methods."[30] Despite the claims of some historians, this Allied reluctance to allow parcel schemes was not limited to aid for Jews.[31] Although the British allowed the delivery of 15,000 tonnes of wheat (and 3,000 tonnes of other material) to the Greeks in 1942, they at the same time rejected small-scale parcel programs for Belgians and Norwegians.[32]

During 1941, the British government increased their appeals to the Americans to limit the activities of the humanitarian agencies that were sending food to occupied Europe. Jewish organizations such as the JDC, the World Jewish Congress, or the Federation of Polish Jews in America, concerned about the question of loyalty at a time of major military conflict, soon stopped their shipments. The Joint Boycott Council, created by the American Jewish Congress and the Jewish Labor Committee, forced dissenting Jewish organizations to comply with the wishes of the British government.[33] They picketed the offices of the Agudas Israel of America, the organization representing Orthodox Jews, until it stopped sending food to occupied Poland in August 1941.[34] The outbreak of war between the United States and Germany then severed all direct communications with enemy territories.

Minor shipments of food to occupied Poland continued throughout 1942 against the wishes of the Allied governments and western Jewish organizations, thanks to the efforts of private individuals in neutral Switzerland and Portugal.[35] Although overall this was an impressive effort on the part of several determined activists, "the entire endeavor amounted to a drop of relief in an ocean of agony."[36] Much more significant shipments would have been needed to improve the situation of the starving population in the ghettos in occupied Poland.

At the beginning of 1942, a number of Jewish activists in the United States and Britain moved away from the boycott stance of 1941 and mobilized to change Allied policy.[37] The JDC, as the main philanthropic agency, had to defend themselves repeatedly against accusations that they were not doing enough for the Jews suffering in Poland.[38]

Jewish refugees from the Nazi-held territories were at the forefront of the information campaign about the starvation among European Jews and of new efforts to send food to Jews in eastern Europe. Hayyim Shoshkes (Henry Szoszkies) had been a member of the executive of the Warsaw Jewish community before the war and served on the Warsaw Judenrat in the first weeks after the German invasion. He escaped with his family and reached the United States by way of Italy in late 1939. In 1941 and 1942, he desperately tried to inform the American public about the horrific conditions in the ghettos and lobbied for new shipments of food to the Jews. His reports from September 1941 depicted apocalyptic stories about naked, emaciated corpses lying in the streets because their relatives lacked the means to pay for their burial. They were published in the *New York Times* and debated in the U.S. Congress.[39] Survival of the Jews, Shoshkes asserted, depended on the support they could receive from the outside world.[40] Half a year later, in the spring of 1942, Shoshkes, not knowing that the Nazis had already begun implementing the "Final Solution," warned the American public that "there will be no more Jews in Poland in five or six years. . . . If that situation continues . . . the complete disaster of the Jewish population in Poland in the next few years is imminent."[41]

Zorah (sometimes Zorach or Zerach) Warhaftig, another refugee who had escaped from Poland to the United States (via Lithuania, the Soviet Union, and Japan), prepared one of the most comprehensive studies on Nazi food policies published during the war.[42] Written together with the American Jewish writer Boris Shub, *Starvation Over Europe (Made in Germany)* was published in early 1943 by the Institute of Jewish Affairs in New York. It warned readers that the Germans were carrying out "a totalitarian war food program [and] those whom Germany has marked for extermination [receive] rations which are but death by another name."[43] Shub and Warhaftig correctly suggested that starvation, "one of the major features of the New Order," was systematically imposed on the Jews to eradicate the whole population and made an explicit call to the conscience of the Allied governments: "German-organized starvation is inexorably destroying the Jewish people. Nothing has yet been done to turn the tide."[44]

Even more forceful calls came from the leaders of Jewish refugee communities in Britain, such as members of the Polish and Czechoslovak exile parliaments in London—Ignacy Schwarzbart, Szhmul Zygielbojm, and Arnošt Frischer—or from organizations of orthodox Jewish refugees from Europe.[45] These leaders considered it their obligation to care for the Jews who were members of their religious, ethnic, *and* national communities. They delivered speeches at various mass demonstrations and attempted to persuade the Allied governments as well as Anglo-Jewish and American Jewish organizations to organize help.[46]

During 1942, Allied leaders received irrefutable evidence about the Nazi massacres of the Jews behind the Eastern Front and in occupied Poland. In December 1942, government leaders in London, Washington, and Moscow finally confirmed their knowledge of the systematic "cold-blooded" extermination and threatened anybody who took part in the crimes with retribution. No other specific relief or rescue measures were officially promised. During the subsequent public campaign, led by Jewish organizations, the advocates demanded renewed relief shipments to the Jews in Nazi Europe. It was, however, not always seen as a top priority. A mass demonstration organized by the American Jewish Congress and other bodies in Madison Square Garden in New York convened on March 1, 1943, presented a long list of proposals. The demand to feed the victims "in the view of the fact that planned mass starvation is the design of the Nazi regime in its inhuman warfare" was only the eighth item on the list.[47] Yet others, such as the Jewish Labor Committee in the United States, "representing 500,000 organized Jewish workers," in their rescue proposals published half a year later, saw humanitarian aid as one of the key avenues in the effort to alleviate the plight of the Jews.[48] Indeed, it was thanks to the reports about the Nazi mass extermination of the Jews received in the summer and autumn of 1942 that the Allied governments finally granted the first licenses to governmental and humanitarian agencies to send food specifically to Jews in camps and ghettos. Government officials evidently wanted to silence the mounting dissent with this gesture. Yet those who wanted to send parcels still faced a long list of obstacles that significantly complicated their efforts.

The Major Obstacles

The Allied economic blockade of the Continent was the main obstacle that impeded humanitarian interventions from Allied and neutral lands. The same applied for the remittances of funds, compounded with the lack of foreign currency in British banks, especially of the Swiss franc. These rules complicated the transfers of funds to neutral countries from which Allied diplomats or Jewish humanitarian organizers could send food parcels and medicine to the occupied territories. Some exemptions from the blockade regulations existed, but only when a scheme was being organized by humanitarian organizations. This was mostly the case with parcels for western Allied POWs, whose treatment based on the Geneva Conventions could be supervised by the ICRC. Civilians from the occupied countries were not accorded similar status, even if they were interned in camps. Under the Geneva Conventions, moreover, deported Jews were considered civilian internees ("unassimilated" or "non-assimilated" persons under the Geneva Conventions) and were thus not covered by its provisions. The Red Cross could not supervise the delivery of the aid parcels and prevent their confiscation by the Germans. The ICRC leadership in Geneva was, in addition, careful not to challenge the German policy.[49] Activists for increasing food relief could, however, point to precedents, in particular the help that the British allowed to reach those starving in Greece in the winter of 1941–42. Historians believe that the concessions to the Greeks were motivated by geopolitical considerations and by efforts to prevent the decline of British prestige and reputation in the region.[50]

The early detailed reports about the massacres of the Jews and a subsequent publicity campaign in London in May and June 1942 made the British Ministry of Economic Warfare (MEW) willing to allow further minor concessions in the strict blockade policies. Minister Roundell Palmer, 3rd Earl of Selborne, was, in his own words, "considering whether the dispatch might be permissible on a very small scale, and as a token of sympathy, of parcels containing goods such as sardines, which are local produce of Portugal."[51] "Local produce" was not imported through the blockade, and the Germans could import the goods from Portugal in any case. The subsequent negotiations between the Board of Deputies, the leading Anglo-Jewish organization, and the MEW lasted several months and led to British permission to allow the transfer of £3,000 per month from Britain to Portugal, where the purchase and shipment of relief parcels took place.[52] This program was intended only for Jews in the occupied Polish territories. It was clear that even if successful, the parcels would reach only a tiny part of the Polish Jewish population, and the scheme was never intended to support any large number of individuals over a long period of time.[53]

At the British government's insistence, the Board of Deputies agreed to cooperate with the Polish government-in-exile and their representative in Portugal, Stanisław Schimitzek.[54] For the purpose of coordinating the program, officials of the JDC represented the Board of Deputies in Lisbon. The Polish Ministry of Social Welfare and Treasury in London facilitated the transfer of the money, but the funds came solely from the coffers of the British Jewish philanthropic agencies (mainly from the Jewish Colonization Agency).[55]

More disturbing news from occupied Europe triggered further Allied concessions on both sides of the Atlantic. At the time of the December 1942 Joint Declaration by Members of the U.N., which confirmed their knowledge of Nazi extermination policies, the U.S. Treasury Department granted permission to the JDC to transfer $12,000 (circa £3,000) a month to Lisbon and use it for food shipments to the Jews in occupied Poland.[56] The negotiations between several Jewish groups and the American government had already started in the summer of 1942, and it was also thanks to the news of the British concession that the U.S. government in the end agreed to support the scheme.[57] Soon thereafter, Czechoslovak Jewish activists, supported by the Czechoslovak government-in-exile, persuaded the British MEW to grant permission to transfer £3,000 per month to Lisbon for the shipment of food to the Jewish citizens of Czechoslovakia, including those who had already been deported to occupied Poland. That permission, granted in early March 1943, concluded the negotiations that Czechoslovaks had conducted with British officials for over a year.[58] Czechoslovak Jewish activists together with the JDC then managed to negotiate for permission from the U.S. government for the JDC to transfer $12,000 per month to Lisbon and send food to Jews in occupied Czechoslovakia regardless of their nationality. This aid could reach some of the tens of thousands of German and Austrian Jews imprisoned in the Theresienstadt ghetto who had been excluded from the Czechoslovak scheme.[59] During the following two years, the JDC also received permission to send money to Turkey, from where they planned the shipment of large five-kilo parcels with the help of the Red Cross to Transnistria, Yugoslavia, Romania, and Bulgaria, as well as additional shipments to Theresienstadt. Further funds were transferred by the JDC to the Red Cross in Switzerland for shipments to concentration camps. And another exemption allowed the JDC to send money to Saly Mayer, JDC representative in Switzerland, who shipped parcels to Theresienstadt and Auschwitz-Birkenau. In the last months of the war, JDC representative Laura Margolis attempted to open another route and send food to Theresienstadt, Birkenau, and Bergen-Belsen from Stockholm.[60]

Allied authorities evidently became more approachable as the war continued and with incoming reports about the Holocaust, but the permitted programs for aiding Jews never reached a scale that could seriously threaten the economic blockade of the Continent. The MEW from the very beginning clearly stated that it would have to be a "strictly limited quantity of parcels."[61] This attitude was summarized by the British MEW in mid-July 1944, at the point when most of the victims of the Holocaust had already been murdered:

> It is clearly only possible to assist a small part of the great population in occupied Europe that is suffering from Nazi tyranny, and I have no doubt whatever that there are great numbers of Jews in every occupied country as well as in Germany and her satellites who are suffering grievously. With such limited funds some must be chosen who may benefit and the others must wait with patience and bravery for the day of liberation.[62]

The prolonged negotiations lead us to another matter that complicated the development of the programs: bureaucracy. Each of the permits that the agencies or exile governments received from American and British authorities stipulated a long list of conditions. The British, for example, insisted that the parcels had to be sent to individuals and not relief agencies in occupied Europe. This demand put considerable pressure on organizers in Britain and United States, who had to collect as many reliable addresses as possible of individuals in ghettos and Nazi camps from relatives and refugee organizations at a time when the Jewish population in occupied Europe was constantly in flux or transit. Furthermore, they had to keep the whole program confidential because the British and Americans did not want to publicize schemes that shipped extra food to Nazi-held Europe. This further complicated the collection of addresses. In the end, information about the scheme was quickly leaked, and Jewish agencies were inundated with requests to send parcels, as we see in the letter quoted at the beginning of this chapter. The British government deeply resented this publicity, and the Trading with the Enemy Department regularly complained about it to the Board of Deputies.[63]

The question of whether to mobilize group or individual shipments and whether to demand return receipts from recipients troubled not only the American and British governments. Jewish agencies themselves extensively discussed the benefits and drawbacks of these options. On the one hand, the shipment of a large group consignment to a relief agency in Poland removed the task of compiling recent and reliable addresses for recipients; it also seemed easier to monitor its delivery to the agency. At the same time, it would be impossible to conceal this help from Nazi institutions, which would quickly determine the origin of the parcels. Parcels sent to private addresses increased the burden placed on the agencies handling the shipments and made it even more difficult to ascertain whether the relief had reached prisoners and internees. On the other hand, Jewish refugees in Britain who had "a brother, sister or other relative in Poland, would regard it as a personal contact when obtaining an official confirmation that his relative has received a gift as small as it may be."[64] The food parcel programs—at least they hoped—offered an opportunity to find out whether their relatives were still alive and raised hopes that they could help sustain them from afar.

Further bureaucratic obstacles complicated the program organized by the Joint. The permission they received from the U.S. Treasury Department stipulated that they could only send the parcels to recognized relief agencies in occupied Poland. The liquidation of the Polish ghettos during 1942 led to the closure of all existing welfare agencies, and the JDC conceded in May 1943 that they simply could not go forward with the program because they were not allowed to send parcels to private addresses.[65] This condition was removed from the license that the JDC received for the Czechoslovak part of their program in May 1943, but further delays occurred. The U.S. legation in Lisbon insisted that the JDC had to provide receipts from the addressees that parcels were arriving at their destination, an impossible demand.[66] It was not until October 1943, five months later, that the U.S. legation in Lisbon stopped insisting on receipts from the Jews in Theresienstadt and the JDC could finally direct their first parcels there.[67] It always took several months before the JDC was able to negotiate even minor amendments to U.S. Treasury licenses, for example, if they wanted to include a new destination for the shipments.

Aid organizations encountered the most frustrating bureaucratic delay in dealing with the Polish government-in-exile, which took several months, from October 1942 until February 1943, to transmit the first installment of £3,000 from Britain to their representative in Lisbon. The Council of Polish Jews in Great Britain, unable to comprehend the situation, made desperate pleas to the Board of Deputies in late December 1942, asking them to speed up the whole process: "To us Polish Jews the matter is not one of sympathy or solidarity with coreligionists, but a matter of trying to prolong the life of our starving fathers, mothers, brothers and sisters, even if only by one single day."[68]

Lack of funds was another matter that troubled the activists. The only agency that evidently had remotely sufficient resources was the JDC, with extensive monetary reserves collected in the American Jewish community. In the end, British Jewish agencies only contributed £9,000 for the duration of the Polish program. The truth is that, as we shall see, more would not have made a great difference: most of the Jewish communities in occupied Poland had already been wiped out. In contrast, the Czechoslovak program was maintained from the very beginning by funds allocated from the meager budget of the Czechoslovak government-in-exile, which originated from British state loans. The idea that it would be possible to keep the scheme running from private collections fell through, and it was only thanks to an exceptional donation from the JDC that the Czechoslovaks did not have to halt the scheme before the end of 1943. The Czechoslovak government then made another contribution of £10,000 for 1944, a sufficient amount for slightly over three months, but money for the rest of the year had to be found elsewhere, especially because the British were willing to increase the amount the Czechoslovak exile government could send to Portugal.[69] Frischer, an informal leader of the Czech Jews in London, hoped for a contribution from the British Jewish organization but encountered a lack of understanding on their side. In a strongly worded letter, so typical of his temperament, he directly reproached British Jewry:

> This is an impossible state of affairs. On the one hand the Government is being reproached for not wanting to help, demonstrations are being organized and leaflets and propaganda material printed, but on the other hand Jewry in this country seems to be unable to make full use of those possibilities that are opened by the Government. The Czechoslovak Jews in this country have done their utmost and will do their utmost also in the future to support the relief action. But their means are limited and insufficient to maintain the whole action. British Jewry, [which] undoubtedly is financially strong enough to

> support the action[,] has so far contributed very little. . . . Personally, bearing in mind those who will have to starve in the internment camps [he meant the ghettos] more than before, I think I shall have to take in despair the last step open to me, namely to approach British Jewry publicly, a step which, so far, as you well know, I have been trying to avoid as best as I could.[70]

British Jewish organizations eventually agreed to support the Czechoslovak shipments from Portugal, but the Allied offensive in France in the summer of 1944 soon cut off Portuguese transport connections to the Reich.

Further obstacles emerged in some of the neutral countries. The Portuguese parts of the programs were dependent on the goodwill of the Salazar government, which was surely aware of the true destination of the shipments. On a more practical side, the Portuguese allowed the export of only certain items, which effectively limited the scope of the program to tins of sardines in oil, dried figs, pine nuts, and fruit jams. Tins of fish appeared to be the most favored item because of their nutritional value. At times, the Salazar government completely banned any exports, for example, in early 1943.[71] The Portuguese also limited the number of parcels they were willing to ship abroad each month because their postal services had already been stretched to the limit. The officials who organized the program from Portugal had to either apply for a license to export large numbers of parcels to Nazi Germany or use the services of one of the local companies that were licensed to export food. In the case of the Czechoslovaks and Poles, it was the Association of Portuguese Exporters of Tinned Fish (Gremio dos Exportadores de Conservas de Peixe), a name that became familiar to many prisoners in the Theresienstadt ghetto.[72] Despite these complications, the organizers did not encounter any major problems from the Portuguese side, at least while transport connections to Germany remained open. In contrast, the Turkish part of the program, negotiated in late 1943 with the ICRC by Joseph J. Schwartz, the European director of the JDC, never reached the volume envisioned at the outset, largely because of transport difficulties and delays in the Balkans.[73]

Destinations and Deliveries: The Polish Government and Board of Deputies Scheme

Efforts to send relief parcels to occupied Poland, where the largest parts of the Jewish communities under the Nazis were concentrated, triggered the negotiations for aid programs in the Allied countries. Yet the first parcels left Lisbon only at a point when most of the ghettos in occupied Poland had already been liquidated, largely limiting the number of locations that could be reached. Furthermore, the exile governments and aid activists were always one step behind the Nazis and were not sufficiently informed about the situation on the ground. Therefore, a large number of parcels they sent could not be delivered because the individuals had already been deported to a new location or, more usually, were no longer alive.

Those involved in the decision-making and the activists putting pressure on them were split in their approach to the shipments. It is beyond any doubt that some of them were aware that not all the parcels could be delivered; they knew that the Nazis would confiscate at least some, if not most, of the relief shipments. It was a price many of them were willing to pay. Herbert Katzki, secretary of the European executive of the JDC with its seat in Lisbon, believed that "every effort [should] be made to send the food to the Jewish people in Poland."[74] Selig Brodetsky, the Zionist leader of the Board of Deputies, articulated this view shortly before the shipment commenced: "I am dealing with the problem on the basis that it is worth taking a considerable risk in the matter, even if a proportion of the food products got lost." At the same time, he conceded that influential people in Britain and the United States, especially among the donors, were skeptical about the program and "they will take some convincing."[75] Even the original licenses from the British MEW and the U.S. Treasury Department stressed the conditionality of the approval. Both governments wanted solid confirmations that the parcels were being delivered, and such sentiments were even echoed in the ranks of the Polish and Czechoslovak exile governments.

It soon became evident that the Polish part of the program had failed. Between February and September 1943, the Board of Deputies in cooperation with the Polish Relief Committee in Lisbon sent 27,295 parcels, half a kilo each, from Portugal to occupied Poland.[76] Almost all of them remained unaccounted for. The first summary of the deliveries came on June 26, 1943. For 12,559 parcels shipped by April 1943, the organizers received only 925 confirmations: 849 from Jewish councils (707 of them from Łódź/Litzmannstadt in the Warthegau) and just 76 from individuals. This, of course, did not mean that the receipts were genuine. A further 549 parcels were returned, and in the case of 4,005 packages, the German authorities simply informed the sender that they had confiscated the parcels.[77] In the words of Herbert Katzki, this "result . . . [leaves] much to be desired."[78] At approximately the same time, a Swedish newspaper published a recent circular by the General Post Office in the Generalgouvernement (the occupied Polish territory under German civilian administration), according to which "all import of all kinds of goods by persons of Jewish origin in Poland is prohibited and [such parcels] are seized by the competent authorities. . . . Nor can compensation be paid for such parcels [to the sender]."[79]

In the following months, the Polish representative in Lisbon sent further parcels to the addressees who had confirmed receipt, but the organizers soon conceded that it was impossible to continue this way. In August 1943 they decided to eliminate the territory of the Generalgouvernement from the scheme altogether. They also stopped sending aid to Upper Silesia, from which they had received returned parcels marked with the ominous words "addressee left for an unknown destination."[80] Although the Board of Deputies and the JDC were determined to keep trying, they stated with resignation that they "have not had very much success" and that "the scheme for sending postal packets of food to the Jews in the Polish ghettos has not worked."[81] In one desperate attempt to determine the fate of at least some of the parcels, the JDC submitted to the ICRC 100 names of people in Poland to whom the organizers had sent parcels, requesting information on whether they had been delivered. The Red Cross simply responded that "due to recent changes," they were unable "to control the arrival of individual packages addressed to Jews in Poland."[82]

Jewish activists and humanitarian workers believed they needed to continue supporting communities under the Nazis for as long as even a theoretical chance existed that they could provide aid.[83] Yet in cases where they had evidently reached a dead end, the activists agreed with Polish government officials—who were generally more skeptical—and decided to stop that part of the program and explore other options. Their source of funding also played a role in this. While Jewish agencies were willing to take more risks, exile governments did not want to waste public money if no proof of success could be obtained. Hence, the fact that the monies came from British Jewish agencies was evidently one reason why the Polish part of the parcel program continued. On the side of the Jewish organizations, the feeling of responsibility of those who had managed to escape toward those trapped under the Nazi heel played a prominent role.[84] It is otherwise very difficult to square the idea that these shipments continued with the almost complete failure of the initial round and the ongoing ominous reports about the fate of the Jews in Nazi-controlled Europe.

The history of the Jewish Aid Agency (Jüdische Unterstützungsstelle für das Generalgouvernement, or JUS) in Kraków is illustrative of the whole story.[85] The JUS was headed by Michał Weichert, a famous Jewish theater scholar and author, who during the war took on a prominent position in the distribution of the aid that reached occupied Poland from abroad. Even in 1942 the JUS offices in Kraków and Warsaw were among the small handful of places in occupied Poland still receiving care shipments from abroad through the German Red

Cross.[86] The JUS was closed in December 1942, but Weichert, with German permission, reopened the office in March 1943, at the moment when the Kraków ghetto was liquidated. He kept the organization running again with only a short break until July 1944. In April 1943, Weichert informed his international contacts about the reopening of the JUS[87] and for more than a year remained in contact with international aid organizations as a representative of the only Jewish agency in occupied Poland that was allegedly allowed to distribute aid to Jewish prisoners in forced labor camps. At this point Polish underground groups accused Weichert of collaborating with the Nazis and of helping them to deceive the world about the real fate of the Jews.[88]

After the initial part of the Polish program collapsed, the Board of Deputies, the Joint, and the Polish Relief Committee invested all their hopes in the JUS. There was still enough money from British Jews in Portugal to pay for 100,000 parcels, but in May 1944, full of optimism, JDC representatives asked for even more funds from London.[89] The shipments to the JUS from Portugal never reached the proportions of other programs, and it is unclear for how long they really continued.[90] Weichert soon confirmed the delivery of some of the parcels, and Schimitzek, the delegate of the Polish Ministry of Social Welfare in Lisbon, considered this a "positive (satisfactory)" result.[91] Others, including the JDC representative in Switzerland, Saly Mayer, and Schwartz in Lisbon, had doubts about Weichert's activities. At the end of February 1944, in a phone conversation, they concluded that Weichert's reports "of course [have] to be taken at face value as the Germans might be up to any damn devilish tricks just to give out the news that there are still Jews in Kraków."[92]

The Polish exile government tried to stop the scheme after receiving reports from home that Weichert was collaborating with the Nazis. Yet representatives of the Board of Deputies and the Joint disagreed, clinging to the hope that they found a way to help. The JDC believed "that [the JUS] could not exist without certain collaboration with the Germans," but it did not necessarily mean that the "assistance does not reach certain number of Jews."[93] Representatives of the Board of Deputies also suggested to Minister of Labour and Social Welfare Jan Stańczyk of Poland that "whilst there was undoubtedly a leakage to the Germans of these food parcels sent to Kraków, the despatch of parcels should be continued because a substantial number of Jews were, in fact, being helped thereby, and the loss to German sources was an inevitable risk that had to be taken."[94] Even the ICRC provided reports suggesting that the help was really delivered.[95] As a consequence, the Polish government reversed its previous decision and sanctioned further shipments "to the fullest extent practicable."[96] As late as in mid-July 1944, the Joint wanted the U.S. Treasury Department to amend its

Joseph Schwartz, European director of the JDC, at work in his office in Lisbon, 1941. Courtesy of the United States Holocaust Memorial Museum, photo 59606.

license, which would allow the organization to take over the program for the JUS, until then funded by British Jewish funds.[97] Only the end of transport connection from Portugal stopped the shipments to Kraków (although attempts were made to send food from Switzerland, Sweden, and Turkey). This shows that some Jewish activists were willing and eager to explore all possible avenues to help—and continued sending food parcels to Kraków at the point when almost no Jews were alive in Poland any more. The total number of food parcels sent this way is not exactly clear, but it seems it went into several tens of thousands.[98]

What happened to the aid sent to Weichert? Most of the parcels were beyond any doubt confiscated by the Germans, while another part apparently did reach the JUS. As in the other cases discussed below, the Nazis realized that if they wanted the parcels to keep coming (and to get their share), they had to deliver at least some of them. Weichert was selling the sardines and other products on the black market and bought basic necessities such as flour, which he sent to labor camps in the Kraków district, especially the Płaszów camp (nowadays familiar from the movie *Schindler's List*). Weichert's communication with Jewish activists abroad possibly helped to paper over Nazi plans, but the food he received, even if minor in total numbers, helped to save lives. As Bauer concludes, "It was only a drop in the sea. But was not a drop in the sea infinitely better than nothing at all?"[99] Did the aid distributed by Weichert outweigh his collaboration? This question continues to be a matter of debate among historians and humanitarians.

The Czechoslovak Program in Cooperation with the Joint Distribution Committee

Programs organized by the Czechoslovak government-in-exile in cooperation with the JDC were more successful. The gradual concentration of the Czech Jews in the Theresienstadt ghetto started in November 1941 and was completed by mid-1943. The fortress town became a temporary holding center for most of the Jews in the Protectorate of Bohemia and Moravia, which was a political unit established by Hitler in the territory of the western parts of interwar Czechoslovakia. From mid-1942 onward, portions of the German and Austrian Jewish communities and later deportees from the Netherlands, Denmark, Slovakia, Hungary, and elsewhere were also sent to the ghetto. In the meantime, the Nazis began to deport the Jews farther east, to occupied Poland and the Nazi-occupied Soviet territories, which further complicated efforts to ascertain their location.

The Czechoslovak government received British permission to transfer £3,000 monthly to Lisbon on March 2, 1943.[100] The scheme could only be used for food parcels for Czechoslovak citizens incarcerated in Theresienstadt and other locations. The Czechoslovak consul in Lisbon, František Čejka, organized the purchase and shipment of the consignments and was obliged to cooperate with the British embassy there and respect their instructions: for example, they stipulated from which company he could buy food for the parcels. No more than four tonnes of food (8,000 parcels) could be sent per month, and he could only use local Portuguese shipping companies.[101]

Čejka began systematic shipments in late April 1943. He gave priority to the people deported to Theresienstadt, but a small portion of the consignments also went to Czechoslovak prisoners in camps in France. Between April 30 and early September 1943, he sent 11,039 parcels (half a kilo each) to Theresienstadt and 1,673 to France.[102] Czech Jewish representatives in Switzerland who were in contact with Theresienstadt soon reported that they had received the first confirmations that the parcels had been delivered. They also sent further group consignments from Geneva with the help of the ICRC.[103]

By contrast, the JDC part of the program experienced a slow start. The JDC sent the first parcels from Lisbon to Theresienstadt only in October or November 1943, after the U.S. consul in Lisbon stopped insisting on individual receipts from prisoners for delivered parcels. The American humanitarian agency eventually spent $12,000 per month on up to 18,000 parcels to 9,000–10,000 Jews in the ghetto, including Austrian and German Jews.[104] JDC representatives closely cooperated with the Czechoslovak consul in Lisbon, which was a condition demanded by the U.S. Treasury license.[105] This coordination was fundamental to avoid duplicating names in the lists of intended recipients, because the Nazis (at least on paper) allowed each prisoner to receive parcels not exceeding one kilo per month.[106]

A total of no less than 140 tonnes of food (over 280,000 parcels[107]) were sent from Lisbon to Theresienstadt (the estimate includes the JDC and Czech programs together), mostly containing sardines, dried fruit, and biscuits. Another part of the JDC program developed in April 1944 in Switzerland, where Saly Mayer began to send 4,000 parcels per month to Theresienstadt and eventually managed to increase the number to 12,000 per month.[108] Further bulk shipments were sent through the ICRC.[109] A large number of prisoners in Theresienstadt confirmed receipt of packages.[110]

Aware of the deportation of the Czechoslovak Jews to the east, Jewish activists tried to persuade the Czechoslovak government to divert part of the shipments to labor and concentration camps in occupied Poland as well. They in particular obtained lists of Czech and Slovak Jewish prisoners from the so-called labor camp Birkenau bei Neu Berun, which in reality but unknown to the activists was the extermination camp Auschwitz II-Birkenau, where more than one million Jews were murdered during the war. The Czechoslovak consul in Lisbon made the first test shipment to Birkenau of 32 parcels in late July 1943. The number of parcels sent to the camp quickly grew, and by late November 1943 Čejka had already sent over 1,000 parcels in one consignment (each parcel containing half a kilo of tinned sardines).[111] Attempts to reach other locations holding Jewish deportees from the Protectorate and Slovakia, such as the ghetto in Izbica or the concentration and extermination camp in Majdanek near Lublin in eastern Poland, failed almost immediately. The parcels were never acknowledged, or they were returned with most of the contents missing.[112]

Other parts of the program ran more smoothly and continued to grow in the second half of 1943 and during 1944. Czechoslovaks kept sending thousands of parcels from Lisbon to Theresienstadt and Birkenau, and their diplomats in Geneva and Turkey (in Istanbul and Ankara) also organized small shipments.[113] They received hundreds of confirmations from Theresienstadt and even some from Birkenau.[114] Only in June 1944 did the optimism of the organizers begin to evaporate. Consul Čejka received a letter from the Theresienstadt Jewish elder Paul Eppstein confirming the receipt of 7,294 parcels.[115] Later Eppstein confirmed that 13,444 parcels had been delivered to Jewish internees between April 10 and

Pour éviter l'eventuelle suspension des envois veuillez accuser réception a l'expéditeur en rappelant le
SAM AMON
Rua do Monte Olivete 16
Lisbon, Portugal
N.º

LISBOA-R.P. N.º 8
N.º

Exp.: Grémio dos Exportadores de Conservas de Peixe
LISBOA PORTUGAL

Destin.:
1483
WEISSOVA Edita
Lager Birkenau Bei Neubrunn
Oberschlesien
ALEMANHA

Sardine shipment label (Lisbon, Portugal) addressed to Edita Weissova at the preprinted address "Lager Birkenau Bei Neubrunn/Oberschlesien." The parcels were officially sent by Grémio dos Exportadores de Conservas de Peixe. According to postwar World Jewish Congress lists, Weissova survived. Courtesy of the Crown family, United States Holocaust Memorial Museum, Acc. 2016.516.2.2.

July 3, 1944. This meant that only about 10–15 percent of the parcels sent by Čejka and the JDC had gotten through.[116] No similar collective confirmation ever arrived from Birkenau. During the debate that followed, supporters of the program successfully persuaded their opponents to continue with the shipments, but the Czechoslovak exile government insisted that the program could no longer be funded from the state budget, only from other available funds (donations from humanitarian organizations and fundraising).[117] This partial financial dependence of the Czechoslovak relief program on its state treasury complicated the efforts of the Jewish organizers to continue with the shipment. Despite looming financial difficulties, it was again not the uncertainty surrounding the deliveries but the Allied military breakthrough in France that stopped the Portuguese part of the program. But the efforts to ship food continued.

During 1943, the JDC successfully established closer cooperation with the ICRC in Switzerland and its representatives in Turkey. In May 1943, Professor Carl Jacob Burckhardt, the head of the Joint Relief Commission of the ICRC (or Commission mixte), offered during his visit in Lisbon for the ICRC to take over parts of the JDC program that had stalled in Lisbon and begin shipment of food from Switzerland. They would distribute the food in occupied Poland, or if they were unable to reach Jews in Poland, "they would see to it that the parcels were distributed among needy Jewish people in other countries."[118] Such an easy solution proved impossible to execute because the U.S. government rejected it. However, the JDC eventually managed to receive permission to send $100,000 (429,000 Swiss francs) to Switzerland to be used for relief shipments for Jews in Europe. The ICRC took over the deliveries and distribution of the aid: 100,000 francs were sent to the ICRC delegate in Romania for helping the Jewish deportees in Transnistria, and 100,000 francs were used for medical aid to Bergen-Belsen, Zagreb and other camps in Croatia, Theresienstadt, Birkenau, and the JUS in Kraków. The remaining balance of 229,000 francs (over $50,000) was used in 1944 to buy food parcels for Kraków, Theresienstadt, Budapest, Birkenau, and Bergen-Belsen.[119]

In September 1943, Joseph J. Schwartz in cooperation with the representatives of the Red Cross in Turkey opened another route with the aim of sending up to 250 tonnes of food to Transnistria. The JDC secured another license for the purpose from the U.S. Treasury Department ($100,000) and after several months negotiated the inclusion of other destinations such as Yugoslavian territory and Theresienstadt in the scheme. These five-kilo parcels contained *bulama* (a product made of grapes), hazelnuts, figs, apricots, raisins, and soap.[120] The first train left Istanbul in March 1944, but it is not clear if it ever reached its intended destination. The second installment of another $100,000 sent by the Joint to Turkey was never spent for the intended shipments and was eventually reimbursed.[121]

What happened to the shipments sent by the Czechoslovak government and the Joint? More than 80,000 parcels were sent to ghettos and camps in the framework of the Czechoslovak governmental scheme. Over 90 percent of the parcels went to Theresienstadt and a smaller part to the Auschwitz complex (in particular to Birkenau), but the help also went to internees in France, Belgium, and concentration camps in Germany (such as Sachsenhausen-Oranienburg).[122] The amount of food sent by the JDC was even larger. That most of the parcels did not and could not reach their destination was due solely to German authorities. They confiscated most of the shipments. More importantly, however, they had deported or murdered the intended recipients before the parcels could reach them.

The real number of parcels delivered to the inmates in Theresienstadt is still a matter for historical research. In recollections after liberation, Moci Kohn, who had worked in the Theresienstadt post office, believed that about 120,000 parcels had reached the ghetto by October 1944.[123] Other survivors also recalled the delivery of parcels. Some historians believe that a high number of parcels reached the inmates and emphasize the moral and psychological value of the packages for the detainees.[124] Yet historian Miroslav Kárný maintained that the Germans had allowed the delivery of only 15.9 percent of all shipped parcels.[125] Another historian, Vojtěch Blodig, reached similar conclusions, suggesting that the Germans confiscated fifty-five tonnes of parcels and allowed the distribution of only about ten tonnes.[126] Even so, this was an exceptionally high number in comparison with other concentration camps and ghettos.

The higher delivery rate was doubtlessly related to the role that Theresienstadt played in German propaganda and attempts to cover up the genocide of the Jews. In June 1944, the Nazis organized for a delegation of the Red Cross a visit to the ghetto to show that the Jews were living almost unhindered in the city that was "given to them by the Führer." Indeed, some of the inmates noticed an increase in the number of parcels reaching the ghetto in the spring of 1944, shortly before the visit, when the SS tried to improve conditions in the fortress town.[127] At exactly that time, Willy Mahler, who worked in the Theresienstadt post office, noted in his diary that the Theresienstadt administration had received permission to distribute the parcels that could not be previously delivered because the addressees had already been deported to the east.[128]

It remains difficult to reconstruct the whole story of parcel deliveries to Theresienstadt, and the behavior of the Nazi officials, including of the German Red Cross, remains unclear. Crucially, a German Red Cross document from August 1943 confirms all parcels sent by Czechoslovaks from Lisbon were reaching the Protectorate, though it is unclear what happened to them then.[129] We can at least ascertain that the parcels were not simply stolen on their way from Portugal to Germany. The meager evidence we have from the German archives is often contradictory. In March 1943, Adolf Eichmann allowed the delivery of food and medical parcels to Theresienstadt, while at the same time stating that shipments for the Jews further in the east were not possible at the time. Yet one month later, Eichmann only grudgingly agreed to a large ICRC shipment of condensed milk and prunes to Theresienstadt, stressing that he would not be willing to approve any similar shipment in the future because of shortages of similar items in the rest of the Reich territory ("angesichts der Knappheit beispielsweise von Büchsenmilch in übrigen Reichsgebiet"). He was clearly unwilling to allow the Jews to enjoy food items that were strictly rationed or even unavailable to the Germans. At the same time, Eichmann confirmed that the shipment of individual parcels was still permitted. Yet the Jewish elders of Theresienstadt, evidently under coercion, sent a letter to Switzerland expressing thanks for the parcels but stating that further shipments were unnecessary, for the Jews in the ghetto had sufficient access to food.[130] The historians Morgenbrod and Merkenich suggest that in mid-1943 the Reich Security Main Office ordered that parcels arriving from abroad should no longer be sent directly to the ghetto and had to go via the German Red Cross regional office in Bohemia and Moravia. Some of the parcels then continued on to the ghetto, some went to other camps such as Auschwitz, and others were evidently confiscated.[131] In January 1944, Eichmann informed the German Red Cross that because the Jews in Theresienstadt had enough food, the recent shipment from the ICRC should go to one of the Jewish labor camps. It seems that Birkenau was selected as the destination, although we do not know if the shipment reached the camp. The German Red Cross tried to persuade Eichmann to approve the shipments, arguing that their coöperation would help improve the conditions of German POWs and civilian internees in Allied hands. As late as in August 1944, the German Red Cross inquired if they could approve the request of the ICRC to send forty boxes of Lactissa (a kind of powdered milk) and twenty boxes of Ovomaltine to Birkenau.[132]

The SS were highly interested in having the scheme continued and included the distribution of the parcels in the tour of the Theresienstadt ghetto they organized for the Red Cross. Around the same time, Deputy Reich Press Secretary (Stellvertreter des Reichspressechefs) Helmut Sündermann told a gathering of foreign correspondents that 20,000 parcels had arrived in Theresienstadt in the course of June 1944.[133] Furthermore, the film *Theresienstadt. Ein Dokumentarfilm aus dem jüdischen Siedlungsgebiet*, about life in the ghetto, prepared in 1944 by a Czech film crew for German propaganda, showed a sequence from the post office during which the inmates received parcels and, later, a family scene in which a prisoner opened a parcel he had received from abroad.[134]

Much less is known about the fate of the parcels sent to Birkenau. Consul Čejka ultimately sent 12,425 parcels—half a kilo each (6.5 tonnes)—containing tinned sardines to this death factory, where prisoners constantly lived and toiled in close quarters with a number of gas chambers and crematoria. The JDC, following the example of the Czechs, also sent parcels to Birkenau. By July 1944, they were sending 4,000 parcels a month to 2,000 inmates.[135] Almost none of those packages were ever delivered to their addressees, who had often been gassed before the food could theoretically reach them. The tins of sardines were confiscated and distributed among the SS camp guards.[136]

Unlikely as it sounds, however, a certain number of parcels did reach the prisoners, even in Birkenau. In late 1942, the SS allowed the delivery of parcels to prisoners in the camp, but Jews were initially excluded. This seemed to change in 1943, when some of the Jews, among them deportees from Slovakia, reported the arrival of food parcels.[137] Other individuals confirmed the delivery of parcels with tinned sardines from Portugal in cards that the German censors allowed to be sent to neutral countries.[138] Auschwitz survivors interviewed by the historian Miroslav Kárný in the 1970s and 1980s likewise confirmed irregular deliveries of parcels to Birkenau.[139] Hella Kounio (Cougno), deported to Auschwitz from Thessaloniki, received tins of sardines from Portugal "three or four times." Kounio was a privileged Jewish prisoner who worked in the Political Division in the camp. She believed that the Germans allowed the delivery of some parcels to encourage more shipments, which they subsequently confiscated.[140] The SS also allowed several prisoners to send confirmations abroad, as "evidence" that they were still alive and that reports about the extermination of the Jews had been invented by Allied propaganda. The prisoners were asked to postdate their cards (they were told that the censorship would delay the mail) and were murdered shortly thereafter. In most cases they were no longer alive when their relatives or the Jewish activists abroad received the cards.[141]

Conclusion

This chapter has shown that attitudes in the Allied countries toward "the obligation to care" for Jewish inmates in Nazi ghettos and concentration camps varied significantly. It is fair to conclude that the Polish and Czechoslovak exile governments, observing the duty of care for their citizens, supported these humanitarian programs. Hence, we need to differentiate between the positions of the exile governments—the official diplomatic representatives of the subjugated communities—and the major Allies. While the former had the obligation of a modern state to look after their citizens, the latter lacked such sentiments. The major Allies grudgingly approved a few minor concessions. This decision to help the persecuted came during 1942 and 1943, at the peak of the military conflict, when the Wehrmacht still maintained firm control over large swaths of Europe and the western Allies were still preparing for major military interventions.

Jewish organizations in the United States and Britain were initially torn between their effort to help their suffering brethren and the feeling that they as true Britons and Americans had to be patriotic and support their governments in wartime. Concerns about the allegations of dual loyalties played a prominent role in some Jewish organizers' decision to stop their initial relief schemes in 1941. Less well-integrated groups, such as the Orthodox Agudas Israel, exile Jewish organizations, and recent refugees were at the forefront of the fight for relief shipments. For them, this was not a matter of generic humanitarian intervention but an effort to directly support their own families, friends, and communities. Once the information about the scheme leaked to the public, refugees such as Symcha Gausman immediately approached the Jewish organizations with requests to include their relatives in the planned program. The realization that they could send food to their families liberated them from some of the agony they had experienced since the beginning of the war. Finally, they concluded, they could do something for their wives, children, elderly parents, and friends abroad.

The relief parcel schemes as they developed in the second half of 1943 raise the question of whether the exile governments and activists were able to comprehend the full lethal nature of the German campaign against Europe's Jews. They attempted to send help to Birkenau and Kraków when the extermination campaign in Poland was almost complete. Some Jewish organizers were aware of the hopeless situation in eastern Europe, but they still tried to help every single individual they could potentially reach. Štěpán Barber, a Czech Jewish activist, articulated this point of view in a letter to the Board of Deputies in March 1943, when he asked the British organization to send parcels to his relatives who had been deported to eastern Poland almost a year earlier: "The only trace I could find so far was the name of my grandfather who is somewhere near Lublin if he is still alive. . . . I am unfortunately only too well aware of the low degree of probability that these parcels will arrive in time, but *still it is our duty to do all in our power to help them as much as we can.*"[142] This, however, does not explain why governmental agencies continued the shipments. It is evident that the governments would have never approved of sending the parcels had they believed that most of the Jews were no longer alive. This research tends to confirm the notion that the Allies were not really able to comprehend Nazi plans. Judging from the parcel schemes, the change only came in mid-1944, when the reports from occupied Europe confirmed that most of the parcels were not delivered. Nevertheless, attempts to send parcels to Birkenau continued even after details from the famous 1944 Vrba-Wetzler Auschwitz report were made available in London.[143]

For prisoners, the arrival of parcels meant much more than a temporarily increased intake of calories or a supply of medicine that could save a life. Heinrich Liebrecht wrote after the war, "Little parcels containing sardines arrived from Lisbon [to Theresienstadt], ordered by the American Joint Distribution Committee. The oil in them was very valuable."[144] The parcels provided moral encouragement and a sense of satisfaction—as Marion Kaplan argues—to both the senders and the recipients.[145] It evoked the feeling that somebody cared, even in a world of complete moral degradation under the Nazis. Rabbi Leo Baeck, a German Jewish leader, recalled that "a package came for me not long after I arrived in Theresienstadt. Its contents had been removed and it was really only an empty cardboard box. But it gave me joy in the knowledge that someone had thought of me in exile."[146] For Miriam Wattenberg in Warsaw, the arrival of a parcel from her gentile friends signified that "in this ocean of misery in which we are living, it is a comfort to find a warm-hearted person."[147] Ruth Bondy, later a famous Czech Israeli writer, remembered a similar feeling in Birkenau when she in February 1944 received a parcel with a loaf of bread. The sole realization that it was addressed with her name, not simply to the prisoner number tattooed on her forearm, recreated the feeling of human dignity for her.[148]

Others paint a less positive image and acknowledge the problems the parcels could cause in the prisoner community. H. G. Adler, the main historian of the Theresienstadt ghetto and himself a survivor, was very critical of relations among prisoners. He suggested that after a slow start in 1942, parcels began arriving in "considerable quantities" by 1944: "The packages gave rise to major social divisions and did a great deal of damage in addition to being a blessing. . . . Few of those who were well supplied were aware of their responsibilities. It is no wonder that jealousy and hatred arose. Throughout rooms and halls, people enjoyed delicious meals while, next to them, wizened old men and women rummaged in the garbage."[149]

The parcels could also play an important role in the economy of the ghetto or camp, for they brought items in high demand into the community that could be sold on the black market or exchanged for other commodities and services. Satirical verses written in Theresienstadt tell the tale of a prisoner who received a parcel and exchanged it for a service from another inmate. The next person exchanged it for another item or service with a third person and so on. Eventually, the parcel made a full round and ended up in the hands of the original recipient. He finally opened it to find that the parcel had been empty all along.[150]

That said, the number of parcels sent in the framework of the JDC, Board of Deputies, and Polish and Czechoslovak programs remained strictly limited and could never have improved the situation of large numbers of Jewish prisoners. The card index created in London and Lisbon by the Czechoslovak government together with the JDC contained fewer than 9,000 names and addresses of Jews trapped in Theresienstadt.[151] A total of almost 150,000 Jews spent some time behind the walls of the fortress town, and the card index thus contained only around 6 percent of all the names of the Jews deported to Theresienstadt.

Although almost 300,000 parcels were sent to Theresienstadt under the auspices of the relief programs, on average only about 2 parcels were sent to each deportee over almost two years—if they shared the parcels (which rarely happened). Much less was received, of course.

There is something unusual about this whole aid operation: although we have a reasonable estimate of the number of parcels sent by all organizations, we do not know how many of the parcels arrived or how many people received the help. We will never know how many people were saved, for the parcels were only one contributing factor. The evidence is purely anecdotal. At the same time, we need to correct the conclusions reached by other authors such as Pamela Shatzkes, who assert that "the claim that food parcels from abroad were instrumental in saving Jews from death is, on the face of it, absurd."[152] The parcels that arrived before 1941 in Warsaw and other ghettos, and later in Birkenau and Theresienstadt, helped the recipients. Of course, they could not ultimately save the Jews as long as the Nazis ruled Europe. Although the Nazi regime sought to murder all of Europe's Jews, its officials also, for various reasons detailed above, allowed some parcels to reach prisoners. In the end, the Nazis clearly benefited from these relief shipments as well. But the physical and emotional support the parcels brought to prisoners helped some survive until the day of liberation. They gave them strength to perform forced labor, pass periodic selections, and endure the last months of the war, when life-threatening conditions and starvation continued to kill Jewish prisoners.

The programs testify to the immense efforts of a few activists, who with uncertain leverage were able to lobby government officials and negotiate the permission to send the parcels. A final example illustrates this well. In November 1945, Ines Regina Goerke, sixty-seven years old, at the time living in the Deggendorf Displaced Persons Camp in Bavaria, wrote to her brother Walter Rothschild in Los Angeles:

> My dear brother Walter, Now that I am again pretty well taken care of, the memory of the starvation period in Theresienstadt and the indescribable blessing caused by the sardine packages are very vivid in my mind. I do not know whom I have to thank for this humanitarian gesture. Should you, my dear Walter, have the possibility, please do it for me and emphasize the fact that innumerable fellow sufferers would have been reduced to real starvation were it not for the generosity of these contributions. In spite of all postal difficulties the dispatches were perfectly well packed and we were all happy and moved by the regularity of their arrival. . . . Your loving sister, Ines.[153]

Walter Rothschild forwarded the letter to the JDC office in New York with the attached comment: "I am sending you this German letter as I am sure you enjoy hearing how the work of your organization is appreciated."[154]

Notes

1 *The Rescue of Stricken Jews in a World at War: A Report on the Work and Plans of the American Jewish Joint Distribution Committee, as Contained in Addresses Delivered at Its Twenty-Ninth Annual Meeting, December 4th and 5th, 1943* (New York: American Jewish Joint Distribution Committee, 1944), 16.

2 London Metropolitan Archives (LMA), ACC/3121/C/11/92, Gausman to Brotman, June 8, 1943.

3 Peter Roessler, a thirteen-year-old orphan at the time, remembers that one day almost three years after his arrival in the Łódź ghetto, he and his brother suddenly received a parcel that contained a moldy loaf of bread. It was sent from Prague by a baker and family friend, Mr. Husák. No further shipments followed (or else they were not delivered).

4 Letter to the editor about relief for Polish Jews, American Jewish Joint Distribution Committee Archives (JDC Archives), NY Office 1933–1944, Poland, folder 800, *Congress Weekly* (December 5, 1941).

5 Yehuda Bauer, *American Jewry and the Holocaust: The American Jewish Joint Distribution Committee, 1939–1945* (Detroit: Wayne State University Press, 1981).

6 Ronald W. Zweig, "Feeding the Camps: Allied Blockade Policy and the Relief of Concentration Camps in Germany, 1944–1945," *The Historical Journal* 41, no. 3 (1998): 849.

7 Ibid., 830, 838.

8 Meredith Hindley, "Constructing Allied Humanitarian Policy," in *Holocaust Studies* 9, nos. 2–3, (2000): 77–102, quote on 98; Meredith Hindley, "Blockade before Bread: Allied Relief for Nazi Europe, 1939–1945" (PhD diss., American University, 2007).

9 Michael R. Marrus, "Holocaust Bystanders and Humanitarian Intervention," in *Holocaust Studies* 13, no. 1 (2007): 1–18, quote on 15.

10 Joan C. Tronto, *Moral Boundaries. A Political Argument for an Ethic of Care* (Routledge: London, 1993), 8.

11 Alice Weinreb, *Modern Hungers: Food and Power in Twentieth-Century Germany* (Oxford: Oxford University Press, 2017), 50; Gesine Gerhard,

Nazi Hunger Politics: A History of Food in the Third Reich (London: Rowman & Littlefield, 2015).

12 Gerhard, *Nazi Hunger Politics*, 85–102.

13 Weinreb, *Modern Hungers*.

14 Boris Shub and Zorach Warhaftig, *Starvation over Europe (Made in Germany): A Documented Record, 1943* (New York: Institute of Jewish Affairs, 1943).

15 Sharman Apt Russell, *Hunger: An Unnatural History* (New York: Basic Books, 2006), 96.

16 Chaim A. Kaplan, *Scroll of Agony: The Warsaw Diary of Chaim A. Kaplan*, ed. Abraham I. Katsh (Bloomington: Indiana University Press, 1999), 333, entry for May 16, 1942.

17 Raul Hilberg, *The Destruction of European Jews*, 3 vols., 3rd ed. (New Haven: Yale University Press, 2003), 3:1320. Hilberg estimated that over 800,000 died due to ghettoization and general privation.

18 Mary Berg, *The Diary of Mary Berg: Growing up in the Warsaw Ghetto*, ed. Susan Lee Pentlin (London: Oneworld, 2006), 177.

19 Dawid Sierakowiak, *The Diary of Dawid Sierakowiak: Five Notebooks from the Łódź Ghetto*, ed. Alan Adelson (Oxford: Oxford University Press, 1998), 13.

20 See www.jta.org/1940/04/03/archive/lublin-letters-ask-food (accessed Aug. 2, 2020).

21 *Daily News Bulletin of the Jewish Telegraphic Agency*, reports from 1940–42. See www.jta.org/1941/07/15/archive/famine-among-jews-in-poland-assuming-serious-proportions; www.jta.org/1942/07/27/archive/jewish-children-in-polish-ghettos-plead-for-food-and-clothes (accessed Aug. 2, 2020).

22 Beit Theresienstadt Archives, 303.014.001, Ida Hermann's undated letter (spring 1942). See also Peter Witte, "Poslední zprávy deportovaných transportem Ax," in *Terezínské studie a dokumenty* (Prague: Academia, 1996), 59. Other letters confirm that Czech deportees indeed received food parcels from Prague.

23 See www.jta.org/1942/04/20/archive/polish-jews-send-desperate-appeal-for-food-to-outside-world (accessed Aug. 2, 2020).

24 JDC Archives, NY Office 1933–1944, Poland, folder 800, J.C. Hyman to Israel Rosenberg, September 11, 1941.

25 Ibid.

26 JDC Archives, NY Office 1933–1944, Poland, folder 800, Memorandum: Program of aid in German-occupied Poland, first half of 1942.

27 JDC Archives, NY Office 1933–1944, Poland, folder 801, Moses A. Leavitt to S. R. Lurio, October 20, 1942.
28 See Bauer's chapter 2 on the JDC in Poland between 1939 and 1941. Bauer, *American Jewry and the Holocaust*, 67–106, quote on 106.
29 This term was coined by Tony Kushner, *The Holocaust and the Liberal Imagination: A Social and Cultural History* (Oxford: Blackwell, 1994).
30 Bauer, *American Jewry and the Holocaust*, 99.
31 For this line of argumentation, see esp. Monty N. Penkower's *The Jews Were Expendable: Free World Diplomacy and the Holocaust* (Urbana: University of Illinois Press, 1983).
32 Meir Sompolinsky, *The British Government and the Holocaust: The Failure of Anglo-Jewish Leadership?* (Brighton: Sussex University Press, 1999), 143.
33 "Campaign Against Sending Food Parcels to Relatives in Nazi-Held Territories," *Daily News Bulletin of the JTA*, July 10, 1941.
34 *Daily News Bulletin of the JTA*, July 16, 1941.
35 Raya Cohen, "The Lost Honour of Bystanders? The Case of Jewish Emissaries in Switzerland," *Journal of Holocaust Education* 9, nos. 2–3 (2000): 159–65.
36 Avraham Milgram, *Portugal, Salazar, and the Jews* (Jerusalem: Yad Vashem, 2012), 204–5.
37 American Jewish organizations, most prominently Agudas Israel, constantly lobbied Allied officials, including the Polish and Czechoslovak governments-in-exile, to continue shipments of food to the Jews. Hoover Institution Library & Archives (HIA), Files of the Polish Foreign Ministry (MSZ), box 578, Jacob Rosenheim (Agudas) to Raczynski, February 24, 1942.
38 JDC Archives, NY Office 1933–1944, Poland, folder 801, Moses A. Leavitt to Eldred D. Kuppinger, February 1, 1943; ibid., folder 800, *Congress Weekly*, December 5, 1941, page unknown (To the Editor About Relief for Polish Jews).
39 See www.govinfo.gov/content/pkg/GPO-CRECB-1941-pt7/pdf/GPO-CRECB-1941-pt7.pdf, Senate hearing on September 25, 1941, 7532–33.
40 "Death Rate Soars in Polish Ghettos," *New York Times*, September 14, 1941, 31.
41 *New York Times*, March 1, 1942, 28.
42 On Zorah Warhaftig, see his memoir, *Refugee and Survivor: Rescue Efforts during the Holocaust* (Jerusalem: Yad Vashem, 1988).
43 Shub and Warhaftig, *Starvation over Europe*, 7–8.

44 Ibid., 60, 86.

45 Exile parliaments—the Polish National Council (Rada Narodowa) and Czechoslovak State Council (Státní rada)—were advisory bodies to the exile governments. They were supposed to represent the population in the occupied homeland, though the selection of the candidates also reflected the priorities of the exile leadership and the pool of candidates available in exile.

46 For more on Frischer, see Jan Láníček, *Arnošt Frischer and the Jewish Politics of Early 20th-Century Europe* (London: Bloomsbury, 2017); Ernest Frischer and Franz Kobler, *Help for the "Ghettoes"* (London: British Section of the WJC, 1942).

47 "Huge Demonstration in New York Appeals to All Governments to Save Jews in Europe," *Daily News Bulletin of the Jewish Telegraphic Agency*, March 2, 1943. See also "American Jewish Organizations Make Public Their Appeals to the Bermuda Policy," *Daily News Bulletin of the Jewish Telegraphic Agency*, April 20, 1943.

48 "We Can Still Rescue Those Who Remain Alive," *Jewish Labor Committee*, published in *The New Republic*, August 30, 1943, *A Special Section: The Jews of Europe. How to Help Them*, 306–7.

49 Jean-Claude Favez, *The Red Cross and the Holocaust* (Cambridge: Cambridge University Press, 1999). See also Gerald J. Steinacher, this volume.

50 Procopis Papastratis, *British Policy Towards Greece during the Second World War 1941–44* (Cambridge: Cambridge University Press, 1984), 115–18. Furthermore, very small shipments were sent with the help of the Polish government-in-exile to the relatives of the Polish exile military personnel, including Jews. HIA, MSZ, box 577, Polish Ministry of Foreign Affairs, to Ministry of Labour and Social Welfare, March 10, 1942.

51 LMA, ACC/3121/C/11/92, Selbourne to Margulies, Council of Polish Jews in Great Britain, July 13, 1942.

52 LMA, ACC/3121/C/11/92, Postal Packets to the Ghettos, July 30, 1942; Relief to Ghettos, July 31, 1942 (memo of a meeting on July 24, 1942).

53 LMA, ACC/3121/C/11/92, Board to R. Bloch, October 6, 1942; Board meeting. Postal parcels to ghettos, September 15, 1942.

54 See also Schimitzek's memoir, *Na krawędzi Europy: wspomnienia portugalskie, 1939–1946* (Warsaw: Wydawnictwo Naukowe, 1970). I would like to thank Adam Sitarek for allowing me access to the book.

55 LMA, ACC/3121/C/11/92, Board of Deputies to Rich (identity is unclear), November 28, 1943. The Jewish Colonization Agency was a

philanthropic organization that primarily focused on supporting Jewish immigration to Palestine.
56 HIA, MSZ, box 577, Hyman (JDC) to Ciechanowski, December 18, 1942 (permit issued on December 11, 1942).
57 See documents about these negotiations in JDC Archives, NY Office 1933–1944, Poland, folder 801.
58 Láníček, *Arnošt Frischer*, 98–114.
59 JDC Archives, NY Office 1933–1944, box 542, License granted to the JDC, May 17, 1943 (applied April 1, 1943).
60 See the correspondence in JDC Archives, NY Office 1933–1944, Relief Supplies General 1943–45, J.D.C. Starts Package Program from Sweden, December 28, 1944.
61 LMA, ACC/3121/C/11/92, Postal packets to the ghetto, July 30, 1942.
62 LMA, ACC/3121/C/11/92, MEW to Brotman, July 18, 1944.
63 LMA, ACC/3121/C/11/92, Trading with the Enemy Department to Brotman, July 6, 1943; Trading with the Enemy Department to Brotman, February 3, 1943.
64 LMA, ACC/3121/C/11/92, Council of Polish Jews in Great Britain to Brotman, February 15, 1943.
65 LMA, ACC/3121/C/11/92, Katzki (JDC) to Brotman, May 13, 1943. Schimitzek mentioned that the Joint had planned to send 12,000–15,000 parcels per month to occupied Poland but had to scrap the plan. Schimitzek, *Na krawędzi Europy*, 556–57.
66 The Jews could hardly send regular mail inside the Nazi empire, and only a few of them could occasionally contact the neutral countries. More research is needed on wartime postal traffic, including letters over borders.
67 JDC Archives, NY Office 1933–1944, box 542, Katzki to Marcellus Parsons, July 29, 1943; AJDC Lisbon to AJDC NY, September 2, 1943. The JDC received a new license from the U.S. Treasury Department only in March 1944. They were thereby allowed to send parcels to individual addresses in occupied Poland.
68 LMA, ACC/3121/C/11/92, A. Babad, Council of Polish Jews in Britain to Brotman, December 28, 1942.
69 Láníček, *Arnošt Frischer*, 120.
70 LMA, ACC/3121/C11/12/92, Frischer to Brodetsky, May 31, 1944.
71 LMA, ACC/3121/C11/12/92, AJDC Lisbon to Brotman, July 2, 1943.
72 Archiv Ministerstva zahraničních věcí, Archives of the Czech Foreign Ministry (AMZV), LA 1939–45, box 515, Ministry of Social Welfare to the Czechoslovak Foreign Ministry, March 19, 1943.

73 JDC Archives, Istanbul Office 1937–1949, War Refugee Board, memorandum from Reuben B. Resnik to Ira A. Hirshmann, March 7, 1944; JDC Archives, Istanbul Office 1937–1949, International Red Cross 1944–46, Mordecai Kessler (American Consulate General Istanbul) to International Red Cross in Ankara, November 29, 1944.

74 YIVO Archives, JDC Lisbon, folder 700, Katzki to Brotman, April 2, 1943.

75 LMA, ACC/3121/C11/12/92, Brodetsky to Frischer, February 23, 1943.

76 LMA, ACC/3121/C11/12/92, Statement of food parcels, sent on account of the Board of Deputies of British Jews (undated, probably May 1944).

77 LMA, ACC/3121/C11/12/92, Caldas da Rainha, summary, June 26, 1943.

78 LMA, ACC/3121/C11/12/92, Katzki to Brotman, July 2, 1943.

79 LMA, ACC/3121/C11/12/92, memorandum from the Commercial Counsellor to H. M. Legation, Stockholm to the MEW, July 19, 1943. See also Schimitzek, *Na krawędzi Europy*, 556–58, 585–86.

80 LMA, ACC/3121/C11/12/92, Schimitzek to Polish Ministry of Labour and Social Welfare, August 23, 1943; Council of Polish Jews in Great Britain to the Board of Deputies, December 6, 1943 (even Galicia did not work); Delegate of the Polish Ministry of Labour and Social Welfare to Ministry of Labour and Social Welfare, October 30, 1943; HIA, MSZ, box 577, Ministry of Labour and Social Welfare to MSZ, August 13, 1943.

81 LMA, ACC/3121/C11/12/92, Board to Barkman, September 24, 1943; Board of Deputies to A. Camps (Ministry of Economic Warfare), September 21, 1943.

82 LMA, ACC/3121/C11/12/92, JDC to the Board of Deputies, November 19, 1943.

83 LMA, ACC/3121/C11/12/92, Professor Samson to Camps, Ministry of Economic Warfare, September 21, 1943.

84 Szmuel Zygielbojm used the term "hell" in his manuscript *Mayne Reyze Durkhn Natsishn Gehenem* (My trip through the Nazi hell), deposited in the YIVO Archives.

85 For more information on the JUS, see the chapter by Alicja Jarkowska, this volume.

86 JDC Archives, Saly Mayer Collection (SM), folder 51, Commission mixte de secours de la Croix-Rouge Internationale to the Schweizerische Israelitische Gemeindebund Sankt-Gallen, August 27, 1942.

87 LMA, ACC/3121/C11/12/92, unsigned note from May 22, 1943 (about Weichert's letter from April 23, 1943).

88 David Engel, "Who Is a Collaborator? The Trials of Michal Weichert," in *The Jews in Poland II*, ed. Slawomir Kapralski (Kraków: Judaica Foundation, 1999), 339–70.
89 LMA, ACC/3121/C11/12/92, Conversation with Schwartz, November 5, 1943; Brotman to Schwarzbart, November 28, 1943; Hurwitz (JDC) to Brotman, March 9, 1944 and June 14, 1944; Brotman to Frischer, March 20, 1944; Robert Pilpel (JDC Lisbon) to Schimitzek, May 9, 1944.
90 LMA, ACC/3121/C11/12/92, Statement of food parcels, sent on account of the Board of Deputies of British Jews until April 30, 1944 (undated, probably May 1944).
91 LMA, ACC/3121/C11/12/92, Schimitzek to the Polish Ministry of Labour and Social Welfare, May 11, 1944.
92 JDC Archives, SM, folder 9, phone conversation with Lisbon, February 23, 1944.
93 LMA, ACC/3121/C11/12/92, Polish Ministry of Labour and Social Welfare to Brotman, July 14, 1944.
94 LMA, ACC/3121/C11/12/92, Note of Interview with his excellency M. Stańczyk, July 21, 1944.
95 YIVO Archives, JDC Lisbon, folder 700, Pilpel to AJDC New York, May 23, 1944.
96 LMA, ACC/3121/C11/12/92, Note of Interview with His Excellency M. Stańczyk, July 21, 1944.
97 YIVO Archives, JDC Lisbon, folder 700, Robert Pilpel, July 19, 1944.
98 The parcels were sent from Lisbon and Switzerland. I have not been able to find a summary document that would list all shipments to JUS. Between November 1943 and April 1944, the Board of Deputies and the Polish government sent 6,200 parcels to the JUS. YIVO Archives, JDC Lisbon, folder 700, Statement of food parcels, sent on account of the Board of Deputies of British Jews (undated, probably May 1944). On other occasions, the JDC in cooperation with the Joint Aid Committee (ICRC) sent 14,500 parcels (meat and tomato concentrate) to the JUS (JDC Archives, SM), folder 51, Joint Aid Committee to Mayer, June 9, 1944.
99 Bauer, *American Jewry and the Holocaust*, 322.
100 [U.K.] National Archives, Kew, FO 371/36653, W3315/49/48, Nichols to Foreign Office, February 24, 1943.
101 AMZV, LA, box 515, Ministry of Social Welfare (MSW) for Ministry of Foreign Affairs (MFA), March 19, 1943.
102 AMZV, LA, box 515, Čejka to MFA, September 3, 1943. According to the information available in London, Czechoslovak citizens were located in

the following camps: Rivesaltes, Gurs, Noé, Nexon, Le Vernet, Brens, and Les Milles. NA, MSP-L, box 58, MFA to MSW, November 22, 1942.

103 AMZV, LA, box 515, Kopecký to Kleinberg, September 25, 1943.

104 JDC Archives, NY Office 1933–1944, box 542, N. Reich to D.L. Speiser, January 31, 1945.

105 The whole group also cooperated with Schimitzek (*Na krawędzi Europy*).

106 JDC Archives, NY Office 1933–1944, box 542, AJDC Lisbon to AJDC NY, Food Packages to Theresienstadt, November 8, 1943.

107 This is an estimate. We do not have any reliable complete statistics for all the programs.

108 JDC Archives, NY Office 1933–1944, box 542, memorandum re Package Service to Russia, Theresienstadt, and Bergen-Belsen February 9, 1945; memorandum N. Reich to D. L. Speiser, Package Service to Theresienstadt and Bergen-Belsen, January 31, 1945; AJDC Lisbon to AJDC New York, November 8, 1943; Buchman to Oscar Gurfinkel, March 24, 1944. (The JDC received permission to transfer $12,000 monthly to Switzerland.)

109 JDC Archives, NY Office 1933–1944, box 542, Schwarz's telegram, received April 11, 1944.

110 JDC Archives, NY Office 1933–1944, box 542, AJDC Lisbon to AJDC New York, September 30, 1944; Henrietta K. Buchman to Hugo Perutz, November 3, 1944. ("We received from our Lisbon office a list containing 8,800 names and addresses of persons in Theresienstadt to whom parcels are currently being sent by our organization and from whom cards have been received in acknowledgment of same.")

111 AMZV, LA 1939–45, box 515, Čejka to Kopecký, December 2, 1943.

112 In late October 1943 Čejka agreed to send a test shipment to Weichert's address in Kraków (JUS), with 26 parcels (one for Weichert) intended for Czechoslovak inmates in Majdanek, Lublin, and Trawniki (AMZV, LA 1939–45, box 514), Čejka to MFA, October 22, 1943; AMZV, LA 1939–45, box 515, Organisation d'Assistance aux Familles Éprouvées (Čejka) to Weichert, October 26, 1943; LA, box 515, Weichert to Organisation d'Assistance aux Familles Éprouvées (Čejka), January 1, 1944; NA, MSP-L, box 75, Čejka to Frischer and exile ministries, May 9, 1943.

113 AMZV, LA 1939–45, box 512, MFA to Hanák, January 10, 1944.

114 Central Zionist Archives (CZA), A320/97; AMZV, LA 1939–45, box 512, MFA to Hanák, January 10, 1944; box 515, MSW to MFA, September 1, 1943; AMZV, LA-D 1939–45, box 515, Čejka to MFA, February 2, 1944; CZA, A320/226, confirmations from March/April 1944.

115 It is not clear how Čejka reached that number. In the letter, Eppstein reported that between November 1, 1943, and March 28, 1944, they had received 6,194 "Postpakete und Paeckchen aus Lissabon." In another letter, Eppstein confirmed the delivery of 1,875 parcels between May 1 and September 18, 1943. That makes 8,069 parcels in all, in contrast to the 7,294 noted by Čejka. Kárný concluded that the difference cannot be explained. Miroslav Kárný, "Terezínské balíčky ve světle archivních dokumentů," *Vlastivědný sborník Litoměřicko* 23 (1987): 210n51.

116 Kárný, "Terezínské balíčky," 204.

117 AMZV, LA 1939–45, box 514, Minutes of the Czechoslovak Relief Action meeting, August 18, 1944.

118 JDC Archives, NY Office 1933–1944, Poland, File 801, Katzki to JDC in NY, May 4, 1943.

119 JDC Archives, NY Office 1933–1944, General Relief Supplies, 1943–45, Pehle to Leavitt, December 12, 1944.

120 JDC Archives, Istanbul Office 1937–1949, Reuben B. Resnik to Ira A. Hirshmann, March 7, 1944.

121 JDC Archives, Istanbul Office 1937–1949, International Red Cross 1944–46, Mordecai Kessler (American Consulate General Istanbul) to International Red Cross in Ankara, November 29, 1944.

122 AMZV, LA 1939–45, box 469, Čejka to MFA, 18 March 1945; AMZV, LA 1939–45, box 513, Čejka to MFA, December 4, 1944.

123 CZA, A320/420, Kohn to Ullmann, August 23, 1945.

124 Mikuláš Čtvrtník, "Balíčková pomoc Terezínu 1942–1944," *Paginae historiae: Sborník Národního archivu*, 17 (2009): 51–52; František Beneš and Patricia Tošnerová, *Pošta v ghetto Terezín* (Prague: Profil, 1996), 111. Tošnerová and Beneš quote a document from February 28, 1945, in which the last chairman of the Council of Jewish Elders, Benjamin Murmelstein (1905–89), informed the SS commandant that between May 1943 and February 1945, 117,083 parcels from Portugal had reached the ghetto. The historians cited conclude that the inmates never received most of the parcels.

125 Kárný, "Terezínské balíčky," 195–210.

126 Vojtěch Blodig, "Poznámky ke zprávě Maurice Rossela," *Terezínské studie a dokumenty 1996* (Prague: Academia, 1996), 216–17n64.

127 ABS, 425-230-7, Social Committee of Jews of Czechoslovakia to Frischer, March 16, 1945.

128 Blodig, "Poznámky ke zprávě," 217n65.

129 USHMM, Report from the German Red Cross (DRK) to Eichmann, August 4, 1943, ITS digital archive, 1.1.0.2/82339788#1/. I thank Marion

Kaplan for the reference to the ITS archive. Cf. report prepared by Čejka, AMZV, LA 1939–45, box 515, Čejka to Kopecký, December 2, 1943.

130 I thank Konrad Kwiet for copies of the documents from the archives of the German Red Cross (BAK, R58/59), Aktenvermerk, March 4, 1943; Aktenvermerk, April 17, 1943; DRK Oberfeldführer to Günther, July 15, 1943 (attached signed confirmations by Paul Eppstein and Jakob Edelstein, June 26, 1943).

131 Birgitt Morgenbrod and Stephanie Merkenich, *Das Deutsche Rote Kreuz unter der NS-Diktatur 1933–1945* (Paderborn: Schöningh, 2008), 389.

132 BAK, R58/59, Niehaus (German Red Cross) to Eichmann, January 4, 1944; Eichmann to the German Red Cross, January 26, 1944; German Red Cross to Reich Security Main Office, August 7, 1944.

133 AMZV, LA, box 469, Frischer to MSW, August 11, 1944.

134 Beneš and Tošnerová, *Pošta v ghetto Terezín*, 113.

135 JDC Archives, NY Office 1933–1944, box 542, Kubowitzki (WJC) to Joseph C. Hyman, July 6, 1944; report by Joseph Schwartz (JDC) to Leavitt, April 11, 1944 (received). Schwartz requested that the JDC should obtain a license for sending parcels to Birkenau; box 802, AJDC Lisbon (Robert Pilpel) to AJDC New York, July 19, 1944.

136 Janusz Gumkowski et al., *Zbrodniarze hitlerowscy przed Najwyższym Trybunałem Narodowym* (Warsaw: Wydawnictwo Prawnicze, 1968), 124.

137 Yad Vashem Archives, O.75/119.

138 CZA, Jerusalem, A320/226.

139 AŽM, Miroslav Kárný Collection, "Dopisy z terezínského rodinného tábora. Analýza souboru 22 dopisů," unpublished manuscript.

140 Kounio, *From Thessaloniki to Auschwitz and Back* (London: Valentine Mitchell, 2000), 110–11.

141 Kárný, "Otázky nad 8. březnem 1944," *Terezínské studie a dokumenty 1999* (Prague: Academia, 1999), 17.

142 LMA, ACC/3121/C/11/12/91, Barber to Salomon, March 15, 1943, my emphasis.

143 On the escape of two Slovak Jewish prisoners from Birkenau and their effort to inform the Allies about the extermination of the Jews, see *London Has Been Informed . . . Reports by Auschwitz Escapees*, ed. Henryk Swiebocki (Oswiecim: Auschwitz-Birkenau State Museum, 2002).

144 Heinrich Liebrecht, "Therefore Will I Deliver Him," in *We Survived: Fourteen Histories of the Hidden and Hunted In Nazi Germany*, ed. Eric H. Boehm (Boulder: Westview, 2003), 237.

145 Marion Kaplan, personal communication.

146 Leo Baeck, "A People Stands Before Its God," in *We Survived*, 291.
147 Berg, *The Diary of Mary Berg*, 191 (October 17, 1942).
148 Ruth Bondy, "The Miracle of the Loaves: Heinz Prossnitz' Package Aid," in *Trapped: Essays on the History of the Czech Jews, 1939–1945*, ed. Ruth Bondy (Jerusalem: Yad Vashem, 2008), 117.
149 H. G. Adler, *Theresienstadt 1941–1945: The Face of a Coerced Community* (New York: Cambridge University Press in association with the USHMM, 2017), 317–18.
150 I thank Lisa Peschel for sending me a copy of the document.
151 JDC Archives, NY Office 1933–1944, box 542, AJDC Lisbon to AJDC NY, September 30, 1944; Buchman to Perutz, November 3, 1944 (8,800 names and receipts).
152 Pamela Shatzkes, *Holocaust and Rescue: Impotent or Indifferent? Anglo-Jewry, 1938–1945* (London: Palgrave, 2001), 197.
153 JDC Archives, NY Office 1933–1944, Relief Supplies General 1943–45, Ines Goerke to Walter Rothschild, undated, November 1945.
154 JDC Archives, NY Office 1933–1944, Relief Supplies General 1943–45, H. M. Picard (HIAS) to JDC NY, March 6, 1946.

4

AN UNDENIABLE DUTY

Swedish Jewish Humanitarian Aid to Jews in Nazi-Occupied Europe during World War II

PONTUS RUDBERG

During the last winter of World War II, feverish activity filled the premises of the Jewish Community of Stockholm next door to the Great Synagogue. Thousands of food packages were prepared to be shipped to Jews in Nazi concentration camps. Two groups of Jewish relief workers were simultaneously compiling lists of prisoners in the Theresienstadt ghetto, Bergen-Belsen, and other concentration camps. These groups collected details about prisoners whose names had been reported by foreign relief organizations, governments, relatives, and friends and were believed to be alive. They negotiated export licenses and agreements with the Swedish authorities and the western Allies. Donors had to be found, and non-Jewish organizations and Swedish retail companies were persuaded to be listed as senders on the packages to increase the chances that they would reach prisoners. The organizers also made deals with suppliers and shipping companies, paid for packages and postage, and printed tens of thousands of address labels.

As a neutral country with good relations with Germany, Sweden was in many regards ideally placed as a bridgehead for sending relief to Jews in Nazi Europe. Yet the Swedish Jewish organizers of the relief schemes faced a number of obstacles imposed by the Swedish authorities, the Germans, and the Allies, as well as by the general difficulties of finding reliable means to communicate under wartime conditions. Other problems stemmed from the organizers themselves, who had diverging views on how to structure the operation. No consensus emerged among Jews in Sweden about where, how, and to whom the food packages should be sent; who would ultimately pay for them; or which of the Jewish organizations in Sweden would be in charge.

This chapter focuses on several programs through which thousands of parcels containing food and medicine were sent from Sweden to Jews trapped in Nazi Germany and occupied countries in Europe.[1] It pays special attention to the scope, scale, and timing of the Swedish contributions and details the role of local Jewish aid organizations as mediators in this process, primarily the relief committees of the country's Jewish communities, the Swedish Section of the World Jewish Congress (WJC), and the American Jewish Joint Distribution Committee (JDC). A long chain of individuals and groups contributed to delivering Swedish aid, including the international organizations operating in Sweden during the war.[2] The chapter also sheds light on the position of Sweden as a neutral in the war, but located inside Europe. Its unique position enabled Jewish activists and relief agencies to operate in and through the country to gather and disseminate information about the fate of Jews living under Nazi control. These networks were vital for this exchange and also played an important role in planning relief and rescue efforts from Sweden. The impact of the Swedish government's export ban and other countries' economic blockades of Germany on Swedish relief forms an important backdrop to this story as well.

Furthermore, the lack of concrete information about the fate of the Jews—and diverse ideas about providing aid under such extreme conditions—led to sharp divisions among activists about the proposed relief schemes and how shipments should be organized. Ironically, such divisions did not cause a failure of the programs but rather contributed to a higher number of shipments sent from Sweden to Nazi Europe, especially in the final months of the war.

Swedish Jews and the Organization of Relief

Approximately 7,000 Jews lived in Sweden in 1933. Membership in a religious body was mandatory for all Swedish citizens, which meant that all Jews with Swedish citizenship had to be a member of an official Jewish community. The Jewish Community of Stockholm was the largest, numbering approximately 4,000 members, while the Jewish communities of Gothenburg and Malmö were the second and third largest, respectively. Already in the spring of 1933, these communities, like their counterparts elsewhere in Europe and the Americas, began forming relief committees to help Jews in Germany. Despite, or possibly because of, their semiofficial status and dependence on money raised through taxation, their relief activities were carried out by fiscally independent subcommittees. Following the patterns of foreign Jewish relief organizations, these committees began to raise funds primarily to facilitate the emigration of German Jews. They gave grants that covered their living expenses in Sweden and set up vocational training programs that would prepare them for further emigration. They also subsidized direct emigration from Germany to Palestine. Beyond such refugee aid, the Swedish Jewish organizations were engaged in different forms of relief and, more explicitly, political responses, such as staging public protests or lobbying Swedish and foreign officials to relax their countries' restrictive immigration policies.[3]

After the outbreak of the war, Sweden declared neutrality and—unlike its northern European neighbors and partly owing to its far-reaching concessions to Nazi Germany—managed to remain neutral throughout the war. Already before the war, the country had issued very few residence or work permits, which Jewish refugees needed to stay in the country. Furthermore, the government issued a decree in September 1938 prescribing that foreign citizens should be turned away at the border if authorities suspected they did not intend to return to their country of origin. Nonetheless, around 4,000 Jewish refugees found refuge in Sweden with the help of local Jews and refugee organizations before the outbreak of war in September 1939.

Soon after the German invasion of Poland, letters from Polish Jews pleading for food aid started to arrive at Jewish communities in Sweden. In response, the chief rabbi of Stockholm, Marcus Ehrenpreis, created a new organization, the Working Committee for Polish Jewish Relief (Arbetsutskottet för hjälp åt Polens judar). Its task was to send food, medicine, and clothes to Poland. The Working Committee was managed and run by the leaders and members of the Jewish Community of Stockholm as an independent organization financed by a mix of private donations and contributions from the Jewish community and other organizations. Calls for donations were usually made in connection with Jewish holidays and were both read aloud in the synagogue and published in the Swedish Jewish press.[4] The rabbis of Gothenburg and Malmö, Hermann Löb and Elieser Berlinger, also created similar relief committees. However, it soon became clear that the material aid sent directly from Sweden could not be very extensive since Sweden had put in place an export ban after the outbreak of the war. Export licenses were issued by the National Trade Commission and were generally only approved for Swedish residents who wished to send aid to close relatives abroad.[5]

Packages to Occupied Poland and France

From the start, the Swedish aid groups looked for partners in other neutral countries. The Working Committee cooperated with the Children's Relief Organization (Œuvre de secours aux enfants, or OSE) in Geneva and the Association

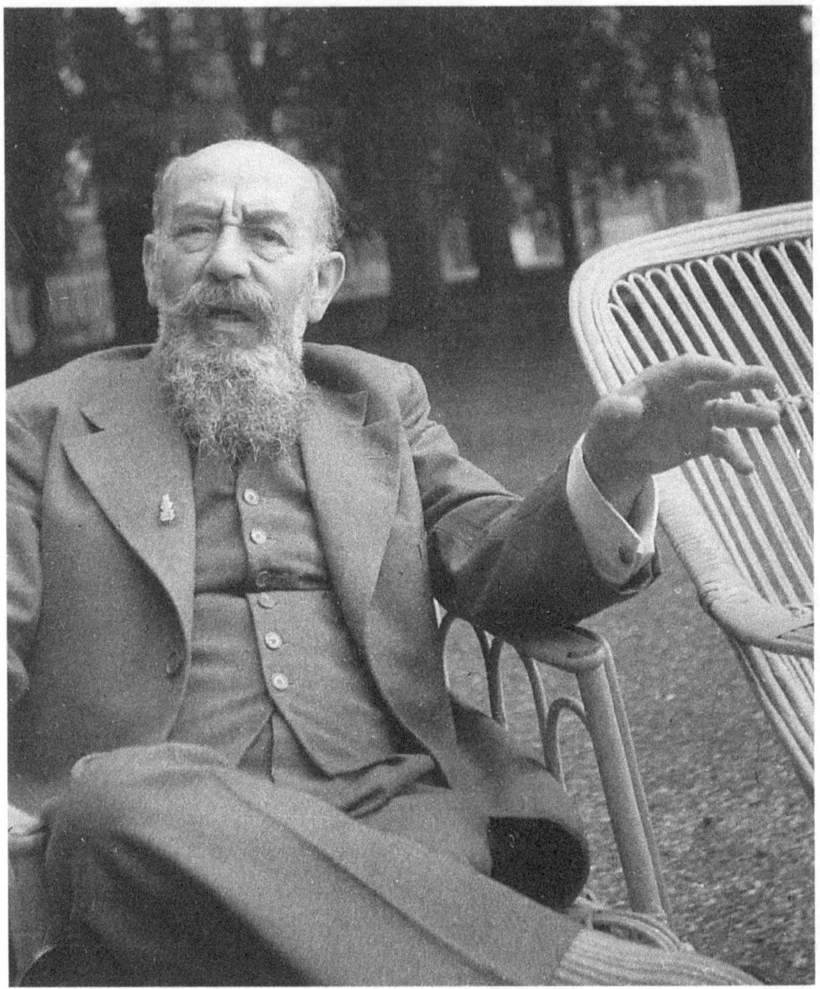

Marcus Ehrenpreis, chief rabbi of Stockholm and leading relief organizer. Courtesy of the Moderna Museet, Stockholm, photo by Anna Riwkin.

of Jewish Swiss Welfare Services (Verband Schweizer Israelitischer Armenpflege, or VSIA) in Zurich in sending medicine to Poland. They also sent money to the Jewish Social Self-Help in Poland (Jüdische Soziale Selbsthilfe, or JSS), as well as to private individuals in Lemberg (Lwów/Lviv). Financial aid was initially sent to recipients in the Lemberg district, Warsaw, Kraków, and the Lublin area. However, according to the committee's own report, it was but "a drop in the ocean." Despite German censors, many desperate letters found their way from

Poland to the committee with requests for aid. They all described how the Jewish population was suffering from the cold and starvation.[6]

To stand out in the flood of requests for aid and to overcome the bureaucratic gulf between them and the relief committees, the requesters frequently emphasized personal connections. Consequently, when the JSS in Lemberg contacted the committee in Stockholm, it usually included personal greetings to Rabbi Ehrenpreis and news from family members and old friends. One letter included greetings from several relatives before informing the rabbi that the JSS committee in Lemberg was serving over 7,000 people daily and needed clothes, shoes, food, and money. At the end of the letter, they asked Ehrenpreis for a personal intervention with the German Red Cross to secure deliveries.[7]

Only in October 1941 did the members of the Working Committee, which had already established contacts with welfare agencies in Europe, take steps to organize the first large shipments of food instead of money to Poland. Rabbi Ehrenpreis contacted Michał Weichert, the chairman of the JSS in Kraków, who like himself was originally from Lemberg, to inquire about possibilities for sending shipments to different parts of Poland. Weichert replied that the Germans required them to rely on official German-controlled channels. All collective shipments needed to be sent exclusively to the JSS through the German Red Cross in Kraków.[8] The Working Committee also sent large sums of money to the Jewish Swiss Welfare Services organization in Zurich to be used for the aid of Jewish children in French refugee and internment camps, among them many refugees from Poland. After having received a request from the Children's Relief Organization (OSE) office in Geneva for assistance in sending medicine to Poland, they also financed a large shipment of typhus fever serum that went from Mexico through Switzerland to Poland. Another shipment of different types of medicines was also sent to the Lemberg district.[9]

Around the same time, the rabbis of Gothenburg and Malmö, Löb and Berlinger, contacted the Relief Committee for the War-Stricken Jewish Population (RELICO), an organization created in Geneva in 1939 by Abraham Silberschein.[10] In part funded by the WJC, RELICO had good contacts within the International Committee of the Red Cross (ICRC) and various diplomats, as well as within the Catholic and Protestant churches. The two rabbis inquired about the possibilities of sending relief to Jews in Poland and in camps in France. Berlinger was also interested in sending aid to Jews in Nazi-occupied Lithuania and Latvia. RELICO offered to act as a mediator, order the packages, and send the lists of recipients to relief workers in France for distribution. This way the shipments would "run smoothly without confiscation," they wrote. Shipments to all parts of Poland, including Galicia, also appeared to be possible. In contrast, it was still impossible to determine whether shipments from Switzerland were really reaching recipients in Nazi-occupied Lithuania and Latvia, although the Portuguese shipping firms that RELICO employed claimed that the shipments from Portugal could reach those places. For bulk shipments of food packages to Poland, RELICO confirmed Weichert's claims that they should go to the German Red Cross in Kraków, which would pass them on to the JSS in that city or in Lublin. RELICO in Geneva was itself using this route for sending "several thousands of packages" to Jews in Kraków.[11]

RELICO and Shipments to Poland

Several issues complicated the cooperation among the Jewish relief committees in Sweden. For example, they disagreed about the use of middlemen such as RELICO. Berlinger in Malmö contacted the committee in Stockholm with a list of addresses of people in Poland whom he wanted to support, inquiring whether it was better to order the packages from RELICO in Geneva or directly from one of the trading firms in Lisbon. The Working Committee believed it was more efficient to negotiate directly with the companies, since middlemen made the shipments more expensive and prolonged the whole process; the committee thus decided to send their packages to Poland through the firm Casa Chinesa in Lisbon, which many other aid organizations used. Berlinger also did not want to ship aid to addresses provided by the refugees, since he thought that only those who happened to have relatives in Sweden would benefit from the packages.[12]

Similar, to Berlinger, Löb in Gothenburg primarily wanted to help those who did not have contacts who could support them. In a letter to the Working Committee in Stockholm, Löb explained that he had recently received a list of 120 addresses of "the poorest of the poor" in Warsaw from the JSS committee there and emphasized that helping the poor was in fact the main aim of his organization.[13] In an appeal for donations before the High Holidays in 1941, Löb stated that the aid should go to Jews who were interned above all in Poland and southern France and that those without relatives in Sweden would be prioritized. The aid had a moral value, showing deportees that they had not been forgotten, Löb wrote. Nearly all of the community members in Gothenburg heeded the call, and within weeks the committee in Gothenburg was able to transfer 2,000 Swiss francs to RELICO to be used for relief packages for the individuals on the list of the poorest in Warsaw.[14]

RELICO generally bought the goods from Portuguese trading firms that shipped the food packages to the German Red Cross representative in Kraków, who was asked to forward them to the JSS in Warsaw. The German Red Cross office in that city had to give preliminary clearance to each delivery, but their decision depended on the approval of their headquarters in Berlin. On December 23, 1941, RELICO informed Löb that according to recent news from Lisbon, an export ban on coffee, chocolate, and other products from Portugal could be expected soon. They therefore decided not to wait for the approval of the Berlin office and ordered packages containing 200 kilos each of coffee, cocoa, sardines, and honey and hoped that the German Red Cross in Kraków would then let the JSS distribute the packages to the addressees on Löb's list. Addressing the shipments to the German Red Cross, RELICO wrote, considerably reduced the risk of loss, and the recipients would not have to pay any fees or taxes.[15] The Stockholm Working Committee also mentioned that the contents of the packages sent from Portugal were initially nutritionally rich and varied and included coffee, cocoa, sardines, honey, and tinned milk but became increasingly rationed with time, as one after another of the foodstuffs became unavailable for export. It was possible to buy other products such as tuna, plums, dried fruit, jam, almonds, figs, and tomato paste. Still, the packages took a long time to reach Poland, in many cases three to six months, and sometimes they disappeared on the way. However, the committee received messages that the packages to a large extent had arrived intact and were of great value to the recipients. Not only were the contents a great morale boost but so was "the joy knowing that there are still people who can and want to aid them," a sentiment shared not only by the recipients.[16]

In February 1942, RELICO confirmed to Berlinger in Malmö that it had made a shipment of 2,500 Swiss francs' worth of food from Portugal on behalf of the Malmö committee to the JSS in Lublin through the German Red Cross in Kraków. The shipment contained 425 kilos of canned fish, honey, and milk powder for 300 addresses in Lublin that Berlinger had provided.[17] Some packages were also sent to occupied Poland directly from Sweden. Individuals who had been able to obtain licenses from the National Trade Commission sent packages with clothes and food with the help of the Working Committee in Stockholm. The committee paid for these approximately 250 packages. The packages, according to the Working Committee, had been extremely valuable to the recipients, not least since they could trade the contents for other badly needed goods. Clothing may have had a greater value than money in Poland.[18] Swedish export licenses were, however, almost exclusively granted to individuals in Sweden who wanted to send packages to close relatives, friends, or acquaintances—both Jewish and non-Jewish. They also had to provide the addresses. Furthermore, letters requesting aid also arrived directly from individuals in Poland who had heard of the committee's work and also from people who had already received packages and wanted to provide more names of possible recipients.[19] Yet many refugees in Sweden chose to turn directly to RELICO instead, most likely thinking that it was more effective to cut out at least one middleman.[20]

The Swedish activists were aware of the constantly shifting situation in occupied Poland, but they tried to explore all possible avenues of aid, even those with uncertain outcomes. In May 1942, Berlinger informed RELICO that his committee wanted to contribute to a shipment that was planned for Jewish deportees who had recently arrived in the ghetto and transit camp in Izbica, in the Lublin district. He was already aware that many of those who had been previously deported to the Lublin area had now been "evacuated" and "replaced" by others, which confirms that the activists in Sweden had access to at least some information about the unfolding genocide in eastern Poland. He had also heard that shipments addressed to Piaski, another small ghetto in the same region, would not be delivered, since the former inhabitants had been deported elsewhere. He therefore wanted to know what had happened to packages sent to those no longer in their original places of residence.[21]

RELICO confirmed the planned shipment to Izbica. It would be addressed directly to the local Jewish council, which had informed RELICO about the arrival of around 8,000 new deportees "from Warszaw and other places," while also confirming that a number of Jews in the Lublin area had been "evacuated again" to make room for the new arrivals. This was the case with the deportees from Stettin, sent to Piaski in 1940. The RELICO staff was not aware that the Jews deported from Izbica and Piaski between mid-March 1942 and mid-April 1942 had already been killed in the Bełżec extermination camp. Nor did RELICO believe that the shipments were likely to be confiscated, since they were primarily addressed to the JSS and their distribution had so far been left intact. They also considered it safe to address new shipments to the Jewish council in Izbica and in other small towns in Poland, which kept RELICO informed about how they used parcels for recipients who had already left. Nevertheless, Silberschein, RELICO's founder and director, advised that in the future all individual packages should be addressed to the Jewish councils as a precaution and also because they would be able to distribute the aid to all in need. RELICO also offered to put Berlinger in contact with Boris Tschlenoff of the children's aid organization OSE in Geneva, who was organizing large shipments of medicine to Poland in cooperation with the ICRC. Yet with the approaching entry of the United States into the war, the Americans restricted funding for relief agencies such as RELICO. Furthermore, they now allowed only medical aid to be sent to the occupied territories. Relief agencies had to collect as much money as possible in the countries of Europe, where funds did not have to pass through the Allied blockade.[22]

Berlinger was not entirely reassured by RELICO's assessment of the situation in Poland and deliveries of the parcels. He had recently received "desperate letters from people in Piaski" who were expecting deliveries and "who have still not received anything." One of Berlinger's sources about the undelivered packages was Elsa Meyring, a former member of the city council in Stettin who had been deported to Piaski; she had miraculously managed to get a Swedish visa and leave Poland for Sweden. Once in Stockholm, she was still receiving letters from Piaski and warned Berlinger about sending large shipments. He followed the advice and ordered new, smaller shipments to ten different addresses in the Lublin area, three for Warsaw, three for France (in Mirepeix-Nay, Camp de Gurs, and Camp Récébédou), and one each for Brussels and Utrecht in the Low Countries.[23] But a few days later, Berlinger again ordered another large shipment for the Lublin area.[24]

Parcels were still being delivered to Jews in ghettos in Poland during the summer of 1942. In June 1942, the Working Committee in Stockholm informed Berlinger it had recently received confirmation that packages ordered from Portugal in October 1941, dispatched in late December, had finally reached a few of their addressees.[25] In August, Berlinger also received news from RELICO that according to the Jewish council in Izbica, shipments had been arriving there since July. Meanwhile, however, the German Red Cross announced that packages to the Radom and Lublin districts had to go indirectly via Kraków in order for shipments to be processed by them.[26] Believing this aid could still reach the ghettos in Poland, Löb and Berlinger ordered thousands of kilos of food through RELICO during the spring and summer of 1942, with the majority of the packages containing canned fish and vegetables such as tomato purée and green peas.[27]

In October 1942 the Working Committee for Polish Jewish Relief changed its name to the Working Committee for European Jewish Relief (Arbetsutskottet för hjälp åt Europas judar). The change reflected the increasing difficulties of getting the packages from Portugal to Poland and "the fact that the destruction of the Jews was extended to all occupied countries."[28] Wilhelm Michaeli, the secretary of the committee, reported that the best way to send food to Nazi-controlled territories was still from Lisbon or, "in an emergency situation," from Hamburg. (Unfortunately, Michaeli did not report on who or what company it was that provided such services in Hamburg.) Smaller packages weighing less than two kilos were more likely to reach the recipients. In contrast to the previous policy of Löb in Gothenburg, Michaeli suggested that priority should be given to relatives of refugees in Sweden.[29]

In the autumn of 1942, RELICO informed the Swedish committees that all its shipments to the Generalgouvernement (part of occupied Poland) were being rerouted. It was no longer possible to communicate with any Jewish organizations in Poland apart from the Jüdische Unterstützungsstelle für das Generalgouvernement (JUS) in Kraków, which had recently replaced the JSS as the only central Jewish relief organization allowed to function in the Generalgouvernement. Furthermore, all shipments, whether addressed to individuals, Jewish councils, or other groups, now had to go through the German Red Cross in Kraków.[30] RELICO still offered to broker shipments of food packages to Poland, but they admitted that they could no longer guarantee delivery to the addressees because of "the constant change of residence" caused by the deportations.[31]

Expansion of the Relief Operation and Uncertainty about the Fate of the Deportees

In September 1942, the Working Committee in Stockholm issued a new call for donations, which they intended to use for new shipments. According to the appeal, the committee had sent around 1,000 food packages (with a weight varying between ten, five, and three kilograms) and 200 packages containing clothes to some of the most populated areas of occupied Poland, including Warsaw, Lublin, and Lemberg. It had also sent medical equipment, medicine, and funds to orphanages in southern France and small amounts of money to individual recipients. The parcels had with a few exceptions been delivered, and hundreds of letters testified that the shipments had contributed to saving many, not least "starving and freezing children." However, since the previous appeal, the situation for the Jews in Poland had greatly deteriorated. The new appeal also referred to the deportations of Jews from Germany, former Czechoslovakia, the Netherlands, Bukovina, Romania, and other territories, which were propelling hundreds of thousands of Jews toward destruction.[32]

In October 1942, Wilhelm Michaeli, the secretary, wrote a long and detailed report about the Working Committee's relief efforts. The report also reveals that Jews in Sweden at this point did not fully understand the systematic nature of the killing. There were considerable barriers to explicit communications. According to the report, a Czech Jewish paper, most likely published in London by Czech Jews in exile there, had recently relayed that addresses of Jews deported to Poland could be obtained through the Working Committee in Stockholm, and as a result, the committee was inundated with hundreds of letters and inquiries from Jews in Czechoslovakia. The news quickly spread to other countries, including Germany, Switzerland, the Balkan states, and Turkey.

The committee, however, was unable to help since it did not have the ability to trace the addresses. All it could do was to recommend that people contact the ICRC in Geneva. Deported Jews also began to send letters to the committee, asking for relief packages. In most cases the committee could only turn down the requests, since it was impossible to help all those in need. Judging by the letters, Michaeli wrote, even Jews in Germany and in occupied countries were as uncertain about the fate of the deportees as the aid workers: "With the deepest desperation and complete irresolution, parents, children, siblings and other relatives turn to us, begging us to try to find a way to contact their family members." The only thing that the Jewish Community of Stockholm could do was to forward the ominous piece of information they possessed: "The person in question had moved to an unknown location."[33]

The committee attempted to establish the fate of Jews from the trickle of information they received. Based on a letter from one of the Jewish elders in the Łódz ghetto, Michaeli tried to figure out the mortality rate among the deportees whom the committee had tried to contact in the ghetto. He concluded that "more than 20%" were most likely dead. He added, however, that since it was unknown how many of those deported to a further destination were still alive, "one must presume the probability of an even higher mortality rate." He also wrote that things had taken a particularly tragic turn for those who had been deported in November and December 1941 and January 1942: "They are thought to have been brought to the region of Kaunas, Riga, and Minsk—but for 11–12 months nothing has been heard from them." The committee had, according to Michaeli, tried to investigate the fate of the deported Jews, but the German authorities had refused to provide any information. The ICRC in Geneva received the same answer. The Working Committee had written to the elders of the Jewish councils detailing a number of locations to where Jews had been deported, but this had not led to any results, and the Germans may have intercepted the letters. The Working Committee attempted to contact the JSS in Kraków on August 13, 1942. They did not receive any response, since the Germans had dissolved the JSS earlier that summer. The committee nevertheless continued to send the names and full details to Geneva, since they assumed that the addresses of "the hundreds of thousands of deported individuals" would at some point turn up—"and then primarily be collected by the Red Cross." They also pressed RELICO and the Verband Jüdische Gemeinden in St. Gallen to petition the German government to make the situation of the deportees "somewhat more endurable" by permitting correspondence, money transfers, and relief packages.[34]

Michaeli reached the following conclusions based on the available information: First, it was absolutely necessary to try to alleviate the suffering of the

Jews in eastern Europe, including those who had been deported there, by using preexisting funds or by starting new fundraising campaigns for this purpose. Second, because of the Swedish export ban, it was important to concentrate on sending food and money, not goods such as clothing. In cases where the intended recipients were unable to collect the money sent, however, the Jewish council had asked for permission to redistribute the aid to others. The most important issue, Michaeli concluded, was to get information about the situation for deportees in the places to where many had been deported and about the possibilities for sending them relief packages at these locations.[35]

By this time details about the pogroms, deportations, and incarcerations in ghettos were reported on in detail in the Swedish Jewish press, and as early as in December 1941 an account of a mass killing of Jews was published. In September 1942, the first part of a series of articles in *Judisk Krönika* (the Jewish Chronicle) reported that, according to sources in London, 700,000 Jews had been massacred in Poland and listed a number of reported mass killings of tens of thousands of Jews in the Baltic countries.[36] Although the Swedish Jews were informed that Jews had been deported and had starved to death and understood that those who had been deported further from the ghettos had most likely been killed, it seems they did not yet see these events as part of a coherent plan by the Nazis to murder the Jews of Europe. However, on December 1, 1942, exactly two months after Michaeli's report, the Jewish Community of Stockholm received a cable from Stephen S. Wise of the WJC and Chaim Weizmann of the Jewish Agency stating that Hitler had ordered the extermination of all Jews in Nazi-occupied countries and that almost two million were already known to have been murdered. Ehrenpreis cabled a reply to Wise the following day, saying that he had declared December 3 a day of mourning for the deported Norwegian Jews and that the European Jews would be included.[37] From this point on, it seems, the question was not what was happening to those who had "disappeared" after liquidation of ghettos and further deportations but rather what could be done to save those who remained alive.

In January 1943, all relief to occupied Poland was stopped for the time being because the Working Committee in Stockholm received word that the Jüdische Unterstützungsstelle in Kraków had been dissolved on December 1, 1942.[38] With shipments to the Polish Jews increasingly difficult, the committee instead began to distribute relief to Jews imprisoned in camps in southern France and elsewhere. In early 1943, RELICO also began taking requests to send packages to Theresienstadt in occupied Czechoslovakia, and in September they informed Berlinger that shipments to Poland had become possible again through the ICRC.[39] But later that month, Berlinger received news from

JÜDISCHE UNTERSTÜTZUNGSSTELLE FÜR DAS GENERALGOUVERNEMENT **JUS** CENTRALA POMOCY DLA ŻYDÓW W GENERALN. GUBERNATORSTWIE

Empfangsbestätigung !

Hiermit wird bestätigt, dass durch die Vermittlung des Beauftragten des Deutschen Roten Kreuzes beim Generalgouverneur, Dienststelle Krakau, der Jüdischen Unterstützungsstelle für das Generalgouvernement / J U S / ein Waggon " Stettin 35663 " enthaltend:

1600	kg	Zellstoffwatte
4000	St.	Papierbinden
197	"	Papierwesten
100	"	Papierbettdecken

im Gesamtgewicht von 2550 kg brutto als Liebesgaben aus Stockholm, ausgeliefert worden ist.

Jüdische Unterstützungsstelle JUS für das Generalgouvernement

Krakau, den 29.4.44.

Weichert

/ Dr. Weichert /

Büro u. Lager — Biuro i mag.: Krakau, Józefińska 2a — Fernruf — Tel.: 202 89 — Postanschrift — Adres: JUS Krakau, Postfach 211 — Bank-Konto — Konto bank: Städt. Sparkasse Krakau Zweigstelle I Nr. 21

Letter from Dr. Michał Weichert (JSS, Kraków) confirming a donation of 2,550 kilos of paper products from Sweden, April 29, 1944. Courtesy of the Riksarkivet Arninge, Judiska Församlingens Arkiv i Stockholm.

RELICO that a large shipment of milk powder they had sent on his orders from Switzerland to Kraków for further distribution "in camps" had allegedly been redirected to "Birkenau," since "no consignment can currently be cleared to Kraków."[40] The situation was constantly changing. The Jüdische Unterstützungsstelle in fact resumed its activities in March 1943 before it was closed down again in August 1943. However, the agency's director, Michał Weichert, was not deported and continued to send packages to camps until he was finally permitted to reopen his organization in February 1944.[41] In the summer of 1944, the committee in Stockholm sent them medicine and medical equipment from Sweden through the German Red Cross in Kraków, with the Swedish Red Cross as the official sender.[42]

Combined Efforts to Reach the Theresienstadt Ghetto

In the spring of 1944, the Working Committee continued to explore further options to help. These efforts again reveal the difficulties of tracing the location of the intended recipients. They put together a lengthy report in English, most likely destined for their American or British counterparts, outlining the possibilities of sending relief to Theresienstadt. According to the report, correspondence with the ghetto was very sporadic. Some people living in Sweden were receiving postcards or letters from their relatives in the ghetto regularly, every two or three weeks. The overwhelming majority, however, were only getting news at irregular intervals, with long silences in between. The Working Committee concluded that whether the inmates were allowed to communicate or not seemed to depend more on the mood of the German guards than on any actual regulations. Those getting food parcels were at least allowed to send a postcard acknowledging receipt. The receipts posed interpretative challenges for the committee in Sweden. Even people who did not receive any parcels at all quite often filled out the receipt postcards. This may have been a means of asking people living in Sweden to send relief parcels to the undersigned as well and to inform them that they were also being held in Theresienstadt. Sometimes the printed receipt cards that came back to Sweden contained a short message such as "kind regards" or a short note from the undersigned that they were well. But sometimes the cards came back only with a signature and perhaps the date.

The Working Committee explained in one of its reports that it had developed a method of tracing persons in Theresienstadt by using the camp's postal system: "When we previously supposed a missing person to be in Theresienstadt we used to write to him or her a postcard with [an] avis de réception [acknowledgment of receipt]."[43] However, for the last year, this way of ascertaining an address had become useless since the receipts were being returned with the stamp of the ghetto's Jewish Self-Administration (Jüdische Selbstverwaltung) as a signature. Therefore, the committee tried writing letters to Theresienstadt with a request for an acknowledgment of receipt to a person whom they knew for certain was in the United States, and even in this case the stamped certificate of receipt came back. The committees' conclusion was that it was impossible to trace a person's whereabouts in this way, even if the method had led to positive results in several cases. Thus, due to concerns that aid was not reaching the intended recipients, the Working Committee abandoned the system and instead started to send small amounts of money through a bank in Theresienstadt, with the dates of birth added to facilitate the identification of the addressees. The bank remitted the money against acknowledgments of receipt with the personal signature of the recipient. In most cases a reply did come, although it could take several months. But the reply was often negative, indicating that the addressee was "dead" or that he or she had "departed." Sometimes, the money was returned without any justification, which the committee interpreted as a sign that the addressee was no longer in Theresienstadt. The report stated that sooner or later the German authorities would probably stop these transactions and admitted that the committee had their doubts that the money was really received by the addressees. They therefore now advised against sending money to Theresienstadt except in cases where they hoped to learn whether an individual was in the ghetto; even in those cases, they only sent small amounts.[44]

The situation constantly kept changing. In the summer of 1944, the route from Lisbon through southern France was cut off as a result of the Allied invasion. Subsequently, at the end of August, the Working Committee applied for a license to send food, vitamins, and other food supplies directly to the ghetto.[45] The National Trade Commission rejected the application on the basis that it wanted to centralize relief shipments to Jews in Germany. It advised the committee to turn instead to a Christian organization that was already sending relief to POWs, called Help the Victims of War! (Hjälp Krigets Offer!, or HKO).[46]

Still other options were available. On August 17, 1944, one of the board members of the Working Committee, Samuel Nisell, informed the Malmö Jewish community of his committee's efforts to send aid to Theresienstadt and his meeting with a representative of the Danish government's refugee office in Stockholm to discuss the matter. Nisell explained that the committee was only sending approximately 100 packages monthly, each containing four boxes of sardines, to individuals in Theresienstadt who had been deported there from Germany and other occupied countries, but not from Denmark. Jews who had been deported from Denmark were already receiving packages directly from the Danish refugee office in Stockholm; the Danish representative had therefore advised Nisell not to send even more packages to the Danish prisoners, since it could "irritate the Germans" and could lead to restrictions.[47]

A Lisbon of the North

The opportunities to send relief changed constantly. However, the established Jewish relief organizations in Stockholm, having long depended on the goodwill of the Swedish authorities to operate, were perhaps too cautious or too dispirited by the many rejections of their petitions to see and take advantage of Swedish officials' changing attitudes when it came to helping Jews. It took an outsider to see new opportunities—and one desperate enough not to let himself be stymied by bureaucratic hurdles or be overly concerned about stepping on toes. In July 1944, Dr. Jacob Hellman—the WJC's leading representative in South America living in Buenos Aires—contacted Gilel (Hillel) Storch, a Latvian businessman and WJC representative who lived in Stockholm as a refugee. Hellman asked if food packages could be sent from Sweden to the Bergen-Belsen concentration camp.[48] The general outlook for sending food from Sweden had improved considerably at that point. The Swedish government was now more inclined to help European Jews, and the international climate had improved as well. Iver Olsen, representative of the newly created War Refugee Board in Sweden, was determined to show Washington that the body was contributing to the rescue of Jews.

Within the ICRC in Geneva, the position on helping the Jews had also changed. Since the end of 1942, the ICRC had worked on two fronts. It sent packages with food to concentration camps and kept appealing for aid from Germany's allies and satellites. The organization, however, faced the formidable demand from the Allies that senders had to know the names and whereabouts of the recipients of the packages in advance. The rationale, theoretically, was to prevent packages from ending up in the hands of the Germans. In practical terms, it clearly complicated efforts to send aid to prisoners who were not considered POWs, that is, political prisoners and those seen as racially inferior.[49] Furthermore, only packages for camps that had been inspected by the ICRC were allowed to pass though the Allied blockade of continental Europe.[50] Thus, packages to Theresienstadt were permitted after the ghetto was inspected by the Red Cross on June 23, 1944, though prisoners known by name before this date also had the right to receive a limited number of packages.[51] As a consequence, Storch together with two other activists in Sweden, Norbert Masur and Fritz Hollander, immediately began preparations for the operation. In August 1944, he applied to the National Trade Commission for a license to ship 100,000 kilos of food from Sweden.[52]

Storch was not only energetic and determined but also unusually bold and exacting. He went straight to the top in his efforts to get all the necessary permits and licenses, and he did not seem to care if that meant stepping on the toes of some lower government officials or Swedish Jewish representatives. This often led to disputes but also to successes.[53] On November 14, 1944, it was announced at the meeting of the Swedish Section of the WJC that 10,000 packages had been ordered and that Storch had personally signed a guarantee for their payment. However, some problems remained before the shipments could be made. First, it was necessary to get permission for the packages to pass through the Allied blockade.[54] It was here that the Swedish aid workers met the same obstacles as the ICRC in Switzerland. Hollander explained that the negotiations with "the Americans" about obtaining permission had been made in the name of the WJC. However, the Americans insisted that the ICRC would have to oversee the delivery.[55] The WJC in Stockholm also needed to get credible lists of Jews who were still alive in concentration camps. According to his biographer, Lena Einhorn, Storch had access to a register of around 12,000 Jews in German concentration camps and received another 17,000 names of imprisoned Jews from Laura Margolis, representative of the JDC, who was in Stockholm at the time. In addition to these, the Working Committee had lists of a couple hundred Jews who had friends and relatives in Sweden.

To increase the chances that the deliveries would be allowed by the Germans, the Jewish organizations in Sweden wanted to avoid having the names of their organizations on the packages, so they looked for alternatives. The secretary of the Swedish Section of the WJC, Herbert Friedländer, first contacted the Swedish Red Cross, which did not answer immediately, and then the Christian relief organization HKO. Storch also later negotiated with the Swedish Cooperative Union (Kooperativa förbundet). Its chairman, Carl Albert Andersson, who was the mayor of Stockholm, granted Storch credit, and an agreement was made that the Cooperative Union would prepare the first 10,000 packages; Storch personally signed a guarantee for the payment. On December 12, 1944, the Swedish Section of the WJC was informed that 9,800 packages had been sent.[56]

Bergen-Belsen was initially their intended destination, but the parcels ended up going to Theresienstadt, for which the committee had more reliable lists of prisoners. By and by, the Swedish packages were also sent to Ravensbrück and other camps. Since the Swedish Section of the WJC did not yet have its own offices in Stockholm and the Swedish Section's chairman, Ehrenpreis, was also the chairman of the Working Committee, it was decided that the "package operation" would be administered and carried out jointly by both organizations. The Working Committee contributed its offices in the building of the Jewish Community of Stockholm. However, the cooperation did not work well, not least because of Ehrenpreis's skepticism about the scheme. Initially he saw the entire operation as the personal responsibility of Storch, Masur, and Hollander, since they had applied for the export licenses without his knowledge: "If it works out well, the merit is yours, if it goes bad it's not my fault" (*Går det bra är det er förtjänst, går det illa är det ej mitt fel*), he declared in a meeting of the Swedish Section of the WJC in November 1944.[57] In Ehrenpreis's view, the main responsibilities of the WJC were in the political and cultural fields, and he also did not believe that the scheme would be effective in saving lives. At the meeting, he said that sending packages was not the best form of aid: "One cannot save any human lives with a few kilos of groceries," he maintained and instead pointed to what he referred to as the successful diplomatic activities in Hungary as an example of what the WJC should be doing to save lives.[58] The statement was immediately challenged by Hollander, who argued, "We have learned from eye-witnesses that small packages have in fact saved the lives of people who have been starving for a long time and are now about to be liberated."[59]

The results of the previous relief efforts shed light on Ehrenpreis's opposition. The Swedish Jewish committees had sent thousands of food packages to communities and ghettos that no longer existed. The Germans dissolved the organizations that had distributed the aid and murdered most of the recipients. Detailed reports of the destruction of the European Jewry had been published in the Swedish Jewish press, some by Ehrenpreis, who had also shared them with government officials and politicians.[60] One must also take into account how international, above all American, relief work was organized. A large contribution from Jews in the United States was funneled primarily through the nonpolitical JDC. The JDC often saw the WJC as unnecessary competition when it engaged in relief work.[61] The Working Committee was already partly funded by the JDC, whose leadership was reluctant to finance activities in which the WJC was involved.

Hillel Storch and His Efforts in the Final Months of the War

During the last months of the war, the leading role in the Swedish relief efforts was assumed by Storch, an ambitious activist who promoted his vision often against opposition in the Jewish organizations. Storch felt hostility from both Ehrenpreis and the visiting JDC representative, Laura Margolis.[62] Personal disagreements and fights over the organization of the relief efforts ultimately led

Storch to withdraw from the Swedish Section of the WJC on November 13, 1944, although he continued to attend the section's meetings until the end of December. Meanwhile, he complained to the WJC in New York, claiming that Ehrenpreis wanted the JDC to take over the Swedish Section's rescue activities. The short and tempestuous cooperation between the Swedish Section and the Working Committee had nonetheless been successful in another way: in less than two months, 25,000 kilos of food packages were dispatched to around 10,000 individual recipients in Theresienstadt and Bergen-Belsen through their combined efforts.[63] In January, the Christian relief group HKO had also received a letter from Josef Wein and Simon Feinberg, signing it as representatives of the Council of Jewish Elders in Bergen-Belsen, confirming that they had indeed received 2,350 packages between November 16, 1944, and January 5, 1945. If the intended recipients were not present, other prisoners shared the contents.[64]

Meanwhile, further news arrived in Sweden of the terrible conditions in some of the remaining German camps. The extermination camps had already been dismantled, but the Jews who were still alive continued to starve to death. In February, the WJC's Swedish Section also informed the Swedish Ministry for Foreign Affairs that the sister of one of the leading persons in the package operation, Jacob Ettlinger, was one of the prisoners who had died of starvation in Bergen-Belsen.[65]

With the approval of the executive committee in New York, Storch decided to open a new WJC branch, with an office in central Stockholm. Because all licenses were issued to Storch personally, he transferred the entire operation to the new organization, which he called the Relief and Rehabilitation Department. According to Storch, they sent a first test shipment on February 3, consisting of a train carload of 4,700 packages from Sweden to Bergen-Belsen, for which the Swedish company Banankompaniet had obtained a guarantee for distribution from a trading company in Hamburg, J. Nootbaar, Jr. The shipment was made with the permission of both the British and the American legations in Sweden.[66]

Storch also succeeded in financing and sending the remaining licensed packages through his new organization. According to Gerhart Riegner, one of the WJC representatives in Geneva, Storch's effort made such an impression on the War Refugee Board that it donated another 40,000 packages stored in Gothenburg to his operation.[67] To be allowed to obtain the packages, Storch turned to Count Bernadotte with the request for the Red Cross to control their distribution, since this was a requirement for collecting the packages from the American Red Cross warehouse. (The ICRC had created a storage facility in

Gothenburg to serve as a new distribution route for packages to Allied POWs in Germany.)[68]

The JDC got fully involved in the relief work from Sweden only in the final months of the war. Although the JDC had already planned to send a representative to Sweden in 1943, it was not until late 1944 that Laura Margolis arrived to report on JDC relief work in Sweden and look at how the Jewish Community of Stockholm was using the funds received from the JDC. At first, she seems to have been rather pessimistic about it, reporting that her work was complicated by the numerous relief organizations and different people involved. Hence, at the point when Storch finally got his funding from the WJC and his new organization dispatched the remaining packages, Margolis appointed Ragnar Gottfarb, a Swedish Jewish lawyer, as the JDC's representative in Sweden and left $75,000 with him to be used in a new package program.[69]

In March 1945, Margolis reported that the Jewish Community of Stockholm was "doing a satisfactory job" and left the country. Her activities in Sweden show how the JDC sought to persuade the Jewish leaders in Stockholm to follow its line that all relief projects should go through them and that the WJC should only be concerned with politics and cultural matters. It is evident that the Swedish Jewish representatives agreed to this without any objection. It is also clear that this international organizational struggle had a direct impact on Sweden. Those critical of the JDC-funded Working Committee gained international support from the WJC.

In addition to the bureaucratic obstacles put up by the Swedish export ban and the Allied blockade, one large issue remained uncertain. Would the German authorities allow the packages to be delivered to Jewish prisoners? On March 15, 1945, Storch received a telegram from the WJC in New York stating that the packages were of great importance but that very few of them had arrived in Bergen-Belsen and the prisoners were starving to death.[70] Storch had previously experienced cases of the Allies stopping food shipments, referring to their guidelines that only parcels to camps that had been inspected by the ICRC would be allowed through. He had thus already contacted both the Swedish Red Cross and the ICRC, inquiring if they (instead of HKO) could act as senders. He concluded that the packages had a better chance of being permitted to pass through both the German controls and the Allied blockade under their banners. Both Count Bernadotte and ICRC representatives agreed.[71]

A few days later, on March 19, Storch contacted the deputy head of the Legal Department of the Ministry for Foreign Affairs, Svante Hellstedt, requesting the Swedish government's permission to ship food, medicine, and clothing at a value of one million Swedish kronor to Jews interned in German concentration camps. Storch wrote that the goods would be distributed by the ICRC, Swedish Red Cross, and HKO, as well as by direct mail, and that delivery of the parcels would be supervised as closely as possible. Storch explained that the WJC in Sweden was in contact with their branches abroad—as well as with the Jewish Agency—and that their register of Jews interned in German concentration camps included around 50,000 names. This number did not represent the actual number of Jewish prisoners the organization thought were being held in the camps, only the names and whereabouts of Jews about whom they had received information. Storch described the desperate situation of the Jews in the camps, attached supporting evidence, and gave a personal account of a meeting with a group of Jews who had been released from concentration camps, where they received Swedish food packages. Storch told Hellstedt that the WJC was shipping food by boat from Buenos Aires and that they were also negotiating with the American Red Cross. He stressed that if help did not come soon, no one would be left to save, and he begged the Ministry for Foreign Affairs to deal with his request as soon as possible. Storch promised them the "eternal gratitude of the Jewish people."[72]

Accounts of how many of the Swedish packages reached Jews in the camps vary. According to Leon Lapidus of the Swedish Section of the WJC, around 72,400 packages were dispatched by the WJC from Sweden during the war, mostly to Theresienstadt, Bergen-Belsen, and Ravensbrück.[73] According to the WJC's Riegner in Geneva, most of these packages did arrive. Meanwhile, others claimed that the Germans stole a large portion of the packages or that many of the packages did not leave Gothenburg until after the war. The many signed receipts for the packages sent by the Working Committee deposited in the archives of the Jewish Community of Stockholm imply that the packages were in fact delivered, although the prisoners may have been forced to sign the confirmations. One recipient of the Working Committee's packages to Theresienstadt was the famous German Jewish leader Leo Baeck. Baeck later said that he had sometimes received empty packages from individuals but that packages from the Red Cross or the JDC were generally delivered. Nevertheless, when on May 6, 1945, the Jewish Council of Elders, which represented the prisoners, took charge of the entire administration in Theresienstadt, including the postal service and storage facilities, large deposits of food and medicine were found. In one of the storerooms, they discovered thirty packages of matzot that the Working Committee had sent to the Danish Jews for a seder.[74] And when on April 14, 1945, British soldiers entered Bergen-Belsen, they found large stockpiles of packages from Sweden that had not been delivered to the addressees. Since it took the British some time to get their own food supplies through to the survivors, the undelivered Swedish packages may have saved a large number of lives.[75]

Conclusion

The Swedish Jewish relief committees' efforts to send food, medicine, and clothing to Jews in Nazi ghettos and camps demanded large and complicated operations. These operations involved many different agents along the way, beginning with the committees' appeals for donations down through final delivery of aid shipments. The committees raised funds through appeals in the Jewish press and during services in synagogues; through personal visits to potential donors, fundraising bazaars, and other events; and through contributions from distant relief organizations. After the committees decided exactly where the aid should go, the money was transferred either to other relief organizations or directly to the trading companies that, with the help of shipping firms or postal services, dispatched food and other items in individual packages or in bulk to a range of destinations in Europe.

In a time flooded with pleas for help, those desperately in need of aid often invoked old personal connections in a bid to have their requests receive priority. Similarly, Jews in Sweden used their contacts elsewhere in Europe to try to ascertain the location or fate of deported Jews. Swedish Jewish relief committees remained in constant contact with foreign Jewish leaders and organizations as well as with international relief agencies. These transnational contacts contributed not only to Sweden's role as a bridgehead for humanitarian relief in Europe at the end of the war but also to its function as a hub for exchanging information about the genocide as it unfolded.

The disagreements between members of the Swedish Section of the World Jewish Congress and the Working Committee for European Jewish Relief, and between Storch and members of both organizations, actually seemed to result in a larger number of relief shipments. If Storch had not applied for export licenses in the name of the WJC, a license for such large shipments would most likely not have been granted. His initiative got the WJC involved in relief work in Sweden, initially in cooperation with the Working Committee. Later, when he finally ended this close cooperation and brought the operation under his new organization, the Relief and Rehabilitation Department, the Working Committee shifted its focus to other relief activities. The resulting scope of their work increased as a whole.

The chances that Jews had of receiving relief shipments in Nazi camps and ghettos varied considerably, both geographically and over time. Many factors contributed to whether relief packages would reach their intended recipients. Consequently, aid organizations had to be ready when a possibility opened up, and testing different ways to reach prisoners also proved critical. However, the arrival of packages in the camps and ghettos did not automatically mean that lives were saved. That several different organizations sent relief shipments using different strategies and routes most likely increased the chances that at least some of the packages would arrive. One prevailing idea at the time was that centralization and unity would lead to a more efficient and successful operation. A more reasonable conclusion may be that—paradoxically—the disunity and competition between Jewish advocates in Sweden in fact saved more lives than would otherwise have been the case.

Notes

1 Different authors have told part of the history of this operation before: Lena Einhorn, *Handelsresande i liv* (Stockholm: Norstedts Pocket, 2006), primarily dealt with the operation from the perspective of refugee activist Gilel Storch, while Sune Persson discussed Swedish Red Cross involvement in *"Vi åker till Sverige." De vita bussarna 1945* (Rimbo: Fischer, 2002).
2 This chapter draws mainly on reports, correspondence, memos, and purchase orders preserved in the archives of the Jewish Community of Stockholm, as well as the JDC Archives in New York and the Central Zionist Archives and Yad Vashem in Jerusalem.
3 Pontus Rudberg, *The Swedish Jews and the Holocaust* (Abingdon: Routledge, 2017); Svante Hansson, *Flykt och överlevnad* (Stockholm: Hillel, 2004).
4 The broader outlines of the activities of the committee have previously been described in Hansson, *Flykt och överlevnad*, 266–68; cf. Rudberg, *Swedish Jews and the Holocaust*, 231–44.
5 Rudberg, *The Swedish Jews and the Holocaust*, 237.
6 Riksarkivet Arninge (RA), Judiska Församlingens Arkiv (JFA), Arbetsutskottet för hjälp åt Europas judar (AHEJ), E1: 3, Report by the Working Committee for Polish Jewish Relief, October 1942.
7 RA, JFA, Arbetsutskottet för hjälp åt Polens judar (AHPJ), E1: 1, JSS Lemberg to Marcus Ehrenpreis, Lemberg, February 17, 1941.
8 RA, JFA, AHPJ, E1: 1, Michał Weichert to Marcus Ehrenpreis, Kraków, October 22, 1941.
9 RA, JFA, AHEJ, E1: 3, Report by the Working Committee for Polish Jewish Relief, October 1942.

10 See the chapter by Anne Lepper on RELICO, this volume.
11 Central Zionist Archives (CZA), C3: 1316, RELICO to Hermann Löb, October 31, 1941 (carbon copy); Elieser Berlinger to RELICO, Malmö, November 19, 1941; RELICO to Elieser Berlinger, November 25, 1941 (carbon copy).
12 RA, JFA, AHPJ, E1: 1, Arbetsutskottet för Polens judar to Elieser Berlinger, Stockholm, December 25, 1941 (carbon copy).
13 RA, JFA, AHPJ, E1: 1, Hermann Löb to Inga Gottfarb, Gothenburg, December 5, 1941.
14 Hermann Löb, "Insamling för svältande barn," *Judisk Krönika* 10, no. 8 (October 1941): 126; RA, JFA, AHPJ, E1: 1, Hermann Löb to Inga Gottfarb, Gothenburg, December 5, 1941; CZA, C3: 1316, Hermann Löb to RELICO, Gothenburg, December 11, 1941.
15 CZA, C3: 1316, RELICO to Hermann Löb, December 23, 1941 (carbon copy).
16 RA, JFA, AHEJ, E1: 3, Report by the Working Committee for Polish Jewish Relief, October 1942.
17 CZA, C3: 1314, RELICO to Elieser Berlinger, February 4, 1942 (carbon copy).
18 RA, JFA, AHEJ, E1: 3, Report by the Working Committee for Polish Jewish Relief, October 1942.
19 See, e.g., JFA, AHPJ, E1: 1, Herbert Israel Finkelscherer to Marcus Ehrenpreis, Piaski, December 15, 1941; Adolf Israel Flater to Marcus Ehrenpreis, December 22, 1941.
20 See, e.g., CZA, C3: 1317. H. Bachner to RELICO, Stockholm, August 20, 1941, and Isak Bieder to RELICO, Halmstad, March 19, 1941.
21 CZA, C3: 1314, Elieser Berlinger to RELICO, Malmö, May 5, 1942, Elieser Berlinger to RELICO, Malmö, May 7, 1942.
22 CZA, C3: 1314, RELICO to Berlinger, May 11, 1942; Christopher R. Browning, *Ordinary Men: Reserve Police Battalion 101 and the Final Solution in Poland* (London: Penguin 2001), 52.
23 CZA, C3: 1314, Berlinger to Melico, Malmö n.d. but stamped by RELICO in Geneva as arrived on June 10, 1942; Else Meyring to Elieser Berlinger, Stockholm, June 6, 1942; Berlinger to RELICO, Malmö, June 15, 1942. See also Helmut Müssener and Wolfgang Wilhelmus, *Stettin, Lublin, Stockholm* (Rostock: Ingo Koch Verlag, 2014).
24 CZA, C3: 1314, Berlinger to RELICO, Malmö, June 19, 1942.
25 RA, JFA, AHPJ, E1: 1, Inga Gottfarb to Elieser Berlinger, June 12, 1942.

26 CZA, C3: 1314, RELICO to Elieser Berlinger, August 27, 1942 (carbon copy).
27 CZA, C3: 1314, RELICO to Elieser Berlinger, February 24, 1942 (carbon copy); RELICO to Elieser Berlinger, April 22, 1942 (carbon copy).
28 JFA, AHEJ, E1: 3, Redogörelse för Arbetsutskottets för hjälp åt Europas judar verksamhet från 12 november 1942–30 september 1944, Stockholm, December 19, 1944.
29 JFA, AHEJ, E1: 3, Redogörelse för Arbetsutskottets för hjälp åt Europas judar verksamhet från 12 november 1942–30 september 1944; RA, JFA, AHEJ, E1: 3, Wilhelm Michaeli, P.M., Stockholm, October 1, 1942.
30 CZA, C3: 1316, RELICO to Hermann Löb, November 3, 1943 (carbon copy).
31 CZA, C3: 1314, RELICO to Elieser Berlinger, November 3, 1942.
32 YVA O.74, 30, "Våra stamfränders nöd . . . ," Working Committee for European Jewish Relief, Stockholm, October 1942. The Working Committee and more than thirty Jewish representatives of all major political and religious factions signed the appeal.
33 RA, JFA, AHEJ, E1: 3, Wilhelm Michaeli, P.M., Stockholm, October 1, 1942.
34 Ibid.
35 Ibid.
36 "Utrotningskriget mot judarna," *Judisk Krönika* 11, no. 7 (October 1942): 122–24.
37 RA, JFA, Huvudarkivet, E1: 5, Stephen S. Wise and Chaim Weizmann to the Jewish Community of Stockholm, December 1, 1942; RA, JFA, Flyktingsektionen B1: 2, Marcus Ehrenpreis to Stephen Wise, December 2, 1942.
38 RA, JFA, AHEJ, Arbetsutskottet för hjälp till Europas judar to Elieser Berlinger, Stockholm, January 28, 1943 (carbon copy).
39 CZA, C3: 1314, Berlinger to RELICO, Malmö, September 7, 1943.
40 CZA, C3: 1314, RELICO to Elieser Berlinger, September 21, 1943 (carbon copy); RELICO to Berlinger, February 4, 1944.
41 Mordecai Paldiel, *Saving One's Own: Jewish Rescuers during the Holocaust* (Lincoln: University of Nebraska Press, 2016), 441.
42 RA, JFA, AHEJ, E1: 1, Arbetsutskottet för hjälp åt Europas judar to Svenska Röda Korsets Överstyrelse, Stockholm, June 22, 1944.
43 RA, JFA, AHEJ, E1: 1, "Memorial regarding Theresienstadt," Stockholm, April 3, 1944.

44 Ibid. Meanwhile, Berlinger's committee in Malmö was also sending packages through RELICO to Theresienstadt. For example, in August 1944 RELICO confirmed that it had sent eighty-five packages containing sardines to eighty-two addresses in Theresienstadt on Berlinger's behalf. Among the names were Danish chief rabbi Max Friediger and many other Danish Jews but also Jews of other nationalities imprisoned there. See CZA, C3: 1314, RELICO to Berlinger, August 4, 1944 (carbon copy).

45 RA, JFA, AHEJ, Working Committee for European Jewish Relief to the [Swedish] State Trade Commission Stockholm, August 24, 1944 (carbon copy).

46 RA, JFA, AHEJ, E1: 1, Hj. Karlberg to Working Committee for European Jewish Relief, Stockholm, August 25, 1944. The HKO was the Swedish equivalent of a cooperative body called the Emergency Committee of Christian Organizations (ECCO) formed in Geneva immediately after the outbreak of the war. See Mikaela Nybohm, "Männen bakom taggtråden: Om H.K.O's hjälp till krigsfångar," in *EB-nytt: Nyheter från Riksarkivet avdelning för enskilda arkiv 2010* (Stockholm: Riksarkivet 2011), 33–42. RA, JFA, Arbetsutskottet för hjälp åt Europas judar, E1: 2, Folke Bernadotte to Wilhelm Michaeli, Stockholm, April 5, 1944.

47 JFA, AHEJ, E1: 1, Samuel Nisell to the Jewish Community of Malmö, Stockholm, August 17, 1944. For an extensive discussion of the Danish case, see the chapter by Silvia Goldbaum Tarabini Fracapane, this volume.

48 RA, JFA, Huvudarkivet, F1 c: 3, Meeting protocol of the Swedish Section of the WJC, Stockholm, December 12, 1944.

49 Jean-Claude Favez, *The Red Cross and the Holocaust* (Cambridge: Cambridge University Press 1999), 7–8, 240; Ronald W. Zweig, "Feeding the Camps: Allied Blockade Policy and the Relief of Concentration Camps in Germany, 1944–1945," *The Historical Journal* 41, no. 3 (1998): 827; Joan Beaumont, "Starving for Democracy: Britain's Blockade of and Relief for Occupied Europe, 1939–1945," *War and Society* 8, no. 2 (1990): 57–82.

50 Walter Laqueur, *The Terrible Secret* (London: Weidenfeld and Nicolson 1980), 17–40; Favez, *Red Cross and the Holocaust*, 7–8.

51 František Beneš and Patricia Tošnerová, *Pošta v ghettu Terezín* (Prague: Profil, 1996), 140; Leni Yahil, *Et demokrati på Prøve* (Copenhagen: Gyldendal, 1967), 268–69.

52 RA, JFA, Huvudarkivet F1 c: 3, Protocol of the Swedish Section of the WJC's meeting, Stockholm, November 14, 1944; Einhorn, *Handelsresande i liv*, 249–50.

53 Einhorn, *Handelsresande i liv*, 249–50.
54 Sweden, as a neutral state, had to negotiate concessions with both belligerents, which allowed it to import and export material through the blockade.
55 RA, JFA, Huvudarkivet, F1 c: 3, Meeting protocol of the Swedish Section of the WJC, Stockholm, November 14, 1944.
56 RA, JFA, Huvudarkivet, F1 c: 3, Meeting protocol, Swedish Section of WJC, Stockholm, December 12, 1944; Einhorn, *Handelsresande i liv*, 251–54.
57 RA, JFA, Huvudarkivet, F1 c: 3, Meeting protocol of the Swedish Section of the WJC, Stockholm, November 2, 1944; see also Einhorn, *Handelsresande i liv*, 254.
58 RA, JFA, Huvudarkivet, F1 c: 3, Meeting protocol of the Swedish Section of the WJC, Stockholm, November 2, 1944.
59 Ibid.
60 Rudberg, *Swedish Jews and the Holocaust*, 216.
61 Yehuda Bauer, *American Jewry and the Holocaust* (Detroit: Wayne State University Press, 1981), 184–85.
62 Einhorn, *Handelsresande i liv*, 264.
63 Ibid.; RA, JFA, F1 c: 3, Meeting protocol of the Swedish Section of the WJC, Stockholm, December 4, 1944; JFA, AHEJ, E1: 3, Report of the activities of the Working Committee for European Jewish Relief from 12 November 1942–30 September 1944, Stockholm, December 19, 1944.
64 CZA, C2: 4429, Josef Wein and Simon Feinberg, Der Judenältesten-Rat, Bergen-Belsen, to Hjälp Krigets Offer, Bergen-Belsen, January 19, 1945.
65 CZA, C4: 301, Swedish Section of the WJC to Gösta Engzell, Stockholm, February 26, 1945.
66 RA, JFA, AHEJ, E1: 3, Meeting protocol of the Working Committee for European Jewish Relief, Stockholm, January 16, 1945; Einhorn, *Handelsresande i liv*, 264–65; CZA, C4: 301, Storch to Engzell UD, Stockholm, February 14, 1945 (carbon copy); WJC Relief and Rehabilitation Department to Gösta Engzell, Stockholm, February 8, 1945 (carbon copy).
67 Einhorn, *Handelsresande i liv*, 265.
68 CZA, C2/4429, Gilel Storch to Folke Bernadotte, Stockholm, March 4, 1945 (carbon copy); *Report of the International Committee of the Red Cross on Its Activities during the Second World War*, vol. 3: *Relief Activities* (Geneva: ICRC, 1948), 165–66, 336.

69 JDC Archives, no. 921, Joseph Schwartz to Laura Margolis, October 1944; Laura Margolis to Joseph Schwartz, Telegram, received in New York (from Stockholm on November 1, 1944); Glen Whistler (the American Red Cross in Sweden), "confidential report" to the American Red Cross in Sweden, January 1, 1945, a copy sent from J. W. Pehle of the WRB to Moses Leavitt of the JDC.

70 CZA, C4: 301, U.S. State Department to WJC, March 15, 1945 (carbon copy).

71 CZA, C4: 421, WJC Stockholm to Dr. Ernhold, ICRC, March 19, 1945; Einhorn, *Handelsresande i liv*, 265.

72 CZA, C4: 301, Gilel Storch to Svante Hellstedt, March 19, 1945. At the same time Storch also played a key role in the Swedish Red Cross mission of the White Buses, which saved a large number of Jewish prisoners from German concentration camps during the very last weeks of the war in April and May 1945. See Persson, "*Vi åker till Sverige*"; Ingrid Lomfors, *Blind fläck* (Stockholm: Atlantis, 2005); Einhorn, *Handelsresande i liv*.

73 "Arbetet inom 'Judiska världskongressens' svenska avdelning," *Judisk Krönika* 14, nos. 5–6 (1945): 106–7. These numbers more or less match the numbers given by Storch, who claimed that 40,000 food packages had been sent from Sweden through his program and that he had obtained a further 30,000 from the War Refugee Board. See CZA, C4: 301, Gilel Storch to Lennart Nylander, Stockholm, December 8, 1945 (carbon copy); Inga Gottfarb gives the same estimate in her 1986 book, *Den livsfarliga glömskan* (Höganäs: Wiken, 1986), 142.

74 See, e.g., RA, JFA, Arbetsutskottet, E1: 1, Heros handel to Arbetsutskottet för hjälp åt Europas judar. Invoice for the shipment of sixty-four packages of sardines to thirty-two recipients in Theresienstadt (two packages each) with a list of the recipients: "Liste über 32 Empfänger zum Auftrag von 7. August 44 (order 93)." Rabbi Baeck is twelfth of the thirty-two names on the list. Dr. Paul Epstein, one of the leaders of the former Berlin Jewish community, appeared on the same list; Leonard Baker, *Days of Sorrow and Pain* (New York: Macmillan, 1978), 289; RA, JFA, AHEJ, E1: 2, Arbetsutskottet för hjälp åt Europas judar to Hjälpkommittén for deporterede fra Danmark, April 13, 1944. See Beneš and Tošnerová, *Pošta v ghettu Terezín*, 164.

75 Hugo Valentin, "Rescue and Relief Activities on Behalf of Jewish Victims of Nazism in Scandinavia," *YIVO Annual of Jewish Social Science* 8 (1953): 230; Gottfarb, *Den livsfarliga glömskan*, 143.

5

"WEAPON OF LAST RESORT"

The International Red Cross and Relief Efforts for Jews during the Holocaust, 1942–45

GERALD J. STEINACHER

> *When future historians are able to analyze the circumstances which made possible the annihilation of one-third of the Jewish people—the bulk of European Jewry—as well as the barbarous slaughter of untold masses of other civilizations during the Second World War, there is one set of problems which will give them the greatest difficulty: where was the enlightened, civilized world, particularly the humane, neutral influences, while all this was going on? Where above all, was the International Red Cross Committee? For the ICRC has a specific obligation, owing [to] its essential character as laid down in its statutes, to safeguard the hard-won principles of civilized conduct in war-time.*[1]
>
> —Jewish Holocaust survivor, May 1945

In the context of the Holocaust, whatever the broader record of its humanitarian efforts, the International Committee of the Red Cross (ICRC) is still best known

---

I wish to thank the following scholars and institutions for their important support for this research: David Forsythe at the University of Nebraska-Lincoln; Bob Moore at the University of Sheffield; Jan Láníček at the University of New South Wales in Sydney; the United States Holocaust Memorial Museum, particularly Elizabeth Anthony, Ron Coleman, Rebecca Erbelding, and Jan Lambertz; the International Institute for Holocaust Research–Yad Vashem; the American Jewish Joint Distribution Committee; the Central Zionist Archives; and the Museum of the Italian Red Cross in Campomorone/Genoa. Thanks also to Dr. Christoph Mentschl of the University of Vienna for his help.

for its failures: its silence on the genocide and its representatives' controversial visit to the Theresienstadt ghetto in June 1944. In 1977, Holocaust survivor and scholar Mark (Meir) Dworzecki wrote, "The World War II era has been engraved in the hearts and minds of the inhabitants of the ghettos and concentration camps as the 'period of bitter disappointment with the Red Cross.'"[2] For many decades after 1945, the ICRC shielded itself against critics by emphasizing its own precarious position during the war and its desire to not endanger its relief operation for POWs. And as early as 1948 the organization saw the need to publish a report defending itself against any accusations that it had not done enough for Jews during the war. But it was not until the 1990s that the ICRC apologized for its silence on the Holocaust and for the limited help the organization had provided to Jewish victims.[3] It is therefore unsurprising that Jewish communities worldwide remain critical of the Red Cross (and Switzerland) in large part due to this wartime experience.[4] But while the overarching failures of the ICRC are well understood, its relief operations when it comes to victims of the Holocaust are less well known.

This chapter gives an overview of the aid efforts made by the ICRC and its cooperation with Jewish aid organizations, most notably the American Jewish Joint Distribution Committee (JDC or the Joint), the World Jewish Congress (WJC), and the Relief Committee for the War-Stricken Jewish Population (RELICO) in Geneva. It addresses the ways the Red Cross worked with these bodies to channel food, clothing, and medicine to Jews trapped in wartime Europe. What help was possible, and what legal, financial, and practical obstacles did the ICRC and aid organizations collaborating with the Red Cross face? And how successful was this cooperation in bringing relief, especially food parcels, to civilian prisoners of the Nazis and populations under siege, particularly the Jews? This chapter also looks at the philosophy of the organization and how (and if) the Holocaust challenged its priorities and operating principles. While the ICRC relief efforts for POWs have rightly received much attention, its efforts on behalf of civilian prisoners are not as well known.[5]

The Red Cross on the Road to World War II

The Red Cross humanitarian movement began in 1859 as a private initiative of Geneva businessman Henri Dunant. The movement initially drew heavily from Judeo-Christian ideas of caritas, performing works of mercy in the footsteps of the biblical Good Samaritan. Espousing the importance of neutrality and independence from all governmental influence, the ICRC had as its main humanitarian goal the alleviation of human suffering through practical voluntary service. The organization remains a private association under Swiss law, its steering committee consisting of up to twenty-five members, men and women who are all Swiss nationals. While the composition of the ICRC is not international, the scope of its activities has long reached beyond Switzerland's borders.[6] It has placed the Geneva and Hague Conventions at the center of its work, a set of international treaties that have prescribed the rules of warfare. The first Geneva Convention of 1864 encompassed the protection of wounded soldiers. After World War I, rules concerning the humane treatment of POWs were added.[7] Although sovereign governments sign and ratify the Geneva Conventions, the ICRC traditionally has functioned as an important guardian and leading promoter of these treaties and their application. National Red Cross societies have worked together with the ICRC in many ways but have remained legally independent organizations. The German Red Cross, for example, is an organization governed by German law with its own goals, rules, traditions, and staff. The ICRC traditionally reserved the right to recognize new national societies and welcome them into the international Red Cross movement. However, once a national Red Cross organization was recognized, the ICRC retained very little oversight or leverage over it.[8] While many national Red Cross, Red Crescent, and Red Star of David societies exist across the globe today—even a national Swiss Red Cross society—none of these organizations has special international status enshrined in the Geneva Conventions. The Swiss-based "mother organization" of the Red Cross therefore holds a special status in the realm of humanitarian work, yet its activities were never limited by the parameters of the Geneva Conventions and other international treaties.

Based on its own statute, the ICRC often uses its own "right of initiative" to intervene in humanitarian emergencies, even if international conventions did not cover all these cases. For instance, the ICRC took over the care and protection of POWs during World War I long before the provision was codified internationally in the Geneva Convention of 1929. Without the goodwill of the countries that were signatories to the conventions, the humanitarians of the Red Cross could (and can) do little. Therefore, national interests and reciprocity in the observation of the treaties have played a huge role in the success or failure of humanitarian work. By international agreement, the ICRC would deliver parcels and mail to the POWs of all countries. A central Red Cross agency collected and exchanged information on POWs and their whereabouts, giving a critical boost to prisoners and their families. The ICRC, as a neutral agency operated by citizens of a neutral country, could also distribute food parcels funded by the national Red Cross societies. "In a way, the ICRC served as an international 'postman' for prisoners of war," one Swiss historian put it.[9]

Wherever possible, ICRC delegates also reported on the living conditions in POW camps.

Humane treatment of prisoners of war was enshrined in the Geneva Conventions of 1929, which Germany had signed and largely respected for western Allied POWs during World War II. The Soviet Union did not sign those conventions, which played into the hands of Hitler's "total warfare" in eastern Europe. Soviet POWs ultimately were left at the mercy of their Nazi captors. Out of some 5,745,000 Soviet POWs in German hands, at least three million died of starvation or neglect or were shot.[10] Because the Nazi government did not recognize Poland's government-in-exile, Polish soldiers were also not protected, nor were imprisoned Jewish civilians covered by the Geneva Conventions. In the decade leading up to World War II, the ICRC had only a small staff in Geneva and limited financial resources. By the end of the war in 1945, the Geneva organization had grown to 3,400 professional employees and volunteers, including delegates whose task was to inspect POW camps.[11]

Humanitarian Relief to Concentration Camps

Urgent requests for aid to concentration camp inmates came just months after Hitler's appointment as German chancellor in January 1933. In the summer of 1933, a Jewish refugee sent a dramatic letter to the ICRC about the brutality in the regime's new camps: "I beg you again in the name of the prisoners—Help! Help!"[12] The writer was referring to Dachau near Munich, the first major concentration camp set up by the Nazis. Before 1938, mostly political opponents—including some Jews—were arrested and imprisoned in concentration camps, but starting with the pogroms in November 1938 this began to change. For the first time, Jews were arrested in large numbers, solely because of their Jewish identity or family background.

When the Nazis came to power, the restrictions imposed on outside help for victims of political or racial persecution rapidly became obvious. Nazi officials deemed the treatment of German citizens in concentration camps to be an internal affair of the country, with prisoners viewed as enemies of the state and criminals. ICRC president Max Huber and his vice president, Carl Jacob Burckhardt, looked for avenues around these obstacles. The German Red Cross itself was not very cooperative; its representatives went so far as to claim that living conditions in the camps were initially much better than what most inmates had enjoyed in their civilian lives prior to detention.[13] When they finally secured the opportunity to inspect early concentration camps, ICRC representatives were well aware of the danger of having such visits exploited for propaganda purposes. Despite some hesitation, Burckhardt proceeded in 1935 with visits to the concentration camps in Esterwegen, Dachau, and Oranienburg, and his subsequent report contained only a mild critique.[14] His main objection was that political prisoners and criminals were not being held separately. Clearly unimpressed, SS-Gruppenführer Reinhard Heydrich reacted to Burckhardt's criticism in a short letter: "From a National Socialist point of view political criminals are on the same level as professional criminals; this is also evident from the new penal code."[15]

By 1937 the German Red Cross had become nazified at almost every level, with the hard-core Nazis and SS officers in its leadership ensuring that the actions of the organization would fall into line with the policies and aims of the Third Reich.[16] The national organization had lost its independence and neutrality and had been completely restructured to serve "the requirements of the Reich, the Nazi Party, and the Wehrmacht."[17]

With the pogroms of November 1938, large numbers of Jews were arrested as Jews and imprisoned in concentration camps for the first time since the Nazi takeover. The widespread and open physical violence both during and following the pogroms took many German and Austrian Jews completely by surprise.[18] With the outbreak of the war the following year, interventions for civilian prisoners of all kinds, not just Jews, became increasingly difficult. One major obstacle was legal in nature. The 1929 Geneva Conventions still protected soldiers—men and women in uniform, wounded or imprisoned—but not civilians. Only a few exemptions existed.[19] The ICRC had attempted to address this gap in international law through the so-called Tokyo draft of 1934, which aimed to protect enemy civilians in the territory of a belligerent power as well as civilians under the authority of the enemy in occupied territories. Although these provisions were not ratified before the war broke out, many countries agreed to adhere to these expanded rules. The German government was among the first to declare its cooperation, and ultimately thousands of "civilian internees" received largely the same status as POWs. These so-called assimilated civilian prisoners who found themselves trapped in an enemy country at the outbreak of hostilities were to receive some protection. Relatives and humanitarian aid organizations were allowed to send parcels to this group. However, the Nazis rejected outside aid and refused legal protection for detained Jews and prisoners considered especially dangerous to the regime, regardless of their nationality. Only in certain cases did the Nazi government allow exceptions to this tough stance. The ICRC had cooperated with aid organizations in the early months of the war and engaged in some test runs in cooperation with Jewish organizations in Switzerland to deliver food parcels

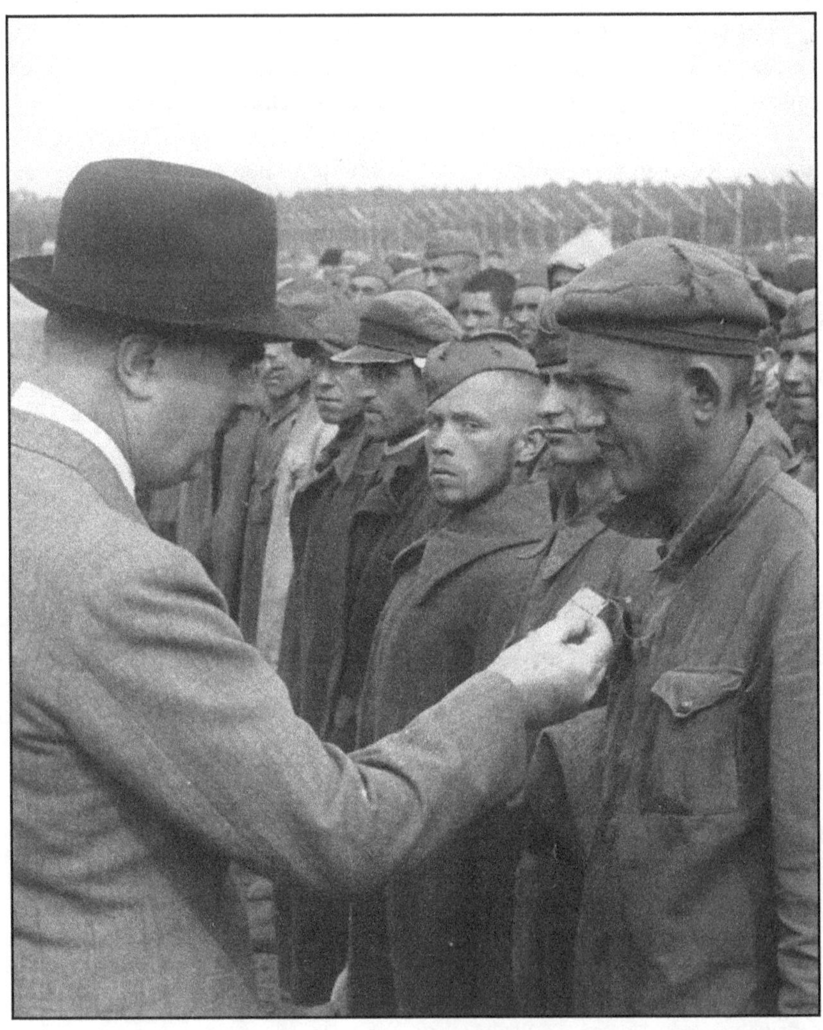

Dr. Carl Jacob Burckhardt, head of an ICRC delegation, visiting a POW camp in Germany, August 1941. Courtesy of ICRC Archives, photo by Mauritius Hartmann, V-P-HIST-01565-49.

and medicine to civilians (non-Jews and Jews) in Poland.[20] However, the scale remained modest.[21] As the Germans seized ever more territory, intervening to improve living conditions in Nazi camps became even more difficult. The Nazi state eventually oversaw a total of more than 42,000 detention sites, which served different purposes and included concentration camps, ghettos, POW camps, forced labor camps, and killing centers.[22] The opportunity to send relief such as food and medicine depended not only on the nature of the camp and the category of prisoner but also on the reigning policies of the Nazi state, policies that changed over time. The ICRC was allowed to inspect nine prison camps for Jews in occupied France during July and October 1941, but the organization was usually barred from inspecting camps and ghettos elsewhere in Nazi-occupied Europe.[23] Officials at the German Red Cross now repeatedly told the ICRC not to intervene on behalf of Jews because such requests would be ignored. In the summer of 1941, the German Red Cross also made very clear to Geneva that inquiries from relatives about individual concentration camp prisoners, forwarded by the ICRC, would no longer be answered for the duration of the war.[24]

Knowledge about the Holocaust

In retrospect, the year 1942 proved to be critical in the ICRC's policies concerning civilian victims of the Nazi regime in general and European Jews in particular. The ICRC leadership learned increasing details during the war about Nazi plans for Jews in occupied Europe. Vice President Carl Jacob Burckhardt, a university professor from Basel, an ambitious diplomat, and essentially the ICRC's "foreign minister," had gained early knowledge about the so-called Final Solution.[25] Burckhardt was arguably the most influential official at the ICRC even before taking over as its president in January 1945. Like many of his contemporaries, he was not immune to antisemitic stereotypes.[26] He had close contacts with German diplomats and officials, as well as with refugee circles and the leaders of Jewish organizations (for example, Gerhart Riegner from the WJC, who was stationed in Geneva during the war). On November 7, 1942, Burckhardt confirmed to the U.S. consul in Geneva, Paul C. Squire, that Hitler had issued an order in 1941 to make Europe "*judenfrei*" (free of Jews). Burckhardt did not use words such as "murder" or "extermination" but seems to have just repeated the language of his German sources. Still, he made clear that *judenfrei* could only mean murder of the Jewish population.[27] Burckhardt likely knew about the Riegner telegram from August 1942 that informed the leaders of the WJC as well as British and U.S. government officials about Nazi plans for a "Final Solution to the Jewish question" through mass murder. Riegner was a former student of his, and the two met regularly.[28] When they met on November 17, 1942, the ICRC diplomat made fairly clear that he already knew what was unfolding. Burckhardt confirmed Riegner's information, which helped convince U.S. diplomats that the reports made by Riegner and others about the Nazi plan to murder all European Jews were accurate.[29] Historian Yehuda Bauer has highlighted the importance of Burckhardt as a neutral source and concluded, "What apparently convinced the Americans of [the Riegner report's] accuracy was, more than anything else, the testimony of Dr. Carl J. Burckhardt."[30]

In a joint public statement dated December 17, 1942, the Allied nations condemned the "bestial policy of cold-blooded extermination" and warned the Nazi perpetrators and their collaborators that they would "not escape retribution" once the war was over. This statement gained some attention, for it was printed in many newspapers in Allied and neutral countries and broadcast over the radio. However, the declaration promised little beyond postwar retribution. And it was followed by very few targeted interventions to rescue Jews and other Nazi victims trapped in Europe.[31]

Silence about the Shoah

Inside the ICRC, knowledge about Nazi atrocities did not translate into immediate action. In October 1942, the ICRC leadership discussed the fate of concentration camp inmates and possible aid work for them. The ICRC felt the need to address the increasing brutality of the war, including both the mass Allied bombing of civilian targets in German cities and the deportation and mass murder of civilians through the Axis powers. A draft appeal addressing these issues was prepared for that month's meeting. It highlighted among other issues the special fate of civilians who had been deported and imprisoned, reading in part: "Certain categories of civilians belonging to various nationalities are being deprived of their liberty for reasons connected with the state of war, and are being deported. Or they have been taken hostage and risk being put to death for acts of which they are usually not the perpetrators."[32] The ICRC called upon the "warring powers" to grant these categories of civilians at least POW status.

Based on its own principles, the ICRC could no longer risk its moral standing by remaining on the sidelines. A majority inside the organization's leadership had become ready and willing to do something by the fall of 1942. The four women on the ICRC leadership committee—Suzanne Ferrière, Marguerite Frick-Cramer, Lucie Odier, and Renée Bordier—sought to address the specific fate of deported civilians. However, at the plenary session of the committee on October 14, 1942, Swiss politicians together with a minority of ICRC assembly members managed to block their colleagues' public appeal about responding to Axis atrocities. Burckhardt played a decisive role in this backpedaling. As the most senior ICRC official at the meeting (President Huber was absent), his opinion was arguably the most influential. Burckhardt did not share his knowledge about Hitler's extermination program with his colleagues at the organization.

He instead supported the stance taken by Swiss president Philipp Etter, who spoke clearly against a public appeal, arguing that such provocations would not be in the interest of Switzerland's neutrality. Fear of a German invasion of Switzerland was also widespread at the time, and Switzerland had no interest in riling the "German tiger." The draft statement was ultimately shelved.[33] Stunningly, in talks with U.S. diplomats less than a month later, Burckhardt stated that the committee decided against "his [Burckhardt's] plan to direct a public appeal throughout the world" for practical reasons. Other committee members, he claimed, had stalled the initiative so as not to "jeopardize their [main] work for POWs."[34] Burckhardt failed to mention an important detail: quite apart from their fundamental humanitarian concerns, some of the defeated pro-appeal members of the ICRC were worried about possible long-term consequences for the Red Cross if it remained silent. As political scientist David P. Forsythe has concluded, "With great prescience, several Assembly members . . . , speaking in advance of President [Philipp] Etter at the 14 October meeting, said that if the ICRC did not issue the public statement under consideration, its future work would be tainted."[35] They worried that the reputation of the humanitarian body was at stake.[36]

The Allied Blockade

Despite the primary impetus of the ICRC to provide aid, its leaders faced a major obstacle in their search for funding and relief supplies: the Allied blockade. Part of the Allied war plans entailed cutting Nazi Germany off not only from international supplies of war materials but also from food. Food had quickly become a scarce wartime commodity in Europe, which in turn created difficulties for the relief parcel planning of the ICRC and other humanitarian groups in Switzerland. Red Cross parcels for POWs were exempt from the blockade and continued to cross the Atlantic on Red Cross ships.[37] Standard Red Cross parcels were often assembled in Switzerland, from where the ICRC would then help to distribute them in the POW camps. They proved an important source of nutrition and moral support for British, U.S., and other Allied POWs in German captivity.[38] The standard food parcels for POWs in 1943 contained 1,845 grams of sugar and dairy products: 600 grams of jam, 430 grams of sweetened concentrated milk, 80 grams of Ovo sport Swiss energy bars, 150 grams of biscuits, 250 grams of smoked sausage, 225 grams of cheese, and 100 grams of chocolate. By late 1943, the parcels contained more variety. They began to include three 100-gram packets of biscuits, two packets of soup in cubes, six packets of vegetable powder for soup, 500 grams of noodle soup, 165 grams or three tins of

Globus goulash, one bottle of salted paprika paste (Pritamin), and a packet of plum marmalade.[39] In the United States, the food shipments were often assembled at the American Red Cross premises in Philadelphia and shipped by the western Allies under an ICRC flag to ports in Lisbon or Marseille. From there, the precious cargo was transported by rail or trucks to Switzerland. The ICRC then delivered the relief funded by the Allies to POW camps in Nazi-controlled Europe.[40]

Relief in the form of food and medicine for civilians was a completely different matter. The ICRC repeatedly pleaded with Allied officials for exemptions for aid shipments to prisoners in Nazi camps, aid that was subject to the tightly enforced blockade. Allied officials proved intransigent, however, for they believed the blockade was working and would therefore shorten the war significantly. Exemptions from this policy were rare. In one exception, in 1941–42, the Swedish Red Cross and the ICRC were permitted to provide aid to the starving Greek population under wartime occupation, what one historian has called "a substantial break in the blockade."[41] Other relief efforts were discussed but not acted upon (for instance, special provisions for Jewish children). In the end, the concessions made to aid the starving Greek population remained the main exception to Allied principles.[42]

The ICRC made renewed attempts to obtain exemptions from the blockade by lobbying the American Red Cross. The request met with little success.[43] The ICRC had little choice but to search for food and supplies for civilians from inside Europe—from neutral countries such as Sweden, Portugal, and Switzerland itself. Further afield, Hungary, Turkey, and Romania afforded some opportunities to secure supplies.[44]

Humble Beginnings of a Relief Plan

Jean (Johannes) Schwarzenberg, an Austrian nobleman with Swiss citizenship, worked in the division for civilian internees at the ICRC headquarters and from 1942 onward began coordinating its relief efforts for concentration camp inmates.[45] The ICRC's aid relief work for civilians was throughout the war carried out under the umbrella of a body called the Joint Relief Commission (Commission mixte), organized under a cooperative arrangement struck between Geneva and national Red Cross societies. The ICRC also worked with a large number of other Jewish and humanitarian organizations, including the Quakers and the Young Men's Christian Association (YMCA). Ultimately, the ICRC's help for Jewish victims was largely financed by Jewish organizations, including the Joint and the WJC in particular.[46] The Joint had been founded on the eve of World War I in New York and was already active in a wide range of rescue activities for Jewish victims. It helped refugees emigrate, sent food parcels to Jewish refugees, opened refugee shelters and soup kitchens in Europe, helped finance the efforts of government aid agencies, and toward the end of the war even considered providing ransom money to save lives.[47] Founded in the 1930s, the WJC was an international organization that fought antisemitism and lobbied for a range of causes such as civil rights for Jews. The two organizations differed in style and philosophy, and the Joint had access to greater financial resources.

Gerhart Riegner and Saly Mayer were among the main Jewish contacts for the ICRC in Switzerland. Riegner, a German Jew, had found refuge in Switzerland and served as a representative of the WJC, which had moved its headquarters to New York City. Mayer was president of the Association of Jewish Communities in Switzerland and later also served as a representative of the Joint. The ICRC worked with both men and their organizations on a regular basis. Riegner's memoirs indicate that he did not have the highest opinion of Mayer.[48] Their personalities and backgrounds differed. Despite Riegner's closer relationship to Burckhardt, Red Cross representatives appear to have favored Saly Mayer, particularly since the Joint provided crucial funds to the ICRC and in many respects shared a similar philosophy about concrete humanitarian work and discreet diplomacy with the Geneva-based institution.

Jewish organizations were disappointed by the ICRC's silence and unwillingness to condemn the mass murder program, hoping for more practical aid for Jewish victims. As a result, cooperation between the Joint (whose headquarters were also in New York) and the ICRC in Geneva increased in early 1943, though the former—as a private organization—lacked leverage and the latter remained constrained by the lack of legal protections covering most imprisoned civilians. The Joint provided financial support and supplies, while the Red Cross took over acquisition, transport, and delivery of food supplies to Jews trapped in Nazi territory and detention sites. Relations between the parties proved difficult at times but also achieved some significant successes, especially later in the war. Cooperation between the Joint and the ICRC had started slowly and with a certain measure of distrust. As one biographer of Saly Mayer writes, "For a long time relations with the ICRC would be difficult for Mayer. Only at the beginning of March 1943 would he meet with its president, Max Huber, to ask for help from what for a Jew was not an unproblematic institution."[49] In March 1943, ICRC president Max Huber wrote to Mayer, assuring him that he would do what he could for Jewish victims. But Huber also cautioned, "You know well all the difficulties which we will have to face."[50]

Difficulties notwithstanding, the WJC demanded action. The organization's men in Geneva, Gerhart Riegner and Paul Guggenheim, demanded that ICRC vice president Carl Jacob Burckhardt at the very least organize some relief missions. Sending food parcels seemed like a feasible option, if only because it had been so widely implemented for POWs. Could this system be extended to civilian prisoners? Many obstacles seemed to prevent any large-scale operation, but the WJC tried to extract concessions from the ICRC by appealing to their anxieties about the Red Cross image. At a May 1943 meeting, Guggenheim of the WJC declared that, after the war, the world would sternly ask if his organization and the ICRC had done enough and that he doubted the question would be answered affirmatively.[51] In early 1943, the ICRC renewed its efforts to aid imprisoned civilians, including Jews. It eventually attempted a two-pronged strategy: stationing delegates in countries allied with Nazi Germany and sending food parcels to camps in Nazi-controlled Europe outside the Reich whenever and wherever possible. Negotiating with German satellites (and not Nazi Germany) for access to Jewish prisoners or populations was more likely to produce results, especially now that the balance of the war was changing after the Axis defeat at Stalingrad in January 1943.

Food Parcels into Concentration Camps

Pushing for aid to Jewish prisoners in known camps in the Reich was never completely abandoned and ran parallel to these efforts. Starting with first mass arrests of Jews during the November pogroms in 1938 ("Kristallnacht"), the numbers grew quickly during the war. In December 1943, there were 315,000 prisoners in concentration camps, for instance, reaching a peak in January 1945 with 714,211 prisoners, not all of them Jewish.[52] Starting in the summer of 1943, Schwarzenberg experimented with sending food parcels to civilian prisoners with privileged status (those who had been given some of the rights granted to Allied POWs), only a relatively small group of internees at that point. In principle, the German government allowed the sending of parcels if a prisoner's location and name were known. This concession proved rather empty since the government typically did not give out information on the whereabouts of most concentration camp inmates and deportees, much less the location of the camps themselves. Despite these obstacles, the ICRC pushed forward with Schwarzenberg's food parcel program on a very small scale. Schwarzenberg stated in his memoirs that the program had started with a list of 18 names of prisoners in the Buchenwald concentration camp.[53] In June 1943, the organization was able to send parcels to 150 mostly Norwegian inmates who were held in Sachsenhausen and a few other camps. Scandinavian aid organizations had provided the names and addresses. Based on the Nazi regime's racial and political views, the Scandinavian prisoners constituted a privileged category. The ICRC received signed receipts from many of these recipients, sometimes with additional names of other nationals appearing on those same forms. In early 1944, the Dutch Red Cross provided the ICRC with the names and whereabouts of about 5,000 prisoners, mostly German Jews but also Norwegians and Dutch. The program grew slowly but steadily, and the ICRC also found it was able to buy supplies for these parcels in Romania, Slovakia, and Hungary.[54]

Schwarzenberg now hoped that he also could send food to less "accessible" civilians imprisoned by the Nazis for political or "racial" reasons. Despite all this and the lack of international treaties protecting these victims, the ICRC began working to extend the parcel scheme to prisoners with little international legal protection, such as Poles, Soviets, and Jews, based on the organization's "right of initiative." In June 1943, the ICRC delegate in Berlin proposed extending the parcel service scheme to camps such as Auschwitz-Birkenau, only to have the idea rejected by Walther Hartmann of the German Red Cross. Hartmann claimed that the Jews were employed exclusively in labor camps in the east, where food and medication were reportedly abundant. This brusque answer from Berlin shattered many hopes in Geneva.[55] But Schwarzenberg was a determined man, and in the summer of 1943 he decided to test whether the parcels were in fact arriving and to confirm that receipts could be obtained. "For this purpose," Schwarzenberg reported,

> we forwarded, by way of experiment, 50 parcels of Swiss origin, containing a receipt form, addressed personally to 50 designated prisoners in various concentration camps and prisons in Germany [Schwarzenberg does not name the camps]. The result was beyond all [of our] expectation[s]. In less than 6 weeks over two-thirds of the receipts, duly signed by the recipients, had been returned to us. This result is all the more striking as, owing to the constant changes in the camps, it was to be expected that a certain percentage of the addressees could not be reached. Unfortunately no more parcels are now available for these civilian prisoners.[56]

The ICRC informed British and U.S. authorities about these developments and again hoped for some support in easing blockade restrictions. The organization viewed the returned receipts as sufficient proof that the aid had reached the intended internees and deemed its experiment a success. In March 1943

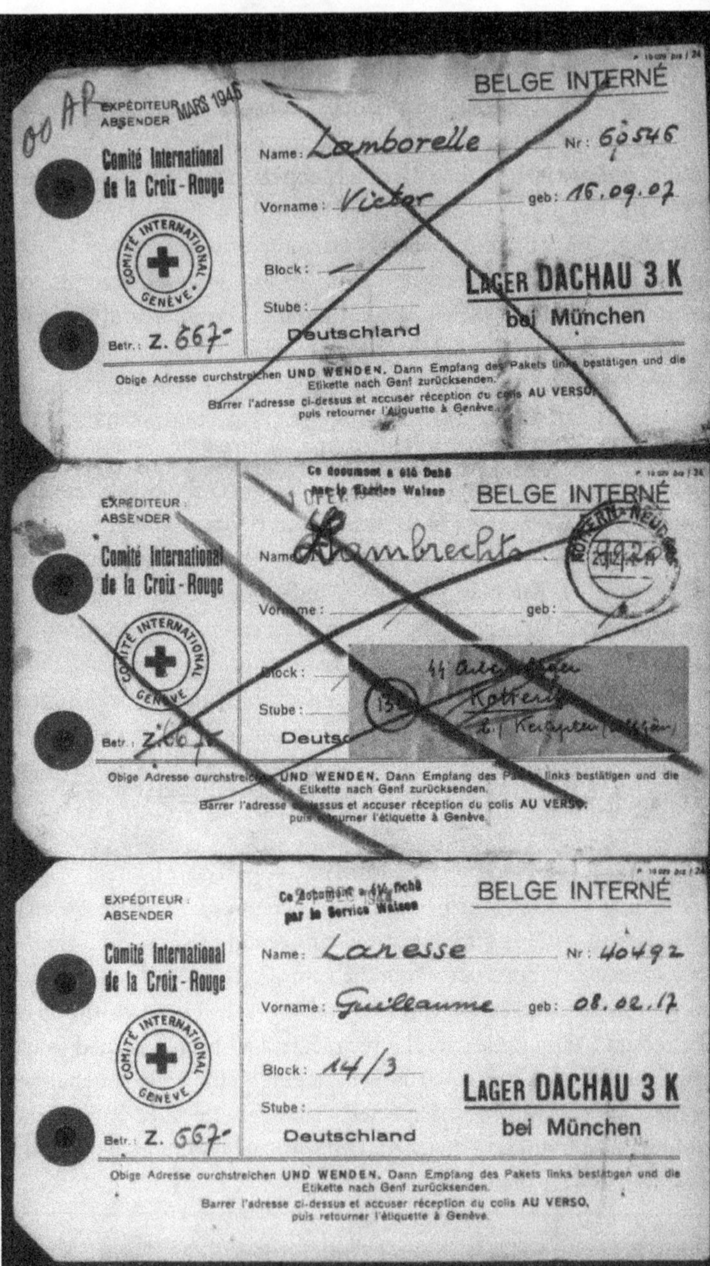

P. 10 029 bis / 24

BELGE INTERNÉ

EXPÉDITEUR: MARS 1945

ABSENDER

Comité International de la Croix-Rouge

COMITÉ INTERNATIONAL GENÈVE

Name: Lamborelle Nr: 60546

Vorname: Victor geb: 16.09.07

Block: —

Stube:

LAGER DACHAU 3 K

bei München

Deutschland

Betr.: Z. 667.

Obige Adresse durchstreichen UND WENDEN. Dann Empfang des Pakets links bestätigen und die Etikette nach Genf zurücksenden.

Barrer l'adresse ci-dessus et accuser réception du colis AU VERSO, puis retourner l'étiquette à Genève.

P. 10 029 bis / 24

Ce document a été fiché par le Service Walsen

BELGE INTERNÉ

EXPÉDITEUR:

ABSENDER

Comité International de la Croix-Rouge

COMITÉ INTERNATIONAL GENÈVE

Name: Lambrechts

Vorname: geb:

Block:

Stube:

Deuts[chland]

Betr.: Z. 667

Obige Adresse durchstreichen UND WENDEN. Dann Empfang des Pakets links bestätigen und die Etikette nach Genf zurücksenden.

Barrer l'adresse ci-dessus et accuser réception du colis AU VERSO, puis retourner l'étiquette à Genève.

P. 10 029 bis / 24

Ce document a été fiché par le Service Walsen

BELGE INTERNÉ

EXPÉDITEUR:

ABSENDER

Comité International de la Croix-Rouge

COMITÉ INTERNATIONAL GENÈVE

Name: Laresse Nr: 40492

Vorname: Guillaume geb: 08.02.17

Block: 14/3

Stube:

LAGER DACHAU 3 K

bei München

Deutschland

Betr.: Z. 667.

Obige Adresse durchstreichen UND WENDEN. Dann Empfang des Pakets links bestätigen und die Etikette nach Genf zurücksenden.

Barrer l'adresse ci-dessus et accuser réception du colis AU VERSO, puis retourner l'étiquette à Genève.

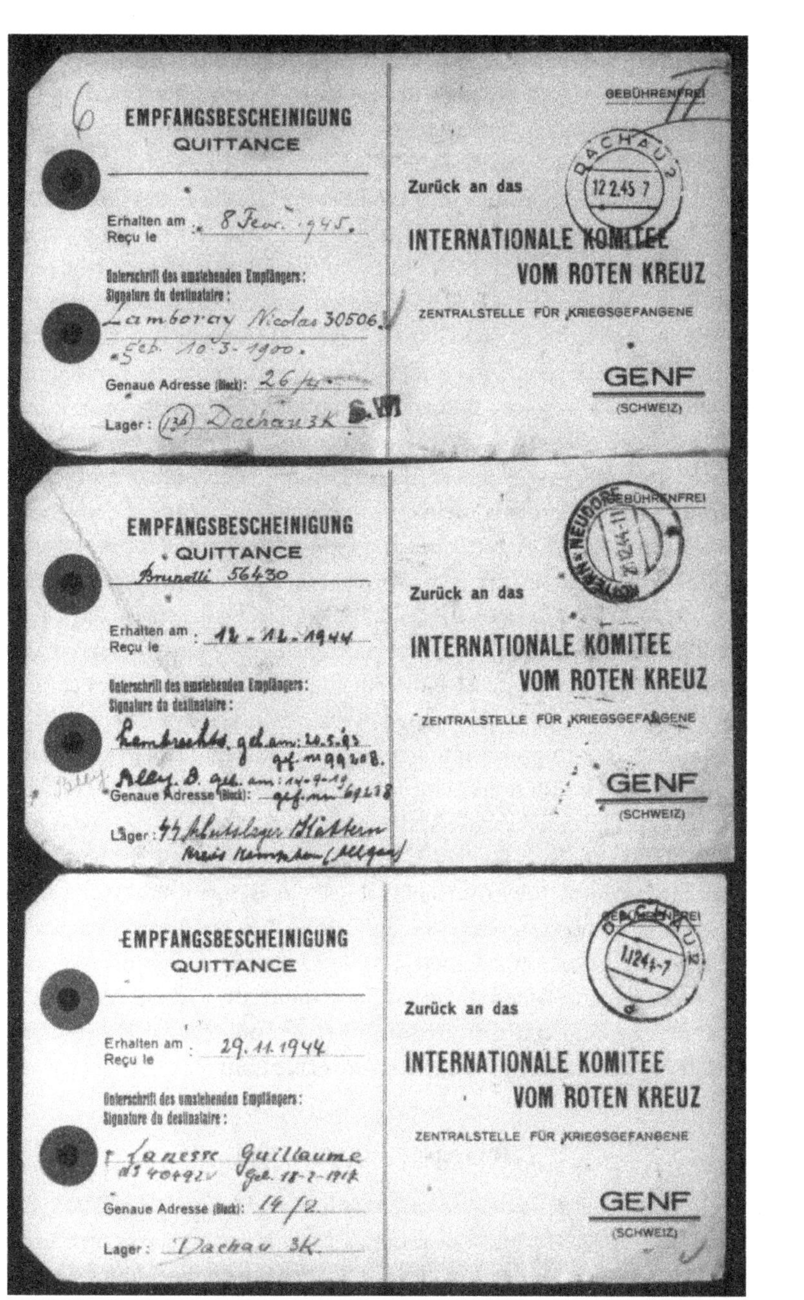
6

EMPFANGSBESCHEINIGUNG
QUITTANCE

Erhalten am / Reçu le: 8 Fevr. 1945.

Unterschrift des umstehenden Empfängers: / Signature du destinataire:
Lamboray Nicolas 30506
geb. 10-3-1900.

Genaue Adresse (Block): 26

Lager: Dachau 3K

GEBÜHRENFREI

DACHAU 2 12.2.45 7

Zurück an das

INTERNATIONALE KOMITEE
VOM ROTEN KREUZ
ZENTRALSTELLE FÜR KRIEGSGEFANGENE

GENF
(SCHWEIZ)

EMPFANGSBESCHEINIGUNG
QUITTANCE
56430

Erhalten am / Reçu le: 12.12.1944

Unterschrift des umstehenden Empfängers: / Signature du destinataire:

Genaue Adresse (Block):

Lager:

GEBÜHRENFREI

Zurück an das

INTERNATIONALE KOMITEE
VOM ROTEN KREUZ
ZENTRALSTELLE FÜR KRIEGSGEFANGENE

GENF
(SCHWEIZ)

EMPFANGSBESCHEINIGUNG
QUITTANCE

Erhalten am / Reçu le: 29.11.1944

Unterschrift des umstehenden Empfängers: / Signature du destinataire:
Guillaume

Genaue Adresse (Block): 14/2

Lager: Dachau 3K

GEBÜHRENFREI

DACHAU

Zurück an das

INTERNATIONALE KOMITEE
VOM ROTEN KREUZ
ZENTRALSTELLE FÜR KRIEGSGEFANGENE

GENF
(SCHWEIZ)

Parcel receipts from concentration camp prisoners, 1944–45. Courtesy of the ICRC (copy at United States Holocaust Memorial Museum, RG-58.002M.0067-00000031-00000032, Selected records of the ICRC, Division Assistance Spéciale).

Schwarzenberg wrote to Saly Mayer regarding help for Jews deported to Transnistria. The ICRC was preparing a delegation for Romania stationed in Bucharest, and now Schwarzenberg asked for Mayer's advice on how to get funds to buy much-needed food and medicine.[57]

Some good news came from the Terezín ghetto (Theresienstadt) near Prague. In early 1943, the ICRC could report that some food parcels had reached this location. The "Jewish Elders" in the ghetto had signed the receipts, which the ICRC again took as an indication that packages had reached their intended recipients.[58] The ICRC knew from the German Red Cross that the situation in Theresienstadt was dire. But the camp's command resisted further relief efforts. To add to the difficulties, the ICRC in Geneva received a suspect letter dated November 30, 1943, signed by Paul Eppstein and Benjamin Murmelstein, the Jewish elders of Theresienstadt: "We confirm most sincerely the receipt of the medication delivery announced in a letter of September 30, 1943. We allow ourselves to remind you repeatedly that the supply of medications for the Jews in our care is so adequate that we ask that you refrain from further deliveries; the health condition of the Jews entrusted to our custody can still be described as quite favorable."[59] The SS obviously intended for this kind of "information" to deceive the outside world about the real conditions in the ghetto, which must have raised eyebrows in Geneva. The Swedish Red Cross had been sending large numbers of gift packages to Norwegian internees and Danish Jews in Theresienstadt for some time.[60] However, Theresienstadt remained a special case because of the ways in which the Nazis used it in their propaganda. In the second half of 1943 and early 1944, the ICRC began receiving ever more information from national Red Cross organizations, government agencies, and nongovernmental organizations. But the knowledge remained limited, contradictory, and sometimes based merely on rumors. As a result, some camps such as Sachsenhausen, Theresienstadt, and Dachau were for a number of reasons getting a disproportionate amount of relief. However, access even to those known camps remained rare exceptions.

Increased Efforts: 1944

In 1944, ICRC relief activities increased for Jews and other civilian Nazi victims, although far too late for most of Europe's Jews. It was a race against time. By early 1944, most Jews in Nazi-controlled Europe—with the major exception of Hungary—were already dead. The increased relief work was in part due to the establishment of the War Refugee Board (WRB).[61] The WRB was created in January 1944 as the first U.S. government agency to explicitly help civilian victims of the Nazi regime. While the U.S. Treasury Department was charged with the administration of the newly founded organization, many of its funds in fact came from private Jewish organizations such as the JDC. The turning tide on the battlefield provided the impetus for increasing its activity. It had become more obvious that Nazi Germany was losing the war, but it remained unclear how long the war would still drag on. The WRB began putting considerable pressure on the ICRC to act and intervene wherever possible. On January 29, 1944, the U.S. ambassador to Switzerland, Leland Harrison, forwarded a message from the newly established WRB to ICRC president Max Huber in Geneva. In it, he asked Huber to facilitate "feeding programs in Romania, Theresienstadt, Slovakia and Croatia." The WRB was willing to provide the necessary funds "at once for necessary operations."[62] However, the ICRC was slow to respond, and time was of the essence. Because relief for POWs and "assimilated civilians" was its essential work, the ICRC remained cautious. Throughout the Nazi years, Huber had considered the Jewish civilians in camps very much from a legalistic point of view. As a trained lawyer and legal scholar, his perspective is not surprising, but this viewpoint narrowed down the possible options for providing help. Max Huber realized that the expectations put on the ICRC were very high and remained wedded to a modest stance in which "to recognize the limits of humanitarian aid is the condition for its survival."[63] Two weeks later, on February 11, 1944, the U.S. delegation in Switzerland followed up with him, reporting that the WRB was requesting more information about relief operations of the ICRC on behalf of Jews and other persecuted groups in Croatia, Slovakia, Romania, Hungary, and Theresienstadt.[64] By 1944, the ICRC had delegations in Bucharest, Bratislava, and especially Budapest actively helping and carrying out relief work for Jews.

Money from the Joint

All such plans and new efforts had to be financed. With the Allied blockade still in force, money was one of the main tools the WRB could provide.[65] According to ICRC sources, the organization had received 22 million Swiss francs from Jewish organizations during the war.[66] In February 1944, the WRB informed Huber that the U.S. Treasury Department had granted the JDC a license (that is, an exemption from the blockade) for $100,000 (300,000 Swiss francs) for the aid project. Saly Mayer would work out the details about how to use the money with the ICRC, which was to buy food and clothing in neutral countries and otherwise carry out relief work. The WRB requested that it be fully informed about the actions taken by Geneva.[67] Mayer could now count on the support of both the WRB and the U.S. embassy, which had promised him "all possible cooperation in this matter."[68] Yet a further complication loomed on the horizon.

The ICRC's traditional mandate was organized along the lines of "nationality." This approach made providing aid for specific ethnic or religious groups more complicated. Jewish victims were citizens of a large number of different countries or had been made stateless. Saly Mayer was well aware of the hurdle, writing in an internal memo that

> with regard to I[C]RC we must not forget that Jewish help is not contained in their charter; on the other hand it does not say that I[C]RC should refuse to help Jews. Considering the neutral character of ICRC one has to handle this matter very carefully. I told and wrote to ICRC to not refuse this offer of $100,000 and considering the new turn the whole matter has taken they should open a new resort for Jewish help.[69]

The memo of March 1944 stated that the Red Cross would probably help with buying food and clothing as well as deliveries. The JDC also hoped to get the names and locations of prisoners from the Red Cross. Saly Mayer and the ICRC agreed that a small portion of the $100,000 could cover administration costs, but most of it was to be used for food, clothing, and medications for the relief of Jewish prisoners. Ultimately, 100,000 francs were sent to Romania to help deportees in Transnistria and Bessarabia. Theresienstadt was to receive standard Hungarian food parcels worth 119,000 francs, and Jews in Kraków would receive food parcels worth 100,000 francs (for instance, vitamin-enriched milk). Small quantities of food parcels were sent to camps in Upper Silesia and the Netherlands. The remaining JDC money was earmarked for the relief of Jews in Rome and the purchase of medicine.[70]

Most of this money was transferred through banks in various ways, but according to the historian Jean-Claude Favez, the ICRC always tried to respect the financial transaction laws in Switzerland and the other countries involved. The JDC's funds were channeled through Swiss banks accounts and used for purchasing Hungarian and Romanian currency. In addition, Red Cross delegates also acquired local currency in those countries in exchange for credits payable after the war and guaranteed by the Joint and the WRB.[71] The system worked, although disagreements arose at the time concerning how Joint money was used and how delegates kept records. Similar problems arose when it came to monies for relief and rescue operations. The Jewish organizations and the WRB wanted to have clear records of what happened with their money and demanded detailed receipts. The demand proved unrealistic in a time of war and chaos. The deficiencies in the receipt system sometimes led to considerable tension between the Joint and the ICRC.[72] However, with this increase of funding and activities, Saly Mayer suggested to Huber that it was time for the creation of a proper office designated for Jewish relief inside the ICRC.[73] Schwarzenberg immediately embraced the idea.

Extension of Food Parcels Relief

News about the availability of substantial new funds made Schwarzenberg euphoric: "This is amazing; 100,000 dollars for free is fantastic. This changes everything; now one has to pursue this work seriously. . . . I have to tell Huber that this has to get done now."[74] In early 1944, Schwarzenberg's and Mayer's wishes for a new relief office in the ICRC materialized: the Special Relief Division (Division d'assistance spéciale) was formally created and put in charge of helping all deported civilians in camps not then under the protection of the Geneva Conventions—Jews, political prisoners, and other imprisoned civilians.[75] The parcel service to civilians in camps was expanded, and the status of Schwarzenberg's office grew. Nevertheless, personnel and resources for his Special Relief Division remained scarce.[76]

The ICRC reported after the war that all individually or collectively addressed parcels contained receipt forms. Those were often signed by the prisoners and returned by the postal service back to Geneva. The ICRC had a card index where the names of detainees and deportees were documented.[77] These acknowledgments provided evidence of the actual camp as well as the name of a prisoner. To the great surprise of the ICRC, the German post office sometimes even forwarded parcels after a prisoner was transferred elsewhere. As mentioned above, the receipts often contained signatures and names of additional prisoners who were also hoping for food parcels. Thus, over time the ICRC collected ever more names and ever more information on the whereabouts of civilian prisoners. By March 1945, the ICRC had a list of nearly 56,000 civilians in camps and their locations.[78]

Although the Allied blockade had not been lifted, the War Refugee Board helped to obtain exemptions for its humanitarian work in Europe. This was not easy to achieve. Even in the last months of the war, the British and U.S. governments were determined not to let food and relief fall into German hands. They were also trying to avoid anything that might upset Stalin and fuel his paranoia. Furthermore, the British and U.S. governments' primary concern remained getting their own POWs back safely.[79] The number of food packages sent to concentration camps and Theresienstadt increased slowly. In June 1944, five months after the WRB had first intervened, Schwarzenberg reported to his superiors on results obtained from the food parcel program. The project had started with a test run of 50 parcels, increased monthly, and had grown to a total of 19,485 parcels delivered between its humble beginnings in November 1943 and May 1944.[80] The cooperation between the JDC, the WRB, and the ICRC now began to produce modest yet real results. Schwarzenberg credited Saly Mayer and described him as an "experienced and discreet friend of our institution" (*erfahrener und diskreter Freund des Hauses*) and as "really the only one who does something and is really useful to us."[81] In September 1944, the American, British, and Canadian Red Cross societies allowed the ICRC to redistribute the 315,120 food packages from the stranded cargo ship, the SS *Christina*, originally bound for Belgian and French POWs.[82]

Relief Efforts in the Last Stages of the War

Despite some progress, the blockade of continental Europe remained tight and resources remained scarce. In February 1944, the American Red Cross also made clear that the U.S. government had not deviated from its policy.[83] Three months later, the ICRC renewed its pressure on the American Red Cross to lobby American officials "for the purchase of supplies for these concentration camps."[84] The U.S. State Department still did not yield.[85] Despite the fact that the Treasury Department had just created the WRB the previous month, views and policies changed only slowly. As in the case of POWs, blockade authorities tied permission to import parcels from Europe to the supervision of the distribution by neutral delegates.[86] The U.S. government wanted to make sure that food packages filled with precious coffee, sugar, and meat would not fall into enemy hands. These were understandable concerns. This was one important reason why the ICRC eventually accepted the invitation by Nazi authorities to visit Theresienstadt with its 35,000 prisoners on June 23, 1944. The visit centered on checking living conditions in the camp and seeing whether people were being deported from there to other camps. The young ICRC delegate Maurice Rossel was joined by two delegates from the Danish Red Cross. The Red Cross visit was painstakingly staged by the SS to deceive the world. Whether Rossel was aware of this remains unclear, but in any case he wrote a positive report about the inspection tour.[87] However, the visit did not change the Allied position concerning the blockade. The ICRC had no further access to the ghetto until its next visit on April 6, 1945.

Relief efforts were stepped up in the last months of the war and particularly during the first postwar months. Hungary became a priority for the

Red Cross in 1944 and 1945. In 1944, German troops invaded Hungary, and the large Jewish population there faced mortal danger. A massive deportation operation to Auschwitz-Birkenau began in May 1944. The ICRC leadership received the WRB's and Jewish organizations' calls for intervention with trepidation. The ICRC delegate in Washington, DC, again explained to WRB director John Pehle that the provision of material relief was the ICRC's proper domain and the best way for the Red Cross to assist Jews in Hungary.[88] Tensions between Jewish activists and the Geneva organization grew sharp. Riegner and others knew that millions of Jews had already been killed and that with the annihilation of the Jews in Hungary, the "complete realization of the Final Solution" seemed in sight.[89] The WJC faced "a black wall of stubbornness and bad will," Riegner's boss Kubowitzky (also Kubowitzki) wrote earlier in 1944.[90] In response to the bureaucratic obstacles thrown up by the ICRC, Riegner and his WJC colleagues ultimately sent false papers and money to Budapest for whatever was needed. Inspired by other diplomats from neutral countries and humanitarians, the local ICRC delegates in Budapest ultimately went well beyond the cautious instructions given by Geneva. According to the ICRC, humanitarians issued 30,000 letters of protection and provided food and shelter for 3,000 Jewish children in Budapest.[91] Some 255,000 Jews, about one-third of those who had lived in wartime Hungary, were ultimately saved in part thanks to aid workers from various nations, such as Friedrich Born, a particularly courageous ICRC delegate in Budapest.[92]

Meanwhile, the ICRC leadership under Carl Jacob Burckhardt engaged in a number of direct negotiations with Nazi officials to allow more aid to reach civilian prisoners. These efforts produced limited results. Himmler eventually preferred the Swedish humanitarian Folke Bernadotte over Burckhardt. Count Bernadotte, vice president of the Swedish Red Cross, used these high-level talks to enhance the standing of Sweden and himself. Thousands of Scandinavian and other Jewish prisoners were collected from selected concentration camps such as Neuengamme and brought to Sweden in Bernadotte's famous "White Buses" operation, which stole Burckhardt's thunder.[93] Only in the last weeks of Hitler's Reich did Burckhardt receive authorization from Himmler's subordinate, Ernst Kaltenbrunner, to station ICRC delegates in some of the remaining concentration camps to manage the distribution of food and medicine.[94] But by the spring of 1945 the situation in Germany had grown increasingly chaotic, with communications and the train system in tatters. Individual ICRC delegates managed to enter some ghettos and concentration camps such as Theresienstadt and Mauthausen, where they prevented last-minute mass executions and organized the orderly transfer of power to Allied authorities.[95] The Allies also made a fleet of trucks available to the ICRC in the last weeks of the war in Europe to keep relief for POWs and other prisoners going.[96] The WRB sent more than "300,000 food packages from the United States and gave the International Red Cross the trucks, tires, and gasoline to deliver them to concentration camps," historian Rebecca Erbelding points out.[97]

The signed receipt slips, still preserved in archives today, show the names of about 116,000 prisoners.[98] The ICRC declared in its 1948 report that "between November 1943 and May 1945 1,112,000 parcels of food, clothing, and medicine were sent to known internees."[99] Based on ICRC sources, Jean-Claude Favez puts the number of food parcels at between 750,000 and 1,112,000.[100] However, the large numbers of Red Cross parcels that reached camps in the first postwar weeks are included in these statistics. The ICRC was in most cases not able to verify the distribution of parcels in detention sites.[101] We have some evidence that parcels reached many prisoners but also that a large (if unknown) number did not.[102] The exact number of concentration camp detainees who received parcels through the ICRC will never be known. These numbers also pale in comparison to the 24 million food parcels delivered to western Allied POWs. An estimated 200,000 British and imperial forces and 95,000 U.S. troops were in German hands during the war.[103] According to Nazi figures, detainees in concentration camps amounted to some 715,000 people in January 1945.[104] Given the number of people detained in these types of Nazi camps alone, the assistance offered by the ICRC seems too little, too late.

Conclusion

The ICRC struggled to find ways to support civilian victims of the Nazis, particularly Jews. It continued to focus its energies on its traditional mandate to help POWs and wounded soldiers. However, early on, the Red Cross identified the needs of civilian victims of the war and of Nazi persecution and was willing to do something for them. The humanitarians in Geneva realized that the obstacles to providing aid were manifold and substantial: the Allied blockade, the lack of a legal basis for humanitarian intervention (civilians were in the main not covered by the Geneva Conventions), and the nature of the Nazi dictatorship and its genocidal program against Jews and other groups. Although ICRC officials had early knowledge about the Nazis' plans to systematically murder Europe's Jews, the organization decided not to speak out publicly against them. The leadership was concerned that too much engagement on behalf of Jews and too pointed a confrontation with the Nazi regime would seriously hamper its main mission of helping POWs.

As the course of the war in Europe changed, the ICRC cooperated more closely with the Allied governments and Jewish aid organizations. Cooperation between the Joint and the ICRC was particularly close and focused on relief through food parcels and medical supplies for camps and ghettos. The ICRC did not traditionally engage in rescue (in the narrowest sense of the word) but had always stressed its mission as a provider of relief through the provision of food, medical supplies, and clothing.[105] The ICRC was so rigid about procedures that it refused to bankroll more clandestine relief programs that did not conform to its POW food parcel "model." Rescue operations remained limited and often occurred only through the initiative and courage of a few individuals.

Starting in 1944, with the creation of the War Refugee Board and Allied victory in sight, larger numbers of food parcels were sent to concentration camps and ghettos, financed in part by Jewish organizations and delivered through the ICRC. The ICRC was mainly a trustee for the financial and material aid provided by other organizations and governments. While many camps in eastern Europe remained out of reach, thousands of food parcels did reach some Jews eventually, mainly in the last months of the war. At some locations, such as Theresienstadt, the ongoing and relatively high numbers of aid deliveries likely saved many lives. But given its propagandistic purpose for the Nazis, Theresienstadt remained an exception in many regards. Aid remained very limited in most camps, especially considering the massive scale of suffering. Still, the concentration camp food parcels program could be seen as "a weapon of last resort" for the ICRC, as Jean-Claude Favez has described it. The program played a critical role in the ICRC's postwar account of its activities during the Holocaust.[106]

By June 1944, Schwarzenberg had detailed knowledge about the unfolding genocide. The Schwarzenberg papers also contain reports about the situation in Auschwitz-Birkenau and other camps, including transcripts of letters from the Auschwitz subcamp Blechhammer in the fall of 1944. Jewish activists such as Abraham Silberschein in Geneva kept Schwarzenberg informed about the Nazi murder campaign.[107] In June 1944, Schwarzenberg forwarded to Dr. Heinrich Rothmund, the powerful chief of the Swiss police, what were apparently reports about Auschwitz and asked him to sacrifice some of his precious time to read them. Schwarzenberg stated, "From all the atrocity reports which I have received so far, and we have legions of them, this one is the most precise so far and gives clarity about the process of gassing the Jews (page II, etc.). I am asking you to treat this copy and the names it references with the utmost confidentiality. The Jewish organization which gave me the document will produce a new edition without stating names."[108] Rothmund's answer is also preserved in the archives. In it Rothmund showed himself mainly worried about "the fate of the ordinary German people" and the future of Europe dominated by people from other continents.[109] This exchange puts a spotlight on the lack of interest and empathy by some Swiss government officials toward the Jewish plight but arguably also their antisemitism. That the ICRC could achieve something for Nazi victims outside of their traditional mandate was ultimately due to a few engaged individuals such as Schwarzenberg, together with their Jewish counterparts. The obstacles were significant: a lack of a legal basis for protecting (Jewish) civilians, the weak leverage of Jewish nongovernmental organizations, the Allied blockade, personal sympathies and antipathies, and a mindset that focused on relief rather than rescue operations. More than anything, the Nazis' determination to commit genocide set clear limits for the humanitarians in Geneva.

Notes

1 S. Z. Kantor, "The International Red Cross Was Silent," *Jewish Frontier* (May 1945): 17–20, quote on 17.

2 Meir Dworzecki, "The International Red Cross and Its Policy vis-à-vis the Jews in Ghettos and Concentration Camps in Nazi-Occupied Europe," in *Rescue Attempts during the Holocaust: Proceedings of the Second Yad Vashem International Historical Conference*, ed. Yisrael Gutman and Efraim Zuroff (Jerusalem: "Ahva" Cooperative Press, 1977), 71–107, quote on 72.

3 David P. Forsythe, *The Humanitarians: The International Committee of the Red Cross* (Cambridge: Cambridge University Press, 2005), 49–50. The Dutch Red Cross in 2017 was much more forthright when its chairman apologized "to the victims and their relatives" for its "lack of courage." See "Dutch Red Cross Apologizes for Failing to Protect Jews from the Nazis," *Jewish Telegraphic Agency*, November 2, 2017.

4 See, e.g., Jean-Claude Favez, *The Red Cross and the Holocaust* (Cambridge: Cambridge University Press, 1999), 282.

5 For a good overview, see, e.g., Bob Moore and Kent Fedorowich, *Prisoners of War and Their Captors in World War II* (Oxford: Berg, 1996); Bob Moore and Barbara Hately-Broad, *Prisoners of War, Prisoners of Peace: Captivity, Homecoming and Memory in World War II* (Oxford: Berg, 2005); Arieh J. Kochavi, *Confronting Captivity: Britain and the United States and Their POWs in Nazi Germany* (Chapel Hill: University of North Carolina Press, 2005); and James Crossland, *Britain and the International Committee of the Red Cross, 1939–1945* (Basingstoke: Palgrave, 2014).

6 David P. Forsythe, *The Humanitarians: The International Committee of the Red Cross* (Cambridge: Cambridge University Press, 2005), 15ff.

7 Michael Barnett, *Empire of Humanity: A History of Humanitarianism* (Cornell: Cornell University Press, 2013), 2ff.

8 See Gerald Steinacher, *Humanitarians at War: The Red Cross in the Shadow of the Holocaust* (Oxford: Oxford University Press, 2017), 16.

9 Sébastien Farré, "The ICRC and the Detainees in Nazi Concentration Camps (1942–1945)," in *International Review of the Red Cross* 94 (winter 2012): 1381–408, quote on 1386.

10 Alfred Streim, *Die Behandlung sowjetischer Kriegsgefangener im "Fall Barbarossa." Eine Dokumentation* (Heidelberg: C. F. Müller, 1981); Christian Streit, *Keine Kameraden. Die Wehrmacht und die sowjetischen Kriegsgefangenen 1941–1945* (Bonn: J. H. W. Dietz Nachf., 1991); Hannes Heer and Klaus Naumann, eds., *Vernichtungskrieg. Verbrechen der Wehrmacht 1941–1944* (Hamburg: Hamburger Edition, 1995); Aron Shneyer, *Pariahs among Pariahs: Soviet-Jewish POWs in German Captivity, 1941–1945* (Jerusalem: Yad Vashem, 2016).

11 *Report of the International Committee of the Red Cross on Its Activities during the Second World War (September 1, 1939—June 30, 1947)* (hereafter *Report*), vol. 1: *General Activities* (Geneva: ICRC, 1948), 63. See also Farré, "The ICRC and the Detainees in Nazi Concentration Camps," 1386.

12 Letter Friedrich K. to the ICRC in Geneva, July 30, 1933, Archives du Comité international de la Croix-Rouge (ACICR), Détenus politiques en Allemagne CR 110/4–3.01 [4992], Yad Vashem (YV) M.75.

13 German Red Cross presidency answers to Swedish Red Cross President Prince Carl, October 5, 1933, signed [Joachim] von Winterfeldt-Menkin, ACICR, CR 110/4–3.01, YV, M.75. See Steinacher, *Humanitarians at War*, 38.

14 Carl J. Burckhardt, *Meine Danziger Mission 1937–1939* (Munich: Callwey, 1960), 54–55.

15 Letter Reinhard Heydrich, to the chief of staff of the Duke of Coburg (German Red Cross), February 13, 1936, ACICR, CR 110/4–3.01, YV M.75.

16 Steinacher, *Humanitarians at War*, 37ff.; Birgitt Morgenbrod and Stephanie Merkenich, *Das Deutsche Rote Kreuz unter der NS-Diktatur 1933–1945* (Paderborn: Schöningh, 2008); Dieter Riesenberger, *Das Deutsche Rote Kreuz. Eine Geschichte 1864–1990* (Paderborn: Schöningh

Verlag, 2002), 354ff.; Bernd Biege, *Helfer unter Hitler. Das Rote Kreuz im Dritten Reich* (Reinbek: Kindler, 2000), 10; Markus Wicke, *SS und DRK. Das Präsidium des Deutschen Roten Kreuzes im nationalsozialistischen Herrschaftssystem 1937–1945* (Potsdam: Vicia, 2002); Stefan Schomann, *Im Zeichen der Menschlichkeit. Geschichte und Gegenwart des Deutschen Roten Kreuzes* (Munich: DVA, 2013), 267–68.

17 "Durch das Reichsgesetz vom 9.12.1937 über das DRK [here: German Red Cross] wurde die Organisation vollkommen neu als einheitl. . . . Rechtskörperschaft unter Schirmherrschaft Adolf Hitlers gebildet . . . je nach den Anforderungen von Reich, Partei u. Wehrmacht." *Meyers Lexikon*, 8th ed. (Leipzig: Bibliographisches Institut, 1942), 598.

18 See Alan E. Steinweis, *Kristallnacht 1938* (Cambridge, MA: Belknap Press of Harvard University Press, 2009).

19 The ICRC nevertheless tried to bring relief where possible; for initiatives after World War I, see, e.g., Kimberly A. Lowe, "Humanitarianism and National Sovereignty: Red Cross Intervention on Behalf of Political Prisoners in Soviet Russia, 1921–3," *Journal of Contemporary History* 49, no. 4 (2014): 652–74.

20 On RELICO, see the chapter by Anne Lepper, this volume.

21 Dworzecki, "The International Red Cross and Its Policy," 72; Sebastián Farré, *Colis de guerre: Secours alimentaire et organisations humanitaires (1914–1947)* (Rennes: Presses Universitaires de Rennes, 2014), 132–33.

22 Ronald W. Zweig, "Feeding the Camps: Allied Blockade Policy and the Relief of Concentration Camps in Germany, 1944–1945," *The Historical Journal* 41, no. 3 (1998): 826.

23 Monty Noam Penkower, "The World Jewish Congress Confronts the International Red Cross during the Holocaust," *Jewish Social Studies* 41, nos. 3–4 (1979): 231.

24 Favez, *Red Cross and the Holocaust*, 56–57.

25 Paul Stauffer, *Sechs furchtbare Jahre. Auf den Spuren Carl J. Burckhardts durch den Zweiten Weltkrieg* (Zurich: Verlag NZZ, 1998), 9. Burckhardt was internationally quite well known as a historian and author. But it was his function as high commissioner of the League of Nations in the Free State of Danzig/Gdansk between 1937 and 1939 that put him in the spotlight of international politics. Though also a historian by training, the ICRC official should not be confused with the famous nineteenth-century historian of the Renaissance who bore the same name.

26 Steinacher, *Humanitarians at War*, 29–30.

27 Memo from the U.S. consul in Geneva, Paul C. Squire, about his interview with Dr. Carl J. Burckhardt, November 7, 1942, regarding "Jewish Persecution" (Strictly Confidential), USHMM, RG-68.045M, reel 232. See also Jürgen Matthäus, *Predicting the Holocaust: Jewish Organizations Report from Geneva on the Emergence of the "Final Solution," 1939–1942* (Lanham, MD: Rowman & Littlefield in association with the USHMM, 2019).
28 Penkower, "World Jewish Congress," 229–56.
29 Favez, *The Red Cross and the Holocaust*, 6, 39.
30 Yehuda Bauer, *American Jewry and the Holocaust: The American Jewish Joint Distribution Committee, 1939–1945* (Detroit: Wayne State University Press, 1981), 191.
31 Favez, *The Red Cross and the Holocaust*, 38ff.
32 Ibid., 87.
33 On July 24, 1943, the ICRC did send a telegram to all the nations at war asking them to respect international standards of warfare. The very generally worded text was also published in the journal of the ICRC and went basically unnoticed. See also Gerald Steinacher, "The Red Cross and the Holocaust: 1942 as a Turning Point for the Humanitarians?" in *The End of 1942: A Turning Point in World War II and in the Comprehension of the Final Solution?*, ed. Dina Porat and Dan Michman (Jerusalem: Yad Vashem, 2017), 279–94.
34 Memo from the U.S. consul in Geneva, Paul C. Squire, about his interview with Dr. Carl J. Burckhardt, November 7, 1942, regarding "Jewish Persecution" (Strictly Confidential), USHMM, RG-68.045M, reel 232.
35 Forsythe, *The Humanitarians*, 49.
36 Ibid., 49. See also Caroline Moorehead, *Dunant's Dream: War, Switzerland and the History of the Red Cross* (London: Carroll & Graf, 1998), 706.
37 In addition, personal parcels were sent from Canada and later from the United States for onward transmission to POWs in Germany through the regular mail system. They were exempt from the blockade but not "protected." The ships carrying these latter parcels were not marked with Red Cross signs and thus became potential targets for German submarines.
38 E.g., S. P. Mackenzie, *The Colditz Myth: British and Commonwealth Prisoners of War in Nazi Germany* (Oxford: Oxford University Press, 2006). The book contains over fifty references to Red Cross parcels for POWs.
39 Farré, "The ICRC and the Detainees in Nazi Concentration Camps," 1406.
40 Ibid., 1387.

41 Forsythe, *The Humanitarians*, 44. See also W. N. Medlicott, *The Economic Blockade*, vol. 2, ed. W. K. Hancock (London: HMSO and Longmans, Green, 1959), 272.
42 Medlicott, *Economic Blockade*, 2:275.
43 U.S. National Archives and Records Administration, College Park, MD (NARA), RG-200, American National Red Cross, box 1018, folder 619.2: "Camps—Europe, General." Note from ICRC, director of the Prisoners of War and Civilian Internees Committee for Mr. James, American Red Cross, Washington, DC, May 7, 1943 (Confidential).
44 *Report of the Joint Relief Commission of the International Red Cross, 1941–1946* (Geneva: International Red Cross Committee and the League of Red Cross Societies, 1948), 12.
45 Steinacher, *Humanitarians at War*, 50ff. For Schwarzenberg, cf. Colienne Meran, Marysia Miller-Aichholz, and Erkinger Schwarzenberg, eds., *Johannes E. Schwarzenberg, Erinnerungen und Gedanken eines Diplomaten im Zeitenwandel* (Vienna: Böhlau, 2013), esp. the contribution of Oliver Rathkolb, "Johannes Schwarzenberg—Eine Persönlichkeit der Zeitgeschichte im 20. Jahrhundert," 251–61.
46 Dworzecki, "International Red Cross and Its Policy," 95.
47 Bauer, *American Jewry and the Holocaust.*
48 Gerhart M. Riegner, *Never Despair: Sixty Years in the Service of the Jewish People and the Cause of Human Rights* (Chicago: Ivan R. Dee in association with the USHMM, 2006), 99.
49 Hanna Zweig-Strauss, *Saly Mayer (1882–1950). Ein Retter jüdischen Lebens während des Holocaust* (Cologne: Böhlau, 2007), 194. "Erst Anfang März 1943 wird er schließlich dessen Präsidenten Max Huber aufsuchen, um Hilfe von dieser für den Juden nicht unproblematischen Organisation zu erbitten."
50 JDC Archives, NY, Saly Mayer Collection (SM), 3/2/2/23b, letter Huber to Mayer, March 12, 1943.
51 Archiv für Zeitgeschichte (AfZG) Zurich, NL Stauffer 14 (V), 31.1.3. Ar WJC. "Aktennotiz über eine Unterredung mit Prof. Carl Burckhardt vom Internationalen Roten Kreuz vom 18. Mai 1943," signed by Riegner, May 19, 1943.
52 Nikolaus Wachsmann, *KL: A History of the Nazi Concentration Camps* (New York: Farrar, Straus and Giroux, 2015), 627.
53 Schwarzenberg, *Erinnerungen und Gedanken*, 169.

54 Zweig, "Feeding the Camps," 830. See also Farré, *Colis de guerre*, "Chapitre IX—Des colis pour les deportes: le CICR et les camps de concentration," 165ff.

55 Favez, *The Red Cross and the Holocaust*, 102.

56 USHMM, RG-58.002M, reel 1; ACICR, B SEC DAS, DAS ZA—1.01, "Despatch of standard food parcels to concentration camps and prisons: note de J.-E. Schwarzenberg du 24 août 1943."

57 Schwarzenberg to Saly Mayer, March 19, 1943, NL Schwarzenberg, Institut für Zeitgeschichte Wien, Mappe 9, Korrespondenz mit div. Briefpartnern, 1.

58 USHMM, RG-19.045M, reel 9, ACICR G 59/6–170, G59/6–169, letter, Suzanne Ferriere to Kullmann, February 16, 1943.

59 Central Zionist Archives (CZA) A 320\25–150. Receipt for medication to Commission mixte de secours de la Croix-Rouge international, Geneva, from the Ghetto Theresienstadt. "Jüdische Selbstverwaltung Theresienstadt, 30. November 1943, Betrifft: Medikamentensendung laut Zuschrift vom 30.9.1943, Dr. Paul Israel Eppstein, Dr. Benjamin Israel Murmelstein." See also H. G. Adler, *Theresienstadt 1941–1945. Das Antlitz einer Zwangsgemeinschaft* (Tübingen: Mohr, 1960), 739.

60 Steinacher, *Humanitarians at War*, 57. See also Adler, *Theresienstadt*, 363.

61 For more on the WRB, see Rebecca Erbelding, *Rescue Board: The Untold Story of America's Efforts to Save the Jews of Europe* (New York: Doubleday, 2018), and her contribution in this volume.

62 USHMM, RG-19.045M, reel 9, ACICR, G596–170, Leland Harrison forwarded a message from the War Refugee Board to Max Huber, January 29, 1944.

63 Archiv für Sozialgeschichte Zürich, Mappe 49.5 ZA 1, "Internationales Komitee vom Roten Kreuz (IKRK)." "Helfen als Kunst des Möglichen. Ein Vortrag von Prof. Max Huber über das Internationale Komitee vom Roten Kreuz," *Neue Zürcher Zeitung*, January 25, 1944.

64 JDC Archives, NY, SM, 3/2/2/23b; Daniel J. Reagan wrote to Max Huber (ICRC Geneva), February 11, 1944.

65 Claude Lanzmann interviews Roswell McClelland, November 1978, USHMM, RG-60.5047. See also https://collections.ushmm.org/search/catalog/irn1002803 (accessed September 4, 2019).

66 Frederic Siordet, *Inter Arma Caritas: The Work of the International Committee of the Red Cross during the Second World War* (Geneva: International Committee of the Red Cross, 1947), 77.

67 JDC Archives, NY, SM 3/2/2/23b; Daniel J. Reagan wrote to Max Huber ICRC Geneva, February 11, 1944.

68 JDC Archives, NY, SM 3/2/2/23b; Daniel J. Reagan, Commercial Attaché, U.S. Legation in Bern, informed Saly Mayer, February 11, 1944.

69 JDC Archives, NY, SM, roll 8, folder 23, "SM Item 15: 100,000 $ 300,000 Frs Red Cross Allegation" (1944).

70 JDC Archives, NY, SM, roll 8, folder 23, Mayer to ICRC Geneva, 17 March 1944. See also JDC Archives, NY, SM, roll 8, folder 23, Schwarzenberg to Saly Mayer, "Verteilungsplan Betrifft: $100.000 des American Joint," March 24, 1944. See also Farré, "The ICRC and the Detainees in Nazi Concentration Camps," 1389.

71 Favez, *The Red Cross and the Holocaust*, 104.

72 See, e.g., memorandum, Dr. Kurt Wehle to Jerome J. Jacobsen (JDC), February 17, 1950, on questions relating to arrangements made between ICRC and JDC for financing rescue work for Jews. JDC Archives, G45–54/4/70/4 RO.31. Saly Mayer wrote to an ICRC official: "Ich werde Ihnen beweisen, dass es nicht Misstrauen ist unsererseits, sondern dass es das System und Kontrolle verlangen, dass ich mir anvertraute Gelder richtig placiert wissen will." JDC Archives, SM, roll 3, folder 10, Telephon mit PB am 12. Juli 1946, 9 Uhr, SM 1.

73 JDC Archives, NY, SM, 3/2/2/23b, letter, Saly Mayer to Max Huber, February 16, 1944.

74 JDC Archives, NY, SM, roll 8, folder 23, Saly Mayer about Schwarzenberg [1944].

75 USHMM, RG-58.002M. Selected records from the International Committee of the Red Cross. Division Assistance Spéciale, reel 1, 0001 0029 DAS / ZA—1.03 (Note non signée du 2 mars 1944 concernant la constitution d'une nouvelle division dite "Division d'assistance spéciale").

76 *Report*, 3:338.

77 Ibid., 3:339.

78 Steinacher, *Humanitarians at War*, 52. See also Favez, *The Red Cross and the Holocaust*, and ICRC website article "The ICRC in WW II: The Holocaust," January 24, 2014, www.icrc.org/en/document/icrc-wwii-holocaust (accessed April 14, 2019).

79 On how the blockade worked, see the official British government history by Medlicott, *Economic Blockade*, vols. 1 and 2 (1952, 1959); Meredith Hindley, "Blockade before Bread: Allied Relief for Nazi Europe, 1939–1945" (PhD diss., American University, 2007).

80 USHMM, RG-58.002M, reel 1, 1998, 0001 0023. DAS / ZA—1.02, "Le Service des colis pour camps de concentration (CCC). Sa création, les résultats obtenus," note de J.-E. Schwarzenberg du 30 juin 1944.

81 USHMM, RG-19.045M, reel 1, ACICR G59/[0]-1.06, Note für Herrn Dr. Bachmann (evtl. für Herrn Burckhardt) from Schwarzenberg, July 26, 1944.

82 See the chapter by Rebecca Erbelding, this volume, and her *Rescue Board*, 250. See also Favez, *Red Cross and the Holocaust*, 98; *Report*, 3:336–37.

83 NARA, RG-200, box 1018, folder 619.2: "Camps—Europe, General." Francis B. James, ARC Special Representative, to R. Gallopin, Director Relief Prisoners of War, Internees and Civilians, ICRC Geneva, February 7, 1944.

84 NARA, RG-200, box 1018, folder 619.2, ARC National Headquarters, memo Henry W. Dunning, May 6, 1944, handwritten note: "Mr Allen—Information. Probably not much that we can do. MP."

85 NARA, RG-200, box 1018, folder 619.2. ARC National Headquarters, memo Henry W. Dunning, May 6, 1944.

86 Zweig "Feeding the Camps," 825–51.

87 Adler, *Theresienstadt*, 135ff. Two officials of the German Red Cross, Walter Hartmann and Heinrich Niehaus, spent two days at Theresienstadt at the end of June 1943, and their leaked information to the International Red Cross was alarming. See Adler, *Theresienstadt*, 121; Favez, *The Red Cross and the Holocaust*, 74. On the Red Cross and Theresienstadt, see also the appendix in Otto Dov Kulka, *Landscapes of the Metropolis of Death: Reflections on Memory and Imagination* (Cambridge, MA: Belknap Press of Harvard University Press, 2013). After the ICRC visit, the Nazis decided to use Theresienstadt to deceive an even wider audience by producing the notorious propaganda film *Theresienstadt: A Documentary Film about the Jewish Settlements*. Unofficially, the film had the even more cynical title *Theresienstadt: The Führer Gives a City to the Jews*. With the film barely finished in the last months of the war, a Red Cross delegation was to attend a special showing by the SS leaders in Prague on April 6, 1945.

88 JDC Archives, NY, AR 193344. 4. 32, Zollinger, ICRC Washington, DC, to Walter Pehle, August 1944, Hungary.

89 Penkower, "World Jewish Congress," 230.

90 Ibid., 232; Riegner, *Never Despair*, 134ff.

91 Siordet, *Inter Arma Caritas*, 76.

92 Favez, *The Red Cross and the Holocaust.*
93 See Steinacher, *Humanitarians at War*, 70ff.
94 Erbelding, *Rescue Board*, 255–56.
95 Steinacher, *Humanitarians at War*, 80.
96 Zweig, "Feeding the Camps," 848.
97 Erbelding, *Rescue Board*, 257.
98 "The International Enquiry Service at Arolsen today holds 96,184 receipts, to which should be added 20,070 supplementary signatures appearing on some of the slips." Favez, *The Red Cross and the Holocaust*, 75.
99 *Report*, 3:335–36.
100 Favez, *The Red Cross and the Holocaust*, 75.
101 Farré, "The ICRC and the Detainees in Nazi Concentration Camps," 1391.
102 See Jan Láníček's discussion of stolen packages, this volume.
103 The numbers are taken from Kochavi, *Confronting Captivity*, 1. Mackenzie gives the number of 164,000 British and imperial forces; see Mackenzie, *The Colditz Myth*, 41. David Rolf states that eventually over 135,000 British men in the armed forces were in Axis captivity in his *Prisoners of the Reich*, 4. Other sources indicate that 130,000 British forces and 102,000 U.S. forces were POWs; see Francois Cochet, *Soldats sans armes. La captivité de guerre: une approche culturelle* (Brussels: Bruylant, 1998), 97.
104 Favez, *The Red Cross and the Holocaust*, 76.
105 Dworzecki, "International Red Cross and Its Policy," 72.
106 Favez, *The Red Cross and the Holocaust*, 98, 279; Steinacher, *Humanitarians at War*, 52.
107 NL Schwarzenberg, Institut für Zeitgeschichte Wien, Mappe 5, Korrespondenz als Vertreter des IKRK.
108 Schwarzenberg to Dr. Rothmund, Chef der Polizeiabteilung, June 26, 1944, NL Schwarzenberg, Institut für Zeitgeschichte Wien, Mappe Prov. Nr. 4, Behandlung der jüdischen Gefangenen. This was most likely Rudolf Vrba and Alfréd Wetzler's April 1944 report on Auschwitz; it was not included in this archival file.
109 Rothmund to Schwarzenberg, June 27, 1944, NL Schwarzenberg, Institut für Zeitgeschichte Wien, Mappe Prov. Nr. 4, Behandlung der jüdischen Gefangenen.

6

MAKING SURE THEY ARE ALIVE TO BE RESCUED

The War Refugee Board's Food Package Program

REBECCA ERBELDING

In the spring of 1945, twenty-year-old Dora Burstein arrived in Ravensbrück concentration camp. Born in Poland, Dora had already survived both the Łódź ghetto and Auschwitz before finding herself transported by train from a forced labor ammunitions factory outside of Berlin, one of the many prisoners throughout the shrinking Reich being shuffled around to keep them out of Allied hands for as long as possible. After a few days in Ravensbrück, Dora and her sister, who remained by her side throughout their imprisonment, were handed food packages.[1]

In an oral history nearly fifty years later, Dora remembered opening the heavy cardboard box with Red Cross markings on the outside. She remembered receiving chocolate, bacon, sugar, and rice and assumed that the German officers stationed in the camp had stolen the cigarettes from the boxes. Dora was right. Her package had originally included a pack of cigarettes, biscuits, processed cheese, powdered milk, margarine, salmon or tuna, sugar, chocolate, dehydrated soup (probably the rice she remembered), canned meat, vitamin C tablets, and a bar of soap. Unbeknownst to her, American Red Cross workers had packed her box between October 22 and November 13, 1944, in a warehouse outside of New York City. It sailed to Europe on a Swedish vessel, the M/S *Saivo*, on December 1, 1944, and was stuck in Gothenburg, Sweden, until March 16, 1945, when two railcars carrying 10,800 packages—including Dora's—left for Ravensbrück. Dora Burstein was one of tens of thousands of prisoners to receive American food packages in the weeks prior to liberation.

An American effort to deliver 300,000 packages to concentration camps seems easy enough on the surface. After all, the Allies had stockpiled more than seven million packages in Switzerland for POWs by the spring of 1945; the Committee of the International Red Cross (ICRC) published an extensive full-color brochure boasting of the streamlined boxing and distribution of these packages.[2] But those parcels were meant for Allied prisoners of war who were covered by the Geneva Convention of 1929, which mandated the humane treatment of POWs but crucially did not extend to protect captured civilians.[3] The distribution of POW packages was not subject to approval by Allied blockade authorities restricting the materials that could be sent into Europe or (generally) not forbidden by the Germans who supervised the POW camps.[4] Sending food and medicine to Jewish and political prisoners within the SS-camp system, however, was entirely different. The War Refugee Board (WRB), the U.S. government agency driving the food package project, had to engage in long and frustrating negotiations with Allied blockade authorities; the difficulties of wartime purchasing, packing, and shipping; and the challenges of Operation Clarion, the Allied endeavor to destroy Axis transportation routes. After nearly a year of planning, the packages finally arrived just as the Allied armies began liberating Nazi camps. The project to deliver 300,000 food packages serves as an example and reminder of the challenges the WRB faced in providing wartime relief to concentration camp prisoners.

In January 1944, after months of public and intra-administration pressure for the U.S. government to do more to assist European Jews and other Nazi victims, President Franklin Roosevelt signed an executive order creating the War Refugee Board.[5] This new agency was tasked with taking "all measures within its power to rescue the victims of enemy oppression" and affording these victims "all possible relief and assistance consistent with the successful prosecution of the war."[6] For the first time, the U.S. government had an official policy for addressing the ongoing mass murder of European Jewry, and it was a policy of relief and rescue. The WRB staff, largely composed of Treasury Department employees (many of whom had been the driving force behind the agency's creation), took their vague "relief and rescue" assignment and immediately began soliciting concrete suggestions from humanitarian aid organizations with extensive networks in Europe. Aiding Jews fleeing to safety was the immediate priority; within hours of the WRB's creation, the staff approved a request of the U.S.-based Union of Orthodox Rabbis to send money to assist Polish Jews crossing the border to safety in Hungary.

Over the next several months, as the WRB staff realized that the number of Jews able to escape enemy territory was limited, they initiated more projects related to relief. The tension between relief and rescue—providing clothing, food, and medicine to the many or expending a tremendous amount of effort and resources to bring small numbers of Jews to safety—remained constant. The WRB staff could not assume that the recipients of relief would survive the war, yet the knowledge that people were suffering compelled them to action.

Paul McCormack, the WRB's relief specialist and a former American Red Cross employee, did not see relief and rescue as mutually exclusive. In a March 13, 1944, memo, he explained, "Appreciating that we must and should continue to think and act in terms of actual release and rescue, it will become necessary, at one time or another, to actually engage in a program of some form of feeding to insure the availability of people to release and rescue."[7] McCormack argued that the WRB should sponsor a stockpile of goods in Switzerland for the ICRC to draw upon, should the possibility arise for this material to be distributed to Jews and other persecuted populations.

The ICRC staff in Geneva had been struggling to purchase clothing and medical supplies in Switzerland, surrounded by Axis powers, and enthusiastically supported the idea of a stockpile. In addition, in September 1943, six months before McCormack's memo and prior to the establishment of the WRB, Nahum Goldmann of the World Jewish Congress (WJC) had proposed a $10 million fund for the International Red Cross as a way to send food, clothing, and medicine to Jews in Europe. The money would be supplied by American Jewish organizations and by the U.S. and British governments. Assistant Secretary of State Breckinridge Long, claiming that the plan would need a congressional appropriation if the United States were to donate directly, instead proposed that the Intergovernmental Committee on Refugees take on the project.[8] This committee, established after the Evian Conference in 1938 to help German Jewish refugees emigrate, had been dormant for most of the war, but the British and American delegates at the April 1943 Bermuda Conference on Jewish refugees had revived it as a public demonstration of their ostensible support for refugee aid. The United States and Great Britain had already agreed to jointly fund any rescue or relief project sponsored by the London-based Intergovernmental Committee on Refugees, but the slow bureaucracy embedded in the structure of that committee meant that when the WRB was established in January 1944, the Red Cross had yet to spend a penny from the still nonexistent fund.

Even before the creation of the WRB in January 1944, Treasury Department staff, while compiling their manifesto against the State Department's obstruction of rescue and relief proposals, had stumbled upon the WJC/ICRC stockpile proposal. They believed that Long had thrown the idea "into the wastepaper basket; namely, the Intergovernmental Committee," and decided to revive it.[9] On January 27, 1944, John Pehle, a Treasury Department official and director of the new WRB, sent a cable to Geneva asking the ICRC for "immediate information concerning what areas you could operate in right now, assuming that necessary funds are made available to you, to provide food and medicine to Jews and other persecuted groups in German-occupied areas who are denied the facilities available to the rest of the population."[10] While awaiting a reply, Pehle asked the American Jewish Joint Distribution Committee (the Joint) to provide a $100,000 donation so the ICRC could begin work immediately. The Red Cross in Geneva, pleased to finally have some funding for aid to civilians, agreed to consult with the Joint's representative in Switzerland, Saly Mayer, and with the U.S. legation in Bern about its use of the money.

The British government, upon learning of the $100,000, protested that the money would certainly fall into Nazi hands and that goods meant for German-occupied territory could not enter Europe through the Allied blockade. Negotiations dragged on, and the Red Cross still did not spend the money. Finally, at the beginning of April 1944, the Red Cross asked permission to purchase medical

Staff of the WRB meet in director John Pehle's office in the Treasury Department, March 25, 1944. Pehle is behind the desk, at right. Courtesy of the Franklin Delano Roosevelt Presidential Library and Museum.

supplies, particularly surgical dressings. The U.S. State Department and the Foreign Economic Administration, a recently created American agency tasked with supervising economic projects overseas, could not agree on whether they needed to seek British approval for this request or for the Red Cross's follow-up request to purchase apple jam and green peas to send to the Theresienstadt concentration camp and to buy premade food packages in Portugal to send to Jews in Croatia. The British finally acquiesced in May, and the Red Cross began to spend the $100,000.

The drama and frustration surrounding the money indicated the necessity of stockpiles inside Switzerland, since such reserves would allow the Red Cross to have supplies at the ready without needing to bring them through the Allied blockade. In June, Dr. Johannes Schwarzenberg of the ICRC wrote to the U.S. legation in Bern, emphasizing the extreme need. The Red Cross could "forward at present roughly 20.000 individual parcels each month," but if French deportees could be included, "the above figures would have to be about ten times larger. . . . Theresienstadt alone could absorb up to 80.000 parcels a month, at a rate of a single parcel per head. Taking into account the requirements in Croatia, Poland, and lastly Hungary—should relief work for the Jews in that country become possible and necessary—several hundred thousand parcels per month would likewise be essential."[11] His message arrived at an opportune time: the WRB had finally reached agreement with the U.S. State Department and the Foreign Economic Administration that the International Red Cross should be given permission to establish stockpiles from which they could fill packages.[12] At least U.S. government agencies were finally in agreement.

On June 12, 1944, less than a week after the D-Day invasion, WRB director John Pehle met with representatives of the U.S. State Department and the British government to hammer out the details and obtain British approval. The Honorable Dingle M. Foot, the parliamentary secretary of the British Ministry of Economic Warfare, which oversaw the Allied blockade, adamantly refused to consider the idea of stockpiles, believing that the U.S. and British governments had already done enough to help Jews. One WRB staff member remembered Foot commenting that "a great deal of pressure now being exerted on both Governments on the feeding question might be removed if the British and American publics were informed of all the steps previously taken with a view to assisting victims of Nazi oppressions"—an apparent reference to the Holocaust.[13] Finally, after two days of meetings, Foot reluctantly agreed to allow the Red Cross to distribute 100,000 prepackaged food parcels per month for three months—approximately two million pounds of food—as a trial, rather than create a large reserve. Since clothing parcels were considered more valuable, the WRB would test the efficacy of the plan using food parcels and would be responsible for supplying them.[14] Pehle proudly informed President Roosevelt of the agreement, along with Secretaries Hull, Morgenthau, and Stimson, writing, "At this stage, sustaining the lives of these unfortunate people may be quite as important as attempting to rescue them from enemy territory."[15]

The British wanted the WRB to find food for the packages in neutral or occupied Europe rather than bring it in from outside the Allied blockade. A fortuitous opportunity immediately presented itself and served as a trial for the plan—although it did not ultimately count toward the WRB's agreed-upon 300,000 packages. In early May, the SS *Christina*, a cargo ship carrying 315,120 relief packages meant for French and Belgian POWS, had been attacked and sunk near Sète, France. While the waterlogged boxes were no longer fit for Allied POWs, the American Red Cross recommended searching the boxes for anything that could be sent into concentration camps. All but 400 packages had been damaged, but after the WRB paid a reduced price to the French and Belgian governments, the ICRC shipped the salvageable remnants to Geneva for drying and sorting. The rescued *Christina* boxes soon revealed usable amounts of powdered milk, margarine, tinned meat, corned beef, salmon, pâté, and jam and some quantity of coffee, soap, sugar, and cheese.[16]

On July 7, Schwarzenberg of the ICRC presented an aide-mémoire to the U.S. legation in Bern. While the Red Cross was pleased that the Allies were willing to send supplies to civilian prisoners, Schwarzenberg cautioned against asking for official German permission, since it was likely to be denied.[17] The Red Cross could handle the *Christina* packing and deliveries, but without a stockpile, the WRB would need to prepare the envisioned 300,000 parcels in the United States and ship them to Switzerland, since such a large amount of material was not readily available in Europe. The project necessitated secrecy to prevent the Germans from learning the origin of the supplies: the packages would be labeled with International Red Cross stickers only after they arrived in Geneva but prior to distribution.[18] To pay for the food and boxes, the WRB requested $1,125,000 from President Roosevelt's emergency fund.[19]

Although the British delegation had approved the trial of 300,000 food packages in June, two more months passed before they agreed to the details. On August 9, the British Foreign Office finally granted permission for the United States to send 300,000 relief packages through the "Gothenburg" shipping route (the route normally used to send POW packages) to distribute the salvaged material from the *Christina*, and agreed to the Red Cross's suggestions regarding the handling and distribution of the food packages. After alerting

Schwarzenberg that the project was finally underway, a British consulate staffer reported that the International Red Cross, "needless to say, is delighted."[20] Over the summer of 1944, the Red Cross sent 25,600 newly created *Christina* parcels to prisoners in various concentration camps, including 3,000 to Dachau. It received back more than 1,500 signed receipt cards from Dachau prisoners; each card bore between one and fifteen signatures. These new names were added to lists for future package deliveries, and the Red Cross could inform some families that new evidence had emerged that their loved ones were still alive.[21]

After the British government approved the Gothenburg shipping route, the WRB immediately convinced the American Red Cross to give up space on the *Gripsholm*, a Swedish humanitarian ship scheduled to depart New York harbor in late August. There was not much time, and while the Red Cross could pack the remaining 285,000 packages over the next several months, the WRB wanted to send the first shipment immediately. Since Roosevelt's emergency fund allocation had yet to materialize in the WRB's accounts, the Joint again stepped in, lending $41,475 to pay for the first 15,000 parcels.[22]

With ten days to go before the shipment was due on the docks, Macy's and Gimbels, the department stores contracted to provide the food packages, both pulled out, claiming they did not have the manpower to handle such a large order on short notice. Paul McCormack sped to New York and worked with the Joint to select two other commercial companies.[23] Wallace, Burton & Davis Co. charged $2.91 for each of 10,000 packages, which contained cheese, Kraft whole milk powder, sugar, dehydrated soup, raisins, and something called prune butter.[24] Prince Company's packages were a bit more expensive, at $3.00 each for the 5,000 parcels, which contained tinned meat and meat spread, cookies, fruitcakes, dehydrated soup, marmalade, tea, and processed cheese.[25] The WRB arranged for the necessary export license for the goods and convinced the Office of Price Administration, which controlled American wartime rationing, to give them the required 73,125 red ration points for the meat and dairy products and 2,000 sugar coupons.[26] On August 23, the *Gripsholm* left New York for Gothenburg carrying 15,002 relief packages. At a meeting with Morgenthau, Pehle boasted, "That is the first time that any food has been sent to people in concentration camps [by the United States]. We had to beat the British down on it. We had to talk the Red Cross out of space on the ship. We had to buy the food in New York. We did the whole thing."[27]

The packages arrived in Gothenburg in mid-September 1944 after a rough voyage. The shipping crates were too large and the contents shifted, resulting in a loss of almost all of the sugar. Moreover, the tape was not secure enough and had to be redone, and the boxes were marked in English, which would make delivery to concentration camps difficult. The ICRC also needed to replace all the receipt cards with an alternate version that they preferred.[28]

Due to other commitments, the American Red Cross could not package the remaining 285,000 boxes until late October, but in the meantime, the WRB took advantage of additional opportunities to distribute relief. In October, Schwarzenberg reminded Roswell McClelland, the WRB's representative in Switzerland, that 260,000 POW packages meant for French prisoners in North Africa were in their warehouse. He suggested that the WRB might obtain permission from American and British authorities to redirect 40,000 of them to concentration camps. With the blessing of the Allies, the Red Cross was able to distribute them. Schwarzenberg also shared a report with McClelland describing the appalling living conditions, meager food allotments, and forced labor in the Ravensbrück concentration camp. The report mentioned that female physicians imprisoned there were attempting to care for their fellow inmates.[29] Using his discretionary fund, McClelland purchased supplies for 500 packages—antibiotics, vitamins, cleansers, Vaseline, and bandages—and sent them through the Red Cross into the camp.[30] In a separate relief effort after the Warsaw Uprising, the WRB approved a request from the Polish Red Cross to assist the more than 240,000 Poles streaming through Pruszków on the outskirts of the city and allowed a shipment of food, clothing, soap, and medical supplies from Sweden as well as 250 tons of canned goods left over from the *Christina*.[31]

On October 26, the American Red Cross began packing the remaining 285,000 packages of the WRB's 300,000-box trial. Working six days a week, the Red Cross staff averaged 14,000 packages a day and, in less than a month, had readied 224,328 boxes. They contained cigarettes, biscuits, cheese, powdered milk, salmon or tuna, margarine, sugar, chocolate bars, dehydrated soup, meat, vitamin C, and a bar of soap.[32] Approximately one-third of the packages were designated as kosher and marked on the outside with a *K*; the rest included pork meat.[33] The Feinberg Kosher Sausage Company of Minneapolis, which sold the canned kosher meat to the WRB, ended up having to make a special road trip to the East Coast to make the shipment deadline.[34] The Europe-bound *Saivo*, carrying 37,388 shipping cartons containing the readied parcels, sailed "with the tide" on December 1, 1944.[35] The ICRC had hoped that the packages could arrive in now-liberated Marseilles for easier transport to Switzerland, but the WRB disagreed, so these cartons, too, sailed to Gothenburg.

Throughout the fall, the WJC protested the distribution plans for the packages—even though they did not know which camps were involved, a tightly kept secret to ensure that the packages could be delivered at all. Due to the terms of the agreement with blockade authorities, the 300,000 packages had to be distributed in camps where the Red Cross could guarantee arrival and distribution, which eliminated sites in occupied Poland, including Auschwitz-Birkenau, from consideration. The WJC wrote to the WRB to "express our deep concern over the probability that the camps specified by the ICRC are not likely to benefit any substantial number of Jews. It appears from recent information that there are still Jews in the following camps in Poland: Czestochowa, Jedrzejow, Kattowice, Kielce, Klimontov, Krakow, Mielec, Myslowice, Opole, Oswiecim, Piotrkow, Radom, Sanok, Skarzyske, Trzebinia, Wieliczka-Bochnia."[36] The WRB forwarded the list to Switzerland, where McClelland dutifully passed it on to the ICRC: "This is the old story . . . a list—largely misspelled and garbled of 'camps' in Poland, with the suggestion that ICRC try to include all or some of these camps in future distributions."[37] McClelland responded to the WRB that since "at least nine-tenths of the sites are quite inaccessible to ICRC (which would not be able to enforce even remotely the minimum necessary control as to allocation and reception of parcels)," he was not optimistic that distribution at alternative sites would be possible.[38]

The International Red Cross was nonetheless willing to send test shipments to these camps, at least the ones that could be located and were near the Eastern Front. But to do so, the United States and Britain would need to release the ICRC from the obligation to supervise the distribution of the packages, "as they have not the slightest hope of securing permission for their delegates to visit these camps."[39] In the absence of that permission, the ICRC reminded McClelland to make sure the WRB kept the list completely confidential since any publicity would endanger their ability to successfully distribute packages. This frustrated the WJC staff even further; in London, one told a WRB representative of his conviction that "the I[C]RC is not sending food to concentration camps in which Jews are kept. He continually stated that he would certainly not say that the I[C]RC was anti-semitic but that he was interested in knowing the camps to which food parcels were being sent."[40]

Bypassing the ICRC and WRB entirely, the WJC set about sending their own food packages with the assistance of the Swedish Red Cross—20,000 five-kilogram packages that included canned meat, pea meal, berry jam, dried milk, hard bread, canned fish, and cod liver oil—to concentration camps with large Jewish populations.[41] By the time the WRB learned of the proposal in late October, the matter was already before the Foreign Economic Administration and blockade authorities in London.[42] It was approved, although the U.S. State Department and British government inserted a provision the World Jewish Congress had been trying to avoid: the Red Cross had to supervise distribution—which it could not do in Bergen-Belsen, Theresienstadt, or most camps with a mostly Jewish population. The Swedish YMCA volunteered to guarantee distribution, and the WJC pledged to stop the program if there were problems.[43] Unfortunately, the WJC struggled to find funds for this program.

On January 8, 1945, McClelland learned that the 15,002 *Gripsholm* parcels had never arrived in the concentration camps. The ICRC reported that Nazi Germany had been holding three freight cars containing the boxes in Warnemünde, Germany, on the Baltic coast, for nearly two months and suspected that an overall halt in freight shipping was to blame. The Germans were using all available rail transport to bring men and supplies to the Western Front in preparation for the Battle of the Bulge and had no interest in sending American-produced parcels to concentration camps. Packages for Allied POW camps were also delayed.[44] Three weeks later, however, the ICRC reported that the *Gripsholm* boxes were finally moving.

By this time, the 224,328 *Saivo* packages had arrived and were waiting in Sweden. The kosher packages (39,324 in this batch) were reserved for Jewish prisoners, with the remaining 185,004 earmarked for the main German camps where both Jews and non-Jews were imprisoned. The *Caritas II* transported 60,672 packages, the last of the agreed-upon 300,000, from the port of Philadelphia to Toulon, France, at the end of December 1944. Worried that these packages would also be caught in the German transportation limbo, McClelland wrote to the WRB asking permission to procure trucks. Four or five large trucks on loan to the Red Cross would enable fast, flexible distribution of packages with a greater degree of control than using German-controlled trains.[45] The WRB agreed with McClelland and prepared a cable granting him permission to find the trucks. Before it could be sent, the War Department balked at the plan. Providing trucks would set a "precedent which would have an adverse effect on the distribution of prisoner of war packages. This Government has taken the firm view that the Germans should provide transportation for the distribution of these packages."[46]

War Department disapproval left the WRB in a tough position. Wartime conditions made transportation within Germany increasingly difficult. In mid-February, the Allied Air Forces launched Operation Clarion, an offensive designed to "deny the enemy the use of the rail system and to limit alternative movement by highway to the night hours. When the enemy has been forced to move . . . he has to move by road thus exposing himself to high daytime losses."[47] By demanding that the Germans carry out their official responsibilities to provide transportation for Red Cross packages—both those meant for Allied POWs and the WRB's packages—the War Department, in hewing so stringently to the rules of war, was only ensuring that the cartons would never arrive.[48] On

February 20, WRB director William O'Dwyer—a New York City politician and district attorney who took over when John Pehle resigned in January—outlined the problem of providing relief inside Germany to Treasury Secretary Henry Morgenthau Jr., Secretary of War Henry Stimson, and Acting Secretary of State Joseph Grew. The WRB's intelligence indicated that while the Germans had abandoned wholesale extermination, prisoners were now threatened with death by starvation, exposure, and neglect. O'Dwyer proposed that he would go to Switzerland himself to negotiate with the ICRC and the Swiss government to purchase food, medicine, and relief supplies; provide the Red Cross with trucks and gasoline to transport the goods; and ask for the empty trucks to bring released prisoners to safety. Though hesitant to commit American relief stocks then in Switzerland to the program, the secretaries, including Stimson, approved, and Assistant Secretary of War John McCloy was instructed to obtain trucks to distribute the WRB packages.[49]

Trucks proved exceedingly difficult to find, and ICRC president Carl Jacob Burckhardt wrote to the U.S. legation in Bern that transportation was the decisive question for preventing the starvation of prisoners: "We are often expected to do miracles. That is of course impossible; but by exerting every nerve and applying all our will, we can do something—provided certain indispensable means for the execution of our task be furnished us."[50] In meetings with McClelland, ICRC representatives stressed the need to send packages to the Hamburg and Munich areas—the sites of the Neuengamme and Dachau concentration camps—where they (correctly) believed the SS were chaotically collecting the survivors of forced marches and evacuated camps. Again, they reminded him, "invaluable aid could be rendered to at least some thousands if a few trucks were available."[51]

While O'Dwyer made plans for his trip, McClelland tried to find transportation and relief supplies within Switzerland, with American guarantees that anything the Swiss lent would be replaced after the war.[52] In a letter to the ICRC, McClelland wrote that he was "happy the War Refugee Board is really 'up on its feet'" and anticipated "full cooperation from them, particularly in the all-important truck question." He was concerned, however, that the WRB wanted to prioritize packages for prisoners deemed by the Nazis to be unfit for labor—concluding that prisoners who could not work were the most vulnerable. While asking the Red Cross whether targeted distribution was even possible, McClelland mused, "It will boil down to the old question of the lesser of two evils: keep people alive with small amounts of food which certainly will not directly benefit the Germans but at the same time keep people alive who are contributing slightly to the German war effort. I would vote for keeping them alive."[53]

On March 7, 1945, O'Dwyer updated Morgenthau with frustration: "We have untold numbers of people dying over there. There isn't any way in the world that I can get a pound of that food in to these people. The Army won't release gasoline and the Swiss government won't release gasoline. We have all the money in the world to buy trucks but we can't get trucks, and if we get trucks, we can't get gasoline because the Army won't release it." He had decided to cancel his own trip, since "this is the place where arrangements have to be made," but planned to send additional WRB staff to Europe in his stead. The next day, after some calls and a trip to the Pentagon, McCloy sent a cable to General Eisenhower asking the military to provide ten five-ton trucks and between 1,500 and 2,000 gallons of gas weekly for use by the International Red Cross. WRB staff proceeded to Allied headquarters in Paris to work out the details.[54]

From Switzerland, McClelland, struck with a bout of influenza that took him out of commission for the first half of March, tried to keep track of the package distribution underway. The ICRC had a few trucks, but they were being used to transport POW packages as well. Four convoys of twenty-five trucks crossed into Germany on March 7, but detailed tracking proved almost impossible: ICRC convoys were diverted and delivered packages to alternate locations, or the headquarters in Geneva lost track of the convoy for weeks. Some WRB packages, rather than being distributed in concentration camps, were handed out to prisoners on forced marches discovered on the sides of roads. Still, the bottleneck was slowly breaking, but not fast enough. On March 16, railcars containing 10,800 WRB packages left for Ravensbrück, including Dora Burstein's. The next day, 9,600 headed toward Neuengamme. Approximately 1,170 went to Theresienstadt on March 23, and 4,900 more left for Jewish forced laborers near Vienna.[55] McClelland reported that the ICRC had rented six twelve-ton trucks. Finally recovering from his illness, he cabled on March 23 that he would be going to Paris within the week to meet with military representatives.[56] Transportation and gasoline were the only way to guarantee that all the WRB packages would reach their intended recipients. WRB representatives Herbert Katzki, arriving from the United States, and James Mann, traveling from London, beat him to Paris.

Before he left Bern, McClelland, who had a good relationship with Burckhardt, sent a cable to the WRB about recent negotiations between Burckhardt and Nazi officials. In mid-March 1944, Burckhardt had traveled to Berlin to meet with SS-Obergruppenführer Ernst Kaltenbrunner and, as a result of these negotiations, secured permission for ICRC representatives to be stationed in larger concentration camps to supervise relief distribution. These representatives would not be permitted to return to Switzerland until the end of the war.

All camps could now receive supplies by truck, provided the distribution was discreet, since German civilians had begun to suffer from food shortages. At the end of his cable to the WRB, McClelland stressed that they could contribute by obtaining as many trucks and tires as possible.[57]

The three WRB representatives—Katzki, Mann, and McClelland—gathered in Paris on March 27, 1945. After several meetings with Brigadier General Morris Gilland—during which the men "made every argument available to us"—the general promised 2,000 gallons of gasoline per week, including oil and grease, and thirty truck tires.[58] They could only obtain six army trucks, but Mann informed O'Dwyer by phone that they could possibly use some French trucks that the Red Cross had recently received. After almost a week of meetings in Paris, McClelland returned to Switzerland to collect the tires on the French-Swiss border. In his last phone call to O'Dwyer, McClelland confided, "I hope we can keep it up, especially at this critical moment, because this is sort of the last lap now. I hope that the Army really finishes it off for us, because that's the only final solution, but if we can get in behind there and save a few of these people, why that's what we are really interested in doing now."[59] The military delivered thirty truck tires to the Pontarlier border station on Monday, April 2, but the French refused to let the tires cross without customs paperwork. Katzki and Mann had to intervene from Paris. The ICRC naturally welcomed the trucks, gasoline, and tires, and McClelland was able to cable Paris that five trucks would leave for Germany that Saturday and ten more the following week, "though geographic area still accessible is rapidly shrinking."[60]

In light of the desperate need for more packages, McClelland approved a request by Isaac Sternbuch, a Union of Orthodox Rabbis representative, to purchase more food for Red Cross distribution. Sternbuch purchased flour in Switzerland to make matzot to send to concentration camps for the Passover holidays and condensed milk, cheese, and canned fish intended for prisoners in Theresienstadt. McClelland also arranged for the WJC to distribute the 39,324 kosher WRB packages, in part to assuage their earlier complaints, and the WJC promised to distribute the WRB packages to inmates in Bergen-Belsen and Theresienstadt.[61] Unfortunately, this did not go smoothly. The Red Cross dispatched 18,000 of the kosher parcels, but the WJC announced that they planned to keep 20,000 in Stockholm as a reserve of kosher food to distribute to rabbinical groups after liberation. The WJC nevertheless asked the WRB to provide 30,000 more packages for immediate distribution. McClelland annotated the cable with the comment, "They have a lot of nerve!" and reminded the WJC that the packages remained the property of the WRB and they were only the distributing agents.[62] All packages needed to be sent into Germany immediately.

In the United States, the WRB staff worked on increasing the number of food packages the ICRC could distribute in camps. At the beginning of November 1944, the WRB had obtained permission from blockade authorities to package and distribute an additional 300,000 three-kilogram packages after the first trial was completed.[63] At the end of January, they began to plan the new batch, which was to include biscuits; tins of cheese, powdered whole milk, margarine, salmon or tuna, and canned meat; bars of chocolate and soap; and packages of cigarettes, multivitamins, and sugar cubes.[64] Although the WRB staff did not commit any deliberations to paper, the WJC's complaints likely registered: this time, half the parcels would be kosher. Due to wartime regulations, the WRB's relief specialist, Paul McCormack, sent five pages of instructions to the Treasury Department's procurement officer, providing details down to the size of the cracker (whole wheat, square, in packages 4″ x 2¾″ x 2¾″).[65] The WRB obtained ration coupons and filled out forms to avoid having to pay tax on the cigarettes (which they later decided to eliminate from the boxes), but by the end of March they were still waiting for bids from three commercial package companies. McCormack also obtained permission from blockade authorities to ship a third set of 300,000 parcels if the WRB finished distributing this round.[66] On April 5, a week before his death, President Roosevelt informed O'Dwyer that due to the "time element" he did not feel it necessary to authorize the third set, since the war would be over soon.[67] With the war clearly coming to an end, the next day the WRB formally canceled the second set of packages as well.[68]

Instead, O'Dwyer embarked on a challenging negotiation with the War Department to purchase POW packages from their stocks in Switzerland. He originally offered to buy 900,000, but the War Department, which had 2 million packages, claimed that was too many. They finally agreed to sell 206,000 parcels—but the War Department and the American Red Cross insisted that there could be no markings designating the packages as former POW shipments. Without new boxes, the War Department argued, "the Germans would then be encouraged to take prisoner of war packages destined for American and Allied prisoners of war, black out the symbols and labels and distribute the packages to German civilians."[69] Even at the end of the war, the War Department and the American Red Cross concerned themselves with packages falling into the hands of the enemy. The WRB would need to purchase and pack the food in new boxes while supervising the old ICRC-marked boxes until they could be destroyed.[70] On April 6, O'Dwyer called McClelland in Switzerland to inform him of the POW packages and to ask him about the prospects of unpacking and repacking the boxes. The news arrived at a good time, since the Red Cross thought the 60,000 WRB packages still in Switzerland would probably be distributed within the next two weeks.[71] The ICRC argued that in light of the desperate need, perhaps just blacking out the insignia would suffice.[72] The War Department also insisted on official payment before the boxes could be turned over to McClelland. The packages themselves would cost $762,200, while repackaging would cost at least one Swiss franc per parcel and could be accomplished at a speed of 2,000–3,000 per day.[73] On April 20, after the WRB filled out the forms and mailed the check, the American Red Cross instructed their representatives to transfer the packages to McClelland.[74] Three days later, the ICRC informed McClelland that war conditions were forcing them to halt any convoys into Germany.[75] The POW packages were never reboxed, and the WRB resold them to the United Nations Relief and Rehabilitation Administration after the war.[76]

With the POW packages no longer a concern and the dust settling at the end of the war, McClelland was able to investigate the distribution of the WRB's 300,000 packages. Despite all the difficulties of Red Cross transportation and even the temporary shutdown of transit at the end of the war, nearly all of them had been delivered. The first 15,000—the ones that had been stuck in the German rail shutdown—were delivered to concentration camps in Germany, though the Red Cross never specified which ones. The legation in Stockholm supplied information about the distribution of the majority of the WRB's 300,000 packages—almost all of the 224,000 Gothenburg boxes had been delivered in March. The WJC directed the 39,324 kosher packages to Jewish internees, mainly in Bergen-Belsen and Theresienstadt. As for the nonkosher packages, 21,600 went to Neuengamme, 13,200 were delivered to POWs to compensate for POW packages given to Norwegian civilians, 9,600 went to Ravensbrück, and 140,376 were listed as being given to civilian internees, though it is unclear whether this was a reference to civilian internment camps or prisoners in unknown concentration camps.[77]

McClelland had more details for the 60,571 packages originally delivered to Toulon and distributed out of Switzerland: they were delivered to a host of camps, forced labor locations, and former camps—Mauthausen, Landsberg, Uffing, Theresienstadt, Salzburg, Linz, Augsburg, and Lustenau. Red Cross records are more specific: trucks carried 1,000 WRB boxes to Mauthausen on April 16; 4,230 to Theresienstadt on April 17; 3,660 to camps in southern Bavaria on April 19; and 8,550 to Landsberg am Lech (Kaufering VII) on April 23. On April 29, after the ICRC liberated Polish and Hungarian Jews on a train near Bienberg, they supplied the newly liberated survivors with 2,500 WRB packages.[78] Nearly 5,000 were sent for relief in northern Italy, and 5,550 were given to refugees in transit through the Swiss border town of St. Margrethen.[79] Though many of the packages were not delivered until after the war was over, McClelland compiled a list of figures and dates for each location. While the difficult circumstances had rendered many distribution details uncertain, it is clear that tens of thousands of WRB food packages were delivered to concentration camps in the final days prior to and just after liberation.

Nearly a year passed from the time that blockade authorities agreed on the project of the 300,000 food packages until the first boxes arrived in concentration camps, and nearly two years elapsed from the time of the World Jewish Congress's proposal for a $10 million aid fund for the International Committee of the Red Cross. The WRB's lengthy and complicated fights surrounding the distribution of food packages and relief goods highlight the fact

Two newly liberated survivors of the Dachau concentration camp pose for the camera, April–May 1945. One holds a food package, almost certainly one of the parcels orchestrated by the WRB. Courtesy of the ICRC Photo Archives, V-P-HIST-02730-22A.

that a determination to assist was not enough to remove all the bureaucratic barriers, even for an agency that was itself part of a government bureaucracy. The complicating factors of transportation, rationing, the availability of materials, blockade regulations, and the ever-changing battle lines of World War II all had a significant effect on who benefited from relief efforts and when and where. While the War Refugee Board could mitigate some of these factors, the staff was still hamstrung by many of them. Yet after its creation, the Board did everything it could think of to expedite relief, working with Allied and neutral governments and Jewish relief organizations, protesting to military authorities, negotiating with commercial companies, and never losing sight of the end goal: to keep people alive long enough to be liberated.

Notes

1 Oral history with Dora Burstein Langsam, November 30, 1994, USHMM, RG-50.462.0112.

2 International Committee of the Red Cross, "Relief for Prisoners of War and Civilian Internees," Geneva, 1942. Copy found in U.S. National Archives and Records Administration, College Park, MD, RG-84, American Legation, Bern, American Interests Section, General Records 1942–47, 814.2, box 38.

3 Gerald Steinacher, *Humanitarians at War: The Red Cross in the Shadow of the Holocaust* (London: Oxford University Press, 2017), chap. 1.

4 The most comprehensive account of the blockade is Meredith Hindley, "Blockade before Bread: Allied Relief for Nazi Europe, 1939–1945" (PhD diss., American University, 2007).

5 For a history of the WRB, see Rebecca Erbelding, *Rescue Board: The Untold Story of America's Efforts to Save the Jews of Europe* (New York: Doubleday, 2018).

6 Executive Order 9417, January 22, 1944, Franklin Delano Roosevelt Presidential Library and Museum, Hyde Park, NY (FDRL), Papers of the War Refugee Board (PWRB), LM0306, reel 1, frames 2–3.

7 Paul McCormack, memo, March 13, 1944, USHMM, PWRB, LM0306, reel 1, frames 262–63.

8 Nahum Goldmann, memo of conversation with Long, September 16, 1943, USHMM, RG-67.011, World Jewish Congress, 107-D; Breckinridge Long, memo of conversation with Goldmann, September 16, 1943, Library of Congress (LOC), Breckinridge Long papers, box 202, folder "Refugees 2."

9 Jewish Evacuation Meeting, January 13, 1944, FDRL, Morgenthau Diaries, vol. 693, frames 187–211.
10 John Pehle, cable to ICRC, January 27, 1944, USHMM, PWRB, LM0306, reel 8, frames 668–70.
11 Johannes E. Schwarzenberg, letter, June 12, 1944, FDRL, PWRB, box 68, folder 4.
12 Unknown, cable to Winant, June 12, 1944, USHMM, PWRB, LM 0306, reel 1, frame 221.
13 Eldred Kuppinger, memos and minutes of discussions, June 17, 1944, USHMM, PWRB, LM0306, reel 24, frames 519–32.
14 Ibid.
15 John Pehle, Pehle memo to Roosevelt, June 22, 1944, USHMM, PWRB, LM0305, reel 1, frames 185–86.
16 Paul Squire, Geneva consulate cables, July 7, 1944, USHMM, PWRB, LM0306, reel 24, frames 490–91.
17 Schwarzenberg confided at a meeting that Red Cross delegates were allowed to visit Dachau, Sachsenhausen-Oranienburg, Buchenwald, and Ravensbrück; the visits were unofficial and tolerated by the camp commandants. He feared that asking formal permission would restrict their access to these camps. Howard Elting Jr., memo of meeting, July 4, 1944, FDRL, PWRB, box 68, folder 4.
18 Edward Stettinius, cable to Bern about relief packages, July 31, 1944, USHMM, PWRB, LM0305, reel 1, frames 166–68.
19 Franklin Roosevelt, memo on relief package program, September 12, 1944, USHMM, PWRB, LM0306, reel 24, frame 772.
20 H. B. Livingston, letter from British consulate in Geneva to Elting, August 9, 1944, FDRL, PWRB, box 68, folder 4.
21 Leland Harrison, cable from Bern about package distribution, September 21, 1944, USHMM, PWRB, LM0306, reel 24, frames 919–21.
22 The Joint decided to donate $15,000 and the WRB reimbursed the remaining $26,475. Moses Leavitt, letter, September 7, 1944, USHMM, PWRB, LM0306, reel 24, frames 751–52.
23 Henrietta Buchman, memo, August 11, 1944, Joint Distribution Committee Archive, New York (JDC), Collection: 1945–1954: New York Records of the American Jewish Joint Distribution Committee (JDC)—NY 45–54, Sub Collection: Administration—NY 45–54/1, File 00193_1108; JDC.
24 Henrietta Buchman, order paperwork, August 14, 1944, USHMM, PWRB, LM0306, reel 24, frame 628.

25 Ibid.

26 John Pehle, letter to the Office of Price Administration, August 16, 1944, USHMM, PWRB, LM0305, reel 1, frames 161–62. John Pehle and Paul McCormack, letter to the Office of Price Administration, August 23, 1944, USHMM, PWRB, LM0306, reel 24, frames 587–588.

27 Henry Morgenthau Jr., "Group" meeting, August 22, 1944, LOC, Morgenthau Diaries, vol. 764, frames 47–75.

28 Roswell McClelland, cable 6263, September 21, 1944, USHMM, PWRB, LM0306, reel 24, frames 919–21.

29 Roswell McClelland, note to Reagan about pharmaceutical supplies, November 17, 1944, FDRL, PWRB, box 68, folder 5.

30 International Committee of the Red Cross, letter to McClelland with pharmaceutical lists, November 24, 1944, FDRL, PWRB, box 68, folder 5.

31 Herschel Johnson, cable from Stockholm about supplies to Pruszków, November 1, 1944, USHMM, PWRB, LM0306, reel 24, frame 795. Cordell Hull, cable to London, September 12, 1944, USHMM, PWRB, LM0306, reel 24, frames 769–70.

32 Paul McCormack, memo to Hodel, October 21, 1944, USHMM, PWRB, LM0306, reel 24, frames 828–29.

33 Ralph Stoddard, letter from American Red Cross, December 26, 1944, USHMM, PWRB, LM0306, reel 25, frames 18–19.

34 Arnold Feinberg, Feinberg Kosher Sausage Co., asks for letter, January 23, 1945, USHMM, PWRB, LM0306, reel 25, frame 172.

35 Paul McCormack, memo to the file, November 27, 1944, USHMM, PWRB, LM0306, reel 25, frame 92.

36 A. Leon Kubowitzki, letter from the World Jewish Congress, October 24, 1944, USHMM, PWRB, LM0306, reel 24, frame 823.

37 Roswell McClelland, note to Schwarzenberg, November 22, 1944, FDRL, PWRB, box 68, folder 5.

38 Roswell McClelland, cable from McClelland, September 9, 1944, USHMM, PWRB, LM0306, reel 24, frame 776.

39 J. Klahr Huddle, cable from Bern, December 16, 1944, USHMM, PWRB, LM0306, reel 25, frames 37–38.

40 James Mann, letter to Pehle, January 13, 1945, USHMM, PWRB, LM0305, reel 15, frames 873–912.

41 A. Leon Kubowitzki, Kubowitzki asks Pehle to support WJC relief package program, September 22, 1944, USHMM, PWRB, LM0306, reel 24, frames 844. Cf. the discussion of Swedish relief efforts by Pontus Rudberg, this volume.

42 John Pehle, draft memo to Stettinius, October 25, 1944, USHMM, PWRB, LM0306, reel 24, frames 840–41.

43 Kurt Grossmann, letter to McCormack, October 27, 1944, USHMM, PWRB, LM0306, reel 24, frame 807.

44 Roswell McClelland, handwritten notes, January 8, 1945, FDRL, PWRB, box 68, folder 5.

45 J. Klahr Huddle, cable from Bern, January 22, 1945, USHMM, PWRB, LM0306, reel 25, frames 174–76.

46 Florence Hodel, memo to the file, February 1, 1945, USHMM, PWRB, LM0306, reel 46, frame 194.

47 Allied Air Forces, "Effect of Allied Bombings of German Transportation System," February 27, 1945, LOC, Morgenthau Diaries, vol. 823, frames 174–76.

48 Paul McCormack and Benjamin Akzin, memo urging procurement of trucks, February 10, 1945, USHMM, PWRB, LM0306, reel 17, frames 190–91.

49 William O'Dwyer, minutes of the Fifth War Refuge Board meeting, February 28, 1945, LOC, Morgenthau Diaries, vol. 823, frames 233–34.

50 Carl Burckhardt, letter to Leland Harrison, February 19, 1945, FDRL, PWRB, box 68, folder 6.

51 Leland Harrison, cable from Bern, February 24, 1945, USHMM, PWRB, LM0305, reel 23, frames 49–50.

52 Joseph Grew, cable to Bern, February 23, 1945, USHMM, PWRB, LM0306, reel 17, frames 163–67.

53 Roswell McClelland, letters to Red Cross, February 28, 1945, FDRL, PWRB, box 68, folder 6.

54 John McCloy, cable to Eisenhower, March 8, 1945, USHMM, PWRB, LM0306, reel 17, frames 140–41. Florence Hodel, memo to the file about trucks and gasoline, March 9, 1945, USHMM, PWRB, LM0306, reel 17, frame 134.

55 Leland Harrison, cable from Bern, March 24, 1945, USHMM, PWRB, LM0306, reel 17, frames 260–62.

56 Roswell McClelland, cable from Bern, March 23, 1945, USHMM, PWRB, LM0306, reel 17, frame 268.

57 Leland Harrison, cable from Bern, March 22, 1945, USHMM, PWRB, LM0306, reel 17, frames 275–77.

58 James Mann, letter to Hodel, April 9, 1945, USHMM, PWRB, LM0306, reel 17, frames 403–10.

59 William O'Dwyer, transcript of phone conversation, March 29, 1945, USHMM, PWRB, LM0306, reel 17, frames 229–36.
60 Leland Harrison, cable from Bern to Paris, April 4, 1945, FDRL, PWRB, box 68, folder 9.
61 J. E. Schwarzenberg, letter to McClelland, March 16, 1945, FDRL, PWRB, box 68, folder 7.
62 Roswell McClelland, letter to Riegner, April 13, 1945, FDRL, PWRB, box 71, folder 3.
63 Edward Stettinius, cable to London, November 10, 1944, USHMM, PWRB, LM0306, reel 24, frames 960–61.
64 Franklin Roosevelt, memo approving food packages, January 31, 1945, USHMM, PWRB, LM0306, reel 25, frame 150.
65 Florence Hodel, memo to Mack, January 31, 1945, USHMM, LM0306, reel 25, frames 143–48.
66 Joseph Grew, cable to London March 1, 1945, USHMM, LM0306, reel 25, frames 399–400.
67 Franklin Roosevelt, letter to O'Dwyer, April 5, 1945, USHMM, LM0306, reel 25, frame 478.
68 William O'Dwyer, letter to Pehle, April 6, 1945, USHMM, LM0306, reel 25, frame 468.
69 Florence Hodel, memo for the file, April 10, 1945, USHMM, LM0306, reel 25, frames 961–62.
70 Harrison Gerhardt, letter to McCloy, March 30, 1945, USHMM, LM0306, reel 25, frames 987–88.
71 Florence Hodel, memo, April 6, 1945, USHMM, PWRB, LM0306, reel 17, frames 199–200.
72 Leland Harrison, cable from Bern, April 6, 1945, USHMM, PWRB, LM0306, reel 25, frame 981.
73 Leland Harrison, cable from Bern, April 10, 1945, USHMM, LM0306, reel 25, frames 964–65.
74 Basil O'Connor, letter, April 20, 1945, USHMM, LM0306, reel 25, frame 942.
75 Leland Harrison, cable from Bern, April 25, 1945, USHMM, PWRB, LM0306, reel 17, frames 345–47.
76 William O'Dwyer, letter to the United Nations Relief and Rehabilitation Administration, June 12, 1945, USHMM, PWRB, LM0306, reel 25, frame 917.
77 Herschel Johnson, cable from Stockholm, June 8, 1945, USHMM, LM0306, reel 25, frames 548–49.

78 USHMM, RG-58.002M, Selected records from the International Committee of the Red Cross. Division Assistance Spéciale, "Logistique et transport, 1940–1946," reel 10.
79 Roswell McClelland, cable from Bern, June 20, 1945, USHMM, LM0306, reel 25, frames 543–46.

II

UNDER REGIMES ALIGNED WITH NAZI GERMANY

7

JEWISH FOOD AID IN VICHY'S INTERNMENT CAMPS, JUNE 1940–NOVEMBER 1942

LAURIE A. DRAKE

Hunger defined daily life for internees inside Vichy's internment camps. Testimonies, memoirs, and excerpts of letters sent from the camps attest to the regime's inability to adequately feed those it interned. For instance, Arthur Koestler, the well-known Jewish Hungarian writer and journalist who spent time at the Le Vernet internment camp, wrote in his memoir, "The nourishment provided by the camp was just sufficient to keep a man alive in a state of permanent, aching, stomach-burning hunger, with constant day-dreams of food."[1] Rudolf Herschmann, an internee at Rivesaltes, complained in a letter, "The staff at the camp hate us so much that they want us to die of hunger."[2] Another internee from Rieucros used humor to describe her woeful situation, "Here life is quite gay, they've put us on a jockey diet. When we leave, we'll be as thin as cigarette paper."[3]

Yet, while hunger reigned in Vichy's camps, famine never occurred due to the important role that international aid organizations played in providing food relief to detainees. In other words, the help provided from abroad was instrumental in ensuring that illness and inanition rather than death characterized the degree of food shortages for most detainees.[4]

The role of providing relief to internees fell primarily to international organizations, which had two key advantages that facilitated work in the camps.[5] First, they had financial resources that made it possible for them to purchase much-needed supplies within France and occasionally on the international market. Second, since they came from abroad, these organizations could more easily deliver help to individuals and groups that the regime had socially excluded

Prisoners in Rivesaltes line up at a food distribution point, March–May 1942. Courtesy of Simone Weil Lipman, United States Holocaust Memorial Museum, Acc. 1990.184.15, photo 80168.

and then detained. Vichy welcomed this international support for internees so long as the organizations refrained from publicly criticizing the new regime and agreed to distribute its resources to those most in need, regardless of faith, ethnicity, or nationality.[6] For many organizations, this last requirement likely appeared benign and would have little impact on how they operated. However, these restrictions placed Jewish groups in an awkward position, since their fundraising efforts focused on asking wealthier members of their community to support their less fortunate Jewish sisters and brothers interned in Vichy's camps. Moreover, the hypocrisy of such a policy was glaring. Organizations understood that the camps detained individuals because of their ethnic or religious backgrounds, making it harder for these agencies to maintain the external facade of neutrality. Despite these restrictions, Jewish aid organizations found creative ways to work around this requirement and deliver aid to Jewish inmates.

In this chapter, I examine the strategies and mechanisms deployed by the two largest Jewish agencies working to provide food relief to the camps: the American Jewish Joint Distribution Committee (the Joint or JDC) and the Camps Commission. What particular challenges did Vichy's requirements create for Jewish aid organizations that wanted to focus their efforts on helping Jewish detainees? How did they react to these rules and work around them? I argue that until the beginning of the deportations in the summer of 1942, the adaptability and creativity of the Joint and the Camps Commission allowed them to become increasingly effective in directing aid to Jewish detainees. For the first six months following the fall of France, the Joint lacked clear pathways for supporting interned Jews directly. Thus, they strategically worked closely with the American Friends Service Committee (commonly referred to as the Quakers), a Christian philanthropic group with aid workers already embedded in the internment camps, to ensure that their help reached Jewish internees. In some instances, this sufficed, for a few camps held mostly Jewish detainees. In other cases where a camp's population was less homogenous, it would have been difficult to earmark these resources for Jews. As time progressed, Joint personnel found their bearings and identified loopholes that allowed them to increasingly direct their assistance to Jewish inmates. They achieved this by supporting the Camps Commission (Commission des camps), a Jewish-led French organization that worked inside the camps and with Jewish inmates directly to provide food relief. The Camps Commission drew on three schemes in particular: organizing and funding camp canteen purchases, creating an internee adoption program for Jewish inmates, and donating kosher food for observant Jews and for holidays. After providing a short introduction to Vichy's camps, this chapter explores the evolution of the Joint and the Camps Commission's strategies over time. Finally, the chapter examines Jewish aid during the deportations and, for many, the journey to mass killing sites.

Internment under Vichy

The Vichy government was born out of France's calamitous military defeat in June 1940, which sent the country into chaos. The armistice agreement between France and Germany drew a line extending from the southwest to the northeast, dividing the country largely into two zones. The German army occupied the northern half of the country, and the newly formed collaborationist government known as Vichy retained full control of the southern half, known as the unoccupied zone.[7] When Vichy's octogenarian leader Marshal Pétain came to power, he inherited a network of camps that the previous regime had used to intern so-called undesirable groups, a euphemism for foreigners. Initially, the camps held several thousand internees, including some 40,000 Germans and Austrians believed to be politically suspicious and several thousand exiled Spanish Republicans who had fled Franco's Nationalist government following the end of the Spanish Civil War in 1939. While the new regime freed some of these inmates, the government, fueled by mounting xenophobia and antisemitism, also went to work creating new laws that made it easier to intern new groups of foreigners, notably Jews, and increased the number of internment facilities in the unoccupied zone. Thus, between 1940 and the summer of 1942, Vichy's camps increasingly became sites of Jewish internment.

During its four years in power, the Vichy regime operated a total of twenty-five camps as well as over sixty small holding centers. Although the number of inmates varied throughout the war, at their peak in February 1941 the camps cumulatively held close to 50,000 individuals, of whom 40,000 were Jewish.[8] The other 10,000 internees consisted of Vichy scapegoats such as communists, anarchists, Spanish Republicans, and "asocials," a catchall term usually used to refer to women of questionable morals and individuals with political views at odds with the regime.[9]

As the number of sites and the size of their inmate populations grew, the facilities were transformed into "camps of misery."[10] Living conditions in the camps had always left much to be desired, but under Vichy they worsened markedly. In a letter written to an American friend, Mrs. Abraham described her first few days at Gurs:

> The camp was not at all prepared for the arrival of 8,000 Jews . . . and we had to arrange ourselves on the straw on the floor, always in fear

> that rats would jump on our faces. Immediately in the first few days, a serious disease, dysentery, broke out, and 15–25 people died every day. . . . Food consisted of a ration of dry bread, black coffee mornings, middays and evenings yellow peas, we called them marble peas because they were so hard as to be barely edible.[11]

Mrs. Abraham's experience was typical of life at the Gurs camp and of Vichy camp experience more broadly. At each facility, inmates lived in crowded barracks that felt like saunas in summer and iceboxes in winter. In addition, camps struggled to maintain adequate sanitation facilities. Internees lacked adequate latrines and access to clean water for washing and laundering clothes. As a result, typhoid, dysentery, and tuberculosis spread like wildfire, to say nothing of the infestations of lice, fleas, and rats that also raged. For example, the International Committee of the Red Cross reported that rat infestations had taken over the camps at Rivesaltes and Gurs and that the vermin gnawed their way through internees' clothes and sometimes even nibbled at their skin.[12] Yet, however bad these material conditions were, inmates complained most about their persistent hunger, which pulled at their stomachs and weakened their bodies. "Darkness, dirt, inactivity, cold, hopelessness does not kill a man quickly. But in addition, there is hunger and sickness. The food situation in France is serious. The refugees in the camps suffer from it not doubly, but three- or fourfold. . . . They get what remains from the poor table of their 'hosts'—the least and the worst," explained one internee at Gurs.[13]

Although food shortages plagued the country throughout the war, it was ultimately those confined to Vichy's internment camps who fared worst of all.[14] A study of diets and nutrition in Vichy's camps undertaken by the International Committee of the Red Cross and the Comité de Nîmes, a coordinating body that brought together over twenty different aid agencies working to improve life inside the camps, found in October 1941 that an internee consumed on average between 950 and 1,188 calories daily. This was well below the League of Nations' recommended average of 2,000–2,400 calories per day and significantly below what the average free civilian living in Marseille was consuming, which was approximately 1,760 calories per day.[15]

In theory, Vichy extended its civilian rationing policy to its internees. Thus, unlike the Nazis, Vichy never implemented a separate rationing policy for inmates.[16] Yet confinement by its very nature increased the likelihood of hunger. As sites of social and political exclusion aimed at cordoning off individuals perceived as threats to Vichy's national security, internment camps removed inmates' nutritional autonomy and transferred the responsibility of procuring food for them to the state. Given the number of people it needed to feed and the gravity of the national food crisis, officials never succeeded in obtaining enough food to feed the thousands of individuals interned inside its camps.[17] Part of this was due to the unreasonable burdens of German requisitioning, which removed substantial quantities of food from the French market.[18] To add insult to injury, the British blockade of Europe applied, now that Vichy was a German ally, preventing France from purchasing supplies on the Allied market.[19] In addition, most camps were located in small villages and often increased the number of people living in a given area by at least a factor of ten.[20] This demographic shock strained local food economies, which were often weak to begin with. For example, an inspector described Gurs, a large camp located in the southwest, as "a veritable little village with more than 3,000 inhabitants that dwarfed the town of Gurs, itself adjoining the camp, which counted a population of only a few hundred individuals."[21] Similarly, Le Vernet, an all-male camp located in the Pyrénées, interned anywhere from a few hundred to several thousand internees throughout the war, whereas the village itself only had a population of some 350 people.[22]

Given the hunger crisis that emerged, international aid organizations stepped in to fill the nutritional gap as best they could. Although it can be challenging to pinpoint the exact quantity of food donated by any one given organization, a number of reports written by various agencies and coordinating bodies point to the fact that relief organizations together played a substantial role in improving the material life of the camps and preventing famine. For instance, the combined volume of donated food sent to the camps by all aid organizations—a sum that exceeded 200,000 kilograms (nearly 441,000 pounds)—was enough to demonstrate its overall significance.[23] Another way to assess the importance of food donations is through their contribution to overall diets, which can be gauged at specific moments. For example, at Gurs in 1941, aid organizations brought or sent in approximately 20 percent of all food that was consumed in the camp that month.[24] The Joint was an important player in this arena, donating significant sums of money that at first bolstered efforts led by other organizations but later supported the Camps Commission. It is to the story of the Joint's early food relief efforts that I now turn.

Phase 1: Supporting the Work of Other Organizations (July–December 1940)

The first six months following France's defeat left aid agencies already working in the unoccupied zone scrambling to adjust, not only to the new political reality and the food and material shortages but also to the thousands of additional people in desperate need of help. The Quakers played a significant role in these early relief efforts since they were already working inside the camps when France fell.[25] They, along with other agencies, worked rapidly to support the 10 million internally displaced people who had sought protection in southern France from the advancing German attack and scrambled to find supplies for the 6,500 Jews that the Nazis had expelled overnight from Baden and the Saar-Palatinate regions in southwestern Germany to internment in the Vichy zone. In short, the volume of work stretched existing resources too thin, and Howard E. Kershner, the head of the Quakers, quickly realized that additional financial resources would be needed. Thus, in the fall of 1940, the Quakers turned to the Joint for financial support to bolster aid efforts for the camps. With the addition of the Jews expelled from Germany, the internee populations had become predominantly Jewish. It was time, the Quakers argued, for the Joint to take some responsibility and step in as the leading American Jewish philanthropic agency. In a telephone conversation with Joseph Hyman, the Joint's executive vice chair, Dr. Joseph J. Schwartz, the Joint's European chief, explained, "The feeling, not only on the part of the Red Cross but that of the Quakers, has been that the Jews can take care of their own group."[26] Hyman was sympathetic to these requests and did not doubt their sincerity or find them inappropriate. In a letter to one of the Joint's board members, Hyman clarified his views on the matter:

> This is not said to impinge in the slightest degree on the motives or the sincerity of the people at the head of the Red Cross or the Quakers. . . . There is no intimation that either the Red Cross or the Quakers would wish in any way to discriminate between Jew and non-Jew, but the feeling does come to us that, over and above what we do as American citizens by making our contributions to the Red Cross, we have a special job to do in many special situations and needs, and for Jewish victims, who no other agency is in a position to meet.[27]

Amid growing pressure to support aid efforts already underway in Vichy's camps, the Joint resolved to offer financial aid.[28] After initially considering an alliance with the American Red Cross, the Joint opted to work with the Quakers because they were "doing a good job and have developed excellent relations with the authorities arising out of the fact that they are helping the French population."[29] Although never setting down a hard and fast rule, the Quakers and the Joint developed a tacit understanding that funds provided by the Joint would be aimed at Jewish internees and Quaker funds would be spent on other groups of internees.[30]

The British blockade, which had come into effect in France after its defeat, further shaped the ways in which the Joint supported the Quakers' aid efforts.[31] The blockade prohibited Allied countries and organizations from sending food and supplies to France, and it also limited how much French currency American aid organizations could transfer. This meant that American agencies needed to purchase all their supplies on the ground in France, which was difficult since French francs were not easy to come by. The U.S. Treasury Department had only approved the Quakers to clear a maximum of 6,000 francs per day (approximately 180,000 francs per month); although essential, this was not enough to support the breadth of their activities in France. As Schwartz explained to his colleagues in New York, the problem lay in the fact that "the Quakers have not enough free francs in France to do any work among Jewish refugees in the camps."[32] In other words, it was not enough for the Joint to simply transfer American dollars to the Quakers, whose head office was located in Philadelphia. Doing that would have done little to help them reach the thousands of Jews in France. The Joint thus sought and received approval from the U.S. Treasury to transfer French francs to the Quakers working in unoccupied France, which it seemingly received with ease.[33] And so in August and September 1940, the Joint sent them 260,000 francs.[34] Another 500,000-franc donation to assist them with their camp relief efforts followed in December.[35] Having found a loophole through which it could support relief efforts on the continent, the Joint began canvassing its American network of supporters in search of additional francs. Between February 1941 and October 1942, they managed to acquire an additional 2 million francs through this channel.[36] Although it did not provide boots on the ground, the Joint cemented itself as a philanthropic benefactor that would secure critical support for those working directly with Vichy's Jewish inmates, namely, the Quakers, who distributed the food to the detainees in Vichy's camps.

Phase 2: A Coordinated Jewish Aid Effort for the Camps (1941–42)

By January 1941, the initial flurry of confusion caused by France's defeat and the subsequent establishment of a new government had been quelled. While the Joint continued to work with the Quakers to fund aid efforts in the camps in unoccupied France, other groups on the ground began to slowly wrap their heads around the reality of internment and the new roles they might play. For example, in January 1941, Albert Levy, Dr. Joseph Weill, and Georges Picard, three French Jewish leaders living and working in the unoccupied zone, formed the Camps Commission, which focused explicitly on supporting internees. The commission's purpose was threefold: to coordinate Jewish assistance efforts for the camps, to ensure more equitable distribution of aid resources, and to procure more food to send to internees. Picard, who became the Camps Commission's general secretary, set up offices in Toulouse on 7 rue Caffarelli because the major camps they worked with—Gurs, Rivesaltes, Noé, Récebédou, and Le Vernet—could be easily accessed from there.[37] With the creation of this new organization focused on aiding interned Jews, the Joint found a new partner to support. Thus, until November 1942, most of the commission's budget came from donations made by the Joint. For example, in 1941, it received monthly donations of approximately 250,000 francs from the Joint, which accounted for 90 percent of its operating budget.[38] The additional 10 percent of its funds came from the grand rabbinate of France, the country's highest Jewish religious authority.[39]

Although never explicitly stated in any of their internal documents, the Camps Commission was likely born out of the recognition that Jewish internees had more acute needs than other detainees and lacked easy access to family members and friends who could help them. As Anne Grynberg, a leading historian of Vichy's camps, has explained, the Jews inside Vichy's camps suffered from a "great solitude."[40] Most were foreign born and thus had few friends to turn to

Prisoners in Rivesaltes in line for food distributed by relief agencies, March–May 1942. Courtesy of Simon Weil Lipman, United States Holocaust Memorial Museum, Acc. 1990.184.4, photo 22138.

who were not being detained themselves. Furthermore, few French-born Jews at that time were able or willing to provide support for foreign Jews.[41] Vichy's antisemitic policies produced a sharp division between French-born Jews and foreign Jews. Until the deportations began, the primary goal of the French Jewish communities was to protect themselves, even at the cost of ignoring and sacrificing Jews from other countries.[42] Moreover, new antisemitic laws increasingly impoverished Vichy's own Jewish communities, making it harder for the minority that did want to help. The Statut des juifs (Law on the Status of Jews) issued on October 3, 1940, closed off top public offices to Jews and imposed quotas on other professions, and a subsequent law also gave prefects, local agents of the state, the authority to intern foreign Jews in camps or force them to relocate to remote villages where they lived under police surveillance.[43] Finally, in some instances, there was simply no Jewish community to mobilize for help. For example, in a report about the situation in unoccupied France, the Joint learned that "Perpignan has no Jewish community, no bureau of assistance of the Consistory."[44] The lack of Jewish people living in the region would have had serious implications for the thousands of Jews interned at Rivesaltes, located a mere eleven kilometers down the road. Without a clear community for these internees to turn to for help, larger organizations had to step in and develop programs and schemes to assist Jewish detainees. These programs included a fund to purchase supplies for internee canteens at Gurs, a coordinated internee adoption program, and targeted kosher food campaigns for Jewish holidays.

Supporting Internee Canteens

Initially, the Camps Commission, like all other aid agencies, became involved in large-scale food donations to Vichy's camps. However, because they were aiming their aid efforts toward Jews, they focused on providing additional food supplies to Gurs and Rivesaltes, two of the largest camps in the unoccupied zone with the highest proportion of Jewish prisoners. Still, like all other relief efforts, these donations could not be directed at any particular internees within the camps. It took a controversy over the administration of Gurs's internee canteens that began in the winter of 1941 to open up opportunities for the Camps Commission to more easily direct their group shipments to Jewish detainees.

The canteen system at Gurs was disrupted in December 1940 when Maurice Eisenring, the camp's director, curtailed its purchasing freedom.[45] Until then, the internee-led canteen system had provided detainees with a high degree of autonomy to purchase the supplies they wanted from the vendors with whom they chose to work. In addition, the canteen used the small profit it generated to provide supplies at discounted rates or at no cost to internees who lacked the means to pay.[46] Despite Eisenring's assertion that the new cooperative—which centralized purchasing—simplified matters, the changes proved problematic for the internees at Gurs. For one, it quickly became apparent that it almost entirely benefited the camp's personnel, who had first dibs on the inventory.[47] Second, losing access to local vendors also severely curtailed the canteens' ability to exercise control over what they purchased. Frustrated with this loss of autonomy, a group of internees wrote to the local prefect in protest. Nothing changed.[48]

Instead, the solution came from outside the camp. To circumvent the changes made by the camp director, Rabbi René Samuel Kapel, who was both chaplain in the camp and conveniently affiliated with the Camps Commission, created his own purchasing cooperative, known as the Coopérative d'achats (Buying Cooperative, commonly referred to by Kapel and the internees as the CDA).[49] Kapel asked internees to tell him what they wanted, purchased food using funds provided by the Camps Commission, and resold it to the canteens at cost.[50] Thus, the CDA went a long way in reestablishing the viability of the former canteen system and its support of Gurs's Jewish inmates, including allowing it to provide discounted and free food to those most in need. But more importantly, it gave the Camps Commission an avenue into the camps. The link between the CDA and the internees provided the Camps Commission with a way to send food and supplies directly to internees and circumvent the camp administration.[51] For instance, in 1941 the CDA at Gurs received food donations worth over 1.25 million francs (roughly $27,000) from Jewish aid organizations.[52] It also gave the Camps Commission a greater understanding of camp conditions and internee morale, allowing them to identify gaps it could fill.[53]

Given the success of this model, the Camps Commission recommended that local committees be formed in each camp and that they develop a comparable canteen model.[54] By the end of the year, internees had established similar committees at Noé and Récébédou, two camps located just outside of Toulouse.[55] At Rivesaltes, resistance from the head of the camp delayed the creation of a committee, but in February 1942 internees from the Jewish quarter launched the Comité de liaison des oeuvres (Committee for Connecting with Aid Organizations).[56] Although none of the committees at any of the camps gave overt instructions to favor Jewish internees, it is likely—given that the Camps Commission and other Jewish aid organizations supported their work—that this was one of the mechanisms through which Jewish internees received aid. In all cases, Jewish men chaired these committees and significant amounts of food aid flowed through them. That only the camps with large Jewish populations developed these *comités* further supports this probability.

Despite being an important success for the Camps Commission, canteens were imperfect solutions to the persistent food challenges facing all internees inside Vichy's camps. As Rivesaltes internee Sophie Caplan recalled, only those with money could purchase food from them.[57] Thus, even with the institutionalization of social committees that provided discounts and free food to internees lacking means, the canteens divided the camp population into two classes based on the availability of money: those who had access to funds and those who did not. As a consequence, a new scheme emerged that aimed to create greater equality between Jewish inmates.

Internee Adoption Program

Because of the growing gap between those with access to funds and those without, the Camps Commission spearheaded a new kind of initiative: an internee adoption program that encouraged Jewish communities in the unoccupied zone and abroad to donate money or send food parcels to a Jewish internee inside one of Vichy's camps. Not only did this scheme allow the commission to target their relief efforts toward Jewish internees in need, but it also alleviated the financial burden of supplying everyone with help. To facilitate the process, the Camps Commission collected the names of interned Jews in need of assistance, centralized them on one list, and sent out requests for support on their behalf to Jewish communities and organizations, both local and international. To ensure that as many detainees could benefit from the program as possible and to avoid having multiple donors send packages to the same internee, the commission acted as an intermediary, collecting the parcels and sending them directly to internees. From the perspective of the internees, however, the packages they received came from an individual on the outside who supported them. In this sense, the Camps Commission's adoption program did more than just provide internees with additional sustenance; it showed them that someone, somewhere, still cared for them. "Individual parcels were a form of aid that was almost as important for the boost to morale it brought as it was for the contents," one report explained.[58] To a certain extent this was true. As one internee wrote, "Our only glimmer of light is the mail and the hope of receiving a little package. . . . When the mailman has come without bringing any relief whatsoever, we are plunged into an even deeper despair than before; we feel like survivors of a shipwreck who have seen a boat, but who have not themselves been seen by those who are in safety and who could rescue them."[59] In addition to creating an important link to the outside world, the parcel program also provided important material support for detainees. For example, in their 1941 annual report, the Camps Commission proclaimed that through this initiative, 800 individual parcels had been sent to internees each month.[60]

Kosher Food in the Camps

Another way the Camps Commission directed aid to Jewish internees was by supplying the social committees created inside the camps with kosher food. Both Gurs and Rivesaltes provided Jewish internees with a special kitchen in which they could prepare their food. In theory, the government agreed to provide observant Jewish inmates with supplemental rations of kosher meat to replace the standard meat allocation. Yet this rarely occurred in practice.[61] Internees at Rivesaltes, for example, never received any kosher meats and fats; instead, the camp gave them more turnips.[62] The Camps Commission thus stepped in and attempted to locate and procure kosher food, mostly meat, on behalf of the internees.[63] It also sent packages with kosher products to internees at Noé and Récébédou, where no special kitchens existed.[64] This initiative certainly provided many internees with much-needed additional calories. However, faced with competing priorities, the Camps Commission struggled to raise the funds they required to fully meet the needs of these kitchens. For instance, the Camps Commission strained to set aside the 2,000 francs they estimated were needed to support Rivesaltes' kosher kitchen.[65]

Passover offered the Camps Commission and other Jewish organizations another opportunity to send Jewish internees additional rations. For example, in 1941 the Joint sponsored the purchase of 50,000 kilograms of matzot for Jewish internees.[66] Within the camps, the *comités* asked their fellow internees to donate money and worked to promote the celebration and register people for seders. Even though these seders were far from well provisioned, Pinhas Rothschild, an internee at Gurs, noted, "The most difficult Passover problem was already solved. Even though many supplies were missing, we were able to obtain matzot."[67] Under the supervision of Rabbi Leo Ansbacher, the internees at Gurs also produced an incomplete Haggadah, which they used to guide the ceremony that took place on the last day of the Passover in 1941 (Hebrew year 5701), in an area outside the camp that was large enough to conduct a prayer service for all the inmates.[68] Similarly, the Camps Commission also purchased fresh fruit and vegetables so that internees at Gurs and Rivesaltes could observe Rosh Hashanah and Yom Kippur.[69]

In the end, the networks built by the Joint and the Camps Commission enabled these organizations to send food and money directly to Jewish internees inside Vichy's camps and to circumvent Vichy's policies governing philanthropic work until November 1942. These networks, forged with Christian and secular organizations—as well as other French Jewish organizations and the internees themselves—proved key. Without them, the Joint and the Camps Commission would have had less success in reaching their coreligionists. The goal of much of this food relief work was to improve the material conditions in the camps, to help Jewish internees continue their religious observance, and, most importantly, to stave off death. Sadly, in this regard the Joint, the Camps Commission, and all the other organizations working inside the camps ultimately proved unable to save the lives of many of the camps' Jews.

Jewish Food Relief during the Deportations and Beyond

On June 16, 1942, the implications of internment dramatically changed for Jewish detainees. That day, René Bousquet, Vichy's general secretary to the police, agreed to hand over 10,000 Jews from the unoccupied zone to German authorities in the occupied zone. Although antisemitic legislation had been escalating since 1940, Jewish inmates found themselves catapulted into mortal danger overnight. The deportations that would send close to 11,000 Jews from the unoccupied zone first to Drancy and then to eastern Europe had begun. The initial 4,663 deported Jews came from Vichy's camps.[70] The police rounded up the remainder, sending them first to a camp and then on to the German authorities.[71]

On August 6, 1942, the same day that the first convoy of Jews left the unoccupied zone, aid organizations received a memorandum from the Ministry of the Interior alerting them to the deportations and notifying them that they were welcome to provide the deportees with food and supplies for their trip.[72] As they learned the news, a number of aid organizations, including the Camps Commission, the Quakers, and the Œuvre de secours aux enfants (Children's Relief Organization), jumped into action, sending food and money to the camps in advance of the next convoys. At Noé and Récébédou, for example, each deportee received a package from the Camps Commission containing 500 grams of biscuits, one can of sardines, 250 grams of raisins or prunes, 500 grams of dried peaches, 500 grams of almonds, 250 grams of onions, 250 grams of apples or pears, and 500 grams of olives.[73] The commission also distributed 25,000 francs among the deportees, probably thinking they could buy supplies as they traveled to the occupied zone.[74] Throughout the period of roundups and deportations, Camps Commission representatives also accompanied many internees to the train station, believing that their presence would help improve the spirits of the Jews being deported. In his account of deportations from Noé and

Récébédou, Georges Picard, the Camps Commission's general secretary, spoke of a conversation he had as he accompanied Jewish inmates to the train station: "Along the way . . . one of the internees told me that two months ago, he would not have been able to walk the distance between the camp and the station. He attributed his improvement to food and treatments arranged by the aid organizations working with the camps."[75] That Picard recounted this conversation demonstrates that he had not yet grasped the full meaning of the deportations.

By September 15, 1942, thirteen deportation trains had left the unoccupied zone, taking 10,614 Jews with them, 600 more than the number Bousquet had promised.[76] In the end, the deportations virtually emptied several of Vichy's camps. For instance, Gurs, which was located in the Basses-Pyrénées, held on average 8,000 individuals in 1941, but only 100 inmates remained by the fall of 1942.[77] Despite this, the Camps Commission and all other organizations continued to work in the camps until November 1942, at which point the Germans—who invaded the unoccupied zone—expelled all international agencies and funding dried up.[78] The Quakers, the largest provider of food aid, fled the country. The Joint also withdrew its funding not long after. Following the deportations and the German occupation of the unoccupied zone, the Joint's board of directors no longer trusted that Vichy was an autonomous state and worried that supporting Jewish leaders had become futile. Thus, although French Jewish organizations, including the Camps Commission, could continue to work, their sources of funding quickly dried up, leaving many of them unable to work.

Conclusion

Long before the deportations from Vichy's camps began, their Jewish inmates faced different challenges than other groups. They lacked important individual networks through which they could secure assistance. Meeting these particular needs would have been easy enough for Jewish aid agencies had it not been for the government's restrictions on targeted aid schemes. However, as this chapter has demonstrated, the Joint and the Camps Commission, the two most influential Jewish aid agencies working to alleviate misery inside Vichy's internment camps, refused to let this restriction prevent them from assisting Jewish internees. The Joint initially worked with other organizations, in this case the Quakers, developing tacit agreements that their contributions would be used to aid the camps' growing Jewish populations. However, over time, Jewish groups developed their own networks and became more sophisticated, identifying loopholes that enabled them to focus their efforts on supporting Jewish inmates. In particular, Jewish leaders leveraged a conflict between inmates and camp administrations to gain greater access to Jews in need. Jewish aid organizations also shifted tactics over time, organizing and promoting an "internee adoption program," which asked individuals who did not face the same restrictions as organizations to send parcels directly to identifiable Jewish inmates. In addition, they used religious holidays and kosher laws as opportunities to send in targeted food aid.

This chapter has, moreover, highlighted how national and local contexts shaped the work of relief agencies, which begs the question: to what extent is the history of aid better told through actions taken on the ground under particular local conditions than through the strategies developed in offices located thousands of miles from the crisis? To answer this, we must also ask how distinct the Joint's efforts were. Did Jewish organizations face similar challenges when directing resources to Jewish internees in other areas of Europe?

More fundamentally, this chapter challenges the dominant narrative of relief work in Vichy France. Most scholars contend that aid groups were balkanized and that organizations competed with each other for stature, often at the expense of serving the needs of inmates.[79] However, the story presented here showcases that this was not the case for every organization. Rather, this case demonstrates that the Joint and the Camps Commission explicitly sought to cooperate with others to ensure that resources could be allocated efficiently to reach Jewish inmates. They did this by being adaptable in their methods and by constantly pushing for new ways to put food in the hands of internees. They made a huge impact by staving off starvation in the camps but ultimately could not save the prisoners once the French decided to hand them over to the Nazis, who deported them to their deaths in eastern Europe.

Notes

1 Arthur Koestler, *Scum of the Earth* (London: Hutchinson, 1968), 119.

2 Rapport mensuel de décembre 1941 for the Camp de Rivesaltes, no date available, Archives départementales des Pyrénées-Orientales 1287W1.

3 Letter from Mme. Laballe to M. and Mme. Cartou, May 17, 1941, Archives départementale de l'Ariège (ADA), 2W2603.

4 Denis Peschanski, "Morbidité et mortalité dans la France des camps," in *"Morts d'inanition." Famine et exclusions en France sous l'Occupation*, ed. Isabelle von Bueltzingsloewen (Rennes: Presses universitaires de Rennes, 2005), 203.

5 The significant role that international organizations played in providing relief to Vichy's camps also explains why the bulk of their work occurred before November 1942, at which point the German military expelled most of their representatives from the country. Although French agencies could provide relief to the camps throughout the war, most did not, choosing instead to focus their energies on helping free civilians, who also demonstrated great need.

6 The Vichy government, working through its national charity Secours national, supervised and controlled the aid environment during the war by disbursing grants to French organizations and according permission to international establishments to operate inside the country. For more information, see Jean-Pierre Le Crom, *Au secours, Maréchal! L'instrumentalisation de l'humanitaire (1940–1944)* (Paris: Presses Universitaires de France, 2013).

7 The armistice with Germany divided France into seven different zones. The occupied zone and the unoccupied zone represented most of the country. However, Italy was given a zone of occupation in the northeast, the Atlantic coast was a military zone, Germany established a forbidden or reserved zone around Lorraine, Alsace was annexed, and a portion of northern France was given to the Military Administration of Belgium and Northern France.

8 Denis Peschanski, *La France des camps. L'internement (1938–1946)* (Paris: Gallimard, 2002), 16, 167; Anne Grynberg, *Les camps de la honte. Les internés juifs des camps français 1939–1944* (Paris: La Découverte, 1991), 12.

9 Although foreign Jews accounted for up to 80 percent of the total interned population in the unoccupied zone for most of the Vichy period, not all camps experienced this trend. Two camps, Gurs and Rivesaltes, interned mostly Jews and are thus commonly referred to as Vichy's Jewish camps. Other camps such as Rieucros and Le Vernet detained mostly Communists, anarchists, and so-called asocials. This distinction is important because when studying certain camps, Jews accounted for only a fraction of the interned population.

10 Grynberg, *Les camps de la honte*, 146.

11 Undated letter from Mrs. Abraham, Ludwig Strauss Collection, Leo Baeck Institute Archives (New York) (LBI), AR 11765, MF 1385.

12 "Rapport Dr. A Cramer Sud-France," 25–09 au 10–10 1941, Archives du Comité international de la Croix-Rouge (ACICR), B G 003 28–02.

13 Undated report, Gurs (Concentration Camp) Clippings Collection, LBI, AR 2273, box 1, folder 6.
14 For a broader discussion of the populations that suffered the most from hunger, see von Bueltzingsloewen, *Morts d'inanition*.
15 Rapport sur la situation alimentaire dans les camps de la zone non occupée et ses suites, July 1, 1942, International Committee of the Red Cross (ICRC) O CMS D-114; Étude sur l'État de Nutrition de la Population à Marseille, Première Enquête (février-juin 1941), ICRC O CMS D-142.
16 Gesine Gerhard, *Nazi Hunger Politics: A History of Food in the Third Reich* (New York: Rowman & Littlefield, 2015); "Alimentation des détenus," March 10, 1942, Archives départementales des Pyrénées-Atlantiques (ADPA), 72W15; Alimentation des internés administratifs, June 16, 1941, USHMM, RG-43.016M, Selected records from the French National Archives—Police Générale, F/7/15089.
17 Ravitaillement des centres de séjour surveillés, August 19, 1942, ADPA, 72W15; Approvisionnement des centres de séjour surveillés, March 23, 1942, USHMM, RG-43.016M, F/7/15089; Peschanski, *La France des camps*, 129.
18 Shannon Lee Fogg, *The Politics of Everyday Life in Vichy France: Foreigners, Undesirables, and Strangers* (Cambridge: Cambridge University Press, 2011), 4; Michel Cépède, *Agriculture et alimentation en France durant la IIe guerre mondiale* (Paris: M.-T. Génin, 1961), 356.
19 On the effects of German requisitioning, see Fogg, *The Politics of Everyday Life*, 4. For more information about the effects of the British blockade, see Meredith Hindley, "Blockade before Bread: Allied Relief for Nazi Europe, 1939–1945" (PhD diss., American University, 2007).
20 Approvisionnement des centres de séjour surveillé, March 25, 1942, USHMM, RG-43.016M, F/7/15089; letter from Inspection générale des camps d'internement du territoire to Docteur Alec Cramer, November 12, 1941, ACICR B G 003.
21 Rapport du 8 juin 1942 sur le camp de Gurs (Basses-Pyrénées), June 8, 1942, Archives nationales 72AJ/3000.
22 Letter from Le Chef de Camp to Le Prefet D'Ariege, May 31, 1941, ADA, 5W135.
23 Rapport sur les activités des Quakers dans les camps d'internement et d'hébergement de 1941 à 1943, September 29, 1943, USHMM RG-67.007, American Friends Service Comittee (AFSC), box 57, folder 17; USHMM RG-43.025M, General Association of Jews in France (Union

général des Isréalites de France), Camps Commission (Commission des Camps), reel 59, 6J39 2 Mi 2/59.

24 Préfet de l'Ariège to Gestionnaire de camp, August 21, 1941, ADA, 5W135; Rapport sur les activités des Quakers dans les camps d'internement et d'hébergement de 1941 à 1943, September 29, 1943, USHMM RG-67.007, AFSC, box 57, folder 17; Kenneth Mouré, "Food Rationing and the Black Market in France (1940–1944)," *French History* 24, no. 2 (2010).

25 The Quakers opened their European office in January 1939, when Howard E. Kershner and his team arrived to provide aid to Spain, which was reeling from a civil war. When the refugee crisis spread into France, Kershner directed the Quakers' relief efforts there and worked to improve daily life for the refugees living in Vichy's newly opened camps. As war broke out across Europe, Kershner decided to remain in France and continue the Quakers' efforts. See Howard E. Kershner, *Quaker Service in Modern War* (New York: Prentice Hall, 1950), 140.

26 Record of telephone conversation with Dr. J. J. Schwartz, August 9, 1940, JDC Archives, NY Office 1933–1944, 4.22 (France), Series 1, file 594.

27 Letter from J. C. Hyman to Mr. Aaron S. Rauh, August 14, 1940, JDC Archives, NY Office 1933–1944, 4.22 (France), Series 1, file 594.

28 Before being asked by the Quakers and the Red Cross for support, the Joint had already decided that they would not send staff to work in the camps. This was standard practice for the Joint, which preferred providing financial contributions over sending personnel abroad. Discussion with American Red Cross, July 23, 1940, JDC Archives, NY Office 1933–1944, 4.22 (France), Series 3, file 618.

29 Letter from J. C. Hyman to Hon. Joseph P. Chamberlain, August 14, 1940, JDC Archives, NY Office 1933–1944, 4.22 (France), Series 1, file 594; Memorandum on Activities of Foreign Non-Jewish Relief Organizations Operating in Unoccupied France, December 30, 1940, JDC Archives, NY Office 1933–1944, 4.22 (France), Series 1, file 594; and Discussion with American Red Cross, July 23, 1940, JDC Archives, NY Office 1933–1944, 4.22 (France), Series 3, file 618.

30 Memorandum on Activities of Foreign Non-Jewish Relief Organizations Operating in Unoccupied France, December 30, 1940, JDC Archives, NY Office 1933–1944, 4.22 (France), Series 1, file 594.

31 Although the United States recognized the Vichy regime diplomatically until November 1942, the British blockade came into effect following Germany and France's armistice agreement. The blockade prohibited

Allied countries from sending supplies to the unoccupied zone of France because they feared that German forces would requisition it. For more information about the U.S. reaction to the British blockade, see Hindley, "Blockade before Bread," chap. 5.

32 Memorandum of telephone conversation with Dr. Schwartz at Lisbon, September 12, 1940, JDC Archives, NY Office 1933–1944, 4.22 (France), Series 1, file 599.

33 French People Do Not Support Vichy Antisemitism, May 9, 1941, JDC Archives, NY Office 1933–1944, 4.22 (France), Series 1, file 595.

34 Letter from Joseph J. Schwartz to Mr. Morris C. Proper, October 9, 1940, JDC Archives, NY Office 1933–1944, 4.22 (France), Series 1, file 594.

35 Outgoing cable to JDC Lisbon, December 12, 1940, JDC Archives, NY Office 1933–1944, 4.22 (France), Series 1, file 594.

36 Memo AJDC, Marseille to AJDC Lisbon, April 4, 1941, JDC Archives, NY Office 1933–1944, 4.22 (France), Series 1, file 599; Record of French Deposits, JDC Archives, NY Office 1933–1944, 4.22 (France), Series 1, file 600.

37 Rapport sur l'activité de la commission des camps pendant l'année 1941, no date available, USHMM, RG-43.025M, reel 1, 2Mi 2/23.

38 Ibid.; Amounts Paid to Various Agencies, December 31, 1941, JDC Archives, NY Office 1933–1944, 4.22 (France), Series 1, file 595.

39 The Joint continued to support the work of other organizations working to help Jewish people. Translation of Camps Commission, June 11, 1941, JDC Archives, NY Office 1933–1944, 4.22 (France), Series 3, file 619; Amounts Paid to Various Agencies, Dec. 31, 1941, JDC Archives, NY Office 1933–1944, 4.22 (France), Series 1, file 595.

40 Grynberg, *Les camps de la honte*, 11.

41 Yehuda Bauer, *American Jewry and the Holocaust: The American Joint Distribution Committee, 1939–1945* (Detroit: Wayne State University Press, 1981), 155.

42 Jacques Adler, *The Jews of Paris and the Final Solution: Communal Response and Internal Conflicts, 1940–1944* (New York: Oxford University Press, 1987).

43 For more information, see Michael R. Marrus and Robert O. Paxton, *Vichy France and the Jews* (Stanford: Stanford University Press, 1981), chaps. 1–3.

44 The Consistory was the body responsible for governing Jewish congregations. It often provided material support to members in need. Exposé,

November 20, 1940, JDC Archives, NY Office 1933–1944, 4.22 (France), Series 1, file 594.

45 Eisenring rescinded the passes that had previously allowed internees to leave the camp to make purchases and refused to allow local merchants to enter the site. Instead, he instituted a weekly two-hour formal market day when merchants could gather just outside the camp's entrance and created a purchasing cooperative through which canteens could buy supplies. Observations concernant le camp de Gurs, dont certaines ont une portée générale, August 11, 1942, USHMM, RG-43.016M, F7/15104.

46 Observations concernant le camp de Gurs, dont certaines ont une portée générale, August 11, 1942, USHMM, RG-43.016M, F7/15104; Rapport à Monsieur le Ministre Secrétaire d'État à l'intérieur, Jan. 24, 1942, F/1a/4553.

47 Claude Laharie, *Le camp de Gurs, 1939–1945, un aspect méconnu de l'histoire de Vichy* (Biarritz: J&D Éditions, 1993), 206.

48 Letter from Préfet des Basses-Pyrénées to Commissaire spécial à Gurs, March 14, 1941, ADPA, 72W21.

49 It is unclear from the archival sources whether the old purchasing cooperative was repurposed during summer 1941 under Rabbi Kapel's leadership or whether a parallel structure with a similar name was created. Regardless, by summer 1941, an internee-led and internee-focused purchasing cooperative was in place.

50 Rapport sur le camp de Gurs, February 1941, Centre de documentation juive contemporaine (CDJC), CCXIX-39.

51 Tableau des secours distribués (en espèces et en matière) pendant la période du 1er juin 1942 au 31 octobre 1942, USHMM, RG-43.025M, reel 7, 6J4 2Mi 2/29.

52 Laharie, *Le camp de Gurs*, 207.

53 Camps Commission Report, April 1941, JDC Archives, NY Office 1933–1944, 4.22 (France), Series 3, file 619.

54 Ibid.

55 Translation of report on Camp de Récébédou, December 1941, JDC Archives, NY Office 1933–1944, 4.22 (France), Series 3, file 620.

56 Letter to the Féderation des sociétés juives de France, February 20, 1942, USHMM, RG-43.025M, reel 7, 6J4 2Mi 2/29; letter from Comité de liaison des oeuvres to Union des sociétés de bienfaisance israélites de Toulouse, February 20, 1942, USHMM, RG-43.025M, 6J16 2Mi 2/52.

57 Interview with Sophie Caplan, October 16, 1995, Visual History Archive, USC Shoah Foundation (VHA), testimony 5444.

58 Rapport sur la situation des centres d'hébergement et des camps en zone non-occupée, undated (ca. Feb. 1942), USHMM, RG-43.025M, reel 1, 2Mi 2/23.

59 Renée Poznanski, *Jews in France during World War II* (Waltham: Brandeis University Press in association with the USHMM, 2001), 183.

60 Rapport sur l'activité de la commission des camps pendant l'année 1941, no date available, USHMM, RG-43.025M, reel 1, 2Mi 2/23. It remains unclear how many people contributed to the program from abroad.

61 Joël Mettay, *L'archipel du mépris. Histoire du camps de Rivesaltes de 1939 à nos jours* (Canet: Trabucaire, 2001), 65.

62 Aumonerie des camps, Rapport de monsieur le rabbin Schilli, Dec. 5, 1941, USHMM, RG-43.025M, 6J16 2Mi 2/52.

63 Letter from Comité de liaison du CAR Perpignan to Mr. Picard, secrétaire générale de la Commission des camps, January 14, 1942, USHMM, RG-43.025M, 6J16 2Mi 2/52.

64 Colis cachère, Mars 1942, USHMM, RG-43.025M, reel 59, 6J39 2 Mi 2/59.

65 Letter from le secrétaire to Jacob Bloch, Ilot B, Baraque 6, August 11, 1941, USHMM, RG-43.025M, 6J16 2Mi 2/52.

66 Letter from Herbert Katzki to Rabbi Kaplan, March 3, 1941, CDJC, CMLV-10. There is no mention in the documents of where the matzot would be purchased. However, given how hard it was to procure food abroad, it is likely that they were procured from a local vendor.

67 The original file is located in ADPA, 72W9. A reproduction is available in Bella Gutterman and Naomi Morgenstern, eds., *The Gurs Haggadah: Passover in Perdition* (New York/Jerusalem: Devora Publishing and Yad Vashem, 2003), 9.

68 Tirza Oren, "Researching the Gurs Haggadah," in *The Gurs Haggadah*, ed. Gutterman and Morgenstern, 48.

69 Rapport succinct sur l'activité de la Commission de février à novembre 1941, CDJC, OSE B I.2.1.

70 By August 1942, Vichy had interned over 20,000 Jews in its camps. See Grynberg, *Les camps de la honte*, 142, 295.

71 Poznanski, *Jews in France*, 279; Grynberg, *Les camps de la honte*, 327.

72 Rapport (de la Commission des camps en date du 7 août 1942), CDJC, CDXV-54.

73 Départ des hébergées des camps-hôpitaux de Noé et de Récébédou en dates des 8 et 10 août 1942, USHMM, RG-43.025M, 6J16 2Mi 2/51.
74 Ibid.
75 Ibid.
76 A total of 38,206 Jews were deported from France to Auschwitz. Of those deported, only 779 survived. Poznanski, *Jews in France*, 287.
77 Report by Directeur départemental de police to the Préfet des Basses-Pyrénées, September 30, 1944, ADPA, 77W4.
78 Following the Allied invasion of North Africa on November 8, 1942, during which Allied forces took control of Vichy's colonial holdings, Hitler ordered his military to take full control of the unoccupied zone, and Vichy accepted the occupation. Shortly thereafter, German authorities ordered all international aid organizations to cease their activities and gave them just a few weeks' notice to leave the country.
79 See, e.g., Jean-Claude Favez, *The Red Cross and the Holocaust* (Cambridge: Cambridge University Press, 1999); Bauer, *American Jewry and the Holocaust*; and Susan Subak, *Rescue & Flight: American Relief Workers Who Defied the Nazis* (Lincoln: University of Nebraska Press, 2010).

8

JEWISH HUMANITARIAN AID FOR TRANSNISTRIAN DEPORTEES, 1941–44

STEFAN CRISTIAN IONESCU

The most extensive atrocities of the Romanian chapter of the Holocaust took place in Transnistria, an occupied area in the southwestern Soviet Union, located between the Bug and Dniester Rivers. Here hundreds of thousands of Romanian and local Jews were murdered or left to die between 1941 and 1944. At the same time, paradoxically, the Jews deported to the Transnistrian camps and ghettos had the highest survival rate among Jews under the Nazi sphere of influence. How was this possible? Many scholars have explained some of the reasons behind this apparent paradox. They focus on Romania's foreign policy opportunism or on the failure of the German blitzkrieg in the east in 1942 and the Axis powers' declining fortunes in the war thereafter. Scholars have yet to pay adequate attention to one of the key reasons for Jewish survival in Transnistria: the central role of a Jewish humanitarian aid campaign and self-help efforts.[1]

This chapter fills that gap in scholarship by exploring the following questions: How did Jewish leaders, individuals, and communities in Romania as well as international organizations manage to aid the deportees in Transnistria? How did deported Jews organize self-help efforts in Transnistria? In addition to examining the aid sent through the official channels, the chapter will investigate private aid organized for deportees by their relatives, friends, and acquaintances, although it is not always easy to distinguish between institutional and private forms of aid.[2] Building on a long and vibrant tradition of assisting those in need, the Jewish communities in Romania, especially its leadership in Bucharest—the Federation of the Jewish Communities from Romania (hereafter the Federation), the Autonomous Aid Commission (hereafter the Aid Commission), and the Secret Rescue Committee—and the Jewish leaders in Transnistria played a crucial role in the survival of tens of thousands of Jewish deportees and local Jews. Their efforts were complemented by the help of the American Jewish Joint Distribution Committee (JDC or the Joint), the World Jewish Congress (WJC), the International Committee of the Red Cross (ICRC), and the Romanian Red Cross Committee, as well as many individual Jews and non-Jews. They provided massive though insufficient material and financial aid to the Transnistrian camps and ghettos and also tried to intervene with Romanian authorities under Antonescu's regime to alleviate the plight of the deportees.

This chapter first presents a brief history of the Antonescu regime and its antisemitic policies, followed by a discussion of the Jewish leadership in Romania and its efforts to help the deportees. It then investigates the Romanian authorities' responses to the Jewish aid campaign and local self-help efforts in Transnistria. Finally, we turn to the role of the leaders of Jewish deportees and communities in Transnistria in the aid campaign, as well as the deportees' perceptions of the aid they received.

The Antonescu Regime and Its Antisemitic Policies

The regime of General (later Marshal) Ion Antonescu came to power in September 1940 when it replaced the royal dictatorship of King Carol II. The new government adopted some of the most radical antisemitic policies among Nazi Germany's partners. Antonescu initially shared power with the fascist Legion of the Archangel Michael (henceforth the Legion).[3] His first antisemitic policies, aimed at disenfranchising the Jews and expelling them from Romania, were adopted in the fall of 1940. Although both Antonescu and the Legion were antisemitic, they disagreed on the best methods to address the "Jewish Question": while Antonescu envisioned a gradual and legal exclusion of the Jews from the economy and society, the Legion pursued a more radical policy. Eventually, their disagreements about governing methods and their desire to monopolize power brought them into open conflict. Supported by the army, Antonescu won a short civil war in January 1941 (known as the Legionary Rebellion) and ruled Romania until August 1944 with a government of army officers and civilian technocrats.[4]

Antonescu sharpened the antisemitic policies adopted by King Carol II during the last years of his regime when, in addition to a number of laws and ordinances, several pogroms—such as those in Dorohoi (with 53 to 200 victims) and Galați (with several hundred victims) in July 1940—were perpetrated by soldiers and policemen.[5] Antisemitic policies, including the pogroms triggered after the territorial losses suffered by the country in the summer of 1940 (when Romania lost Northern Bukovina, Bessarabia, Southern Dobrogea, and Northern Transylvania to its Soviet, Bulgarian, and Hungarian neighbors), became more radical in 1941. Jews were henceforth targeted in a further series of pogroms, such as in Bucharest (in January 1941, which resulted in around 120 victims) and Iaşi (in June 1941, with 8,000 to 14,000 victims).[6] The main reason for Antonescu's hostility against the Jews was his suspicion that they, in particular those located in eastern parts of the country, were disloyal to Romania and sympathetic to its hostile neighbors, in particular the Soviet Union. This was seen as a major security threat to Romania's national community and territorial integrity. He also saw Jews as economic exploiters of the nation.[7] Suspecting them of sympathizing with and actively supporting communism, the Carol II and Antonescu regimes blamed them for the losses and humiliations suffered by the country and the army when the Soviet Union annexed Bessarabia and Northern Bukovina without a fight in the summer of 1940. To recover the lost provinces, Antonescu joined the Axis in the fall of 1940 and took part in the Nazi invasion of the Soviet Union the following summer. During the first months of the war, German and Romanian troops pushed back the Red Army and engaged in mass killings of many local Jews and political "enemies" in what was known as the "purification of land." Antonescu recovered Northern Bukovina and Bessarabia and also acquired Transnistria, which was held under military administration. Transnistria and its camps and ghettos—so far 150 of them have been identified—became the dumping ground and execution site for Romania's domestic "enemies," especially Jews.[8] Around 186,000 Jews from the provinces of Bessarabia and Bukovina and from Dorohoi County out of 478,000 Romanian Jews were deported there by 1942. The whole campaign became part of Antonescu's ethno-nationalist and biological-racial policies of rebuilding and purifying Greater Romania.[9]

Antonescu envisioned different solutions to the so-called Jewish Question based on the location of the Jewish communities: while most of the Jews from the Northern Bukovina and Bessarabia provinces and Dorohoi County were killed locally or were marched to Transnistria in the fall of 1941, the rest of the Jews in the Old Kingdom (Romania's borders before World War I), Southern Transylvania, and Banat were subjected to antisemitic legislation, economic dispossession, and forced labor, but only selective deportations.[10] Run by inefficient, corrupt, and antisemitic bureaucrats, Transnistrian ghettos and camps became deadly places for the Romanian and local (Ukrainian) Jews, many of whom died as a result of mass executions, forced labor, disease

Jewish forced laborers returning home at the end of their shift in Transnistria, 1942. Courtesy of Yad Vashem, Photo Archive, Jerusalem, 3517.

(especially typhus), starvation, and exposure. Due to the changing tides of the war, Antonescu moderated his antisemitic policies, especially from the fall of 1942 onward, and refrained from any further mass executions. He postponed and later abandoned new deportations to Transnistria, allowed the Jewish organizations in Romania to send aid to deportees and repatriate orphans, and even permitted a limited immigration to Palestine. The Jews located in Transnistria continued to die after 1942 but at a lower rate, especially due to the neglect of the Romanian authorities. The deportees lived in terribly overcrowded camps and ghettos and suffered from lack of food, fuel, shelter, medicine, and health care. Beyond this, Romanian officials in Transnistria handed over some of the Jews to the German authorities in the nearby Reichskommissariat Ukraine, who used them for forced labor and subsequently executed them.[11]

The Jewish Community in Romania and Its Efforts to Help the Deportees

Responding to these radical antisemitic policies, Jewish leaders played a crucial role in the survival of parts of their communities. They skillfully navigated political and military challenges, continually petitioned authorities, and mobilized support from influential gentiles. Their efforts were initially led by the Federation under the leadership of the lawyer Wilhelm Filderman. Building on a strong tradition of philanthropy within the Jewish community, he established the Aid Commission, whose mission was to collect and distribute aid to the victims of fascist violence, needy Jews, members of forced labor battalions, and deportees to Transnistria.[12] After December 1941—when he was sacked by Antonescu—Filderman remained the unofficial leader of the Romanian Jews but continued his struggle to help the Jewish deportees. In the meantime and following the Nazi model, Antonescu established a centralized organization to replace the Federation and control the Jews, the Centrala Evreilor din România (Jewish Center), which also supported the work of sending aid to Transnistria. The Bessarabian and Bukovinian Jews who escaped the first waves of mass murder and the death marches to Transnistria were particularly vulnerable. For many of them, the aid from the Romanian Jewish communities proved crucial for survival between 1942 and 1944.

Most of the aid reaching the deportees was sent through the Aid Commission.[13] After Antonescu dismantled the Federation and replaced it with the Jewish Center, the Aid Commission continued to function formally within the Jewish Center but retained its autonomy. This happened even though the Jewish Center's director, Nandor Gingold, was initially reluctant (and remained hesitant) to help the deportees in Transnistria. Gingold claimed that his organization had no jurisdiction outside of Romania and that the Jews in Transnistria were Bolsheviks, which delayed the Aid Commission's relief operations.[14] Distrusting the Jewish Center, Filderman and several of his close associates and other Jewish leaders—including Chief Rabbi Alexandru Safran, Elias Costiner, Mihai Benvenisti and Wilhelm Fischer of the Zionist Organization, Freddy Froimescu, and Moses Zimmer—established a secret Jewish committee to aid the Jews. They collected funds from local wealthy Jews, international Jewish organizations (the JDC and the WJC), and the ICRC. At the same time, Filderman persuaded several of his collaborators—including David Rosenkranz, Moses Zimmer, and Arnold Schwefelberg—to remain part of the Aid Commission to help the Jews through official channels and to oppose, when needed, the decisions made by leaders of the Jewish Center, which usually complied with Antonescu's policies.[15]

Initiatives to organize aid for the deportees started in late 1941, several months after the mass killings that were instigated following the invasion of the Soviet Union and the beginning of the major deportations from Bessarabia and Northern Bukovina that aimed to radically eliminate Jews from those provinces; Antonescu only approved Filderman's and the Federation's request to help their coreligionists on December 10, 1941.[16] Bureaucratic inertia, inefficiency, and corruption caused many delays, and the first winter was the deadliest for the deportees.[17] Even after Antonescu allowed the relief program of the Jewish community to launch, some government departments sabotaged the process through various forms of administrative chicanery. For instance, in the crucial spring of 1942, when a deadly typhus epidemic was still raging among the deportees, on March 7 the Ministry of National Economy authorized the Jewish Center to send a shipment of medicine to the Transnistrian ghettos and camps, but only if they paid export tariffs; as a result, the first shipment of medicine did not reach Moghilev until two weeks later, on March 22.[18] Moghilev was a Transnistrian town through which most of the transports entered the province and that also housed the second largest ghetto, with a population numbering between 15,000 and 20,000 Jews. Struggling to cope with hunger, cold, and disease, the Jewish deportees felt abandoned during the first months by the Romanian authorities as well as by their coreligionists from the central organizations in Bucharest, as Siegfried Jagendorf, one of the heads of the Moghilev ghetto Jewish Council, remembered in his memoir.[19] Some of the delay was also due to difficulties in communicating between the deportees and the Jewish leaders in Bucharest. Such contacts were forbidden by the authorities and depended on gentile couriers. The Jewish Center members sometimes did not answer the desperate calls for help from Transnistria, as Jagendorf reproached the Jewish Center in a report from September 1942.[20] Due to the additional restrictions imposed by the Romanian authorities, such as those on money transfers and currency exchange, very little aid arrived from Bucharest during the first winter (1941–42), and a systematic aid campaign only took place from the spring of 1942 on. To bypass the obstacles to money transfers and currency exchange, the Jewish deportees and their leaders had started to use gentile couriers, often recruited from among the Romanian, German, and Italian civilian and army doctors and nurses who worked in or passed through the area to and from the front line. These couriers usually transported money and other valuables for a hefty fee.[21]

Such transactions were not without risk. The couriers sometimes did not deliver the money and claimed that it had been confiscated by Romanian border officials. Jagendorf suspected that this excuse was false, because those caught illegally transporting money into Transnistria were usually arrested and tried by the local military courts.[22] Sending aid to Transnistria could prove dangerous even for the Jews in Romania who wanted to help their relatives. Hers Ber Sternberg from Bucharest, for instance, was arrested and investigated after a gentile woman and her lawyer husband (the Melinte family)—together with a German officer—promised to help his relatives in Transnistria. The Melinte spouses claimed they were friends with Sternberg's sister and brother-in-law, natives of Czernowitz, who had been deported to Moghilev. Later, the gentile helpers blackmailed Sternberg, threatened him with a gun, and extorted money (200,000 lei) from him before denouncing him to the authorities.[23]

The Jewish leaders considered using other methods beyond the couriers. Crucial for Bucharest Jewish leaders' efforts to understand the situation and local needs in Transnistria was an officially approved delegation to Transnistria led by Fred Saraga, a Jewish leader from the city of Iaşi. Saraga first visited the area in January 1943 and collected information about the harsh conditions in local camps and ghettos. His report describing the atrocious conditions in Transnistria mobilized support from domestic and international donors such as the ICRC, the JDC, and the WJC—which sent money to help the deportees.[24] Jagendorf remembered how after Saraga's first visit to Transnistria, when he promised to help the deportees, the deliveries of aid from Bucharest increased significantly.[25] The material aid was usually collected in Romania by hundreds of subcommittees of the Aid Commission, deposited in several warehouses throughout the country, and sent to Transnistria by rail.[26] While controversy still exists over how those funds were used and how effective they were, most scholars agree that the aid campaign provided critical help in difficult times and saved many lives.[27]

Matatias Carp, the former secretary of the Federation, estimated that during a period of only two years, the Aid Commission in Bucharest, using funds from the aforementioned foreign organizations and funds collected from Jewish communities throughout the Old Kingdom, sent aid in the form of money, medicine, clothes, food, and other goods to Transnistria valued at 481,807,045 lei (the equivalent of $1,350,000). Beyond this, the Aid Commission delivered important quantities of valuable materials that improved the living conditions of the deportees and increased their chances of survival: 150 tons of salt, 300 tons of coal, window glass, 180 cubic meters of wooden planks, sodium, 10 tons of wire and nails, 10,000 shovels, and 352 crates of other tools.[28] The JDC sent the Aid Commission in Romania the sum of 25,000,000 lei (the equivalent of $70,000) between October 1942 and March 1943; 10,680,000 lei (approximately $30,000) between March 1943 and November 1943; and another $25,000 (the equivalent of around 8,900,000 lei) between November 1943 and December 1943. JDC funds were delivered with the help of Swiss envoys, the WJC, and the Romanian Red Cross. For 1944, the aid sent to Romania by the Joint amounted to $1,059,883, which represented a sharp increase from previous years. This was due to the collapse of the Antonescu regime in August 1944, which made it easier to send funds to help returning survivors.[29] The JDC also used Turkey and the Balkans as land routes to send material aid to the deportees in Transnistria via railway: on December 20, 1943, the Joint announced in New York that it was about to send parcels in January 1944, a total of 250 tons of food (flour, vegetable oil, dried fruit, and vegetables) and soap. The items had been bought in Turkey, and the Joint had already secured the Turkish government's export authorization. The shipment and distribution on the ground were supervised by the ICRC with the help of local Jewish committees.[30]

Itzhak Artzi, an organizer of the Zionist youth movement Hashomer Hatzair, was one of those involved in the aid operation for Transnistrian deportees. Artzi visited Transnistria in December 1943 as part of Saraga's second delegation.[31] During the war, Artzi also helped Wilhelm Fischer to organize an illegal network that sent money to Zionist activists deported to Transnistria, with the help of Nathan Klipper. A Jewish businessman who supplied wood for the German army in Transnistria, Klipper traveled frequently to the area and maintained good relations with local German officers. According to Artzi, most of those German officers were willing to deliver money to the Jewish deportees in exchange for a bribe.[32]

From the fall of 1942 on, the Antonescu regime implemented a less radical, more cautious and politically opportunistic Jewish policy, as he and his officials lost faith in a short and victorious German military campaign. Profiting from this situation, the ICRC took concrete steps to deliver aid to Romanian Jews from the fall of 1943. It was financed by funds received from the JDC and the WJC through Swiss banks.[33] The participation of the ICRC in the aid campaign evolved gradually as a result of Romania's involvement in the war and the willingness (from 1942 on) of the Geneva organization's leaders to aid Europe's Jews, in close collaboration with the JDC.[34] Constantly urged by the Swiss ambassador René de Weck to send a delegate to Romania who would investigate the fate of the persecuted Jews and help them, the ICRC initially adopted a cautious stand, aiming to avoid overstepping its remit and antagonizing the Romanian government. As a result, only in the fall of 1942 did the organization send a delegate, Vladimir de Steiger, to Bucharest. The organization started to pay more interest to the fate of the Jews in February 1943, when it asked Steiger to inquire "discreetly" about the conditions under which it could organize a relief program for the Jewish deportees in Transnistria—under the pretext of helping the suffering civilian population in occupied countries. Things moved slowly, and only in the fall of 1943 did the second delegate, Charles Kolb, obtain from the Romanian authorities concessions in favor of the deportees; the aid started to be distributed the following year, in 1944.[35] To that end, the ICRC enlisted the help of the Romanian Red Cross, the Jewish Center, and Jewish leaders such as Filderman. The ICRC focused on transferring money to Romania and delivering it to Jewish communities. The ICRC faced formidable obstacles in various parts of Nazi Europe, and in Romania, too, its relief activities often required breaching the legal provisions regulating transfers of money and currency exchange, exports, as well as other laws adopted by the Antonescu dictatorship.[36]

Alongside the ICRC, the Romanian Red Cross was also involved in the massive relief campaign on behalf of the Jewish deportees. Its president, Dr. Ion Costinescu, repeatedly intervened with the Romanian authorities for Jews each time his help was solicited.[37] Overall, the Romanian Red Cross adopted a favorable attitude toward the persecuted Jews, especially in the second part of the war, which was in line with the new position of the ICRC rather than adhering to the Romanian government's antisemitic policies. Its delegates accompanied Charles Kolb during his visit to Transnistria, and its network later helped with the purchasing and distribution of aid to the deportees.[38] On January 10, 1944, Dr. Costinescu announced that the ICRC would send 10,000 parcels (each of them containing five kilograms of food products, delivered from Turkey) with aid for the children interned in Transnistria and requested free railway transportation and tax exemptions from the Romanian authorities.[39]

Romanian Authorities' Responses to the Aid Delivery for Deportees and Their Self-Help Efforts

As part of Antonescu's broader antisemitic policies, his official stand toward the Jewish deportees in Transnistria and their struggle to acquire sufficient food, clothes, medicine, shelter, and income was to keep them under surveillance and confinement and to avoid spending state resources to support them. He preferred to direct all resources to ethnic Romanians, especially war invalids, veterans, widows, orphans, and poor people.[40] Antonescu believed that the Jewish deportees should work to provide for themselves and that the Jewish communities in Romania and abroad should send them financial and material aid. As I argued earlier in this chapter, the Jewish Center and other organizations and individuals based in Romania delivered aid in Transnistria through official and unofficial channels. While the Romanian authorities allowed and even encouraged such initiatives to deliver aid, they opposed unofficial efforts and tried to identify, control, and arrest those involved. These gentile couriers came from diverse backgrounds and were usually recruited from the people who had direct access to Transnistria, such as civilian administrators, the military, and clergy.

After arresting one of the Jewish Center's couriers—engineer Băcanu Sebastian of Bucharest, who transported money and letters to the deported Jews—Transnistrian gendarmes interrogated him and found out that the Jewish

Center used numerous other such couriers.[41] As historians Ion Popa and Ionuţ Biliuţă have shown, a few Orthodox priests aided the Jews in Transnistria but were arrested.[42] One of these gentile couriers caught by the authorities was a priest from Craiova, Marin Coşereanu, who worked in Transnistria until July 1943 and returned there clandestinely with money and letters for several Jewish deportees in the Balta ghetto (a medium-sized ghetto containing around 2,800 Jews).[43] Coşereanu enlisted the assistance of another priest to help with the distribution of the letters and money. Unfortunately, his new collaborator got scared and informed his superior, who reported the case to the authorities. They arrested and indicted Coşereanu at the Tiraspol Military Court.[44]

Individual members of the army aided the Jewish deportees more than the members of police agencies such as the gendarmerie. While both the military and the gendarmerie were riddled with antisemitic personnel, the latter had a direct role in guarding the ghettos and camps in Transnistria. Also involved in the general surveillance of the Jews and control of rural areas, the gendarmes perceived the Jewish deportees and their activities as a security threat. The gendarmerie was thus less inclined to help the deportees and was more feared by the Jews.

Individual civilians and military officials who visited Transnistria delivered aid to the deportees from their families and friends in Romania in spite of the authorities' measures to prevent such activities; these actions included bringing food, medicine, and especially money in the Romanian currency (lei), which was more valuable than the German occupation currency, RKKS (*Reichskreditkassenscheine*). The gendarmes blamed the Jews who received money from Romania for contributing to the growing food prices and inflation, thus making life harder for lower- and mid-level ethnic Romanian civil servants.[45]

The Romanian intelligence authorities in Transnistria kept tight surveillance on Jews and their visitors and identified many of the gentiles who aided Jews. Some of these intelligence reports confirm individual cases of material aid mentioned in survivors' firsthand accounts.[46] According to the reports, the gendarmes emphasized that Romanian and German military personnel were especially active in smuggling money and mail for the deported Jews, as well as in maintaining personal relations with the Jews. For example, the January 5, 1943, General Directorate Gendarmes' report mentioned specific ethnic Romanians—engineers, business owners, and artists—who were suspected of acting as couriers for the Jews.[47] Another gendarmerie report from January 15, 1943, mentioned the first visit of the Saraga delegation on behalf of the Jewish Center (and the Aid Commission), accompanied by a governmental envoy, to the ghettos of Moghilev, Balta, and Jmerinca (or Zhmerinka, a medium-size ghetto numbering between 1,500 and 1,700 Jews).[48] The delegation spoke to members of the Jewish communities from the three ghettos and provided material aid with a total value of 80,000 RKKS, of which 56,000 RKKS went to the Jews of Moghilev County and 24,000 RKKS went to the Jews of Jmerinca County.[49] These sums ultimately proved insufficient, if we take into account the number of Jews located in these ghettos and the high cost of living. According to gendarmerie reports from April 1943, this first visit of the Saraga delegation nonetheless boosted the deportees' morale and gave them hope for the future. The local gendarmes were particularly concerned that foreign diplomats and governments (as well as some Bucharest officials) were expressing interest in the fate of the Jewish deportees. They also worried about defeatist rumors—allegedly launched by the Jews—and about the impending visit of an apostolic nuncio from the Vatican.[50] These were not just rumors. Earlier, on March 3, 1943, Romanian diplomats from the Ministry of Foreign Affairs had informed the government that the Vatican wanted to visit the "non-Aryan internees" from the Bug River area of Transnistria and distribute aid. The Vatican visit eventually took place in the spring of 1943.[51] The SSI, the main intelligence agency in Romania, kept Red Cross representatives and the diplomats from the Vatican and other countries under surveillance and constantly reported on their moves and efforts to help the deportees.[52]

The government in Bucharest paid more attention to the Jews between 1943 and 1944 than earlier. This was due to foreign policy considerations and the government's worries about the postwar peace negotiations with the Allies, whom Antonescu believed were under Jewish influence.[53] As a result, the Romanian government sent various inspectors to investigate conditions in Transnistria. These envoys reported back on material conditions, including Jewish aid efforts. For example, after visiting 4 (Odessa, Tiraspol, Râbniţa, and Balta) out of the 150 Transnistrian ghettos in the spring of 1943, an envoy determined that while the first three ghettos were well organized and functioned in good conditions, Balta was in a precarious state. The envoy also reported that all the aid sent from Romania by the Jewish Center and the Aid Commission had reached its destinations but remained insufficient for the increasingly high cost of living. In Balta, the Jews faced added shortages due to local authorities' refusal or delay in paying them or the insufficient compensation they received for their work.[54]

The Romanian government aimed to isolate the Jewish deportees in Transnistria because of officials' concerns that information about the Jews' suffering and other "dangerous news" might reach the Allies or the neutral countries. Antonescu's officials in Transnistria thus censored the correspondence of Jewish deportees with their relatives and friends remaining in Romania through the

Schoolchildren (probably in the Zhmerinka ghetto in Transnistria), circa 1942–44. Courtesy of Reuven Bronshtein, United States Holocaust Memorial Museum, photo 48892.

police and gendarmerie and branches of the Jewish Center.[55] Such measures did not produce the expected effect, and the deportees in fact continued to correspond with their relatives and friends in Romania with the help of gentile couriers.[56]

Matching the trend of Antonescu's willingness to allow Jewish communities in Romania to help the deportees, even the government envoys who visited Transnistria became more sympathetic toward the fate of the deportees as the end of the war drew near.[57] They warned central authorities about the potential loss of life and asked them to improve material conditions in the camps and ghettos.[58]

Jewish Leaders in Transnistria and Their Self-Help Efforts

Several leaders among the Jewish deportees in Transnistria were able to organize relatively successful ghetto communities by providing housing, employment, and a variety of social services through their own efforts and with the help of the

Jewish communities in Romania, as well as by negotiating with the Romanian authorities. In this way, they contributed to the survival of many deportees in spite of harsh living conditions and the violence inflicted by Romanian and German authorities and local gentiles. Two of the most prominent Jewish leaders in Transnistria, Meir Teich and Siegfried Jagendorf, illustrate these efforts.[59]

Meir Teich from Suceava headed the Jewish committee in the Shargorod ghetto between 1941 and 1944. Teich worked tirelessly on behalf of his community in what he termed "a tenacious struggle for the organization of our own administration by peaceful methods of resistance," which would fit the broader understanding of Jewish resistance—under the Hebrew term *amidah*—adopted in the current historiography of the Holocaust.[60] Teich and his colleagues managed to establish vital institutions such as bakeries, canteens, cooperatives, and hospitals, which allowed many deported (an estimated 70–80 percent) and local Jews to survive.[61] In a 1958 autobiographical article that appeared in *Yad Vashem Studies*, Teich mentioned that in January 1942 the Aid Commission in Bucharest started to send them small monthly subsidies of 4,000–5,000 RKKS and that his community also received individual voluntary donations. Unfortunately, both forms of aid proved insufficient in the face of limited resources and great need. Teich argued that the material aid sent by the Aid Commission was more important than the financial subsidies, which depreciated in value due to the official restrictions. The shipments included commodities such as salt, kitchen utensils, clothes, and other items. Because those commodities were cheap in Romania but extremely rare and therefore pricey in Transnistria, the Shargorod community sold many of them to local Ukrainians for good prices (for example, salt was fifty times more expensive in Transnistria than in Romania). They were able to use the money for social welfare projects, such as building and maintaining an orphanage.[62] These aid initiatives significantly boosted the local economy by increasing the number of transactions with goods, services, and money between Jews and local gentiles and thus contributed to the survival of many deportees. Still, this commercial activity was dangerous since those commodities were supposed to be used in the ghettos and not sold on the black market and also because some deportees complained that they did not receive their rightful share of these precious items. Teich also remembered that his ghetto received large quantities of medicine from Bucharest, which proved extremely helpful in fighting disease, especially the typhus epidemic.

According to Teich's article, Romanian authorities visited Transnistria in November 1943 to identify "well-kept" ghettos, such as Shargorod. These were to be displayed to Swiss delegates of the ICRC as examples of Romania's decent treatment of the deported Jews, which resembled Nazi efforts to display a sanitized Theresienstadt ghetto to Danish Red Cross and ICRC visitors in June 1944.[63] Even though the Romanian officials tried to keep the Red Cross delegation and the Jews under tight surveillance, Teich managed to meet in private with one of the Swiss representatives, Charles Kolb, and gave him a detailed report with documents about the real conditions prevailing in the ghetto. Kolb provided those crucial documents to Fred Saraga from the Aid Commission in Romania. Saraga later visited Transnistria for the second time, in December 1943, to investigate the reigning situation in the camps and ghettos and to organize repatriation of Dorohoi deportees and the orphan children to Romania.[64]

The engineer Siegfried Jagendorf from Rădăuţi was another energetic Jewish leader who had a crucial role in the survival of many Jewish deportees. He managed to reopen a metal foundry and establish various workshops in Moghilev ghetto, thus offering jobs, food, and a chance for thousands of workers and their families to avoid deportation farther east to the deadlier ghettos and camps near the Bug River.[65] Using his professional credentials, his knowledge of German, his Habsburg Army war veteran status, and his personal charisma, Jagendorf functioned as the head of the Moghilev Jewish Council between November 1941 and June 1942. He persuaded the Romanian officials that he could organize the Jewish deportees into a productive, well-organized, and useful community. Obtaining authorizations for thousands of Jewish workers to stay and work in Moghilev, Jagendorf and his work crew repaired the electric plant of the city and public administration buildings, put the public infrastructure in order, and produced much-needed industrial metal products. Jagendorf sold or bartered the products of the foundry and the other workshops to various companies and institutions all over Transnistria. He thus obtained the respect and trust of some Romanian and German officials and acquired money and food for his community. Jagendorf was also in contact with the Jewish leadership in Romania, to whom he sent several reports about the Moghilev ghetto and Transnistria, and constantly requested material and financial help for the deportees. He and his colleagues managed to establish a network of canteens, retiree homes, orphanages, hospitals, pharmacies, and bakeries with the funds and the food products obtained as a result of their economic activities and with those received from the Jewish communities in Romania.[66]

Not everything that was connected with the reception of the aid from Romania worked harmoniously among various communities in Transnistria. The first winter (1941–42) proved the deadliest for the deportees, with a death rate of up to 30 percent in many ghettos. The deaths were caused by authorities' neglect and restrictions imposed on the camps and ghettos, deportees' disorganization, lack of aid, insufficient health care provisions, a harsh winter, and the typhus epidemic. In subsequent years, the death rate decreased significantly.[67] Tensions and mutual accusations sometimes reared up between various groups of Jews or between Jewish leaders.[68] For example, Teich accused Jagendorf and the other leaders of the Moghilev ghetto of establishing an unjust system of distribution of the aid received from Romania, which he believed favored the Moghilev community and discriminated against residents from other places. In a letter sent in August 1942 to the gathering of Jewish leaders from twenty ghettos and camps, Teich further accused the Moghilev Jewish Council of monopolizing the positions in a planned regional Jewish committee, refusing to consult with the representatives of other ghettos, and confiscating and postponing the distribution of money and medicine sent from Romania. In response, Jagendorf accused the leaders of other ghettos and camps of betraying public interests and abusing their position to obtain various personal benefits.[69] Beyond this, the leaders of the Jewish communities in Transnistria were always at risk of being denounced for their actions around the organization and distribution of aid and for corresponding with the Jewish communities in Romania.[70]

The Perspective of Ordinary Jewish Deportees in Transnistria

Survivors of the Transnistrian ghettos and camps remembered the aid they received as an important material and psychological support. Erica Antal was one of the lucky survivors. She remembered in a 2002 interview that some of her relatives (her aunt and grandparents) from Czernowitz who had managed to avoid deportation sent her money and clothes through a non-Jewish man who visited the Obodovca ghetto, where she lived with her family.[71] But not every deportee was lucky enough to have entrepreneurial relatives back in Romania who could organize help. Survivor Lya Schenker remembered that several Romanian officers brought aid from Romania to their Jewish acquaintances in the Moghilev ghetto. However, her family did not have any such contacts and received only a few items from one of their luckier relatives in the camp (personal hygiene products such as cotton wool, rubbing alcohol, and toothbrushes): "This was the only help we received in four years [of deportation]."[72] Survivors also remembered cases of unreliable couriers and failed attempts to send aid. For instance, Moghilev ghetto survivor Rosza Gotlieb found out a few years after the war that her cousin from Braşov had sent her a large suitcase with clothes, food, medicine, soap, and money, which was stolen by the courier, a soldier named Mate.[73]

Survivor Silvia Hoişie from Câmpulung Moldovenesc remembered in her 2002 interview that her grandparents from Botoşani, who were not deported to

Transnistria, sent them money in 1942 through a Romanian officer, who was paid for the service. Hoişie noted that many other people sent money to Jews in Transnistria and that even though such middlemen were paid, they provided "very useful" help to the deportees.[74] Another survivor, Frima Acs from Suceava, remembered how "after Stalingrad" her family in the Murafa ghetto received a package of food and medicine from their relatives living in the Romanian city of Galaţi.[75] Sarina Ionescu, living with her family from Câmpulung Moldovenesc in the Shargorod ghetto, also recalled that they received money from one of her father's high school colleagues, who lived in Bucharest and was contacted by a Romanian officer on leave who agreed to visit their relatives and friends. She argued that even though the officers and soldiers who acted as couriers for Jewish deportees received money for their services, they in the end saved the lives of some of the deportees.[76] Jagendorf also remembered the case of the ethnic Romanian businessman Ion Larionescu, who visited Transnistria under various pretexts in order to bring money to his deported Jewish friends and who also engaged in official transactions with the Jewish-run Moghilev foundry. He thus helped the foundry to consolidate its productiveness and contributed to the good reputation of its Jewish managers and workers in the eyes of Romanian authorities.[77] Sonia (Follender) Palty also reported in her memoir that her family and other deportees from their ghetto received aid from Captain Paul Constantin Virtolaş, a Romanian reserve officer working for the military justice branch. He was a non-Jewish lawyer in civilian life and the husband of Sonia's aunt. Virtolaş searched the region to find his relatives, bring them food and money, and boost their morale with news about his and other relatives' interventions on their behalf.[78]

The aid for the Transnistrian deportees was also organized by the few former Jewish deportees who were repatriated to Romania before 1944.[79] Judge Simon Hilsenrad from Rădăuţi was repatriated earlier thanks to his good connections to Major Dănulescu, commander of the Moghilev Gendarmerie Legion. He attempted to organize a transport of food and clothes to the Moghilev ghetto with the help of two policemen, but the Secret Service arrested him together with his gentile helpers. The two policemen were tried and sentenced to prison, Dănulescu lost his position, and Hilsenrad was sent back to Transnistria.[80]

Other deportees pulled off even more spectacular aid interventions. Determined to save his seriously ill brother who needed surgery, Mark Brandman—a deportee from Gura Humorului (Southern Bukovina) in the Murafa ghetto—asked a young Jewish woman to introduce him to her lover, the Romanian military commander of the ghetto, who put him in touch with a reliable officer. In exchange for a "generous commission," the officer brought the necessary medicine and surgical tools from Bucharest, which a Jewish doctor then used to perform the operation and save Brandman's brother's life.[81] This case also illustrates the crucial role of some Jewish women who engaged in relations with Romanian officials to help their families and friends. Navigating the complex borders between intimate connections, corruption, sexual violence, and resistance strategies, Jewish women negotiated the boundaries of antisemitic laws and local practices and contributed to the survival of at least some deportees.

Some deportees received crucial material aid such as tools, medicine, and household items even before the deportation started. For example, Sonia Palty mentioned in her memoirs that in the fall of 1942 her group of Bucharest Jews received assistance from the Bucharest Jewish community while awaiting transport at the local railway station.[82] This most likely happened because by the time of their deportation, September 1942, the local Jewish leaders were aware of what was needed to increase the chances of survival in Transnistria.[83] The Romanian authorities in Transnistria moved the deportees from one place to another until they ended up in a camp in the town of Golta. In the winter of 1943, the Bucharest Jewish community sent them six chests with food, blankets, medicine, and clothes.[84]

Social class and gender mattered a great deal in the Transnistrian universe. Czernowitz survivor Gertrude Reicher recollected that she worked for several dentists in the Moghilev ghetto who lived in much better conditions than her family because they practiced their lucrative profession in the ghetto, sold dental materials they brought from Czernowitz, and "received aid from their relatives back in Romania."[85] She also mentioned that she had asked the president of the Jewish community, a lawyer named Katz, for some clothes and shoes for her parents from those items he received from Romania, but he postponed filling her request and demanded sexual favors in return. Outraged by his request, Reicher refused the proposition and did her best to avoid the ghetto leader.[86] The deportees who were able to bring valuables to Transnistria, who had "connections" among Jewish and gentile officials, or who received help from Romania had a better life and higher chances of survival and could sometimes help or hire other (poorer) fellow deportees. This created sharp class differences.[87] Czernowitz deportee Klara Ostfeld remembered that she was hired in the Moghilev ghetto by the Kerns, a well-off family originally from Southern Bukovina, who received money from Romania and had good relations with the authorities. Ostfeld worked as a tutor for their children in exchange for food and shoe leather, which improved the material situation of her family.[88]

Conclusion

In spite of the tremendous difficulties arising from the lack of funds, the war context, an antisemitic central government and local administration, a mostly hostile or indifferent local gentile population, and a limited transportation and communications infrastructure, the Jewish leaders, individuals, and communities from Romania and Transnistria managed to provide aid and organize self-help on a massive scale for the tens of thousands of Bessarabian and Bukovinian Jewish deportees and Ukrainian Jews held in Transnistria between 1942 and 1944. In addition to the help mobilized by organizations, many individual Jews and some gentiles sent goods and funds to their deported relatives and friends. This critical aid was delivered in two main ways, through official and unofficial (or illegal) methods. Much aid undoubtedly arrived through the official channels—via the Aid Commission, the Jewish Center, the WJC, the JDC, and the local and International Committee of the Red Cross—and was transported by rail, trucks, and horse carriages to most ghettos. Such relief programs had the approval of the Romanian authorities. Yet the Romanian authorities kept Jews under tight surveillance because they were suspicious about aid transfers and potential negative propaganda; they thus imposed various export restrictions, sabotaged the communication between the Jewish communities in Romania and the deportees, and sometimes delayed, partially confiscated, or banned the shipments. Simultaneously, unofficial transfers, which are impossible to quantify, also delivered aid, particularly money and other easily movable valuables, to the Jews in Transnistria through a network of gentile couriers, often friends or acquaintances of the deportees or just benevolent civilians and employees of the Romanian and German administration and army. Gentile couriers were usually paid for their services. The Romanian authorities uncovered some of these illegal networks and arrested both their Jewish and their gentile members, and some of the couriers stole the money and valuables. Still, a considerable portion of this aid reached Transnistrian camps and ghettos. The delivery of individual illegal aid was organized mostly by the Jews in Transnistria or their relatives in Romania, who struggled to find non-Jews—usually civilian administrators and members of the Romanian army—willing to transport aid and correspondence to their friends and relatives.

While at first the Romanian authorities forbade and prevented such transports of aid to Transnistria, from 1942 on—and especially in 1943 and 1944—they proved willing to allow and even encouraged the Jewish communities in Romania to send relief shipments of money, food, clothing, and other items. This change of attitude toward the delivery of aid reflected a shift in the

Romanian authorities' attitude toward the "Jewish Question." Concerned about the outcome of the war and believing in the myth of the Jewish world power that allegedly controlled the Allies, Antonescu adopted a more moderate antisemitic policy. At the same time, the dictator refused to spend public resources to aid the Jews and wanted the deportees to support themselves through work or aid from their coreligionists in Romania.

The aid organized by the Jewish leaders, individuals, and communities in Romania and those located in Transnistria played a major role in the survival of tens of thousands of Jews. Such a massive aid campaign proved insufficient to meet all the needs of the deportees. Yet, the tireless work of self-help networks, deployed exactly at the height of the "Final Solution," shows the unique characteristics of the Holocaust that unfolded in one part of Europe's southeastern periphery. It also shows that when political and military circumstances permitted, Jewish leaders managed to navigate the complicated wartime context and regional power structures and deliver substantial aid to their coreligionists, thereby contributing to the partial survival of their communities.

The efforts of the Romanian Jews and their international helpers to provide relief to the deportees in Transnistria fit into a broader pattern of aid initiatives that took place all over Nazi Europe during World War II. Jewish and international humanitarian organizations from occupied, neutral, and Allied countries, such as the Joint Distribution Committee, the World Jewish Congress, and the International Committee of the Red Cross, all played a crucial role in providing aid for the Jewish deportees in many regions under the Nazi sphere of influence, including territories that belonged to prewar Poland, Czechoslovakia, France, Romania, and the Soviet Union. This massive relief effort—though insufficient—was part of a broader humanitarian effort that sought to mitigate the negative consequences of the war not only for deportees but also for POWs, forced laborers, and subject civilian populations by sending them relief aid, even in the face of huge obstacles, such as travel and communication bans, export and currency exchange restrictions, bureaucratic chicanery, surveillance, the difficulty of finding of reliable, trustworthy suppliers and transport routes, shortages, and crumbling economies and infrastructure. Despite these limitations, a massive effort to save lives developed from a long and vibrant Jewish charitable tradition and created a formidable network of "humanitarian resistance" to the Nazis and their collaborators.[89]

Notes

1 For the few scholars who provide a partial examination of the Jewish and gentile humanitarian aid campaign and self-help efforts, see Jean Ancel, *The History of the Holocaust in Romania* (Lincoln: University of Nebraska Press, 2010); Andrei Şiperco, ed., *Crucea Roşie Internaţională şi România în Perioada Celui De-al Doilea Război Mondial* (Bucharest: Editura Enciclopedică, 1997); Andrei Şiperco, ed., *Acţiunea internaţională de ajutorare a evreilor din România. Documente, 1943–1945* (Bucharest: Hasefer, 2003); Sarah Rosen, "The Djurin Ghetto in Transnistria through the Lens of Kunstadt's Diary," and Gali Tibon, "Two-Front Battle: Opposition in the Ghettos of the Mogilev District in Transnistria 1941–44," in *Romania and the Holocaust: Events, Contexts, Aftermath*, ed. Simon Geissbühler (Stuttgart: Ibidem Verlag, 2016).

2 The two forms of aid—institutional and private—are difficult to distinguish because they often overlapped, as in the cases when the Jewish communities sent help to Transnistria from the money raised from individual Jews in Romania. In addition, in their testimonies, survivors did not always differentiate between the communitarian and individual help they received.

3 On the Legion and its antisemitism, racism, eugenics, and violence, see Maria Bucur, *Eugenics and Modernization in Interwar Romania* (Pittsburgh: Pittsburgh University Press, 2002); Roland Clark, *Holy Legionary Youth: Fascist Activism in Interwar Romania* (Ithaca: Cornell University Press, 2015); Armin Heinen, *Die Legion "Erzengel Michael" in Rumänien. Soziale Bewegung und politische Organisation. Ein Beitrag zum Problem des internationalen Faschismus* (Munich: Oldenbourg Verlag, 1986); Constantin Iordachi, *Charisma, Politics and Violence: The Legion of the Archangel "Michael" in Inter-War Romania* (Trondheim: Trondheim Studies on East European Cultures & Societies, 2004); Mihai Stelian Rusu, "Domesticating Viragos: The Politics of Womanhood in the Romanian Legionary Movement," *Fascism* 5, no. 2 (2016): 149–76; Valentin Săndulescu, "Fascism and Its Quest for the 'New Man': The Case of the Romanian Legionary Movement," *Studia Hebraica*, 4 (2004): 349–61.

4 Ancel, *The History*; Dennis Deletant, *Hitler's Forgotten Ally: Ion Antonescu and His Regime, Romania, 1940–1944* (Basingstoke: Palgrave Macmillan, 2006); Tuvia Friling et al., eds., *International Commission on the Holocaust in Romania: Final Report* (Iaşi: Polirom, 2004); Armin Heinen, *România, Holocaustul şi logica violenţei* (Iaşi: Editura Universităţii "Al.

Ioan Cuza" din Iaşi, 2011); Radu Ioanid, *Evreii sub regimul Antonescu* (Bucharest: Hasefer, 1998); Vladimir Solonari, *Purifying the Nation: Population Exchange and Ethnic Cleansing in Nazi-Allied Romania* (Washington, DC: Woodrow Wilson Center Press, 2010).

5 On the 1940 pogroms, see Adrian Cioflâncă, "Informaţii noi despre masacrele antisemite din 1940," *Revista 22*, August 11, 2015, https://revista22.ro/dosar/informaii-noi-despre-masacrele-antisemite-din-1940 (accessed January 21, 2020).

6 See Jean Ancel, *Preludiu la asasinat: Pogromul de la Iaşi, 29 iunie 1941* (Iaşi: Polirom, 2004); George Voicu, *Violenţă şi teroare în istoria recentă a României* (Bucharest: Editura Universitară, 2006).

7 Stefan Cristian Ionescu, "Theorists of Economic Nationalism in 1930s–1940s Romania," *Nationalities Papers: The Journal of Nationalism and Ethnicity* 47, no. 2 (2019): 264–79.

8 On the findings of researchers for the United States Holocaust Memorial Museum, see Martin Dean, ed., *USHMM Encyclopedia of Camps and Ghettos*, vol. II (Bloomington: University of Indiana Press in association with the USHMM, 2012).

9 On the Romanian chapter of the Holocaust and Antonescu's biological-racial policies, see, e.g., Ancel, *The History*; Deletant, *Hitler's Forgotten Ally*; Raul Cârstocea, "Path to the Holocaust: Fascism and Anti-Semitism in Interwar Romania," *S:I.M.O.N. (Shoah: Intervention, Methods, Documentation)* 1, no. 1 (2014): 43–53; Chris R. Davis, *Hungarian Religion, Romanian Blood: A Minority's Struggle for National Belonging, 1920–1945* (Madison: University of Wisconsin Press, 2019); Diana Dumitru, *The State, Antisemitism, and Collaboration in the Holocaust: The Borderlands of Romania and the Soviet Union* (Cambridge: Cambridge University Press, 2016); Geissbühler, ed., *Romania and the Holocaust*; Heinen, *România, Holocaustul*; Ioanid, *Evreii sub regimul Antonescu*; Stefan Cristian Ionescu, *Jewish Resistance to "Romanianization," 1940–44* (Basingstoke: Palgrave Macmillan, 2015); Mihai Poliec, *The Holocaust in the Romanian Borderlands: The Arc of Complicity* (London: Routledge, 2019); Ion Popa, *The Romanian Orthodox Church and the Holocaust* (Bloomington: Indiana University Press, 2017); Solonari, *Purifying the Nation*; Jean Ancel and Ovidiu Creangă, "Romania," in *The USHMM Encyclopedia of Camps and Ghettos, 1933–45*, vol. III, ed. Joseph R. White (Bloomington: Indiana University Press in association with the USHMM, 2018), 570–84; and Marius Turda, *Eugenism şi antropologie rasială în România, 1874–1944* (Bucureşti: Cuvântul, 2008).

10 On forced labor battalions that drafted Jewish men for performing heavy labor, mostly in construction and agricultural projects all over the country, including in Transnistria, see Dallas Michelbacher, *Jewish Forced Labor in Romania, 1940–1944* (Bloomington: Indiana University Press, 2020).

11 Deletant, *Hitler's Forgotten Ally*, 183, 194, 275.

12 Matatias Carp, ed., *Cartea Neagră: Suferințele Evreilor din România, 1940–1944*, vol. 3 (Bucharest: Diogene, 1996), 278–79; Wilhelm Filderman, *Memoirs and Diaries*, vol. 2 (Tel Aviv: Yad Vashem, 2015); Arnold Schwefelberg, *Amintirile unui intelectual evreu din România* (Bucharest: Hasefer, 2000), 124–44; on the Jewish tradition of welfare, focusing on Bucharest women social activists, see Alexandra Ghiț, "Loving Designs: Gendered Welfare Provision, Activism, and Expertise in Interwar Bucharest" (PhD diss., Central European University, 2020), 181–94.

13 Carp, *Cartea Neagră*, 314–15.

14 Ibid., 278–79; Filderman, *Memoirs and Diaries*; Schwefelberg, *Amintirile*, 130–32.

15 E.g., one of the three secretaries of the Federation, lawyer David Rosenkranz, wanted to resign from his position when Antonescu sacked Filderman and replaced the Federation with the Jewish Center; however, taking the advice of Filderman, he decided to stay. Rosenkranz headed the Labor Department and later the Social Welfare Department (1943–44) at the Jewish Center and was involved in the effort to aid the deportees. This included visiting the camps and ghettos in Transnistria three times. Adina Rosenkranz-Herscovici, *Dadu: Viața și activitatea avocatului David Rosenkranz* (Sydney: Rexlibris, 2018), 21–22, 61–62; see also Schwefelberg, *Amintirile*, 130–32; Alexandre Safran, *Resisting the Storm, Romania, 1940–1947: Memoirs* (Jerusalem: Gefen Books, 1996), 91, 93–94, 119.

16 According to Chief Rabbi Safran, Queen Mother Elena had a crucial role in persuading Antonescu to allow the delivery of aid to Transnistria. Safran, *Resisting the Storm*, 86.

17 See Prime Minister Chancellery's letter sent to the Federation on December 10, 1944, referring to Antonescu's approval, in Carp, *Cartea neagră*, 338.

18 See the letter sent by the Ministry of National Economy to the Jewish Center on March 7, 1942, in Carp, *Cartea Neagră*, 349–50. On the deadly typhus epidemic affecting especially the Transnistrian camps and ghettos, see Ancel, *The History*, 395–416.

19 Siegfried Jagendorf, *Minunea de la Moghilev: Memorii, 1941–44* (Bucharest: Hasefer, 1997), 65.
20 See Jagendorf's report from September 1942, in USHMM, RG-25.004M, SRI, reel 10, file 2699, 777–812.
21 Dalia Ofer, "Life in the Ghettos of Transnistria: A Special Case of Genocide," *Yad Vashem Studies* 25 (1996): 229–74; Şiperco, *Acţiunea internaţională*; Jagendorf, *Minunea*, 68–69; Carp, *Cartea Neagră*, 284; Schwefelberg, *Amintirile*, 130–36.
22 Jagendorf, *Minunea*, 68–69.
23 See Erna Sternberg's petition, May 26, 1942, requesting the release of her husband, in USHMM, RG-25.004M, SRI, reel 10, file 2699, 772–74.
24 The JDC, which helped Romanian Jews during the interwar period, intensified its efforts in 1940, even though it faced Romanian authorities' increased suspicion and surveillance of nongovernmental organizations after the establishment of King Carol II's royal dictatorship in 1938. The organization was stripped of its legal status as a result of its efforts, and local organizations were prevented from receiving financial help from abroad. The JDC's activities were made even more difficult due to U.S. restrictions on financial transactions with "countries under the domination of aggressing nations" (as Romania was labeled beginning in November 1940, when it joined the Axis). It managed to bypass these obstacles and sent funds to Romanian Jewish communities through the help of the American Joint Reconstruction Foundation, the ICRC, and the WJC. For more details on the JDC's effort to help the Romanian Jews, see Natalia Lazar and Lya Benjamin, eds., *The American Joint Distribution Committee in Romania, 1916–2016: Documente* (Bucharest: Hasefer, 2017); Şiperco, *Crucea Roşie Internaţională*; Şiperco, *Acţiunea internaţională*; Doina Anca Creţu, "'For the Sake of an Ideal': Romanian Nation-Building and American Foreign Assistance (1917–1940)" (PhD diss., Graduate Institute of International and Development Studies, 2018).
25 Jagendorf, *Minunea*, 128–29; see also Schwefelberg, *Amintirile*, 132–37; Carp, *Cartea neagră*, 289, 291, 454.
26 See Schwefelberg, *Amintirile*, 132–35.
27 See, e.g., Ancel, *The History*; Deletant, *Hitler's Forgotten Ally*; Lazar and Benjamin, *American Jewish Joint*, 32–35.
28 Carp, *Cartea Neagră*, 314–15.
29 Ibid., 310, 314–15; Lazar and Benjamin, *American Jewish Joint*, 33, 258–62.

30 See the December 20, 1943, statement of the JDC, in Lazar and Benjamin, *American Jewish Joint*, 259–60.
31 Itzhak Artzi, *Biografia unui sionist* (Bucharest: Hasefer, 1999), 104.
32 Artzi, *Biografia*, 91, 99.
33 Schwefelberg, *Amintirile*, 134.
34 See the chapter by Gerald J. Steinacher, this volume.
35 Şiperco, *Crucea Roşie Internaţională*, 111–35.
36 Şiperco, *Acţiunea internaţională*, 8–328; on the crucial help provided by Steiger and Kolb, see also Safran, *Resisting the Storm*, 109–10.
37 Safran, *Resisting the Storm*, 68, 93.
38 Şiperco, *Crucea Roşie Internaţională*, 105–6, 111–35.
39 Lya Benjamin, ed., *Evreii din România intre anii 1940–1944: Bilanţul tragediei, renaştrea speranţei, 1943–1944*, vol. 4 (Bucharest: Hasefer, 1998), 290.
40 On welfare policies in wartime Romania, see Şiperco, *Crucea Roşie Internaţională*; Ghiţ, *Loving Designs*.
41 Benjamin, *Evreii din România*, 277.
42 Popa, *The Romanian Orthodox Church*, 61; Ionut Biliuţă, "'Christianizing' Transnistria: Romanian Orthodox Clergy as Beneficiaries, Perpetrators, and Rescuers During the Holocaust," *Holocaust and Genocide Studies* 34, no. 1 (2020): 29–30.
43 Ovidiu Creangă and Alexander Kruglov, "Balta," and Ovidiu Creangă, "Balta/120 Labor Battalion," in *USHMM Encyclopedia of Camps and Ghettos*, III:597–600.
44 See the Ananiev Gendarmes Legion's October 13, 1943, report to the Bucharest General Gendarmes Inspectorate, in Benjamin, *Evreii din România*, 274–75.
45 Cf. Benjamin, *Evreii din România*, 268–69.
46 See the March 1943 bulletin of the Transnistria Gendarmerie Inspectorate, which identified several couriers who delivered money and material aid to Jewish deportees in the Golta ghetto. Benjamin, *Evreii din România*, 233–34. See also the case of a Bucharest military justice captain, Paul C. Vartolaş, who visited the Golta ghetto and delivered aid to Sonia Palty's family and other ghetto inhabitants, which confirms the gendarmes' report. Sonia Palty, *Evrei treceţi Nistrul*, 2nd ed. (Tel Aviv: Papyrus, 1989), 94–99.
47 See the January 5, 1943, note of the General Directorate Gendarmes, in Benjamin, *Evreii din România*, 214–16; firsthand accounts produced by some of these gentile helpers confirm the gendarmerie reports that the

authors delivered aid (food and medicine) to the deported Jews. See, e.g., the memoir of George Tomaziu, *The Witness: Memoir of an Artist and Spy for MI6 during World War Two* (London: Theed Street Publishing, 2015), Kindle ed.

48 See Creangă and Kruglov, "Balta," and Ovidiu Creangă, "Moghilev-Podolsk," in *USHMM Encyclopedia of Camps and Ghettos, 1933–1945*, III:597–98, 715–17. On the Jmerinka/Zhmerinka ghetto, see Vadim Altskan, "On the Other Side of the River: Dr. Adolph Herschmann and the Zhmerinka Ghetto, 1941–1944," *Holocaust and Genocide Studies* 26, no. 1 (2012): 2–28.

49 See the January 15, 1943, note of the Transnistrian Gendarmes Inspectorate, in Benjamin, *Evreii din România*, 217.

50 See the April 19, 1943, note of the Balta Gendarmes Legion, in Benjamin, *Evreii din România*, 237.

51 See the internal report of diplomat G. Davidescu to his Ministry of Foreign Affairs superiors, in Benjamin, *Evreii din România*, 226.

52 See, e.g., the SSI's note no. 37274 of December 14, 1943, about the Red Cross representatives' activity in helping the Jews in Transnistria, including their meeting with Vatican Nunzio Andrea Cassulo and the Swiss ambassador in Romania, Rene de Weck, in Benjamin, *Evreii din România*, 285; Safran, *Resisting the Storm*, 101–11.

53 On Antonescu's fears that the victorious and philosemitic Allies would blame Romania for its antisemitic policies at the peace conference at the end of the war, see Benjamin, *Evreii din România*, 223–24; see also Ionescu, *Jewish Resistance*, 41–42, 53.

54 See the April 19, 1943, government note, in Benjamin, *Evreii din România*, 239–40.

55 See the March 12, 1943, letter sent to the government by the High Command of the Army and the Civilian Government of Transnistria and the September 12, 1943, report of the Gendarmes General Under-Inspectorate to IGJ, in Benjamin, *Evreii din România*, 227–28, 267–69.

56 See, e.g., Benjamin, *Evreii din România*, 267–69; Benjamin M. Grilj et al., eds., *Schwarze Milch. Zurückgehaltene Briefe aus den Todeslagern Transnistriens* (Innsbruck: Studien Verlag, 2013).

57 See the letter sent by Lt. Col. Gervescu (from the Bacău Territorial Recruitment Precinct) on January 11, 1944, to the Bacău Jewish community, requesting them to send thicker and more durable clothes to the Jewish forced labor detachment in Râbniţa, in Benjamin, *Evreii din România*, 291.

58 See, e.g., the January 1944 report of Inspector I. Stănculescu on the situation of Jews in Transnistria, in Benjamin, *Evreii din România*, 291–94.

59 Several studies have been written on specific ghettos in Transnistria. See, e.g., Dennis Deletant, "Ghetto Experience in Golta, Transnistria, 1942–1944," *Holocaust and Genocide Studies* 18, no. 1 (2004): 1–26; Rosen, "The Djurin Ghetto," 131–50; Sarah Rosen, "Surviving in the Murafa Ghetto: A Case Study of One Ghetto in Transnistria," *Holocaust Studies: A Journal of Culture and History* 16, nos. 1–2 (2010): 157–76; Iemima D. Ploscariu, "Institutions for Survival: The Shargorod Ghetto during the Holocaust in Romanian Transnistria," *Nationalities Papers: The Journal of Nationalism and Ethnicity* 47, no. 1 (2019): 121–35.

60 Meir Teich, "The Jewish Self-Administration in Ghetto Shargorod, Transnistria," *Yad Vashem Studies* 2 (1958): 226; on *amidah*, see Yehuda Bauer, *Rethinking the Holocaust* (New Haven: Yale University Press, 2001), 145–66.

61 Teich's claims about the good organization of his community, which enabled the survival of many deported and local Jews, are supported by the recollections of survivors from Shargorod ghetto. See, for instance, the interview with Sarina Ionescu, in Andrei Pippidi, ed., *Holocaustul evreilor români: Din mărturiile supraviețuitorilor* (Iași: Polirom, 2004), 188–89. See also Ancel, *The History*; Deletant, *Hitler's Forgotten Ally*; Gali Tibon, "Am I My Brother's Keeper? The Jewish Committees in the Ghettos of Moghilev Province and the Romanian Regime in Transnistria during the Holocaust, 1941–1944," *Dapim: Studies on the Holocaust* 30, no. 2 (2016): 93–116.

62 Teich, *The Jewish Self-Administration*, 226, 234–36, 244–45. On the importance of such commodities, see the testimony of survivor Bernard Guttmann in Pippidi, *Holocaustul Evreilor*, 164; see also Carp, *Cartea Neagră*, 315.

63 On aid initiatives on behalf of Jews from Denmark imprisoned in Theresienstadt, see the chapter by Silvia Goldbaum Tarabini Fracapane, this volume.

64 Teich, *Jewish Self-Administration*, 245–46; on the visit of the ICRC delegation in Transnistria in December 1943 and the Romanian administration efforts to beautify the selected ghettos and control the visit, see Carp, *Cartea Neagră*, 314, 316; on the fate of Jewish orphans in Transnistria as reflected in their early testimonies, see Dana Mihăilescu, "Networks of Sutured Consciousness in Early Holocaust Testimonies of Orphaned Jewish Child Survivors from Romania" in *Starting Anew: The*

Rehabilitation of Child Survivors of the Holocaust in the Early Postwar Years, ed. Sharon Kangisser Cohen and Dalia Ofer (Jerusalem: Yad Vashem, 2019), 145–69.

65 In addition to the Moghilev ghetto, the surrounding Moghilev region contained fifty-two smaller ghettos. Dalia Ofer, "The Ghettos in Transnistria and Ghettos under German Occupation in Eastern Europe: A Comparative Approach," in *Beiträge zur Geschichte des Nationalsozialismus* 25 (2009): 30–53.

66 Jagendorf, *Minunea*, 31–96.

67 Ancel, *The History*; Ofer, "The Ghettos in Transnistria," 38–39.

68 Ofer, "The Ghettos in Transnistria," 30–53; Rosen, "Djurin Ghetto"; Tibon, "Two-Front Battle," 131–50, 151–70.

69 Jagendorf, *Minunea*, 100–101; Tibon, "Am I My Brother's Keeper?," 93–116.

70 See Emil Călinescu's letter to the head of the SSI agency, in which he denounced Jagendorf for sending a detailed report (including requests for aid) to the old leadership of the Jewish communities instead of the Jewish Center (whom he did not trust) through Călinescu. See also Jagendorf's report to the Jewish Center, in USHMM, RG-25.004M, SRI, reel 10, file 2699, 777–812. Jagendorf also remembered the case of two Bucharest gentile architects who brought letters for him but who were tricked by a police informer into handing him the letters instead. As a result, the authorities arrested and sentenced the couriers to twenty-five years in prison. Jagendorf, *Minunea*, 114–15.

71 See the interview with Erica Antal in Pippidi, *Holocaustul evreilor*, 22.

72 See the interview with Lya Schenker in ibid., 48.

73 Rosza Gotlieb, *Katița prințesa ghetoului* (Bucharest: Fortuna and Glykon, 2003), 79.

74 See the interview with Silvia Hoisie in Pippidi, *Holocaustul evreilor*, 88.

75 See the interview with Firma Acs in ibid., 139.

76 See the interview with Sarina Ionescu in ibid., 184.

77 The Romanian authorities uncovered Larionescu's activities on behalf of Jewish deportees and arrested and sentenced him to ten years in prison; see also the case of the physician Chiriță, who acted as a courier between Bucharest and Moghilev. Jagendorf, *Minunea*, 59, 63–64.

78 Palty, *Evrei treceți Nistrul*, 94–95, 97–99.

79 Some individual Jews managed to obtain repatriation before 1944 through the help of relatives and friends in Romania. In addition, the Antonescu regime repatriated 6,035 Jews from Dorohoi in December

1943 and early 1944 (who were seen as a lesser threat and wrongfully deported) and around 1,846 orphan children (as a humanitarian measure). Tuvia Frilling et al., eds., *International Commission on the Holocaust in Romania: Final Report* (Iaşi: Polirom, 2004), 218–20.

80 Jagendorf, *Minunea*, 54–55.

81 See the interview with Mark Brandman in Jagendorf, *Minunea*, 73.

82 According to official documents, the Bucharest Jewish community supplied further material aid to Jewish would-be deportees to Transnistria on May 12, 1943, while they were waiting for the deportation train in a Bucharest railway station. See the May 14, 1943, report of the Bucharest Military Territorial Circle in Benjamin, *Evreii din România*, 246–47.

83 Palty, *Evrei treceţi Nistrul*, 29.

84 On Golta, see Deletant, *Ghetto Experience in Golta*, 1–26.

85 See the interview with Roza Schachter in Pippidi, *Holocaustul evreilor*, 61–62.

86 Ibid., 65.

87 Tibon, "Am I My Brother's Keeper?"; Rosen, *Surviving in the Murafa Ghetto*.

88 Klara Ostfeld, *Lumini şi umbre în viaţa mea* (Bacău: Multistar, 1992), 49–50.

89 I used the term "humanitarian resistance" as employed by historian Khatchig Mouradian, who examined the network of Armenian individuals and organizations engaged in the self-help efforts aiming to rescue the victims of the Ottoman Empire's genocidal policies. Khatchig Mouradian, "Genocide and Humanitarian Resistance in Ottoman Syria, 1915–1916," *Études Arméniennes Contemporaines* 7 (2016): 87–103.

III

UNDER NAZI OCCUPATION

9

"STAY HEALTHY. SEND PARCELS"

Relief in the Warsaw Ghetto

KATARZYNA PERSON

At the beginning of August 1939, Janina Halperson (referred to by her family as Janka), an eighteen-year-old from an assimilated Jewish family in Warsaw, set off on a journey from Poland to Lund in Sweden to attend a language summer school for foreigners. It was her first trip abroad, and her parents were understandably worried. Her mother sent her a stream of letters—sometimes two a day—making sure that she was keeping appropriate company and eating enough (Janka had never cooked for herself before). She also provided her daughter with addresses of acquaintances in Sweden who could help should she encounter difficulties. When war broke out on September 1, 1939, Janka Halperson was still in Sweden, and her parents decided that it would be best for her to remain there until the situation in Poland became clearer. On August 21, 1939, another Varsovian, forty-year-old Jewish journalist and Hebrew publishing house director Chaim Finkelsztejn, traveled to Switzerland to attend the Zionist Congress in Geneva. The outbreak of the war found him in Paris. Unable to return home, Finkelsztejn decided to go to the United States and from there attempt to organize entry visas for his wife and two daughters, who had stayed behind in Warsaw. Soon after the war began, both Janka Halperson and Chaim Finkelsztejn began sending parcels home. Despite the many differences in their circumstances, material aid sent from these two individuals became in a short space of time one of the few sources of hope of survival for their extended families trapped in Poland and living in the Warsaw ghetto. Their distinct yet linked stories exemplify how aid reached the Warsaw ghetto from thousands of individual Jews abroad.[1]

Mail, both letters and parcels, passed into and out of the Warsaw ghetto at an astonishing rate.[2] Due to the constraints imposed by censorship, the letters in particular provide only limited details on many aspects of life in the ghetto. Yet they remain invaluable in reconstructing social dynamics and the emotional register of those caught up in the horror of the Holocaust. They also show the importance of family links in such difficult times, with ghetto inhabitants and Jewish refugees abroad sharing their meager and often rapidly dwindling resources with family members whom they considered to be even worse off.

This chapter explores the diverse avenues through which people communicated with residents of the ghetto and reveals the complex information networks embedded in parcels and ghetto mail. Relief shipments became much more than simply physical relief. They revealed a "circle of responsibility," consisting of both those in the ghetto and those outside it. What was sent into the ghetto and with what assumptions about ghetto conditions? Parcels became part of what historian Evgeny Finkel described as "coping": trying to survive through "nonviolent 'everyday' or 'hidden' forms of resistance" in the face of Nazi plans for annihilating Europe's Jews.[3]

Functioning of the Postal Service

Correspondence between Janka Halperson and her family began on her departure to Sweden in August 1939 and lasted almost three years, until the beginning of the deportation operation in July 1942.[4] During that time, Janka received 164 letters, mainly from her parents, Dawid (b. ca. 1870) and Luba (née Kahan, b. ca. 1880). The Finkelsztejn family correspondence exchanged between Chaim, his wife, Rywka (née Eisenberg, b. 1897), and the couple's daughters—Tusia (Estera) (b. 1925) and Aviva (b. 1930 or 1931)—was likewise of long duration and extensive, consisting of 140 letters and postcards.[5] Unlike the Halperson family collection, the Finkelsztejn story involves two sides of surviving correspondence: original letters sent from Warsaw to the United States and carbon copies of Chaim Finkelsztejn's letters to Warsaw. They date from December 1939, when he arrived in New York City, until December 1941, when the United States entered the war and the correspondence stopped.

Both the Halperson and the Finkelsztejn families were trapped in the Warsaw ghetto, the largest ghetto in occupied Europe. The ghetto, sealed off in November 1940, was meant to be isolated from the outside world. An incubator of hunger and illness, it became a prison for 450,000 people, both natives of Warsaw and those resettled there from other Jewish communities, many in the environs of Warsaw. Of those imprisoned in the ghetto, 100,000 died there and a further 270,000 were deported to and murdered in the Treblinka death camp during the deportation operation staged from July through September 1942. The ghetto was dissolved in May 1943 following the Warsaw Ghetto Uprising.

Despite these vast quantities of letters sent and received by the Halpersons and the Finkelsztejns, exchanging correspondence proved far from easy. Just two months after the sealing of the ghetto in January 1941, the Deutsche Post Osten (German Post Office East), which organized postal service in the Generalgouvernement, placed the burden and cost of organizing the postal service on the Warsaw Jewish Council (Judenrat) and its postal department.[6] Since the Jewish Council was severely underfunded, letters and parcels had to be paid for not only when sending them but also upon receipt, typically by paying the postman who delivered them. Peretz Opoczynski, a ghetto postman and contributor to the underground archive of the Warsaw ghetto (the Ringelblum or Oyneg Shabes Archive), left a unique written testimony on this subject.[7] As Opoczynski noted, up to 80 percent of the families on many ghetto streets did not have enough money to cover the postman's fee. He wrote in his reportage in 1941, "It often happened that the recipient of the letter knocked on all doors on his floor, the floor below and floor above, on the first floor, on the second floor, and so he journeyed from the fourth to the ground floor, until he finally managed to borrow those meager few grosze [pennies]."[8] Letters arriving at and leaving the ghetto were strictly regulated: to comply with regulations, they had to be written in Polish or German, with other European languages also allowed in the correspondence to certain countries (but not Hebrew or Yiddish).[9] Remarks about developments in the war or the political situation were thus out of the question, and all letters received by Halperson and Finkelsztejn focused almost solely on everyday life and the struggles of the correspondents. Tellingly, Jews in the ghetto were not allowed to use stamps bearing Hitler's portrait but instead had to use those displaying "buildings or scenes from nature."[10]

As with letters, parcels to the Warsaw ghetto could only be sent from countries that were not at war with Germany. Thus, while Janka Halperson could send parcels from Sweden until the summer of 1942, Chaim in New York City had to stop sending them in the summer of 1941. Still, some people who remained in the countries at war with Germany managed to send parcels through intermediaries: individuals, specialized agencies, or aid organizations that would buy products and mail them from neutral countries to Warsaw. It is important to note that parcels came not only from the West. Until the German attack on the Soviet Union, the majority of parcels reaching the ghetto came from Jews who in the first weeks of the war had managed to escape from German-occupied western to eastern Poland, which was occupied and annexed by the Soviet Union on the basis of the August 1939 Molotov-Ribbentrop Pact. Until the Nazi invasion of the Soviet Union in the summer of 1941, Jews considered eastern Poland much safer than western Poland.[11] The vast majority of refugees were impoverished, and sending parcels to Warsaw proved to be a huge financial undertaking for them. Yet their situation was still considerably better than that of their relatives left behind in Warsaw. Postman Peretz Opoczynski noted:

> Parcels [from the Soviet Union] were sent by husbands to their wives and children, sons or daughters to their parents, relatives to relatives, friends to friends. Parcels from Russia arrived carefully wrapped in canvas and stamped with seven stamps, so that the best items would not be stolen from them on the way, as indeed they contained food that was very expensive here. Relatives from Russia sent rice, tea, coffee, chocolate, and initially even vodka or tobacco. They sent smoked meat, sausage, bacon, butter and cheese, and even caviar. Once a Warsaw Jew received such a package, he sold part of it, such as tea, coffee, tobacco, vodka, and so on, for good money, which was enough to feed him for a few weeks, and the rest he took for himself. Homes where such parcels arrived regularly did not know poverty.[12]

In the first months of the war, parcels were also sent to the city from smaller Jewish communities in German-occupied Poland that did not have such severe food shortages as Warsaw, which had been heavily damaged in the September 1939 bombardment.[13] This also continued after the sealing of the city's ghetto. As one of the leading ghetto personalities claimed in 1942, "Jews from the provinces make sacrifices . . . and send parcels to relatives, acquaintances, and even strangers in Warsaw."[14] Many Warsaw ghetto prisoners in turn sent parcels to poorer relatives, often parents and siblings, in smaller Jewish communities and forced labor camps outside the ghetto. This took place until February 1941, after which ghetto inhabitants were only allowed to issue aid parcels to forced labor camp prisoners.[15] A study dealing with parcels was compiled by the Jewish Social Self-Help (Żydowska Samopomoc Społeczna) in the Warsaw ghetto, a grassroots organization that created an extensive social support network supplementing the aid organized by the German-approved official Jewish administration of the ghetto. In the Warsaw ghetto, the Jewish Social Self-Help was also the key element of unarmed resistance against the Nazi authorities.[16] Its study found that parcels coming from relatives were also one of the most important methods of alleviating poverty in the ghetto. According to their estimates, through 1941,

MAX SOSEWITZ
Shipping Service & Bus Center
3212 W. Roosevelt Rd.
CHICAGO, ILL.

Agent for Maritime Commercial Corp.

Repeating
Order No.
dated

ORDER No. S.E. 22831

or shipment of 1 package. . No. SPECIAL delivered free destination, excl. duty
H2 + 1 LB. SOAP

TO SZMUL KLIGER
Please always give Full first name, not only initial!

Destination WARSZAWA

Street & No DZIELNA 4/62

Prov. GERMAN POLAND Country:

Arrival of package at destination is guaranteed. If non-arrival is proved, a replacement package will be shipped promptly. If this is not possible the amount paid will be refunded, less cost of radio transmittance of order.

Sender's name and address
S KELLER
4110 JACKSON BLVD
CHICAGO, ILL.

Price $ 7.65
Rec'd payment 7.65
Date: 3/29/41

Receipt for a food parcel sent from Chicago to Szmul Kliger in the Warsaw ghetto, March 1941. Courtesy of Esther Tenenbaum Sonheim, United States Holocaust Memorial Museum, photo 28571.

inhabitants of the Warsaw ghetto received altogether 877,491 food parcels. They came both from individual relatives and as part of organized aid from Jewish agencies based abroad.[17] According to data gathered by historian Ruta Sakowska, in May 1941 alone almost 109,000 parcels reached the Warsaw ghetto and a month later the figure reached 113,000 parcels.

The postal system could never be described as working well. Letters often arrived long after they had been sent, and both letters and parcels went missing. Sometimes all or some of the contents of packages were stolen by post office employees or requisitioned by the Germans. In October 1941, Rywka Finkelsztejn wrote to her husband of "many parcels getting lost."[18] Problems with the postal service meant that correspondents could never predict when and if their letters or parcels would reach the addressee. As a result, in both collections of letters discussed here, significant gaps occurred, as did references to missing correspondence. Because both parcels and letters often arrived late or went missing, the correspondents used to number their letters so that their recipients would know if one of them had gone astray. For the same reason, their letters almost always described in detail what the parcels contained. Starting in the spring of 1941, collecting parcels became even more complicated, with recipients required to present the post office with numerous documents, including proof of one's relationship with the person who sent the package.

Sending letters from the ghetto was forbidden as of July 22, 1942, which was the beginning of the Great Action, the deportation of 270,000 Jews from the Warsaw ghetto to the Treblinka death camp. On that day, German authorities responsible for the deportation introduced a one-week postal blockade of the ghetto. After a week, parcels were again distributed, but starting from August 8, 1942, no incoming parcels were accepted.[19] The post office (processing only incoming letters) continued to function until the outbreak of the Warsaw Ghetto Uprising on April 19, 1943. Many of the letters reaching the ghetto in the later period, preserved in the underground archive of the Warsaw ghetto, were directed to the Judenrat and inquired about friends and relatives missing after the major deportation operation.

Beyond Material Help

Discussions around material help, while crucial, formed only part of the contents of letters exchanged by members of the Finkelsztejn and Halperson families. Both those who were left behind and those who emigrated spoke above all of bygone family life and of longing, for each other and for the (often idealized) past experiences they had shared.[20] Due to censorship—both that imposed by the authorities and the self-censorship of correspondents not wishing to upset their loved ones—we learn little about the harsh contours of ghetto life or the struggles of living as refugees. Homesickness and loneliness were thus the only negative aspects of their current life that our correspondents were willing to acknowledge. On September 1, 1940, a year after the family parted, Chaim Finkelsztejn wrote to his wife in Warsaw:

> I know that your life is difficult, I know that in every respect you have it worse than I do, but believe that I suffer a great deal as well. Over that horrible year of being apart I went through various stages, I lived as if asleep, I often did not know what was happening to me, in a word, I was half unconscious. I went through sleepless nights, days when I could not swallow anything, when I traveled on the subway from one end of the city to another, with no aim and no need, only because I could not find a place for myself. In a word, I lived on the memory of your last letter and hope for the next one.[21]

On December 14, 1941, he wrote to her, "This is not normal life, only day-to-day vegetation."[22] Nine days later he added, "You at least have our children next to you, and who do I have? Nobody is waiting for me at home, nobody is worried about me, nobody cares about me. And I don't care for anyone here, and I don't wait for anyone, because from the first moment when I wake up in the morning to the last conscious moment before I fall asleep, I think only of you, I remember you, I am filled with you."[23]

People constantly asked for news and expressed concern about each other's well-being, suspecting (usually rightly) that their correspondents were hiding information from them about illnesses or other struggles. Janka Halperson's parents, for example, focused much of their letters on her nephew, little Stefan, describing his development in detail and sending his photographs. They very rarely if ever complained about their own living conditions or mentioned their needs, but rather showed concern for those abroad. Still, as news of the reality of life in the ghetto reached the refugees from other sources, they became increasingly proficient at decoding their correspondents' real situation. On March 16, 1941, Finkelsztejn addressed his wife directly: "For God's sake, how do you support yourself? Do you think that I just believe all your claims that you and the children look good and have clothes to wear? I know with complete certainty that you are not well and that there is nobody to look after you, so how can you cope?"[24] It was finally from his wife's unsteady handwriting that Finkelsztejn deciphered that Rywka was hiding a serious illness from him.

Refugee letters similarly made no admissions of financial concerns and struggles, even though it is clear (and clear to their families in Warsaw) that in most cases the refugees had no resources or family networks to fall back on, possessed no or only limited knowledge of the local language, and were suffering extreme financial stress. Janka Halperson's parents repeatedly brought up her lack of adequate clothing (she had meant to spend only one summer month in Sweden), her work, her living conditions, and her health. On December 23, 1940, her mother wrote that she "would give half of my life to be able to see you and see for myself how you live there, to see that you don't work too hard."[25] There is no doubt that the predominant theme in these letters is guilt: families in the ghetto expressed guilt for having to ask for help, while those abroad felt guilty for not being able to help more and for being in a safer place. At the same time, attempts to aid family members gave them purpose, gave them strength in daily struggles, and helped them to overcome the emotional difficulty of adjusting to life abroad.

While Finkelsztejn wrote openly about his emotional state, he underlined in his letters that he was an exception, that other refugees "made up stories in their letters about their life here."[26] As a result, the recipients of letters, often fully conscious of the glossing over of difficulties, attempted to read between the lines or asked others for information on the true state of their families. Finkelsztejn often directly addressed his daughters with questions about the well-being of their mother, assuming that they were more likely than her to tell him the truth. On February 2, 1941, he asked his friends in the Warsaw ghetto:

> My dears! Again and again I ask you to write me the truth about my Rywka and my girls. Please write me the truth without communicating first with her about what you are to write (I know that she is dictating your letters to me!). I have to know, after all, if she and the children are healthy, how they look, what they wear. A good few months ago she promised to send me a photograph, but she did not send it and I suspect that it is because they do not look well.[27]

Letters reaching the Warsaw ghetto show the extent to which information was circulated among Jewish émigrés abroad. They formed networks, piecing together news from the letters they each received, attempting to gain a fuller picture of ghetto conditions and the fate of Jews in Poland from them. Disseminating news from letters became a critical foundation stone for expatriate communities during the war.

Letters and parcels from abroad also became a community-building element in the lives of Warsaw's Jews as they faced increasing persecution. A letter was usually written by one family member, with the others each adding a few lines. They usually affirmed one another's sentiments. In turn, a correspondent sometimes devoted different parts of a letter to each family member. The importance of letters was not limited to the family circle but also included friends or neighbors; information was at times provided for them or about them. In Halperson's case, more distant family members (including aunts and cousins) as well as former schoolfriends wrote to her, and in some cases she also sent them aid.[28] Importantly, letters to Janka Halperson from those outside her immediate family circle, in particular school peers, were clearly different, for they contained more facts about the struggle of everyday life, sometimes to the point that they were cut out by censors.[29] Thus, writing became an "epistolary ritual." As historian Laura Martinez Martin has argued in her study of writing and reading practices of migrant families, "Epistolary exchanges are commonly understood as experiences shared by two or more people, but in a social context in which family and community were strong these social structures also interacted with the practices of letter writing and letter reading."[30] In both collections of Warsaw ghetto letters, we see the whole family writing to one person abroad, often passing information from a wider network of family or friends. To echo Martinez Martin, reading and writing letters was no longer merely an intimate undertaking. Instead, one can see a "formation of communities of writers and readers who not only shared information and news, but also shared the act of writing and reading."[31]

Help Solicited and Given

Both Chaim Finkelsztejn and Janka Halperson immediately volunteered (even against their families' wishes) to send aid, despite having to overcome complicated bureaucratic procedures and their own financial difficulties. Although Finkelsztejn initially struggled financially (his parcels were financed by fellow Jewish writers and journalists), he began sending parcels almost immediately after arriving in the United States.[32] Despite her family's protests, Janka Halperson began sending them small sums of money as early as in February 1940, six months after her arrival in Sweden.[33] A month later she began sending clothing for her newborn nephew (she probably knitted them herself) and sent a large parcel for her parents' thirty-fifth wedding anniversary. While the family implored her to limit her help, her sister-in-law in a letter from the end of March 1940 confirmed Janka's fears about her family's situation, acknowledging that clothing for the baby would be very useful; they could not afford to buy him an overcoat and thus could not take him out for walks.[34] A month later, in April 1940, a cousin informed Janka that she should be sending her parents food parcels ("if they accept them"), in particular tinned food, and from July 1940 she began doing so.[35] By that point her parents were hinting at the hardships they were facing. Her father wrote: "If it does not cost too much and if it will not be too much trouble, we would like to ask for rice, butter, and sugar in cubes, one kilogram each, and 10 decagrams of tea (not more)."[36] In this case, it was her father who asked for help, while her mother focused in her letters on Janka's own well-being and comfort. This blurring of gender roles, where it was men who became concerned with providing food, is not unique and is, as Nehama Tec noted, characteristic of letters from that period in general.[37] This signaled a shift in interfamilial dynamics in the ghetto more widely, with women increasingly taking on the role of breadwinners.[38]

While in time Janka Halperson's family members began to inquire about more aid—a clear sign that their situation was becoming desperate—as late as April 1941, her parents still implored her to stop sending them parcels and instead spend her money on her own needs.[39] It was only in March 1942 that her father openly wrote to her for the first time that her parcels were necessary for their survival. At that point no one in the family was employed (until then, Janka's brother, who worked as a clerk, had supported them financially), and more likely than not they were suffering from hunger. This reflected the general situation of many prewar middle-class families in the ghetto, who at that point had already run out of belongings they could sell or use to barter for food—be it with other Jews or with Poles illegally entering the ghetto. They thus lost a crucial means of supplementing food rations provided by the Judenrat, and their situation became similar to the poorer members of the community, dying of starvation, malnutrition, and associated diseases before the deportation operation.

Understandably, Rywka Finkelsztejn had fewer qualms about asking for help from her husband. "Stay healthy. Send parcels," she simply wrote at the end of her letter of March 9, 1941.[40] However, she rarely dwelled on her economic and financial needs and the hardship of providing for their two daughters alone. Families headed by women were among the poorest in the ghetto.[41] Unable to find other work, Rywka was most likely supporting them by selling her scant prewar belongings. Despite differences between them, without parcels from abroad, both families—solidly middle-class before the outbreak of the war—faced starvation in the ghetto. Family members outside Poland very quickly became their only lifeline. To quote the ghetto postman Peretz Opoczynski, "[A parcel] being sent decided the fate of the family, it solved the question: life or death."[42]

Parcels as Discussed in the Ghetto Community

The exchange of information around sending and receiving parcels was not limited to the refugee community abroad but also took place in the ghetto. Because letters were often read aloud and passed on even outside one's immediate family circle, ghetto residents were aware of the contents of their neighbors' letters as well as parcels. They were well versed in the technicalities of sending packages, instructing their correspondents on what they needed and how to send it. They were also conscious of costs and explained to their correspondents how to reduce them, both to economize and to send them more goods. Because recipients of "valuable" packages required a permit from the *Devisenstelle* (exchange control office), they often implored their family members to send small quantities of more expensive products to remain under the permitted limit.

Chaim Finkelsztejn, who was older and probably had much better access to information than Janka Halperson, proved more skilled at choosing appropriate products to send to Warsaw. On December 4, 1940, he purchased a parcel for his wife through a company based in Copenhagen, consisting of two pounds of butter, two pounds of cheese, two pounds of ham, two pounds of bacon, and one pound of salami. On January 19, 1941, he sent her two pounds of vegetable fat, two pounds of sugar, three pounds of sardines, and one pound each of salami and cocoa.[43] On October 1941, it was a small quantity of cocoa with sugar, coffee, and chocolate, two tins of sardines, two tins of cereal, two tins of honey, and one tin of condensed milk.[44] As Ewa Koźmińska Frejlak estimates, throughout 1940 and 1941, Chaim Finkelsztejn sent a total of about twenty large and at least as many smaller (one-pound) packages.[45]

It took Janka Halperson longer to learn what was really desirable in Warsaw. Initially she did not know how perilous her family situation had become, and instead of much-needed basic provisions she repeatedly sent her parents homemade fishcakes.[46] After one such package, her mother politely asked her to stop because the fish spoiled in transit. The same applied to oranges, and Halperson's family asked her to send bags of barley and flour instead.[47] In September 1941, they wrote, "As for the parcels. Meat and fish tins are too much of a luxury for us and it is not worth your hard work, unless it costs very little there. . . . We need real things like butter, melted pork fat or lard, possibly some barley. We could do with some tea, but not more than 10 decagrams [3.5 ounces, or less than a quarter pound]."[48] On the same day, her mother described jams as "too much luxury for us and not useful." An exception was made for products that Janka Halperson sent for her little nephew, Stefan, for whom the family accepted chocolate, cocoa, or items of clothing. Neither the Halpersons nor

Rywka Finkelsztejn and her daughters ever asked for money, most likely for fear of theft.[49]

The recipients discussed each parcel in detail and expressed their thanks. They not only actively asked for help for themselves but also alerted the senders to the fate of others who were in a particularly perilous living situation. Typically, they asked their correspondents to get in touch with relatives abroad on behalf of their friends and neighbors. On June 16, 1941, Rywka Finkelsztejn told her husband to go to "Wsandowa's sisters, [and ask them] to send parcels, because they are literally dying of hunger."[50] Sometimes they asked for direct help. Janka Halperson's parents—who in the autumn of 1940 still rarely admitted to their own suffering—nonetheless asked her to send warm clothing to their neighbor's son, who was in a POW camp in France.[51] Janka's friend in February 1942 inquired if she could send a letter to children in Janusz Korczak's orphanage and write to them about life in Sweden.[52]

Conclusion

The story of parcels and letters arriving in the Warsaw ghetto provides an important insight into the informal aid initiatives undertaken during the Holocaust, but it can also contribute to a wider analysis of aid in that period. Such aid should be seen not only in terms of the food or clothing sent and received but also in terms of its emotional impact on both aid recipients and aid providers. Analyzing the evolution of informal aid, however insignificant or modest it may seem, can also be an important contribution to understanding the spread of information on the Holocaust and how it was interpreted by those outside occupied Europe.

This chapter has discussed only one aspect of Jewish networks of support during the war. These networks can be seen as a form of resistance: working to survive despite Nazi plans for annihilating the Jewish population. Those without such networks, be they made up of family, prewar professional contacts, or support from youth organizations, were almost certain to be among the 25 percent of the population who died in the Warsaw ghetto before the deportations in the summer of 1942, succumbing to hunger or illness.

Due to the extreme situation in the Warsaw ghetto, material aid provided by food parcels always remained insufficient, so those abroad also attempted to secure help in other ways. Though far away, refugees still tried to find aid for their families by contacting acquaintances with some perceived influence: a friendly doctor, a neighbor in the Jewish ghetto police, or a colleague in the Judenrat. Chaim Finkelsztejn wrote to David Guzik, head of the American Jewish Joint Distribution Committee in Warsaw, whom he had known from before the war, requesting help for his family. At the same time, many refugees were focused on organizing documents that would allow their families to leave Poland. Throughout the period discussed here, Chaim Finkelsztejn made desperate attempts to obtain visas for his family to join him in the United States. His letters are filled with frustration and continuous disappointment as he tried to overcome formidable bureaucratic hurdles. He also sent assurances to his family that he was still trying. While he did not succeed during the war, his letters show how important it was for both him and those left behind to sustain this hope.

But hope was never enough. Even food parcels sent by Janka Halperson and Chaim Finkelsztejn could not save their families in the face of Operation Reinhard, the German plan to exterminate Poland's Jews in the Generalgouvernement in 1942 and 1943. The only survivor of Finkelsztejn's immediate family was his younger daughter. His wife and older daughter were murdered, probably in the Warsaw Ghetto Uprising in April 1943. His younger daughter was sent out of the ghetto a few days before the outbreak of the uprising. She survived in hiding with a Polish family and was reunited with her father after the war ended. They both remained in the United States, where Chaim Finkelsztejn lived until the age of 102.[53]

Janka Halperson lost all of her closest family members. Her parents were murdered in Treblinka during the first deportation operation in the summer of 1942. Her brother, Michał, was shot on the street by a Jewish policeman around the same time. Her sister-in-law, Paulina, and nephew, Stefan, managed to get out of the ghetto and went into hiding for a short time on the "Aryan" side. Not able to secure further help, they returned to the ghetto, where Paulina committed suicide, poisoning herself and her son. Janka Halperson returned to Poland after the war but immigrated back to Sweden following the anti-Jewish campaign in Poland in 1968.[54]

As Zoë Waxman writes, "The threat to the Jews was a threat to families—to family life and to the creation of new life—as well as a threat to individuals."[55] The letters discussed in this chapter give us an intimate glimpse of the last moments of the lives of two families, which, despite physical distance, remained tightly knit. They represent the last chapter in these family histories, for the correspondents were doomed never to be reunited physically. The deportation operation and later the uprising in the Warsaw ghetto claimed the lives of those who stayed behind. These letters belong to the rare category of sources on the Holocaust that were produced by those who were murdered and thus add another dimension to our understanding of these events.

Because they are a kind of micronarrative, limited to feelings and intimate family life, such letters alone offer a very imperfect picture of life in the ghettos or in exile. They are above all a form of self-presentation: we cannot learn the truth about forced migration or the full-scale horrors of ghetto life from them. They do, however, advance our understanding of family relations and the history of emotions in times of extreme peril. As a unique source for the quotidian reality of ghetto life, the letters also provide a rare source for history of women in the Holocaust, showing how women narrated changing familial dynamics and shifts in gender roles. Finally, the transnational character of the Halperson and Finkelsztejn correspondence offers a unique source for linking micro- and macrohistories of the Holocaust.[56] The letters show the links between Jews across the entire globe—sometimes on what we would consider the "margins of the Holocaust"—who were also affected by Nazi policy.[57] They take us one step closer to understanding the extremely multifaceted Jewish experience of the Holocaust and its long reach.

Notes

1 These stories are taken from just two of the many other large collections of letters sent to and from the Warsaw ghetto that have survived, among them a collection of sixty-two letters written to Dawid Naimark and his cousins (D. Solarz, A. Naimark, and Rabbi A. Kronenberg in New York City) from his relatives and acquaintances in Poland and other countries from November 1938 through October 1941: Jewish Historical Institute Archive (Żydowski Instytut Historyczny, ŻIH), no. 236. See also Wanda Lubelska, *Listy z getta* (Warsaw: Biblioteka Narodowa, 2000); Marcin Urynowicz, "Abrahama Gepnera listyz getta waszawskiego," *Dzieje Najnowsze* 38, no. 1 (2006): 163–84; Jakub (Janek) Gelbart, *Adresat nieznany*, ed. Ewa Koźmińska-Frejlak (Warsaw: Baobab, 2009); Marcin Urynowicz, "'Jeśli starłem choć jedną łzę.' Abraham Gepnera listy z getta warszawskiego," *Kwartalnik Historii Żydów* 250 (2014): 364–87.

2 We only have fragmentary data on the number of letters reaching the ghetto but know, e.g., that in the first half of May 1941 alone the postal service delivered 113,697 letters to the ghetto. "Praca poczty żydowskiej," *Gazeta Żydowska*, May 30, 1941, 2.

3 Evgeny Finkel, *Ordinary Jews: Choice and Survival during the Holocaust* (Princeton: Princeton University Press, 2017), 99.

4 The collection also contains letters by Janka's older brother Michał (b. 1906); his wife, Paulina (b. 1906); and other relatives. A key family

member constantly mentioned in the correspondence was Stefan (also referred to as Stefanek), Michał and Paulina's son, born in January 1940. Janka preserved all of these letters and deposited them in the ŻIH Archive in 2000. See Spuścizna Rodziny Halpersonów (Halperson Legacy Collection), no. S. 363. On the collection, see Aleksandra Karkowska, "Przemilczane—czyli listy z getta. Korespondencja warszawskiej rodziny Halperson 1939–1942/Unsaid—or the letters from the ghetto. Correspondence of the Warsaw Halperson family 1939–1942," in *Izraelska Orkiestra Filharmoniczna w 70. Rocznicę Powstania w Getcie Warszawskim/The Israel Philharmonic Orchestra on the 70th anniversary of the Warsaw Ghetto Uprising*, ed. Marcin Fedisz (Warsaw: Teatr Wielki-Opera Narodowa, 2013).

5 The letters in the collection were deposited in the ŻIH Archive in 2002, a year after Chaim's death. ŻIH, Spuścizna Chaima Finklesztejna (Chaim Finkelsztejn Legacy Collection), no. 346. An edition of the letters was published by Ewa Koźmińska-Frejlak, *Tęsknota nachodzi nas jak ciężka choroba . . . Korespondencja wojenna rodziny Finkelsztejnów* (Warsaw: Stowarzyszenie Centrum Badań nad Zagładą Żydów, 2012).

6 The main studies of the post office in the Warsaw ghetto are Ruta Sakowska, "Łączność pocztowa warszawskiego getta," *Biuletyn Żydowskiego Instytutu Historycznego*, nos. 45–46 (1963): 94–109; and Barbara Engelking and Jacek Leociak, *Getto warszawskie. Przewodnik po nieistniejącym mieście* (Warsaw: IFiS PAN, 2013), 395–409.

7 This clandestine documentation and research project in the ghetto was organized by historian Emanuel Ringelblum. The team succeeded in collecting almost 35,000 pages of documents relating to social life in the ghetto. On the archive, see Samuel D. Kassow, *Who Will Write Our History? Rediscovering a Hidden Archive from the Warsaw Ghetto* (Bloomington: Indiana University Press, 2007).

8 *Archiwum Ringelbluma. Konspiracyjne Archiwum Getta Warszawy*, vol. 31. *Pisma Pereca Opoczyńskiego*, ed. Monika Polit (Warsaw: ŻIH, 2017), 421.

9 For example, letters sent from the Warsaw ghetto to Romania could be written in German, Italian, Romanian, or French. Engelking and Leociak, *Getto warszawskie*, 399.

10 Engelking and Leociak, *Getto warszawskie*, 399.

11 According to Ruta Sakowska, parcels from the Soviet Union constituted up to 84 percent of all parcels reaching the ghetto until March 1941. See Sakowska, "Łączność pocztowa warszawskiego getta," 101. On the life of

Jewish refugees in the Soviet annexed territories, see Andrzej Żbikowski, ed., *The Ringelblum Archive: Accounts from the Borderlands, 1939–1941* (Warsaw: Żydowski Instytut Historyczny, 2018).

12 *Archiwum Ringelbluma. Konspiracyjne Archiwum Getta Warszawy*, vol. 31, 416. For additional information on these shipments from the east, see the chapter by Eliyana R. Adler, this volume.

13 For references to sending parcels to Warsaw in various testimonies from smaller ghettos in the Generalgouvernement, see *Archiwum Ringelbluma. Konspiracyjne Archiwum Getta Warszawy*, vol. 6, *Generalne Gubernatorstwo*, ed. Aleksandra Bańkowska (Warsaw: ŻIH, 2012), 33, 137, 350.

14 *Archiwum Ringelbluma. Konspiracyjne Archiwum Getta Warszawy*, vol. 26, *Utwory literackie z getta warszawskiego*, ed. Agnieszka Żółkiewska and Marek Tuszewicki (Warsaw: ŻIH, 2017), 37.

15 *Archiwum Ringelbluma. Konspiracyjne Archiwum Getta Warszawy*, vol. 16, *Prasa getta warszawskiego: Bund i Cukunft*, ed. Martyna Rusiniak-Karwat and Alicja Jarkowska-Natkaniec (Warsaw: ŻIH, 2016), 409.

16 Describing resistance that he refers to as *amidah* (Hebrew: to stand against), historian Yehuda Bauer includes "smuggling food into ghettos; mutual self-sacrifice within the family to avoid starvation or worse; cultural, educational, religious, and political activities taken to strengthen morale; the work of doctors, nurses, and educators to consciously maintain health and moral fiber to enable individual and group survival." See Yehuda Bauer, *Rethinking the Holocaust* (New Haven: Yale University Press, 2001), 120.

17 *Archiwum Ringelbluma. Konspiracyjne Archiwum Getta Warszawy*, vol. 27, *Żydowska Samopomoc Społeczna w Warszawie (1939–1943)*, ed. Aleksandra Bańkowska and Maria Ferenc Piotrowska (Warsaw: ŻIH, 2017), 494.

18 Rywka to Chaim Finkelsztejn, October 15, 1941, Warsaw, in Koźmińska-Frejlak, *Tęsknota nachodzi nas*, 400.

19 According to Opoczyński, the German civilian administration of Warsaw made an attempt to confiscate parcels coming from abroad. See *Archiwum Ringelbluma. Konspiracyjne Archiwum Getta Warszawy*, vol. 31, 453–54.

20 ŻIH, S. 363/4, Warsaw, April 5, 1942, Michał Halperson to Janina Halperson. See also the discussion of letters sent from the Kraków ghetto in Nechama Tec, "Through the Eyes of the Oppressed," in *Every Day Lasts a Year: A Jewish Family's Correspondence from Poland*, ed. Christopher R. Browning, Richard S. Hollander, and Nechama Tec (Cambridge: Cambridge University Press, 2009), 60–100.

21 New York, September 1, 1940, in Koźmińska-Frejlak, *Tęsknota nachodzi nas*, 93.
22 New York, December 14, 1940, in ibid., 180.
23 New York, December 21, 1940, in ibid., 184.
24 New York, March 16, 1941, Chaim Finkelsztejn to Rywka Finkelsztejn, in ibid., 243.
25 ŻIH, S. 363/3, Warsaw, December 23, 1940, Luba Halperson to Janina Halperson.
26 New York, March 30, 1941, in Koźmińska-Frejlak, *Tęsknota nachodzi nas*, 255.
27 New York, February 2, 1941, Chaim Finkelsztejn to Estera and Chaim Alter Rochman, in ibid., 216–17. I did not find a reply to this letter.
28 See ŻIH, S. 363/5 and S. 363/5. On letters to schoolfriends, see Katarzyna Person, "'I Sometimes Think That I Grew Up on a Different Planet': The Assimilated Jewish Community of the Warsaw Ghetto in the Letters of Wanda Lubelska and Hala Szwambaum," in *Who Is a Jew? Reflections on History, Religion, and Culture*, ed. Leonard Greenspoon (Purdue: Purdue University Press, 2014), 257–66.
29 ŻIH, S. 363/6, Warsaw, March 26, 1940, Paulina Halperson to Janina Halperson.
30 Laura Martínez Martín, "Shared Letters: Writing and Reading Practices in the Correspondence of Migrant Families in Northern Spain," *History of the Family* 21, no. 3 (2016): 434.
31 Ibid.
32 Ewa Koźmińska-Frejlak, "Wstęp," in Koźmińska-Frejlak, *Tęsknota nachodzi nas*, 17.
33 ŻIH, S. 363/3, Warsaw, March 4, 1940, Dawid Halperson to Janina Halperson.
34 ŻIH, S. 363/3, Warsaw, March 26, 1940, Pola Halperson to Janina Halperson.
35 ŻIH, S. 363/5, Warsaw, March 2, 1940, Rafał Wundheiler to Janina Halperson; ŻIH, S. 363/3, Warsaw, July 30, 1940, Dawid Halperson to Janina Halperson.
36 ŻIH, S. 363/3, Warsaw, July 30, 1940, Dawid Halperson to Janina Halperson.
37 Tec, "Through the Eyes of the Oppressed," 96.
38 On this, see Zoë Waxman, *Women in the Holocaust: A Feminist History* (Oxford: Oxford University Press, 2017), 52.
39 ŻIH, S. 363/4, Warsaw, April 27, 1941, Dawid Halperson to Janina Halperson.

40 Warsaw, March 9, 1941, Rywka Finkelsztejn to Chaim Finkelsztejn, in Koźmińska-Frejlak, *Tęsknota nachodzi nas*, 233.
41 Waxman, *Women in the Holocaust*, 47.
42 *Archiwum Ringelbluma. Konspiracyjne Archiwum Getta Warszawy*, vol. 31, 420.
43 New York, January 19, 1941, Chaim Finkelszejn to Rywka Finkelsztejn, in Koźmińska-Frejlak, *Tęsknota nachodzi nas*, 203.
44 ŻIH, S. 363/4, Warsaw, October 5, 1941, Dawid Halperson to Janina Halperson.
45 Koźmińska-Frejlak, "Wstęp," in Koźmińska-Frejlak, *Tęsknota nachodzi nas*, 19.
46 ŻIH, S. 363/4, Warsaw, February 26, 1941, Michał Halperson to Janina Halperson.
47 ŻIH, S. 363/4, Warsaw, April 10, 1940, Dawid Halperson to Janina Halperson; ŻIH, S. 363/4, Warsaw, May 6, 1941, Luba Halperson to Janina Halperson.
48 Up to ten decagrams of tea were treated as a parcel of little value and escaped import duties. ŻIH, S. 363/3, Warsaw, September 10, 1940, Luba Halperson to Janina Halperson.
49 Money orders came both from and into the ghetto. Their amount was restricted, and the sum of money leaving the ghetto on a certain day could not be higher than the sum of money arriving into the ghetto.
50 Warsaw, June 16, 1941, Rywka Finkelsztejn to Chaim Finkelsztejn, in Koźmińska-Frejlak, ed., *Tęsknota nachodzi nas*, 321.
51 ŻIH, S. 363/3, Warsaw, October 26, 1940, Dawid Halperson to Janina Halperson; they asked for two woolen sweaters, two undershirts, two pairs of long johns, and two pairs of woolen socks (new or used but in good condition).
52 ŻIH, S. 363/6, Warsaw, February 21, 1941, Lucyna Bigielman to Janina Halperson.
53 Ewa Koźmińska-Frejlak, *Wstęp*, in Koźmińska-Frejlak, *Tęsknota nachodzi nas*.
54 ŻIH, S. 363, Aleksandra Bańkowska, *Wstęp do inwentarza zbioru Spuścizna Rodziny Halpersonów*.
55 Waxman, *Women in the Holocaust*, 52.
56 On microhistories of the Holocaust, see Tomasz Frydel, "The Ongoing Challenge of Producing an Integrated Microhistory of the Holocaust in East Central Europe," *Journal of Genocide Research* 20, no. 4 (2018): 624–31; Claire Zalc and Tal Bruttmann, eds., *Microhistories of the*

Holocaust (New York: Berghahn Books, 2017); Evgeny Finkel and Scott Straus, "Macro, Meso, and Micro Research on Genocide: Gains, Shortcomings, and Future Areas of Inquiry," *Genocide Studies and Prevention* 7, no. 1 (2012): 56–67.

57 This term is used by Jan Grabowski in *Hunt for the Jews: Betrayal and Murder in German-Occupied Poland* (Bloomington: Indiana University Press, 2013), 1.

10

THE JEWISH AID AGENCY IN THE GENERALGOUVERNEMENT IN OCCUPIED KRAKÓW, 1942–44

ALICJA JARKOWSKA

Anton Musiał

Anny Mari 14–16. Statue manufacturer
March 25 [1943?]

Dear Mr. and Mrs. Musiał,

Several times now have I written to you begging you to send me 5 thousand zloty. As you may know, Jews of Kraków have been in exile for eighteen months. I am at the labor camp in Kraków, where I am nearing death of starvation and cold. My husband is not here—only his sister, Renia, is at the camp with me. We are both sick and swollen from hunger. I am pleading with you once more: please save me from starvation. Please give the addressee of this letter 5 thousand zloty, and if W.G. does not have any cash at his disposal, please give them my husband's fur coat lined with otter fur and [illegible] pig leather, along with some underwear; or maybe you would be so kind as to sell those items yourself and give the money to the addressee. I am relying on your help, knowing your ability to help us, and your kindness toward my husband. God

This work was supported by the National Center of Science (SONATINA 2), project no. 2018/28/C/HS3/00108.

willing [illegible], I shall be grateful to you until my dying day. I sincerely hope for your help and assistance.

Yours sincerely,

Maria Kapellver, wife of Bernard Kapellver, dentist[1]

Between 1942 and 1944, approximately 30,000 Jews were detained in the German forced labor camp in Płaszów, approximately five kilometers from the center of Kraków, capital of the Generalgouvernement, an artificial political unit created from parts of German-occupied Poland. Their fate depended not only on the policies of the occupation authorities but also on the individual and organized forms of aid they were able to obtain. The author of the letter above was one of many prisoners seeking help from her prewar friends; it seems, however, that she was in a better position to find help outside the camp than Jewish detainees in other locations. Kraków was the seat of a major self-help aid agency that operated in the area from the first days of the German occupation: the Żydowska Samopomoc Społeczna (Jewish Social Self-Help, or JSS), renamed in 1942 as the Jewish Aid Agency in the Generalgouvernement (in Polish: Centrala Pomocy dla Żydów w Generalnym Gubernatorstwie; in German: Jüdische Unterstützungsstelle für das Generalgouvernement, or JUS).[2] Between 1940 and July 1944, the institution distributed parcels from foreign organizations such as the American Jewish Joint Distribution Committee (the Joint) and the International Committee of the Red Cross containing food, medicine, and other essentials among inmates of the Kraków ghetto and camps throughout the Generalgouvernement. Much of this aid went to Płaszów, but it also went to its subcamps in Prokocim, Bieżanów, and Kabel, where Maria Kapellver was held. Communications between the detainees and representatives of the JSS-JUS and its chairman occurred on a daily basis, which gave rise to new networks. To fully understand JUS activity in these years, one needs to look not only at the dynamic of the war period and the Holocaust but also at the character and scope of the JSS, its predecessor in 1940–42. The history of both organizations provides critical insights into how Jews coped with life inside Nazi camps and ghettos, when these institutions were compelled to negotiate directly with the occupiers to ensure support for ghetto and camp communities. Who benefited most from the help offered by the JUS? How significant were the locations of the camps or the network of contacts the JUS maintained within Kraków? Were some groups privileged over others, and, if so, what role did they play in those closed communities?

This chapter gauges the impact of JSS-JUS activity on the lives of Jewish prisoners and scrutinizes the concrete work of Jewish self-help networks and the people central to these operations, such as Michał Weichert, chairman of both organizations. Weichert was born on May 5, 1890, in Podhajce, Podolia, to Berisz and Sara Weichert (née Geller).[3] He studied philosophy and law at universities in Vienna, Lviv, and Berlin, completing his doctorate in law in Vienna. Returning to Poland in 1918 to study Jewish theater history in Warsaw, he abandoned these studies after just a month and started organizing Jewish cultural institutions across the country. Weichert was involved in a range of cultural ventures before 1939 and taught at a boys' secondary school in Warsaw. He published articles in many Yiddish-language theater journals, but at the same time continued his legal practice, which he only closed when the war broke out.[4] After the German invasion, Weichert acted as chairman of the Commission for Coordination of Jewish Social Institutions operating under the aegis of the Capital City Committee for Social Self-Help and several secular Jewish philanthropic endeavors. On October 20, 1940, he and his family moved to Kraków, where he coordinated the activity of the JSS and, from late 1942, the JUS.

Weichert's behavior in organizing social help under the genocidal Nazi regime provides a unique window for analyzing these questions. During the war he faced many difficult ethical dilemmas, leading contemporaries to accuse him of collaboration with the Nazis. He was a controversial figure who polarized opinion in Jewish circles, especially when he decided to continue organizing aid after 1943, against the wishes of underground Jewish organizations. Without his assistance many people would most likely have perished during the war. Yet he and his closest associates (such as members of the Jewish police) were already accused of treason during the war by some of their fellow Jews. When the war ended, Polish and Jewish bodies investigated him and tried him repeatedly in liberated Poland. Weichert's activities and his postwar troubles remind us of the difficult choices prominent Jewish activists had to make under Nazi rule. This chapter assesses his wartime behavior and suggests that regardless of the allegations against him, he genuinely supported Jewish communities and Jewish prisoners in concentration camps with help, even if it meant acting against the orders issued by Jewish and Polish resistance cells.

Jews in Occupied Kraków

Kraków's city fabric during the German occupation was heterogeneous, as in other cities during the period. It was the capital of the Generalgouvernement and at the same time the administrative center of the Kraków province and district, housing all the region's central civil and political institutions as well as its police headquarters.[5] According to 1939 statistics, nearly 60,000 Jews lived in Kraków, making up approximately 23 percent of the city's population. Their situation changed dramatically when the Kraków ghetto was created in March 1941 and, later, when the Germans established a forced labor camp in nearby Płaszów. The new Jewish quarter was located in a neglected district of Kraków named Podgórze, devoid of an adequate sanitary infrastructure. Henceforth, Jews were barred from living on the "Aryan" side, an act that later even became punishable by death. Suspected Jews caught outside the ghetto were transferred to prisons and eventually executed in Płaszów. Some Jews, however, decided to risk staying on the forbidden side or fled there because of deteriorating conditions in the ghetto.

The Kraków ghetto consisted of 320 mostly one- or two-story houses and covered approximately twenty hectares.[6] According to information in the official Jewish newspaper *Gazeta Żydowska* in March 1941, "three persons per window" lived in each apartment.[7] A total of 11,000 Jews were initially forced into the ghetto, coming from Kraków and surrounding towns and villages, but the number grew constantly. By June 1942 the number had reportedly grown to 19,000 or 20,000 people. The quarter was fenced off with barbed wire and later by a wall with four gates.[8] The Judenrat headquarters and a German police station stood near the main gate at the intersection of Limanowskiego Street and the Podgórze Market Square. The Judenrat was the official Jewish "self-administration" created on German orders in December 1939. It replaced the preexisting Jewish community structures. So-called Polish Blue Police troops were stationed near the rest of the gates.[9] The ghetto was not completely cut off from the rest of the city, but the Vistula River formed a natural border between them.

After the ghetto was created, the Jewish administration, self-help and charity organizations, and care and education facilities transferred their work inside its boundaries. The most important were the Judenrat, the Jewish Police (Jüdischer Ordnungsdient), CENTOS (the Central Office of the Union of Societies for the Care of Orphans and Abandoned Children), and the JSS.[10] On November 27, 1942, the SS and Police Leader in the city, SS-Oberführer Julian Scherner, ordered the concentration of all Jews working in arms factories, private companies, and military facilities at the forced labor camp (ZAL) Płaszów.[11] Weichert visited them twice weekly, reportedly providing food, medicine, and other basic commodities and acting as an intermediary, delivering correspondence to families detained in other camps or living on the "Aryan" side.[12]

The gradual liquidation of the Kraków ghetto started in June 1942, when German troops under the command of SS-Sturmbannführer Wilhelm Haase carried out the first deportations of between 5,000 and 7,000 Jews to the Bełżec extermination camp as part of Operation Reinhard, the mass murder of the Jews in the Generalgouvernement. On October 27, 1942, German authorities carried out another *Aktion*, murdering around 300 Jews in the ghetto and deporting 7,000 to Bełżec. The final liquidation of the ghetto started on March 13, 1943, at 6:00 a.m., when the SS, police, and paramilitary Sonderdienst units gathered 6,000 to 8,000 Jews from the "A" section of the ghetto and transported them to Płaszów.[13] Haase commanded the entire operation, assisted by members of his staff, including SS-Oberführer Julian Scherner.[14] SS-Untersturmführer Amon Göth, SS-Sturmscharführer Rudolf Körner, SS-Sturmscharführer Wilhelm Kunde, SS-Oberscharführer Albert Hujar and SS-Rottenführer Wiktor Ritschek, and SS-Unterscharführer Horst Pilarzik from the Kraków Gestapo proved particularly ruthless.[15] German authorities liquidated the "B" section of the ghetto the following day. German soldiers divided people by age, sex, health, and fitness for work.[16] People who were found in the streets, hospitals, and shelters were murdered.[17] Children aged fourteen and under, the elderly, and the sick were shot on the spot, their bodies buried in a mass grave.[18]

During the final liquidation of the Kraków ghetto, the Germans killed between 700 and 2,500 people.[19] The remaining residents were transported to Auschwitz (ca. 3,000) and Płaszów (ca. 8,000).[20] Those who arrived in Płaszów were placed in 180 hastily constructed barracks without electricity, heating, or sanitary facilities. Living conditions in the ghetto and in Płaszów made any longer-term survival of the inmates dependent on aid from Jewish self-help agencies.[21]

Activities of the Jewish Social Self-Help (1940–42)

During the war, Weichert was allowed to move freely inside the Kraków ghetto, the Płaszów camp and its branches, and other places under the care of the JSS-JUS. This was mainly due to the nature of the organization he presided over between September 1940 and July 1944. His interpersonal skills, combined with his experience and fluency in German, allowed him to distribute food parcels and medicine among Jews at these sites regularly. Shortly before taking up the job at the JSS, he had been a member of the coordinating committee of the United Committee for Jewish Craftsmen (Zjednoczony Komitet dla Spraw Rzemiosła Żydowskiego), of which he was chairman and in charge of communications with German authorities.[22] He actively participated in negotiations for the creation of the JSS at the German administrative offices for the Generalgouvernement.[23]

The JSS was a central care organization for Jews living in the Generalgouvernement, established by the Office of the General Governor (Amt des Generalgouverneurs) on May 29, 1940, under the bylaws of the Main Welfare Council (Naczelna Rada Opiekuńcza, or NRO). It distributed foreign humanitarian aid collected by the International Committee of the Red Cross and the Commission for Polish Relief (Hoover Commission), as well as Generalgouvernement grants.[24] Other Jewish social welfare organizations had to become subsidiaries of the JSS. Joint-affiliated associations such as the TOZ (Society for the Protection of Jewish Health) and CENTOS also became affiliates of the JSS board while maintaining some autonomy. The Joint thus lost its monopoly on distributing foreign aid in the Generalgouvernement.[25]

The JSS headquarters were located in Kraków, with several field agencies under its jurisdiction.[26] Before 1941, 10 committees and 104 delegations connected to the JSS umbrella had already begun operations, and by the beginning of the following year as many as 412 such committees had been created across the Generalgouvernement.[27] Seven core members ran the JSS: Marek Bieberstein, Dr. Chaim Hilfstein, Dr. Eliasz Tisch, the engineer Józef Jaszuński, Dr. Gustaw Welikowski, Beniamin Zabłudowski, and Dr. Michał Weichert. Weichert and Bieberstein were particularly prominent, organizing many charity initiatives in the Kraków ghetto through negotiations with the German authorities.[28] JSS leaders also negotiated for a share of funds and resources distributed through the general Polish Central Welfare Council (CWC).[29] For instance, on June 26, 1940, at the CWC meeting concerning the distribution of American financial contributions, Bieberstein, representing Kraków's Judenrat, and Weichert and Tisch of the JSS established a system for distributing parcels, as a consequence of the aforementioned changes of late May 1940.[30] From July 1940 onward, aid from the United States was directed to the CWC, which in turn gave a 17 percent share to the JSS board for Jews.[31]

In some cases, the JSS provided support for people seeking work, acquired certificates of employment for them, and supplied Jewish workers with food and clothing, but their main mission was to distribute food, clothes, and financial assistance, as well as medical aid.[32] Jews were also encouraged to actively request help from abroad. They could send cards requesting food or money to their relatives through the JSS Department for the Aid of Foreign Relatives, which forwarded them to the Joint headquarters in Lisbon.[33] The Joint sent the cards to different countries, not only in Europe but also in South America, and acted as an intermediary in transferring parcels to Poland from prisoners' relatives living in the United States. Additional parcels also came from citizens of Switzerland, Portugal, Argentina, and Brazil.

The JSS became the main relief and social agency in occupied Poland that coordinated the activities of other Jewish welfare institutions in the Generalgouvernement.[34] Among them were kitchens, shelters, orphanages, and child-care centers. By all accounts, until June 1942, the JSS had opened 426 kitchens serving hot meals in ghettos and labor camps across the entire Generalgouvernement.[35] The number of people receiving some form of aid from foreign institutions thanks to the JSS in its first year of operations amounted to 500,000. The organization drew aid from several sources, including the Generalgouvernement administration subsidy provided through the Central Welfare Council from the Joint, the International Red Cross, and Jewish councils. The Joint had moved large sums of money to Poland before the war had even started and was entitled to keep its own accounts while the United States was still a neutral country. The organization was the only one able to communicate with institutions across the entire Generalgouvernement and some areas that had been incorporated into the Third Reich. In mid-March 1940, it opened offices in provincial capitals: Kraków, Lublin, and Radom. However, by the beginning of 1941, their headquarters moved to Kraków under pressure from German authorities.[36] Beginning on February 1, 1941, the Joint transferred the vast majority of its funds to the executive of the JSS, which was responsible for distributing the monies among local committees.[37] Between September 1939 and December 1941, representatives of the Joint donated $4.6 million to Jewish communities in occupied Poland.[38] All legal transfers were halted in December 1941, when the United States entered the war. Though no longer legally permitted to operate inside German-occupied territories, the Joint continued to funnel clandestine funds into ghettos in Poland through its office in Switzerland.[39]

The activity of the JSS was strongly dependent on German government policies, and its representatives had to maintain regular and good relations with occupation authorities, who had to approve all decisions made by the organization's leaders. JSS representatives, in particular the chairmen, also met regularly with the Germans to seek additional social assistance. Their reports often mentioned that aid provided to their constituents was insufficient and continued to deteriorate: food and basic necessities were in short supply, and care for children and orphans was insufficient. Ghetto dwellings were often unheated, and sanitary conditions were very poor.[40] The difficulties grew more acute when the JSS started supporting prisoners in labor and concentration camps because this strained their limited resources even further. Tadeusz Pankiewicz, who witnessed the distress of this period, recalled: "Many survived the crises at the ghetto and the Płaszów camp, or even in villages and settlements outside Kraków, only because they were given money and other essentials that had been deposited outside the ghetto. Dr Michał Weichert acted as intermediary in that process, for he had access to different, smaller camps beyond the borders of the ghetto and of Kraków."[41]

JSS officials were forced to cooperate with the Germans to keep assistance flowing. For instance, in the fall of 1941, Weichert managed to obtain permission from German authorities to buy typhus vaccines at the Lviv institute run by Professor Rudolf Weigl and at the Kraków facility run by Professor Otto Bujwid.[42] Fortunately, Weichert, who often spoke with the Germans about the difficulties in supplying food to kitchens and refugee shelters, proved adept at negotiating with the occupation authorities.[43] He participated in many conferences organized by the Germans in the first years of the occupation.[44] In the second half of 1940 he also tried to convince occupation officials of the need to support the Jews of Kraków and the refugees from other cities in occupied Poland by subsidizing the JSS and increasing food allocations to Jewish institutions.[45]

Prior to the creation of the Kraków ghetto in March 1941, the JSS headquarters were located at Stradom Street 10, not far from the office of Hans Frank, the German head of the Generalgouvernement. The JSS office was later moved to the ghetto, initially to the building at Józefińska Street 18, near the Labor Office and the Jewish police station.[46] It remained at that address until July 29, 1942, when the German authorities decided to dissolve the organization, most likely due to Operation Reinhard, which had been initiated in the spring of that year. The organization continued to operate but was gradually forced to cut its staff, and its headquarters were transformed into a lumberyard. It officially terminated its activity in October 1942, when, in line with a decision of the occupation authorities, the JUS replaced the JSS, taking over its funds and facilities. The new organization was under strict control of the Germans. Such cooperation with the occupiers met with objections from part of the Jewish community, especially members of the Jewish Combat Organization (Żydowska Organizacja Bojowa, or ŻOB), an underground armed self-defense organization created in the Warsaw ghetto. From this point on, Weichert, who continued to run the organization, was regularly accused of collaborating with the occupation authorities and using his position for personal gain. But not all Jews shared this opinion, and many thought that Weichert's involvement with the JSS and later the JUS helped to save lives.

The Jewish Aid Agency in the Generalgouvernement (1942–45)

Despite his prominent position in the ghetto, Weichert was constantly in danger of being sent to Bełżec. On June 2, 1942, he offended SS-Sturmscharführer Wilhelm Kunde, who was in charge of Jewish Affairs (Judenreferent) in the German security apparatus in Kraków.[47] Kunde shot him in the arm for trying to save Mordechaj Gebirtyg, a poet, from being transported to the death camp.[48] During the next deportation in October, Weichert was ordered to be transported to Bełżec along with his family, and the Germans rejected the certificate guaranteeing their safety. At the very last moment, he and his family managed to escape and hide in the Judenrat building, where they remained until the end of the operation.[49] Despite the radicalization of the Nazi policies, Weichert continued organizing help, entering the dangerous territory of cooperating with the occupiers when he must have been aware of their genocidal plans.

The JUS officially began its work on October 16, 1942. Its activity did not last long, for on December 1 the Germans decided to liquidate the organization temporarily. They only allowed Weichert to distribute food, clothes, and medicine that had already been collected to the poorest Jews in ghettos and prisoners in Jewish forced labor camps. As he recalled:

> In the days that followed, the same officers came three times; they sealed the warehouses and medicine distribution points and allowed us to take some of it to give away. We gave a lot of medicine and other essentials to three hospitals, two orphanages, and one shelter in the Kraków quarter, and to JULAG I camp [a Jewish camp, *Judenlager*] in Płaszów, JULAG II in Prokocim; we gave clogs and trousers to the Jewish Council to be sent to the camps. We left the meager amount of food we had at the kitchen, for they had allowed it to keep operating. We stored the food at the shipper's facility.[50]

Faced with this new situation, Weichert sought to protect his family and himself from deportation by taking a position as a clerk at the Optima factory in the Kraków ghetto.[51] He worked there until March 1943. On the day of the final liquidation of the Kraków ghetto, March 13, Weichert was reinstated as the head of the JUS. The JSS's former warehouses at Józefińska 2a became the new JUS office, and Weichert moved there with his family.[52] This allowed camp prisoners to continue receiving support from foreign institutions through the

Płaszów camp in the Generalgouvernement, 1943–44. Photo by Raimund Titsch. Courtesy of the Leopold Page Photographic collection, United States Holocaust Memorial Museum, photo 03407.

organization.[53] However, the fact that Weichert was allowed to remain living outside the Płaszów camp most likely gave the impression that the JUS as well as its chairman were collaborating with the Germans.

According to Weichert, the JUS was reactivated in 1943 due to growing pressure from the International Red Cross, which demanded that the Jewish organization in the Generalgouvernement confirm receipt of medicine and threatened to stop all aid to German POWs. He even drew up a plan for distributing a large transport of medicine sent by the Red Cross.[54] The JUS officially resumed its activity in April 1943, and Weichert began requesting further aid from foreign organizations.[55] All former JUS branches were liquidated, and only the Kraków headquarters remained. Its activities were limited to receiving parcels from foreign organizations and distributing them among Jews detained in various German labor or concentration camps, at least on a small scale.[56] Between May and July 1943, the JUS delivered a mere fifty-five parcels to camps throughout the Generalgouvernement.[57] However, the organization was reportedly supporting forty-four camps, twenty-four workplaces, and the last eight remaining ghettos in the Generalgouvernement.[58]

The JUS remained the main recipient of donations from Portugal, including those originating from London, sent by Jewish organizations and the Polish exile government. Due to the deteriorating situation in occupied Poland

and the reorganization of the institution, those activities were undertaken with more caution, more so because the local Polish underground press had begun warning against collaborating with the JUS. The warnings about the German handling of foreign donations reached the policy makers abroad. The *Małopolska Agencja Prasowa*, a periodical published in occupied Kraków, informed its readers on June 4, 1943, that the German authorities had confiscated food parcels addressed to Jews from Portugal and Sweden using the signature and stamp of "the Jewish community" to confirm their receipt. The article argued that "this is a ruse that the German government has been using for a long time, and foreign charity institutions keep sending new shipments, because the previous ones have been officially confirmed. Large quantities of real coffee, tea, and other colonial goods have appeared in the Kraków market of late, but they have been stolen, and they are now sold by German citizens or their middlemen."[59]

Evidence for these accusations remains inconclusive. When writing about the Jewish community, the authors may have meant the Judenrat, which operated in Kraków until the liquidation of the ghetto in March 1943. However, foreign organizations in fact addressed their parcels to the JUS. Although the Polish resistance on several occasions sent reports to London about the JUS, we also do not know how well informed the underground was about the activities of Jewish social and self-help organizations in Kraków.[60] Faced with ambiguous information about the functioning of the JUS, the executive of the Joint nonetheless decided in the autumn of 1943 to send a new "test shipment" of food and medicine from Portugal to Kraków consisting of 1,000–1,500 parcels, with a list of items they contained. The Joint, after receiving confirmation of receipt for some of the parcels, was then willing to increase the number to 10,000 parcels per month, even twice a month. Weichert was instructed to distribute the shipments based on his assessment of current needs and the number of people in need of assistance, should he be unable to find the actual addressees. This gave him a free hand.[61] We do not know if the Joint really increased the shipments as proposed or how often they sent parcels to Kraków. Weichert only confirmed the receipt of parcels half a year later. According to correspondence that survived the war, a total of 6,200 parcels containing figs, almonds, sardines, juice, and jam were sent to Weichert between November 1943 and April 1944. Up to May 1944, Weichert had confirmed the receipt of 2,097 parcels, which meant that around two-thirds of the donations were lost or confiscated. At the same time, Stanisław Schimitzek in Lisbon, delegate of the Polish Ministry of Social Welfare in exile—probably not knowing what had happened to the parcels—considered the result "positive (satisfactory)," and the Joint thus proposed to increase the supply to 2,500 parcels per week.[62]

The JUS prioritized helping prisoners in camps around Kraków, especially Płaszów, Prokocim, Bieżanów, and Kabel, which were close to JUS headquarters and made logistics and direct supervision from the JUS easier. Many of Weichert's coworkers were among the prisoners, and some of them cooperated with him.[63] Weichert and others made sure that younger prisoners in Płaszów were given some special rations.[64] Maria Chilowiczowa, the wife of the head prisoner functionary in the camp, bought rolls and sometimes sweets using JUS funds.[65] One of the young beneficiaries, Marcel Tesse, recalled: "I was given a lump of bread a day, sometimes with some marmalade, and pea or cabbage soup for dinner; but I liked 'justowa zupa' [a hearty soup] best. We also got 'justowy chleb' [special bread from the JUS]. I was never hungry."[66]

Conflicting Views of the JUS

Soon after the JUS was established, Jewish organizations called for shutting down the organization, characterizing its work as treasonous and criminal. In particular, this opinion was espoused by Ferdynand Marek Arczyński, a leading official for the Kraków and Lviv branches of the Council for Aid to Jews (Rada Pomocy Żydom, or RPŻ [code name Żegota]); Witold Bieńkowski, also from the RPŻ; and Adolf Pan, of the Jewish Coordinating Commission (the ŻKK).[67] By all accounts, Weichert received the cease and desist order from Arczyński himself in October or November 1943.[68] Arczyński reportedly characterized JUS activities as "pernicious" and "criminal" to Weichert.[69]

Weichert's actions also came under scrutiny by the Government Delegation for Poland, the official representation of the exile government based in occupied Poland. The delegation sent Witold Bieńkowski, their representative at the Office for Jewish Affairs, to assess the situation. Based on information he obtained, Bieńkowski concluded that the Germans had in fact only handed over part of the foreign shipments to Weichert, somewhere between 10 percent and 30 percent.[70] To confirm the negative opinions expressed by members of the Jewish organizations, the Central Committee of the Bund, also hostile toward the JUS and its head, sent letters to its branches in London and to the Council for Aid to Jews, calling on them to stop sending new parcels to Kraków.[71] In a comprehensive report of the Bund sent on November 16, 1943, to Emanuel Scherer, the Bund member of the National Council (Rada Narodowa) in London, the Central Committee of the Bund outlined the reasons for breaking off all contact with the JUS. The document declared:

> This organization [JUS] is supposed to distribute medicine and other items sent by the Jews from abroad through the International Red Cross to the [Generalgouvernement] camps. In fact, however, it is a diversion carried out by the occupation authorities, who intend to keep lying and manipulating foreign public opinion regarding their attitude toward Jews, and keep the medicine for themselves.[72]

The decision was supported by the Council for Aid to Jews, which together with the Coordinating Committee asked the Polish Jewish representatives in London (Ignacy Schwarzbart and Scherer) to negotiate suspension of all shipments of medicine and other items to the JUS.[73] Members of the Coordinating Commission of the Jewish National Committee (Żydowska Komisja Narodowa) and the Bund adopted a clear position concerning the JUS. They agreed that its activity was used by the Germans for propaganda purposes; they claimed that the occupation authorities had seized as much as 90 percent of the foreign parcels sent to Jews. In fact, those organizations declared that any form of cooperation with the Germans amounted to treason.[74]

A similar stance was adopted by the Council for Aid to Jews, which supported the decision to shut down the JUS and hand over any supplies in reserve to other Jewish organizations.[75] However, Weichert disagreed: he chose not to abide by that decision and continued his activities. Foreign institutions did not stop sending parcels to Kraków either, especially since they had received detailed reports about JUS activities, prepared by Weichert, covering the period between June and December 1943.[76] The JUS received parcels from abroad at least until September of the following year. As historian Elżbieta Rączy has rightly pointed out, the continued willingness of the foreign donors to cooperate with the JUS could be explained by the fact that from their perspective, this organization was a continuation of the JSS. Weichert also offered continuity in personnel. Moreover, many Jews in need of JUS assistance clearly remained living in camps and ghettos.[77] The Coordinating Commission and the Council for Aid to Jews nonetheless continued their campaign against Weichert.[78]

On March 23, 1944, the Council for Aid to Jews once more called for closing down the JUS and breaking all contacts with its chairman.[79] Further reports and telegrams were sent to London in May and September 1944.[80] Weichert's opponents tried to disseminate a claim not only that the occupation authorities had seized the parcels sent from abroad but that Weichert was being financially rewarded for his collaboration. In 1944, information concerning this matter was reportedly provided by Jews who had escaped from Płaszów. Szymon Gotesman from the Jewish National Committee, formerly a secret political organization that had operated in the Warsaw ghetto, cited an account by one of the prisoners who reported that parcels from the JUS never reached the camp.[81] More incriminating information came from the forced labor camp in Poniatowa.[82] Consequently, Weichert was accused of collaborating with Płaszów commandant Amon Göth and Wilhelm Chilowicz from the Order Police. After the war, rumors of banquets and drinking bouts organized by Chilowicz for Göth, Weichert, and Dr. Leon Gross, the camp doctor, began to circulate.[83] In reality, however, the relationship between Weichert and Chilowicz appears to have been very hostile.[84] Chilowicz reportedly obstructed Weichert's activity in the camp, particularly his contacts with Göth and Jewish physicians.[85]

Members of the Warsaw Jewish Combat Organization joined the ranks of those expressing skepticism about the JUS's aid work and Weichert's honesty, implying that the shipments were seized by the Germans and were not reaching the Jews. But even the Jewish underground was not united in its condemnation of Weichert. Stanisław Bagniowski (aka Yitzhak Zuckerman), a Zionist activist and one of the leaders of the underground and later of the Jewish Combat Organization in the Warsaw ghetto, for example, claimed that prisoners of camps under the JUS's care received small parcels, particularly bread, and occasionally also medicine.[86]

Other witnesses suggested that Weichert had visited the Płaszów and Prokocim camps twice a week, in particular when delivering bread.[87] According to Jakub Sternberg, a prisoner and formerly a JSS adviser to the chiefs of districts in charge of administrative and personnel matters, this helped improve the condition of prisoners, who were given additional food rations; thanks to those deliveries, in September 1943, the price of a loaf of bread in the camp decreased from 300 to 40 zloty.[88] Stanisław Smreczyński, manager of the Polish CWC storehouse of medical material, testified that in 1943 Weichert had personally distributed aid packages to the Jewish prisoners in Płaszów. According to Aleksander Bieberstein, one of the Płaszów doctors, the camp hospital was well stocked with medicines delivered by the JUS.[89] From February 1944, food and drugs were also smuggled into the camp by Dawid Liebling, a Jewish functionary prisoner responsible for the cleanliness of camps' latrines and an activist in the Jewish underground, who collected them from the JUS warehouses.[90] Moreover, following Liebling's appeal, Weichert immediately sent the badly needed medicines to the Kabel camp. Bieberstein added: "I firmly believe that if it had not been for Dr. Weichert's assistance, we would have been unable to treat patients at all. I am convinced that many people are now alive thanks to his help."[91]

Weichert issued monthly reports with detailed manifests of goods received from the International Red Cross, the Joint, and the Board of Deputies of British

Jews in London.[92] In total, he collected 649 parcels from those organizations between January and March 1944.[93] Thousands of food parcels continued to arrive in the months that followed. Between 1943 and 1944, parcels from abroad were almost the only source of aid given to the Jews in the Generalgouvernement, apart from the very low official rations. The JUS was reestablished after the Kraków ghetto was closed down. Contributions from the Polish Central Welfare Council were now also very limited. The SS gave the JUS permission to resume its activity, provided that it would be limited to the distribution of medicines sent by the Red Cross among prisoners of Jewish camps. Weichert, however, tried to circumvent that restriction and negotiated for including parcels from other sources in those transactions. He also managed to obtain authorization from the German authorities to distribute food, clothing, and medicine sent by different Jewish organizations in Switzerland and Sweden (such as the Children's Relief Organization [OSE], HAFIP, CPR, RELICO, the Sankt-Gallen Bikur Chaulim Society, Arbetsutskottet för hjälp åt Europas judar in Stockholm, and many others).[94] For them, Weichert and the JUS remained the only contact in occupied Poland that could officially receive aid for Jews from abroad, and they continued to send parcels, even though they had to be aware that most of them would be confiscated.

As we have seen, the relationship between Weichert and foreign humanitarian agencies remained good. Representatives of Jewish organizations abroad were kept informed of the situation of Jews in occupied Poland and allegations against the JUS.[95] The Polish government-in-exile tried to stop the shipments out of fear that the Germans would confiscate them.[96] Yet for Joseph J. Schwartz, representative of the Joint in Lisbon, the fact that Weichert worked with the consent of the Germans did not necessarily mean that the "aid did not reach a certain number of Jews."[97] A similar stance was adopted by representatives of the Board of Deputies, who suggested to Polish authorities that "whilst there was undoubtedly a leakage to the Germans of these food parcels sent to Kraków, the dispatch of parcels should be continued because a substantial number of Jews were, in fact, being helped thereby, and the loss to German sources was an inevitable risk that had to be taken."[98] The Polish Ministry of Labor and Welfare decided to investigate the allegations but did not receive any convincing evidence and lacked the power to intervene in any event.

In March 1944, the Joint proposed sending 2,500 food parcels once a week from Portugal, in view of an "entirely positive" assessment of the JUS's activity. The shipment commenced at the beginning of May 1944.[99] A few delivery confirmations of parcels from different camps in the Generalgouvernement were preserved, for example, from the forced labor camp in Andrychów, near Auschwitz.[100] Food and medicines from the JUS also reached camps in Skarżysko, Częstochowa, Prokocim, Bieżanów, Bochnia, and Trzebinia. They were probably the last foreign shipments sent to Weichert; a month later, he stopped all JUS operations, though parcels were sent to camps even after the JUS was closed down for good in July 1944.[101] The JUS's cooperation with the Joint lasted until the late summer of 1944, and the Joint even arranged to send food parcels from Switzerland and Sweden.[102] The decision to continue the shipments was taken in full awareness of the fact that only a small percentage of the parcels were probably reaching their Jewish addressees.[103]

Weichert had been aware for some time that his life was in danger.[104] In 1944, with the end of the war approaching, the Germans decided to finally liquidate the JUS and get rid of Weichert. He simply knew too much. JSS and JUS reports contained information on the number of Jews held in camps and their living conditions. At the end of July 1944, he was warned by Mieczysław Pemper, a prisoner of Płaszów, of the Germans' plans. The warning allowed Weichert to find refuge and hand over the management of JUS warehouses to the CWC. Juliusz Madritsch, the owner of a textile plant, offered to find shelter for Weichert in Vienna; the Council of Aid to Jews proposed a hiding place at the Tyniec monastery outside of Kraków. In the end, Weichert at first hid for a short time in the CWC's warehouses and later accepted help from Stanisław Dobrowolski, president of the Kraków Council for Aid to Jews, who placed him in several "safe houses" in the city. A Polish woman, Wanda Drewnicka, organized another haven in her apartment, where Weichert stayed between August 1944 and January 1945.[105]

After the JUS was shut down, representatives of the Jewish underground decided to take over the goods stored in its warehouses. According to a detailed list, the Council for Aid to Jews received almost 140 kilograms of tea, 20.5 kilograms of coffee, 315 kilograms of almonds, 6,315 tins of sardines, and 150 bottles of juice, all of which was sold bit by bit on the black market. The estimated value of those goods was approximately 1.7 million zloty, which allowed the Council for Aid to Jews to increase the number of people it aided, including prisoners in Płaszów.[106]

Postwar Judicial Proceedings against Weichert

Following Poland's liberation, Weichert was indicted by the Special Criminal Court in Kraków, an institution established by Polish authorities to pursue and punish Nazi criminals and their collaborators.[107] He was arrested on April 7, 1945, charged with collaboration with the occupation authorities, and placed in a jail in Kraków. The arrest warrant was issued under article 1, section 2, of the Decree of August 31, 1944, "on the penalties imposed on fascist and Nazi criminals guilty of homicide and abuses of civilians and prisoners of war, as well as on traitors of the Polish Nation."[108]

Weichert was mainly criticized because of his position and the privileges he enjoyed after the liquidation of the Kraków ghetto: his status in the JUS allowed him to move freely around Kraków, without the mandatory armband marked with the Star of David. Furthermore, he was often seen with German officials who formally were his superiors, in particular whenever he visited the Płaszów camp. At the trial, Weichert was also accused of misappropriating items sent to the JUS and of leading an ostentatious, luxurious lifestyle on the "Aryan side."[109] These were, in all probability, baseless insinuations.

The investigation lasted nine months; several dozen witnesses testified, including former prisoners of concentration camps as well as members of Polish and Jewish aid organizations. Representatives of the Jewish underground for the most part criticized Weichert's activities. Jewish survivors of the Płaszów camp and its subcamps outside Kraków did not, however, share their opinion and supported him. On January 7, 1946, the Special Criminal Court exonerated Weichert on the following grounds:

> So far no fact has come to light that would condemn the defendant both ethically and morally. Under present circumstances, it would be unfair to say that the defendant did knowingly collaborate with the occupation authorities, as neither the defendant's actions, nor the defendant himself give rise to such accusations—there is no evidence that the defendant agreed to collaborate with the occupation authorities. . . . Therefore, these allegations shall be rejected by the Court, and the defendant is thereby exonerated.[110]

Weichert was released from the jail five days later. However, his troubles with the postwar legal order were far from over.[111] His case was submitted for reexamination to the Najwyższy Trybunał Narodowy (Supreme National Tribunal), the war crimes tribunal in Warsaw. In September 1946, Stanisław Kurowski, one of its prosecutors, rejected this appeal.[112]

Still others disagreed. The decision of the Kraków court was questioned, among others, by Adolf Berman, chairman of the Central Committee of Jews in Poland (Centralny Komitet Żydów w Polsce, or CKŻP), and members of the Bund. One of the events that triggered the smear campaign against Weichert was the article "Obrzydliwość, brzydź się nią! O pisarzu, który jest oskarżony o zdradę"

(A detestable abomination! Writer accused of high treason), published on October 7, 1946, in the *Folkscajtung* by Leo Finkelstein, a writer and journalist associated with the Bund.[113] Finkelstein demanded that Weichert be punished; he called him "a detestable traitor" and "[Hans] Frank's buddy" and argued that Weichert should appear before the Jewish Social Court, a kind of "honor court."[114] Finkelstein's main allegations against Weichert, based on hearsay and testimony of "an eyewitness from Lviv," included deliberately collaborating with the occupation authorities, participating in the Nazi propaganda, intentionally misleading foreign public opinion concerning the situation of Jews in Poland, and benefiting from the suffering of the Jewish community.

It is possible that Finkelstein's article caused a shift of opinion in the postwar Jewish community. Weichert did not send a rebuttal until November 8, 1946. The *Folkscajtung* never published it, nor did the editor mention it in any way.[115] The following month, the *Nasze Słowo* (Our word) journal published a commentary on Finkelstein's article, entitled "Zdrajcy pod sąd" (Traitors should be tried), echoing elements of the original article.[116] Over the next two years, several other texts criticizing Weichert—but some also supporting him—appeared.[117]

As a consequence, Weichert's case became a matter of interest to the executive board of the CKŻP, the Jewish umbrella organization in liberated Poland. Its members supported Weichert's adversaries and indicted him once again in 1949. The trial before the CKŻP Social Court took place in November and December 1949. Crucially, the court did not have official legal standing, but it did have the power to exclude Weichert from the postwar Jewish community.[118] Unlike the Kraków prosecutor's office, the Social Court mainly evaluated Weichert's attitude toward other Jews rather than his work as chairman of the JUS.[119] This was a result of their limited powers: they focused only on crimes against the Jewish people and community. The same people who had testified a few years earlier were named as witnesses in the new trial, but not many witnesses of those events survived, and many of the remaining survivors had left Poland. Two radically opposing worldviews clashed in the courtroom. One viewpoint saw the honor of the Jewish people on trial. The other gave primacy to the question of how the largest number of Jews could be saved during the occupation.

The atmosphere grew tense primarily within left-wing groups previously associated with the Jewish Combat Organization, which were particularly invested in putting Weichert on trial. They were outraged by the fact that Polish judges had not fully considered Weichert's activities as proof of collaboration. As historian Andrzej Żbikowski rightly pointed out, Weichert, according to his adversaries, had been guilty of "not complying with the Jewish National

Committee's decisions, claiming to be the only entity representing Polish Jews who had been murdered."[120] His wartime behavior, they believed, had benefited German propaganda. Gabriel Finder, another historian of these events, adds that Weichert's case also fulfilled a need in the survivor community to name a small group of traitors, thereby magnifying the integrity of the rest of the community.[121] Weichert's active postwar cooperation with the Chief Commission for the Investigation of German Crimes in Poland[122] (predecessor of the Institute of National Remembrance) was frowned upon as well, probably because he was not considered reliable by the postwar Jewish leadership. Ultimately, Weichert and others were used as important witnesses and experts in trials of German war criminals. A strong personal animosity was another reason why Weichert was so vehemently and obsessively pursued by other Jewish activists. Weichert was a man with a strong personality and an individualist who had acted according to his own principles. These personality traits proved effective in his relations with the German authorities but led to conflicts with other members of the Jewish community.[123]

Many old tensions were revisited with renewed fervor at the trial. The Bundist Berman testified, "I saw the JUS back then as a knife in the back of the Jewish fight against the fascists, as an organization that facilitated Hitler's propaganda and conspiracies of the Anglo-Saxon reactionaries. Both in 1943 and in 1944, as well as today, I perceive the JUS clearly as a bunch of collaborators."[124] Furthermore, witnesses testified that the Jewish Combat Organization had condemned Weichert to death in 1944, though the sentence was never carried out.[125] Nevertheless, as in the previous trial, most witnesses, including important functionaries from the Płaszów camp and Weichert's associates, testified in his favor. A letter signed by forty former prisoners of concentration camps in occupied Poland declared that aid provided by the JUS at the end of the war had been crucial for their survival.[126] Strong emotions persisted around decisions about wartime aid and the conditions under which it was distributed. They continued to animate Polish Jewish survivors long after the war was over.

A sentence was passed on December 28, 1949, when the Social Court of the CKŻP found Weichert guilty and "severely condemned" his actions. Furthermore, the judgment stated that the "JUS had been, in its essence, an organization of collaborators."[127] The court's findings concerning the most significant part of the matter under investigation were questionable: the sentence mentioned that the court failed to find evidence that Weichert had obtained any financial or personal profit during the war. The most likely reason for the condemnation of Weichert was contained in the comments of the president and several members of the court: "Dr. Weichert's behavior should be condemned all the more severely because it diverged so sharply from the behavior of that part of our society that decided to fight the occupation authorities."[128] Accusations of collaboration through certain wartime aid initiatives for Jews caused deep divisions in the Jewish community, both during and after the occupation. Assessments of JUS activity remained divisive but inconclusive. Furthermore, Weichert's case was used within antisemitic circles, which also attempted to accuse parts of the Jewish community of collaboration with the German authorities.[129]

Conclusion

The postwar proceedings in Polish and Jewish courts failed to end the public debate about Weichert's wartime actions.[130] The Social Court run by the CKŻP discredited the legitimacy of the JUS, condemning Weichert for collaborating with German authorities and for being complicit in the theft of shipments sent to Kraków by foreign organizations. Germans regularly stole from the Jews, and Jewish property had been confiscated from the first months of the war. Another problem was the seizure of Jewish property by local Germans in high-level positions in the Kraków Gestapo (such as SS-Sturmscharführer Wilhelm Kunde) or at the German camp in Płaszów.[131]

The issue that sparked the greatest ire among Weichert's opponents appears to have been his refusal to submit to the decisions made by the Bund and the Jewish National Committee, which demanded that the JUS close its doors. He openly stood up to other Jewish leaders, while his contacts with the occupation authorities were unacceptable to underground leaders from a moral standpoint. The Jewish underground then tried to no avail to exert pressure on foreign institutions that supported Weichert, in particular the Joint and the Board of Deputies of British Jews. Yet these foreign agencies, like Weichert, chose to aid their fellow Jews in a time of mass extermination of the Jewish people, even if most of the parcels sent from abroad were eventually seized by German authorities. According to some reports, nearly two-thirds of those parcels were lost or confiscated; Weichert denied such allegations until the very end, referring to records of deliveries that he claimed to have kept regularly. This may have been a calculation on his part, but it succeeded in keeping some stream of aid packages coming from foreign organizations. Unfortunately, it is uncertain how the JUS monitored the receipt of parcels. The only surviving receipts for packages are those for deliveries between January and March 1944.[132]

The array of postwar investigations left their mark on Weichert. Several of his requests for permission to immigrate to Israel were denied. The decision of the Social Court excluded him from the social and cultural life of Polish Jews for years after the war. His employment applications submitted to the Central Administration for Theater, Opera, and Philharmonics were denied, as were those sent to theaters in Warsaw and Łódź. He did not find work in his profession again until 1957. Rafał Węgrzyniak was right in concluding that "the plan of Weichert's adversaries to discredit him was fully successful."[133] He was finally permitted to emigrate from Poland in October 1957, and in early 1958 he left for Tel Aviv, where he died on March 11, 1967.[134]

Notes

1 Archives of the Institute of National Remembrance in Kraków (Archiwum Instytutu Pamięci Narodowej, AIPN), sign. Kr 1/1212. Translated from Polish. Her fate is unknown.

2 For a more detailed account of the JUS, see Alicja Jarkowska-Natkaniec, *Wymuszona współpraca czy zdrada? Wokół przypadków kolaboracji Żydów w okupowanym Krakówie* (Kraków: Kraków Universitas, 2018).

3 AIPN, sign. SSK Kr 240, Weichert's criminal case file, 20.

4 Rafał Węgrzyniak, "Sprawa Michała Weicherta," in *Pamiętnik Teatralny*, 1997, 46, book 1/4, 279–81. See also Rafał Węgrzyniak, *Procesy doktora Weicherta* (Warsaw: Państ. Instytut Wydaw, 2017).

5 Bogdan Musiał, *Deutsche Zivilverwaltung und Judenverfolgung im Generalgouvernement. Eine Fallstudie zum Distrikt Lublin 1939–1944* (Wiesbaden: Harrassowitz, 1999), 87.

6 *Gazeta Żydowska*, 2, no. 19 (March 7, 1941): 4; Tadeusz Pankiewicz, *Apteka w getcie Krakówskim* (Kraków: Literackie, 2012), 16.

7 *Gazeta Żydowska* 2, no. 19 (March 7, 1941): 4.

8 Pankiewicz, *Apteka w getcie Krakówskim*, 16.

9 The Blue Police was the common name for Polish police operating in the Generalgouvernement. Adam Hempel, *Pogrobowcy klęski. Rzecz o policji "granatowej" w Generalnym Gubernatorstwie 1939–1945* (Warsaw: Państwowe Wydawn. Nauk., 1990); Jan Grabowski, *Na Posterunku: udział policji granatowej i kryminalnej w zagładzie Żydów* (Wołowiec: Wydawnictwo Czarne, 2020).

10 Alicja Jarkowska-Natkaniec, "Żydowska Służba Porządkowa w okupowanym Krakówie. Nowa elita w getcie Krakówskim i niemieckim obozie Płaszów. Wybrane historie," in *Elity i przedstawiciele społeczności żydowskiej podczas II wojny światowej (1939–1945)*, ed. Martyna Grądzka-Rejak and Aleksandra Namysło (Kraków: Instytut Pamięci Narodowej, 2017), 197–215.

11 Ryszard Kotarba, *Niemiecki obóz w Płaszowie 1942–1945* (Warsaw: Instytut Pamięci Narodowej, 2009), 67. According to Roman Kiełkowski, "Obóz pracy przymusowej i koncentracyjny w Płaszowie," *Przegląd Lekarski*, no. 1 (1971): 27, the number of Jewish prisoners was ca. 20,000; in accordance with the report of the Council for Aid to Jews (RPŻ, code name Żegota), that was the number of detainees as of August 1, 1944; see Archive of the Jewish Historical Institute in Warsaw (ŻIH), 209/28, KL Płaszów. Notice concerning the Płaszów camp, 4. In Mieczysław (Mietek) Pemper's opinion, 22,000 to 24,000 were being held at the camp. However, this number applies to mid-1944.

12 AIPN, sygn. SSK KR 240, Weichert's criminal case file, an account by Natan Stern, 100; tamże, sygn. 010/6582, Sprawa Michała Weicherta, an account by Jakub Perlsm, 102; ŻIH, sygn. 313/137, Weichert's case before the CKŻP Social Court, an account by Jakub Sternberg, 33, 43; accounts by Dawid Liebling, Felicja Rosenblatt, and Szymon Szlachet, 85, 86, 94; AIPN, sygn. 010/6582, Weichert's criminal case file, an account by Feliks Rogowski, 143.

13 Michał M. Borwicz, Nella Rost, and Józef Wulf, eds., *W trzecią rocznicę zagłady getta w Krakówie: (13.III.1943–13.III.1946)* (Kraków: Centralny Komitet Żydów Polskich, 1946), 58; Kotarba, *Niemiecki obóz w Płaszowie*, 28.

14 Tadeusz Wroński, *Kronika okupowanego Krakówa* (Kraków: Wyd. lit., 1974), 259.

15 Archiwum Okręgowej Komisji Badania Zbrodni przeciwko Narodowi Polskiemu (AOKBZpNP), sign. KPP 62/73, 31; Kotarba, *Niemiecki obóz w Płaszowie*, 30; Pankiewicz, *Apteka w getcie Krakówskim*, 182.

16 An account by Roman Kraftlos, in *Dokumenty zbrodni i męczeństwa*, ed. Michał M. Borwicz, Nella Rost, and Józef Wulf (Kraków: Centralna Żydowska Komisja Historyczna w Polsce, 1945), 115.

17 See account by Janina Nehaus, Yad Vashem Archives (YVA), sign. O.3/1249.

18 An account by Leib Salpeter, in *Dokumenty zbrodni i męczeństwa*, ed. Michał M. Borwicz, Nella Rost, and Józef Wulf (Kraków: Centralna Żydowska Komisja Historyczna w Polsce, 1945), 111; Nachman Blumental, ed., *Proces ludobójcy Amona Leopolda Goetha przed Najwyższym Trybunałem Narodowym* (Warsaw: CŻKHwP, 1947), 276.

19 Elżbieta Rączy, *Zagłada Żydów w dystrykcie Krakówskim w latach 1939–1945* (Rzeszów: Uniwersytet Rzeszowski, Instytut Pamięci Narodowej, 2014), 285. Rączy explains the discrepancies between the numbers of victims in note 107.

20 Danuta Czech, *Kalendarz wydarzeń w KL Auschwitz* (Oświęcim: Wydawnictwo Państwowego Muzeum w Oświęcimiu-Brzezince, 1992), 370; Rączy, *Zagłada Żydów w dystrykcie Krakówskim*, 284; Kotarba, *Niemiecki obóz w Płaszowie*, 30.

21 ANKr, "Małopolska Agencja Prasowa," no. 22–23/12 VIII 1943, "Przegląd Polski," no. 16/31, 16 VIII 1943. ŻIH, 302/8 (Z. Szpingarn's diary), 21; 301/3731 (account by B. Steif), 6; 301/247 (account by D. Ansübel), 2; 302/25 (M. Weichert's diary), cz. II, 50.

22 On the creation of the executive committee of the JSS, see Aleksandra Bańkowska, "W poszukiwaniu elit: rekrutacja członków komitetów lokalnych Żydowskiej Samopomocy Społecznej w Generalnym Gubernatorstwie w latach 1940–1942," in *Elity i przedstawiciele społeczności żydowskiej*, 119–31.

23 ŻIH, sign. Ring II/118/28, vol. 30. On the first years of operation of the JSS in the Generalgouvernement and occupied Kraków, see also Weichert's unpublished memoirs (ŻIH, sign. 302/25).

24 The general governor's office decided to set up three separate welfare organizations, one for Poles (Polish Central Welfare Council—Rada Główna Opiekuńcza), one for Jews (JSS), and one for Ukrainians (Ukrainian Central Council). The Central Welfare Council was financed with private donations and subsidized by Polish institutions as well as occupation authorities. See *Statut Naczelnej Rady Opiekuńczej i Rady Głównej Opiekuńczej. Regulamin RGO* (Warsaw: Rada Główna Opiekuńcza, 1941); Bogdan Kroll, *Opieka i samopomoc społeczna w Warszawie 1939–1945. Społeczny Komitet Samopomocy Społecznej i warszawskie agendy Rady Głównej Opiekuńczej* (Warsaw: Pańswowe Wydawn. Naukowe, 1977); Bogdan Kroll, *Rada Główna Opiekuńcza 1939–1945* (Warsaw: Książka i Wiedza, 1985); Adam Ronikier, *Pamiętniki 1939–1945* (Kraków: Wydawnictwo Literackie, 2013); Janusz Kłapeć, *Rada Główna Opiekuńcza w dystrykcie lubelskim w latach 1940–1944* (Lublin: Wydawnictwo Uniwersytetu Marii Curie-Skłodowskiej, 2011); Katarzyna Kocik, "Pomoc charytatywna Kościoła Krakówskiego w czasie okupacji niemieckiej," in *Kościół Krakówski 1939–1945*, ed. Łukasz Klimek et al. (Kraków: Muzeum Historyczne Miasta Krakówa, 2014), 97–125. It changed on December 9, 1940, to the Government of the Generalgouvernement (Regierung des Generalgouvernements). Kroll, *Rada Główna Opiekuńcza*, 142–50.

25 Aleksandra Bańkowska, "Jewish Social Welfare Institutions and Facilities in the General Government from 1939 to 1944: A Preliminary Study," *Studia z Dziejów Rosji i Europy Środkowo-Wschodniej* 53 (2018): 137.

26 For additional information on the activities of the KOP and the KOM, see Rączy, *Zagłada Żydów w dystrykcie Krakówskim*, 233–43.

27 Lucy S. Dawidowicz, *The War against the Jews, 1933–1945* (New York: Henry Holt, 1975), 244; Rączy, *Zagłada Żydów w dystrykcie Krakówskim*, 238.

28 Bieberstein acted as chairman of the Kraków Judenrat from September 1939 to September 1940. He was removed from office for helping Jews who wanted to stay in the city. Between the summer of 1942 and March 13, 1943, he served as head of the newly established orphanage.

29 German authorities established the institution on March 29, 1940, to unify social welfare and humanitarian aid for all nationalities residing in the Generalgouvernement, except for Germans. Its members were representatives of three autonomous social welfare councils: seven from the Polish council (Central Welfare Council), one from the Ukrainian Central Council, and one from the Jewish council (the JSS). Kłapeć, *Rada Główna Opiekuńcza*, 129; Kroll, *Rada Główna Opiekuńcza*, 96. Contrary to the intentions of the German occupiers, the CWC cooperated with Jewish care organizations (the Joint, JSS, and later JUS). The Kraków CWC included a Department of Care for Prisoners and Their Families, and its activities provided aid for prisoners in Płaszów. Permission to begin assisting the prisoners (especially by providing bread) was not granted until the end of October 1943, and systematic help only began at the end of that December. (Families also sent packages to individuals.) See ANKr, DOKr 21, 71 (letter from CWC director Seyfried of October 7, 1943); PolKO 37, 503 (report for October 1943); ANKr, PolKO 37, 841, 843–44; AIPN, 502/283, 44.

30 ŻIH, sign. 210/69, AJDC correspondence with CWC, VI–XI 1940, 2–3. The distribution of parcels from abroad and other aid were organized along similar lines. The CWC operated through a network of care councils and their delegates in individual districts, counties, and cities, distributing food, clothing, and cash to the most needy and running institutions such as community kitchens, shelters, and nursing homes.

31 Yehuda Bauer, *American Jewry and the Holocaust. The American Jewish Joint Distribution Committee 1939–1945* (Detroit: Wayne State University Press, 1982), 99.

32 ŻIH, sign. 211/171, JSS executive committee department notes, 26–28.

33 At the end of May 1940, an office for foreign letters, run by the Jewish Emigration Aid Society (JEAS) (affiliated with the JSS), was established. The JEAS was an institution that had operated in Poland

since 1924 and was charged with searching for addresses of relatives living abroad and acting as an intermediary in forwarding letters from abroad. They also took requests to find relatives in America, Russia, Palestine, and elsewhere. Such letters were also sent through the Polish Red Cross. Aleksandra Bańkowska and Maria Ferenc Piotrowska, eds., *Archiwum Ringelbluma. "Konspiracyjne Archiwum Getta Warszawy,"* vol. 27, *Żydowska Samopomoc Społeczna w Warszawie 1939–1943* (Warsaw: Żydowski Instytut Historyczny im. Emanuela Ringelbluma, 2017), 393, 483.

34 Aid provided by the JSS in 1942 reportedly covered 412 facilities. Medicine distribution points were located in 207 cities and towns across the Generalgouvernement. See the case of Weichert before the CKŻP Social Court, ŻIH, sign. 313/137, Weichert's testimony, 383.

35 ŻIH, sign. 211/171, JSS executive committee department notes, 26.

36 Bańkowska, "Jewish Social Welfare Institutions," 136–42.

37 They were previously sent to Warsaw; at the end of March and in April and May 1940, large amounts—from 840,000 to 1 million zloty per month—were sent to the Warsaw office. ŻIH, AJDC, 210/8–10, 210/186–190, 210/109, as cited in Bańkowska, "Jewish Social Welfare Institutions," 146.

38 Rączy, *Zagłada Żydów w dystrykcie Krakówskim*, 240–41; Dawidowicz, *The War against the Jews*, 329–30.

39 Joint aid reached the Polish ghettos, thanks to the efforts of Saly Mayer, director of the organization's Swiss branch, and Isaac Gitterman, director of the Polish branch. Mayer had contact with individuals in Switzerland, who in turn had links to Polish underground organizations.

40 ŻIH, sign. 211/594, JSS executive committee department notes, 21, 40.

41 Pankiewicz, *Apteka w getcie Krakówskim*, 65.

42 Katarzyna Zimmerer, *Zamordowany świat: losy Żydów w Krakówie 1939–1945* (Kraków: Wydawnictwo Literackie, 2008), 97.

43 Pankiewicz, *Apteka w getcie Krakówskim*, 55.

44 ŻIH, sign. Ring II/1, Mf. ŻIH—793, GG Conference Report, Kraków, February 29, 1940, concerning the financial situation of the Jewish community in Kraków, 40.

45 See ibid., 53.

46 Marek Jóźwik, "Wstęp," in *Inwentarz Żydowskiej Samopomocy Społecznej*, ed. Marek Jóźwik et al. (Warsaw: Archiwum Żydowskiego Instytutu Historycznego im. Emanuela Ringelbluma, 2004).

47 Kotarba, *Nazistowski obóz w Płaszowie*, 72.

48 ŻIH, sign. 313/137, Weichert's case before the CKŻP Social Court, Tadeusz Pankiewicz and Weichert's testimonies, 373, 504.

49 Pankiewicz, *Apteka w getcie Krakówskim*, 81; Aleksander Bieberstein, *Zagłada Żydów w Krakówie* (Kraków: Wydawn. Literackie, 2001), 60; ŻIH, sign. 302/25, Weichert memoirs, 567.

50 ŻIH, sign. 302/25, Weichert memoirs, 67–68.

51 During the war, the prewar Optima chocolate factory facilities at Węgierska Street no. 7/9 served as a concert hall and craft workshop facilities for Jews.

52 Jóźwik, "Wstęp," 4; Andrzej Żbikowski, *Sąd Społeczny przy CKŻP. Wojenne rozliczenia społeczności żydowskiej w Polsce* (Warsaw: Żydowski Instytut Historyczny im. Emanuela Ringelbluma, 2014), 135–36; ŻIH, sign. 313/137, Weichert's case before the CKŻP Social Court, 11. The new board of the JUS consisted of Dr. Chaim Hilfstein, Dr. Eliasz Fisch, Natan Stern, Aleksander Bieberstein, Artur Jurand, secretary Anna Schneeweiss, and Koppel Woller.

53 Jóźwik, "Wstęp," 4; Żbikowski, *Sąd Społeczny przy* CKŻP, 135–36, 312; ŻIH, sign. 313/137, Weichert's case before the CKŻP Social Court, 11, 214.

54 Bańkowska, "Jewish Social Welfare Institutions," 142.

55 London Metropolitan Archives (LMA), ACC/3121/C/11/12/92, Board of Deputies of British Jews report of May 22, 1943.

56 Węgrzyniak, "Sprawa Michała Weicherta," 285.

57 LMA, ACC/3121/C/11/12/92, report of the International Red Cross of September 14, 1943, concerning, among other things, cooperation between the Red Cross, JUS, and Weichert.

58 Ibid.; Rączy, *Zagłada Żydów w dystrykcie Krakówskim*, 251, mentions a total of sixty-six facilities supervised by JUS; forty-nine of them were to be located in the Kraków district. See also Michal Weichert, Żydowska Samopomoc Społeczna, manuscript, 58–72, National Library of Israel, Michael Weichert Archive, 371.11.1.

59 *Małopolska Agencja Prasowa*, no. 12, June 4, 1943.

60 *Wolność*, no. 24, June 10, 1943, 2.

61 LMA, ACC/3121/C/11/12/92, conversation with Schwartz, November 5, 1943; Brotman to Schwarzbart, November 28, 1943; Hurwitz (JDC) to Brotman, March 9, 1944, and June 14, 1944.

62 LMA, ACC/3121/C/11/12/92, statement of food parcels, sent on account of the Board of Deputies of British Jews (undated, probably May 1944).

63 For more on this subject, see Alicja Jarkowska, *Operating against the Individual: The Structures of Power in the Plaszow Concentration Camp* (forthcoming, Kraków 2022).

64 AIPN, sign. SSK KR 240, Weichert's criminal case file, an account by Natan Stern, 100; AIPN, sign. 010/6582, Weichert's case, an account by Jakub Perlsman, 102. Perlsman also mentioned condensed milk delivered by Weichert to mothers.

65 ŻIH, sign. 301/5312, an account by Amalia Hofstäter-Mandelbaumowa, 4–5; ŻIH, sign. 301/3205, an account by Szymon Koch, 2.

66 An account by Marceli Tesse, ŻIH, sign. 301/571, 1. Józef Horn also mentioned the "zupa justowa"; see AIPN, sign. 010/6582, Weichert's case, 104–5.

67 The Council for Aid to Jews was an underground social organization created in December 1942 with the approval of the Delegation of the Government of the Republic of Poland in the Generalgouvernement operating in Warsaw. It functioned until the end of the war. RPŻ's help consisted mainly of providing material aid, organizing accommodations, preparing hideouts and false papers, and caring for children who had escaped from the ghetto, placing them in care institutions. The Jewish Coordinating Commission was an affiliate of the Jewish National Committee and the Bund and was established in October 1942 in the Warsaw ghetto.

68 Węgrzyniak, "Sprawa Michała Weicherta," 285. AIPN, sign. 010/6582, Weichert's case, an account by Marek Arczyński, 9; AIPN, sign. SSK Kr 240, Weichert's criminal case file, an account by Stanisław Dobrowolski, president of the RPŻ in Kraków during the war, 56, 67, 72.

69 AIPN, sign. 010/6582, Weichert's case, an account by Marek Arczyński, 9. According to Stanisław Dobrowolski, the decision to dissolve the JUS was a result of the report prepared at the turn of 1943/1944 by Marek Arczyński; ibid., 11.

70 AIPN, sign. 010/6582, Weichert's case, an account by Witold Bieńkowski, 14, 75.

71 The General Jewish Labor Bund in Lithuania, Poland, and Russia was a leftist, working-class, anti-Zionist Jewish party that existed from 1897 to 1948. Its members actively organized the Jewish resistance movement during World War II.

72 Władysław Bartoszewski and Zofia Lewinówna, eds., *Ten jest z ojczyzny mojej. Polacy z pomocą Żydom 1939–1945* (Kraków: Wydawnictwo Znak, 1969), 991.

73 Ignacy Schwarzbart (1888–1961) was a Zionist activist and member of the National Council of the Republic of Poland in exile. He represented the Jewish community and organized aid for Jews persecuted in occupied Poland.

74 AIPN, sign. 010/6582, Sprawa Michała Weicherta, 76; AIPN, sign. 010/6582, report of the Jewish National Committee in Poland, sent from Warsaw on May 24, 1944, 14, 80; Węgrzyniak, *Procesy doktora Weicherta*, 227–39, 248–49.

75 Teresa Prekerowa, *Konspiracyjna Rada Pomocy Żydom w Warszawie 1942–1943* (Warsaw: Państwowy Instytut Wydawniczy, 1982), 401; Bartosz Heksel, "Krakówska Rada Pomocy Żydom," in *Żegota. Ukryta pomoc*, ed. Bartosz Heksel and Katarzyna Kocik (Kraków: Muzeum Historyczne Miasta Krakówa, 2016), 125–26.

76 LMA, ACC/3121/C/11/12/92, report on the functioning of the Jüdische Unterstützungsstelle für das Generalgouvernement received from Geneva by Ernest Frischer, member of the Czechoslovak State Council, sent in May 1944 to the Board of Deputies of British Jews.

77 Rączy, *Zagłada Żydów w dystrykcie Krakówskim*, 253; ŻIH, sign. 344/147, Weichert's case file, 21.

78 ŻIH, sign. 313/137, Weichert's case before the CKŻP Social Court, 46.

79 Marek Arczyński and Wiesław Balcerak, *Kryptonim "Żegota." Z dziejów pomocy Żydom w Polsce 1939–1945* (Warsaw: "Czytelnik," 1979), 240. The document bears the date "28 III 1944." See AIPN, sign. 010/6582, Weichert's case, 3. In the spring of 1944, a final decision on liquidation of the JUS was also sent from Warsaw; see AIPN, sign. 010/6582, Weichert's case, an account by Stanisław Dobrowolski, 11.

80 Kazimierz Iranek-Osmecki, *Kto ratuje jedno życie . . . Polacy i Żydzi 1939–1945* (London: Orbis, 1968), 232.

81 Ibid.

82 Żbikowski, *Sąd Społeczny przy CKŻP*, 137.

83 AIPN, sign. SSK Kr 240, Weichert's criminal case file, 8.

84 AIPN, sign. 010/6582, Weichert's case, testimony of Mieczysław Pemper, 138.

85 ŻIH, sign. 313/137, Weichert's case before the CKŻP Social Court, testimony of Mieczysław Pemper, clerk at the camp commandant's office, 42; AIPN, sign. SSK Kr 240, Weichert's criminal case file, testimony of Natan Stern, 100.

86 AIPN, sign. SSK Kr 240, Weichert's criminal case file, testimony of Stanisław Bagniowski (aka Icchak Cukierman), 29. It was confirmed by Maria Górecka, who testified that parcels sent by the RPŻ to the camps

reached the Jewish prisoners; see ŻIH, sign. 313/137, Weichert's case before the CKŻP Social Court, 14. Natan Stern vouched for Weichert; food was mostly supplied by the JUS; ŻIH, sign. 313/137, 40.

87 ŻIH, sign. 313/137, Weichert's case before the CKŻP Social Court, testimony of Jakub Sternberg, 33; AIPN, sign. 010/6582, Weichert's case, testimony of Feliks Rogowski, 143.

88 ŻIH, sign. 313/137, Weichert's case before the CKŻP Social Court, testimony of Jakub Sternberg, 33; AIPN, sign. 010/6582, Weichert's case, testimony of Teodor Dembitzer, 140.

89 ŻIH, sign. 313/137, Weichert's case before the CKŻP Social Court, testimony of Aleksander Bieberstein, 41–42; see also his 1949 testimony before the Voivodship ŻKH in Kraków, in AIPN, sign. 010/6582, Weichert's case, 125–26; AIPN, sign. SSK Kr 240, Weichert's criminal case file, testimony of Natan Stern, Mieczysław Pemper, and Helena Anisfeld-Dobrowolska, 102, 108, 136–38.

90 See Alicja Jarkowska-Natkaniec, "Powojenne procesy członków Jüdischer Ordnungsdienst w okupowanym Krakówie. Casus Dawida Lieblinga," *Studia Żydowskie. Almanach* 4 (2014): 97–114; AIPN, sign. SSK Kr 240, Weichert's criminal case file, testimony of Dawid Liebling, 46.

91 ŻIH, sign. 313/137, Weichert's case before the CKŻP Social Court, testimony of Aleksander Bieberstein, 41–42.

92 LMA, ACC/3121/C11/12/92, AJDC Lisbon (Robert Pilpel) to Dr. Stanisław Schimitzek (manager of the Polish Refugee Assistance Committee in Portugal, Lisbon), May 9, 1944.

93 LMA, ACC/3121/C11/12/92, Jüdische Unterstützungsstelle für das Generalgouvernement report for the months January–May 1944 sent to the Board of Deputies of British Jews.

94 LMA, ACC/3121/C11/12/92, Board of Deputies Papers, a letter by Stanisław Schimitzek, delegate of the Minister of Labor and Social Care in Lisbon, to the Ministry of Labor and Social Care in London, May 11, 1944; LMA, ACC/3121/C11/12/92, AJDC Lisbon (Robert Pilpel) to Dr. Stanisław Schimitzek (manager of the Polish Refugee Assistance Committee in Portugal, Lisbon), May 9, 1944; Œuvre de secours aux enfants (OSE), Committee for Relief of the War-Stricken Jewish Population (RELICO) in Geneva, Hilfsaktion für notleidende Juden in Polen (HAFJP) in Zurich, the Commission for Polish Relief (CPR). Bańkowska, "Jewish Social Welfare Institutions," 143.

95 AIPN, sign. 010/6582, Weichert's case, report by the Jewish National Committee in Poland, sent from Warsaw on May 24, 1944, 80; ŻIH, sign.

344/147, Weichert's case file, Agencies, 21; Iranek-Osmecki, *Kto ratuje jedno życie . . .*, 232.

96 Jan Stańczyk (1886–1953), between October 2, 1939, and November 24, 1944, Minister of Labor and Social Welfare in the governments of Władysław Sikorski and Stanisław Mikołajczyk.

97 LMA, ACC/3121/C11/12/92, Polish Ministry of Labor and Social Welfare to Brotman, July 14, 1944.

98 LMA, ACC/3121/C11/12/92, interview with Stanczyk, July 21, 1944.

99 A letter by Stanisław Schimitzek, delegate of the Minister of Labor and Social Care in Lisbon, to the Ministry of Labor and Social Care in London, May 11, 1944; LMA, ACC/3121/C11/12/92, AJDC Lisbon (Robert Pilpel) to Dr. Stanisław Schimitzek (manager of the Polish Refugee Assistance Committee in Portugal, Lisbon), May 9, 1944.

100 See AIPN, sign. SSK Kr 240, Weichert's criminal case file, 13–14, 33.

101 Bańkowska, "Jewish Social Welfare Institutions," 143.

102 JDC Archives, NY Office 1933–1944, box 802, AJDC Lisbon (Robert Pilpel) to AJDC New York, July 19, 1944.

103 Ibid.

104 AIPN, sign. 010/6582, Weichert's case, an account by Tadeusz Pankiewicz, 139; ŻIH, sign, 313/137, Weichert's case before the CKŻP Social Court, testimony of Mieczysław Pemper, 361.

105 Węgrzyniak, *Sprawa Michała Weicherta*, 290; ŻIH, sign. 313/137, Weichert's case before the CKŻP Social Court, testimony of Stanisław Dobrowolski, 620.

106 ŻIH, 230/136, accounts for the second quarter of 1944, vol. 48, cited in Bartosz Heksel, "Krakówska Rada Pomocy Żydom," in *Żegota. Ukryta pomoc*, ed. Bartosz Heksel and Katarzyna Kocik (Kraków: Muzeum Historyczne Miasta Krakówa, 2016), 125.

107 For a detailed analysis of the trial, see Węgrzyniak, *Sprawa doktora Weicherta*.

108 AIPN, sign. SSK Kr 240, Weichert's criminal case file, 225.

109 AIPN, sign. SSK Kr 240, Weichert's criminal case file, testimony of Izaak Scheindlinger, 85; ibid. Władysław Wójcik estimated that Weichert's monthly spending amounted to ca. 40,000 zloty; ibid., sign. 010/6582, Weichert's case, testimony of Emilia Hiżowa, 19.

110 AIPN, sign. SSK Kr 240, Weichert's criminal case file, 138.

111 See Gabriel N. Finder and Alexander V. Prusin, "Jewish Collaborators in Poland on Trial 1944–1956," *Polin: Studies in Polish Jewry* 20 (2008): 122–48. The Social Court (from 1948 also known as the Citizens' Court)

was established by the Central Committee for Jews in Poland in 1946 to investigate persons suspected of collaboration with the occupation authorities, and it operated until the beginning of 1950; 153 files of defendants were preserved. See Żbikowski, *Sąd Społeczny przy CKŻP*.

112 Węgrzyniak, *Sprawa Michała Weicherta*, 294.

113 For the full article, see AIPN, sign. 010/6582, Weichert's case, 89; ŻIH, sign. 313/137, Weichert's case before the CKŻP Social Court, 267–68.

114 ŻIH, sign. 313/137, Weichert's case before the CKŻP Social Court, 268.

115 Michał Weichert, "Moje zabiegi o sąd społeczny" and copy of the document from February 12, 1945, to President of CKŻP, E. Sommerstein, manuscript, 27, ŻIH, sign. 313/137, Social (Citizens') Court of the CKŻP, 1946–1950, Michał Weichert case; ŻIH, sign. 313/135, Social (Citizens') Court of the CKŻP, 1946–50, Wang Mendel Mieczysław, case file, 300–301.

116 Węgrzyniak, *Sprawa Michała Weicherta*, 295; see AIPN, sign. 010/6582, Weichert's case, 88.

117 Copies of articles are preserved in AIPN, sign. 010/6582, Weichert's case, 82–84.

118 Information concerning the CKŻP Social Court can be found in Żbikowski, *Sąd Społeczny przy CKŻP*; Finder and Prusin, "Jewish Collaborators in Poland on Trial," 122–48; David Engel, "Who Is a Collaborator? The Trials of Michał Weichert," in *The Jews in Poland*, ed. Sławomir Kapralski (Kraków: Jagellonian University, 2009), 339–70; David Engel, "Why Punish Collaborators?," in *Jewish Honor Courts: Revenge, Retribution, and Reconciliation in Europe and Israel after the Holocaust*, ed. Laura Jockusch and Gabriel N. Finder (Detroit: Wayne State University Press, 2015), 29–49.

119 A detailed analysis of the trial appears in Żbikowski, *Sąd Społeczny przy CKŻP*, 133–58.

120 Ibid., 35.

121 Gabriel Finder, "'Sweep out Evil from Your Midst': The Jewish People's Court in Postwar Poland," in *Beyond Camps and Forced Labour: Current International Research on Survivors of Nazi Persecution (Proceedings of the International Conference, London, 29–31 January 2003)*, ed. Johannes-Dieter Steinert and Inge Weber-Newth (Osnabrück: Secolo Verlag, 2005), 27. Other trials have also aroused much controversy, such as that of Wiera Gran and Szapsel Roholc. See Gabriel N. Finder, "The Trial of Shepsl Rotholc and the Politics of Retribution in the Aftermath of the Holocaust," *Gal-Ed: On the History and Culture of Polish Jewry* 20 (2006): 63–89; Agata Tuszyńska, *Vera Gran: The Accused* (New York: Knopf, 2013).

122 Główna Komisja Badania Zbrodni Niemieckich w Polsce.
123 AIPN, sign. 010/6582, Weichert's case, testimony of Felicja Bennet, 128, and see testimony of Władysław Wolter, who spoke of Weichert's negotiations with the Germans in a similar manner, 131.
124 ŻIH, sign. 313/137, Weichert's case before the CKŻP Social Court, 89.
125 AIPN, sign. SSK Kr 240, Weichert's criminal case file, 29, an account by Stanisław Bagniowski; ŻIH, sign. 313/137, Weichert's case before the CKŻP Social Court, Marek Edelman's testimony, 526.
126 ŻIH, sign. 313/137, Weichert's case before the CKŻP Social Court, 85.
127 ŻIH, sign. 313/137, Weichert's case before the CKŻP Social Court, Operative part of the judgment, 268, 269.
128 Ibid., 861.
129 Jarkowska-Natkaniec, *Wymuszona współpraca czy zdrada?*; Alicja Jarkowska-Natkaniec, "Wybrane formy kolaboracji w obozie Płaszów. Charakterystyka zjawiska," *Krzysztofory. Zeszyty Naukowe Muzeum Historycznego Miasta Krakówa* 38 (2021).
130 Engel, "Who Is a Collaborator?," 339–70.
131 Martyna Grądzka, "'Wszystkim tym zarzutom przeczę zdecydowanie i stanowczo': proces Amona Leopolda Götha (1946)," *Zeszyty Historyczne WiN-u*, no. 35 (2012): 85–101.
132 After the war, Weichert insisted that he had kept records of all parcels in his notebook and that Jewish camp doctors had to confirm the receipt of parcels and drugs he distributed on the copies of invoices. These documents were never found. Żbikowski, *Sąd Społeczny przy CKŻP*, 147.
133 Węgrzyniak, *Sprawa Michała Weicherta*, 313.
134 Ibid., 304–8.

11

PARCELS SHIPPED FROM DENMARK TO INMATES OF THERESIENSTADT

SILVIA GOLDBAUM TARABINI FRACAPANE

Nineteen-year-old Ruth Salm was one of 470 Jews from Denmark who were caught by the Nazis in October 1943 and deported to the Theresienstadt ghetto.[1] Upon arriving on October 5, 1943, she like other deportees from Denmark was ordered to write reassuring postcards to friends and family.[2] Ruth Salm, who had come from Germany to Denmark in late 1939 through the Youth Aliyah, wrote a card to her Danish foster parents, including a question: "Could you send me some food?"[3] It was not uncommon for the deportees to use these cards to request food, even though they mostly did so in code. Cards like this one soon became a starting point for a group of people in Copenhagen to contemplate food shipments to Jews deported from Denmark.

After the deportations, the Danish civil administration became deeply invested in organizing aid for its deportees. A group of Danish Communists had been deported to the Stuffhof concentration camp at the same time as the first transports of Jews. On October 30, 1943, a formal permit to send them food was obtained.[4] A few days later, on November 4, 1943, the Danish Red Cross sent a first shipment of food to Stutthof.[5] On February 21, 1944, when a group of private individuals (the Fund of 1944) sent its first parcels to the Jews in Theresienstadt (even though a formal permit had not yet been granted), the Danish Red Cross sent its sixth shipment to the Communist prisoners in the Stutthof camp. Only after formal permission was granted to send food to Jews in Theresienstadt did the Danish Red Cross take over these shipments; the first Danish Red Cross parcels reached the ghetto in early September 1944. The Danish state was the main financial sponsor for virtually all the parcels. The questions at the heart of this chapter are: How were the shipments organized? Who did the actual work?

How were the parcels received in the ghetto, and what did the parcels mean to the ghetto inmates?

Danish-German Relations during the War

After Hitler's rise to power, a number of Jewish refugees sought a safe haven in Denmark. However, during the 1930s, Danish refugee policy became increasingly restrictive, as in other European states. Thus, in April 1940, 1,680 Jewish refugees were registered in Denmark, which had 3.8 million inhabitants at the time.[6] Among the refugees were about 640 young German, Czech, and Austrian Jews who had come to Denmark through Zionist organizations such as the Youth Aliyah and Hechalutz.[7] When German troops crossed into Denmark on April 9, 1940, what was then called a policy of cooperation or policy of negotiation was installed. Denmark and Germany were not formally at war. The two countries maintained diplomatic relations through their respective Ministries of Foreign Affairs, and Denmark continued to have a legation in Berlin. Due to this policy of cooperation, no anti-Jewish measures were implemented until after the government resigned on August 29, 1943.[8] Its resignation was a response to having received an ultimatum through Werner Best, the plenipotentiary of the Reich in Denmark, demanding that the Danish government establish special courts and impose martial law, including the death penalty for sabotage and illegal possession of firearms. The ultimatum followed a period of unrest in the country marked by strikes and growing acts of sabotage staged by the resistance. Because government officials refused to follow through with these demands, they tendered their resignation to King Christian X. Up to this point, no executions or deportations had taken place. The resistance viewed the resignation of the government as a victory, but the actual situation changed very little, with the permanent secretaries of the ministries continuing a policy of cooperation.[9]

One effect of this policy was that the Germans did not exploit or force the delivery of goods from Denmark's farmers. The foods exported to Germany were negotiated every year as "almost normal international trade deals under highly abnormal conditions."[10] Denmark did not suffer from severe food shortages: bread, groats, butter, and some other foods were rationed, and the population had to adjust its eating habits, for example, by replacing white bread with rye bread and eating less meat. The fat content of milk and cheese was lowered, but the products were not rationed, and eggs, potatoes, and meat could also be purchased without ration cards. Butter rations were among the most generous in Europe: at 300 grams per week from July 1, 1942, the rations were more than

50 percent larger than German butter rations.[11] Food conditions were such that Denmark was nicknamed the "cream front" (*Sahnefront*) by German soldiers, who to a certain extent took advantage of their deployment in Denmark to provide for their families in Germany.[12] However, it remained illegal to send food or other goods out of the country without a permit from the Danish Administration of Goods Supply (Direktoratet for Vareforsyning). When applying for a permit to send food out of Denmark, the prospective sender had to record what relationship she or he had with the recipient. It was easier, at least before the deportations took place, to obtain a permit if the food was being sent to relatives and, according to some testimonies, only if they were close relatives.[13]

Private Parcels Organized by Refugees

In January 1940, a Jewish couple, Cäcilie and Ludwig Pels, arrived in Copenhagen from Hamburg.[14] A year earlier, Ludwig Pels had been forced to hand over his store in Hamburg. Like many older Jews in Germany who had lost jobs and possessions, the couple was forced to move to a home for the aged run by the Jewish community at Sedanstrasse 23.[15] When their daughter in Denmark heard about their poor living conditions, she began to send them food every week. She and her husband also applied for Danish residence permits for her parents. After some rejections, the Pels couple were finally cleared for entry into Denmark after their daughter and her husband declared that they would pay all maintenance expenses.[16] Once in Denmark, the couple lived with their daughter's family until in April 1940 they moved into a Jewish seniors' home at Dyrkøb 3 in central Copenhagen.[17] From here the Pelses began to send food parcels, *Liebespaketen*, as they were called in German, to orphanages and old-age homes in Hamburg, as well as to individuals in need. In many cases two or more people shared one parcel.[18] The parcels could contain up to 1 kilo of meat, 1 kilo of cheese, and 1–2 kilos of sausages, dried vegetables, eggs, soup stock cubes, or jam, with a maximum total weight of 5 kilos.[19]

Around fifty of the recipients were over time deported to Theresienstadt, where many continued to receive food parcels from their friends in Copenhagen.[20] They included such prisoners as the legal adviser of the Hamburg Deutsch-Israelitische Gemeinde, Nathan Max Nathan, and his wife, Dora, who were deported to Theresienstadt from Hamburg on July 20, 1942.[21] They had begun receiving parcels through Mrs. Pels's network while still in Hamburg. In fact, the earliest documentation available for Mrs. Pels's parcels initiative stems from the summer of 1941, when a parcel was sent to Dr. Nathan in the name of Denmark's chief rabbi, Max Friediger.[22]

Headed by Mrs. Pels, a growing number of parcel senders managed in the years from 1941 to 1943 to ship parcels to at least 200 Jewish addressees in Germany and occupied countries such as the Netherlands, Poland, France, Italy, and the Czech lands.[23] The recipients of these parcels were Jews who either were living in dire straits in Germany or had fled or been deported. A portion of the parcels were shipped to people held in the Westerbork transit camp; others went to residents of the Warsaw, Łódź (Litzmannstadt), and Theresienstadt ghettos. While only a few of the recipients survived the Holocaust, the many thank-you letters they wrote show how vital the food proved for the individuals who received it. Typical was a letter from the staff of the Paulinenstift orphanage in Hamburg, written on behalf of the children on December 21, 1941:

> Dear Mrs. Pels and dear Mrs. Kunstadt,
>
> We have received your latest parcel with heartfelt thanks. Friday evening we had a fantastic soup from it, and then sausage with mashed potatoes. Now we have curly kale with meat, and we are all very happy. We always think of you when we eat these delicious things, that you are the loving donor of all these delicacies.[24]

It seems clear from a number of such letters that the food was critically important, but so was the fact that someone had cared and taken the trouble to perform these acts of kindness.

Because only sending food out of the country to close relatives was permitted, the Pels network had to invent or "strengthen" family ties for the purpose of sending these food parcels: in many cases the senders had no family ties to the recipients.[25] Among the seventy-one parcel senders who can be identified, at least forty were Jews born in Germany, Austria-Hungary, or Czechoslovakia. They had either come to Denmark as refugees or put down roots there before 1933. Some had married into Danish families. Another eleven were born in either Poland or Russia. Fifteen people were born into Jewish families in Denmark, several of them with a spouse from Germany, while one sender was born in Sweden. Only four of the known senders were non-Jewish, albeit one of them had Jewish ancestors. Nineteen additional parcel senders whose names have not been identified in other sources had surnames that suggest they may have been Jewish.[26]

Certain details about this parcels initiative are clearer. The costs of the contents were in part covered by the Jewish Sewing Club (Jødisk Syklub af 1/12 1924), a group for Jewish women in Copenhagen. They held a yearly handicrafts sale, and until April 1940 the proceeds had been sent to a yeshiva in Jerusalem. After the German occupation, the money was instead spent to ship food to Jews abroad.[27] In late September 1943, when the small Jewish community in Denmark was warned about the imminent roundup of Jews, the vast majority of its members tried to reach Sweden.[28] Most succeeded in making the crossing, among them the Pels couple and most of the other parcel senders. However, seven of the senders ended up among the deportees.

Jews from Denmark in the Theresienstadt Ghetto

As a result of the Nazi "*Judenaktion*," 472 Jews were caught and deported in four transports. All but two men reached the Theresienstadt ghetto, which had been established in November 1941 in a small garrison town in the so-called Protectorate of Bohemia and Moravia, northwest of Prague.[29] The Danish deportees arrived in the ghetto short of everything. Some brought a little luggage with them because they had been arrested during their attempted escape to Sweden; others arrived empty-handed, with only the clothes on their backs. They were housed among approximately 40,000 Jewish prisoners from the Czech lands, Germany, and Austria and forced to live in poor conditions.

After receiving the written "greetings" from Theresienstadt—like the card that Ruth Salm wrote to her foster parents—some friends and relatives in Denmark sent parcels to the ghetto by ordinary post.[30] Among them was the family physician of the Oppenhejm family, who sent a package with cheese, bacon, apples, and stock cubes; it arrived in the ghetto on December 16, 1943.[31] The doctor had simply applied for an export permit from the Danish Administration of Goods Supply, packed up the food, and mailed it.

Soon it became clear to the senders that parcels like these did arrive at their destination. The Ministry of Foreign Affairs in Copenhagen inquired through a range of channels about the possibility of sending food but were told that it was not permitted.[32] Despite this, private citizens continued shipping parcels to Theresienstadt, and nothing was done to prevent it, neither in Denmark nor in the ghetto. As a result, preparations began in Copenhagen to coordinate shipments of parcels to all the deportees from Denmark in Theresienstadt. Because the Danish authorities in Copenhagen did not know who had arrived safely in Sweden and who had been deported, they also asked for lists of deportees and information about where they had been brought. For some time they believed that only those over the age of sixty-five had been taken to Theresienstadt.[33] All requests for lists of the deportees were made in vain. As a result, the arrival of mail from Theresienstadt in early November set in motion a whole new chain of relief work. After being read by the German censors, the cards were handed over to the Social Service (Socialtjenesten) and distributed to the intended addressees.[34] Social Service employees quickly made lists of the senders of cards from Theresienstadt and the people in Denmark who had received them.[35]

On November 2, 1943, a month after the first two transports had left, Adolf Eichmann from the Reichssicherheitshauptamt (Reich Security Main Office) visited Copenhagen to meet with Werner Best, the Reich plenipotentiary, and Rudolf Mildner, commander of the Sicherheitspolizei (Sipo) and Sicherheitsdienst (SD)—Security Police and Security Service—in Denmark. The subject of food parcels to the Jews from Denmark may have been broached during the meeting, though it was not mentioned in the telegram sent by Best to the German Foreign Office afterward. But a follow-up telegram from Horst Wagner (of the German Foreign Office), listing what the Reich Security Main Office would agree to, stated that the Danish Jews in Theresienstadt would be allowed to correspond with people in Denmark, whereas the shipment of food parcels was not desirable "for the time being."[36] A further issue discussed at this meeting was a Danish request to visit those being held in the ghetto. Permission was granted but delayed until spring. In the end, the visit did not take place until June 23, 1944, when two Danes visited the ghetto together with the International Committee of the Red Cross (ICRC).[37] In preparation for this visit, major renovations took place in Theresienstadt in the spring of 1944: houses were painted, grass sown, and playgrounds installed, among other things. A big effort was put into making the ghetto look like a nice little town. By mid-May, approximately 7,500 additional people were also sent on to Auschwitz-Birkenau to make the "town" seem less crowded. The day before the visit, several Danish families were moved from the overcrowded attics or "dormitories" where they had been living, separated by sex, and installed in newly furnished private family rooms. Dr. Rossel of the ICRC headed the delegation, which included Dr. Eigil Juel Henningsen of the National Board of Health, delegated for the Danish Red Cross, and Frants Hvass of the Danish Ministry of Foreign Affairs. A delegate of the German Red Cross participated in the visit, as did a number of high-level Nazi officials. The foreign visitors believed what they were shown and wrote positive reports about conditions in the ghetto.[38]

Theresienstadt was used as a transit camp from which the vast majority of ghetto inmates were sent to extermination sites (Birkenau, Izbica, Treblinka, and Maly Trostinec). By contrast, the deportees from Denmark remained in the ghetto, with the exception of one stateless man who was included in a transport to Auschwitz-Birkenau, where he was killed upon arrival.[39] The exact reason behind this exemption and the person who instigated it remain unclear, but they seem to be related to the propaganda; it may well have been part of Himmler's various plans to exchange Jews for goods or his attempts to make contact with western Allies.[40]

On April 15, 1945, the ghetto inmates from Denmark, citizens and stateless alike, were released from Theresienstadt, picked up by the so-called White Buses and taken via Germany and Denmark to Sweden in a Scandinavian relief cooperation.[41] During their eighteen months in the ghetto, fifty-one Danish adults died, as did two babies born there. That not more Danish prisoners died in the ghetto was due to the critical amount of food they received from Denmark.

Activists in Denmark and the Shipments of Parcels

A small group of highly engaged volunteers played an important role in the shipment of parcels from Denmark. Shortly after the deportations had taken place, Dr. Poul Brandt Rehberg mentioned to his colleague Dr. Richard Ege that something ought to be done for the Jewish deportees.[42] Both were physiologists working at the Rockefeller Institute at Copenhagen University, where Ege, a nutrition specialist, headed the Institute of Biochemistry. Along with Ege's wife, Vibeke, and his secretary, Ruth Bredsdorff, the two doctors had been involved in aiding Jews fleeing to Sweden in October 1943. These individuals and the bishop of Copenhagen, Hans Fuglsang-Damgaard, and a Copenhagen pastor, Fritz Lerche, came to form the core of what would a few months later be named the Fund of 1944.[43] They worked in close collaboration with high-ranking officials at the Ministry of Social Affairs, who made sure that money was allocated for the project.[44]

While this group was awaiting a formal permit to send food, preparations began in Copenhagen to ship parcels with clothes.[45] Beginning in November 1943 these private individuals contacted relatives who had received mail from Theresienstadt and whose names had therefore been listed on the correspondence lists, to ask if they would send clothing to the deportees.[46] This effort was coordinated with the Danish Red Cross, which from December 1943 was responsible for shipping the clothes. The clothing was packed in parcels addressed to individuals and put in wooden crates.[47] These were sent through a private Danish moving company with a strong international network care of Chief Rabbi Friediger—a prisoner in the ghetto—who was to distribute them when they arrived in Theresienstadt.[48] The parcels contained either clothes found in the empty apartments of the deportees or, in some cases, secondhand clothes of good quality collected by pastors from among their parishioners.[49] Basic toiletries were also added to these packages. A lawyer in Copenhagen representing the

Jewish community in Swedish exile deposited 15,000 Danish crowns as a warranty should the clothes or other items from the apartments of the deportees be lost during shipping.[50] The first shipments reached the Theresienstadt inhabitants by the end of January 1944.[51] Salomon Katz, who had been deported with his wife, Hella, and their teenage daughter, Frida, noted in his diary: "Hella receives a *Forladung* [notification] for a Red Cross Parcel. It was underwear, dress shirts, shoes, socks, 1 piece of soap for me. For Hella and Frida there were dresses, a skirt, shoes, a smock, soap, a handkerchief, and other clothes. Of course we were happy for the parcel, but we would have been happier for food."[52]

Some people were pleased to receive familiar clothes from home, but for others it was a cruel reminder of life before deportation.[53] In most cases, the clothing was desperately needed, for many had been deported with nothing or only very little luggage.[54] The clothes became a valuable commodity for some, as when Leo Säbel, age nineteen, and a friend each received a parcel containing a winter coat. Säbel recalled years later: "We proudly went on a stroll with our coats on; then we sold them. His for bread, and mine for cigarettes."[55]

In early December 1943, the physiologists Ege and Brandt Rehberg floated the idea of producing and sending high-dose A, D, B1, and C vitamin tablets to the ghetto inmates.[56] Ege thought these pills could be delivered by representatives of the Danish Red Cross the following month, since he believed their visit to the ghetto would be allowed by mid-January.[57] Instead, with the visit on hold, the concentrated vitamins were simply added to select parcels of clothing and arrived in Theresienstadt by the end of March for distribution among the Danish detainees.[58] As one Danish ghetto inhabitant wrote in his diary, "Received vitamin tablets for 2 months. 8 white, 24 red. 1 white pill every 8 days, and one red pill every 2 days."[59] Even though the vitamins gave extra nourishment, some of the young men chose to barter them for something more filling. Heinz Blitzer exchanged his for more bread.[60] While the Danish shipments of food were well known among all Theresienstadt prisoners and mentioned in a wealth of testimonies and historical accounts, the vitamins have remained much more invisible.

Ruth Bredsdorff and Vibeke Ege seem to have played a critical role in the parcel scheme. Their involvement began early on and is documented in the card index created by the group (most likely by Bredsdorff). The card index was based on the lists of incoming correspondence from the ghetto.[61] "Mrs. E[ge]" and "Mrs. B[redsdorff]" are mentioned several times in the index that was created in November and December 1943 and that referred specifically to the parcels of clothing.[62] At first the women contacted people who had received cards from the ghetto, asking them to get involved and send clothes. In cases where friends or relatives could not be located, they went themselves to the apartments of deportees together with workers from the Social Service to sort out suitable clothes and make sure they were shipped to Theresienstadt.[63] Following the "*Judenaktion*," the Nazis did not permit looting or the organized seizure of Jewish belongings. The abandoned apartments of the deported Jews were in many cases protected by the Social Service, which either put the inhabitants' belongings in safekeeping so the apartments could be rented out or paid the rent and insurance. In other cases, neighbors or guardians took care of this, although some abused their role and stole property.[64]

Only a single card in the card index noted that "Jensen does not wish to be listed as sender"; the responses were otherwise generally helpful and favorable. The parcel senders included not only relatives but also several neighbors and colleagues of the prisoners.[65] In addition, many architects, doctors, and clergymen joined their ranks, as did members of women's charitable organizations.[66] Ruth Bredsdorff's extensive commitment to helping the deportees has left traces in the form of personal letters. On June 30, 1944, she wrote to one woman: "Dear Miss Sommer, I just received this card through the door, and general strike or not, you should really have it right away. I know this will make you happy to a degree that we cannot even imagine. You can rest assured that I, even though I do not know your fiancé, am happy to see a sign of life from him."[67] Such empathetic communications clearly show Bredsdorff's involvement and care for the deportees and their relatives.

When Chief Rabbi Friediger invited Dr. Ege to the reopening of Copenhagen's main synagogue in June 1945, Ege excused himself but suggested that his wife should go instead. He added a request that she be joined by the Bredsdorffs, "who together with us have worked for the food shipments to Theresienstadt."[68] In a 1963 article, the modest Dr. Ege again emphasized the work of his wife, Vibeke, and Ruth Bredsdorff.[69] In a letter to Dr. Friediger about how the parcel shipments actually came about, Dr. Ege praised the involvement of the Ministry of Social Affairs, headed by Permanent Secretary Hans Henrik Koch and Head of Division Mogens Kirstein.[70] Koch in turn underlined that Richard Ege had been the actual driving force behind the parcel scheme.[71]

Organized Food Parcels

On January 16, 1944, five deportees who were considered "mistakenly deported" were returned to Copenhagen by train. They either had a non-Jewish parent and were not members of the Jewish community or were married to non-Jews.[72] Upon arrival in Denmark, they were not supposed to talk about the conditions in the ghetto, but they inevitably did pass on information to the Danish Ministry of Foreign Affairs about living conditions in Theresienstadt.[73] Efforts to obtain permits to ship food to the ghetto increased as a result of this information. By the end of January, the Danish legation in Berlin confirmed that the German authorities would still not allow official food parcels for Danish ghetto inmates, arguing that those held in Theresienstadt received the same food rations as other civilians in the Protectorate.[74] A meeting between high-ranking civil servants from Denmark's Ministry of Foreign Affairs and Ministry of Social Affairs and people from the Fund took place on January 21, 1944, to discuss how to proceed. The Ministry of Social Affairs agreed to allocate funds for parcels, despite the fact that formal permits to ship them had not yet been granted, and the Danish Red Cross was approached to organize the shipments.[75] It soon became clear, however, that the organization would not participate in sending food parcels as long as a formal permit had not been granted.[76] A less official solution therefore emerged. From the end of January 1944, the "Ege Group," now under the name "Fund of 1944," again contacted the deportees' friends and relatives who had received postcards from Theresienstadt, asking them to apply for individual permits from the Administration of Goods Supply to send food. The Fund informed them about their intention to begin shipping private food parcels, even though a formal permit had not yet been granted. Because of the correspondence, they knew that individual parcels had been reaching their destination and thus hoped that private parcels would continue to find their way into the ghetto without running afoul of the German authorities.[77]

The shipping firm O. Evensen was in charge of packing and sending the food parcels, and the first 70 were conveyed by ordinary post between February 21 and March 2, 1944. The group then learned that the transport time would be shorter if the parcels went as registered mail.[78] And so indeed, while the first parcels took about three weeks to arrive, the registered parcels were only underway for eight or nine days.[79] After four weeks, 180 parcels had been sent. From the beginning of April, 40 parcels were sent at a time, often with only a few days between. Later, up to 60 parcels were shipped together. Still, it was not until the end of May before almost all of the deportees from Denmark had received their first parcel.[80] Each package contained cheese, sausage, sugar, jam, barley groats, stock cubes, and some butter, for a total of 4.5 kilos of food. In a number of cases, the Fund knew that people ate only kosher meat, and therefore a small number of parcels were sent with lamb sausage instead of pork. This continued when the Red Cross took over the shipments.[81]

Overview of parcels sent through the Fund of 1944

Month	Number of parcels	Number of shipments
February 1944	50	4
March 1944	329	19
April 1944	439	11
May 1944	718	16
June 1944	540	12
July 1944	700	14
August 1944	354	7
September 1944	449	10
October 1944	398	9
November 1944	699	16
December 1944	691	14
January 1945	696	15
February 1945	797	18
March 1945	584	13
Total	7,444	178

Until August 1944, approximately one parcel per month was sent to each deportee from Denmark, whether they were nationals, foreigners, or stateless. In addition, the direct beneficiaries also included deportees from other countries to the extent that the Danish organizers knew their names. Among them were several people who before October 1943 had received parcels through the Pels network, and because they had sent cards expressing gratitude from the ghetto, their names ended up on the shipment lists.[82]

Along with the fact that the Danes remained in Theresienstadt and were exempted from the transports to Auschwitz-Birkenau, many survivors would later list the food parcels as a reason for their survival.[83] By the end of the war in Europe, the Fund of 1944 had sent 7,444 parcels to 837 named individuals, of whom 444 had been deported from Denmark.[84] The numbers of deaths within the Danish group of ghetto inhabitants speak for themselves: from October 1943 to March 1944, 39 deportees died. From April 1944 until April 1945, while parcels were being received, only 12 people died.[85] Furthermore, as already mentioned, one man was included in a transport to Auschwitz-Birkenau in March 1944. Altogether 11 percent of the Danish ghetto inmates died. In comparison, about 23 percent of the ghetto inmates from elsewhere died in Theresienstadt, and more than 88,000 people—or 63 percent—were sent to Auschwitz-Birkenau or other extermination camps.[86]

Parcels from the Danish Red Cross

On June 23, 1944, the aforementioned international delegation headed by Dr. Rossel from the ICRC finally visited Theresienstadt with its two Danish representatives, Frants Hvass and Dr. Eigil Juel Henningsen. During this visit, the Danish representatives finally obtained a permit to ship food to the inmates from Denmark through the commander of the Security Police in Bohemia-Moravia, Erwin Weinmann, who was present during the visit.[87] This meant a major change in the parcel scheme when the Danish delegates returned to Copenhagen.

With the formal permit, the Danish Red Cross now took over the shipments for the deportees from Denmark. The first food parcels sent by the Danish Red Cross began reaching the ghetto in early September 1944.[88] From that point onward, two parcels per month would be sent to each prisoner from Denmark. These parcels contained 1 kilo of oatmeal, 500 grams of butter, 750 grams of sugar, 1/2 kilo of sausages, 1/2 kilo of cheese, 500 grams of powdered milk, 500 grams of jam, and 1/2 kilo of flatbread, for a total of 4 kilos and 750 grams per parcel. Contents of the second monthly parcel varied slightly, with additions of 450 grams of powdered milk, dried vegetables, and stock cubes.[89]

Parcels continued to arrive until the Danes were liberated on April 15, 1945. The last known shipment arrived on April 6, 1945.[90] Like the parcels of the Fund, these were primarily financed by the Danish state.[91]

From the prisoners' point of view, the change of sender resulted in one important problem: the packaging. The shift from the private fund, whose parcels had been packed by a professional shipping firm, to the Danish Red Cross, whose parcels were packed by volunteers, meant less efficient wrapping, spoiled food, and in the worst case spilled contents. In September 1944, Salomon Katz wrote in his diary: "It is now the Danish Red Cross that sends the parcels. But they are not as good as Evensen. Neither is the wrapping. The parcels are almost completely destroyed. The butter has nearly melted and has greased the box. The jam has leaked out. All in all poor packaging, but we are nonetheless happy to get it."[92] A few days later, Katz wrote about another parcel: "Hella [Mrs. Katz] receives a parcel from Denmark. The sausage was moldy. The sugar scattered, so about 1/2 pound lost. The [pack of] powdered milk was also torn, the butter melted, but not so much. Hella sold the powdered milk and a bit of butter. Hella

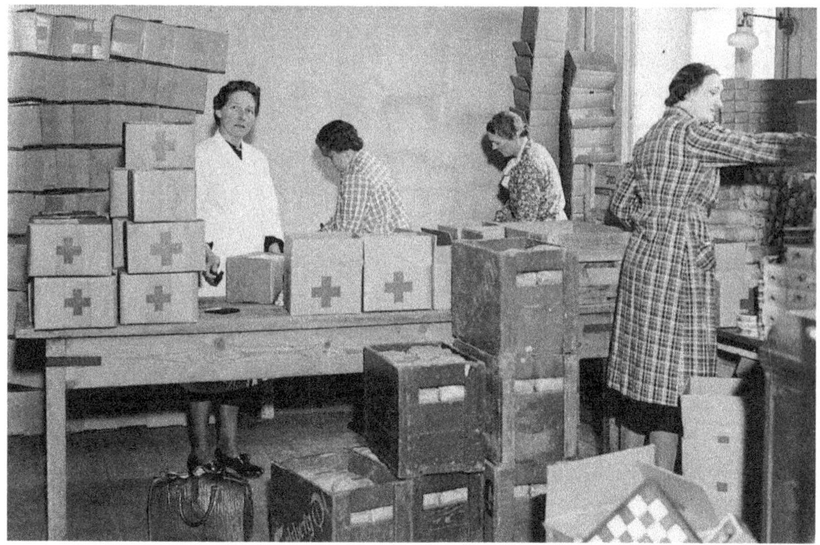

Danish Red Cross volunteers pack parcels. Photo by Vermehren. Courtesy of the Museum of Danish Resistance/National Museum of Denmark.

is on cloud nine. Now we can again buy bread and other edible things."[93] Even spoiled food could be bartered in the ghetto.

December 1944 was a special month, since the shipments were doubled for Christmas. Elias Leiman, age fifty-two, stated shortly after his liberation that during December 1944, his family of five had received no fewer than 25 parcels from Denmark and 2 small parcels from Sweden.[94] Perhaps because of the high number of parcels arriving in December, two shipments that arrived in the ghetto on December 23, 1944, and January 2, 1945—altogether 864 food parcels—were at first withheld by the ghetto commander, Karl Rahm. The Danish prisoners were furious about this decision, angry not only at the commander but also at Dr. Friediger, the Danish chief rabbi, who had signed for the not yet distributed parcels.[95] Finally, on January 21, 1945, the parcels were released but had to be picked up at the Central Supply Depot and not the post office, as was the usual procedure. People who went to pick up their parcels were urged (in writing and orally) to give a share of their food to a collection for people from other countries.[96] This was a compromise reached between Benjamin Murmelstein, the elder of the Jews at that point, and Dr. Friediger. Murmelstein had demanded that Friediger make the "wealthy" Danish prisoners give part of what they received to support others. Murmelstein claimed that Friediger agreed with him, but he faced opposition in his own ranks, making wider implementation of the plan impossible.[97] Friediger and Murmelstein also disagreed about what to do with parcels that arrived in care of Friediger for people who had died or been deported. (Danish parcels were in a number of cases sent care of Friediger, even when sent to people not deported from Denmark.) Murmelstein wanted to use these extra parcels for the benefit of the entire ghetto, while Friediger sought to distribute them as he saw fit.[98] In the end, Murmelstein confiscated these parcels, stirring up considerable resentment among Danes in the ghetto and leading to the conviction that Murmelstein had "seized" or even "stolen" Danish parcels.[99]

Parcels Sent to People from Other Countries

When the Danish Red Cross took over shipments for ghetto inmates from Denmark, the people behind the Fund did not stop their involvement. Instead, they continued the shipments to non-Danish people deported from other countries, and new names were continuously added to the lists when they reached the Fund.[100] All in all, close to 7,500 food parcels were shipped through the Fund of 1944; about 4,900 of them were sent to people who had been deported to Theresienstadt from countries other than Denmark. Only a few of these recipients of parcels survived in the ghetto or were included in the special exchange convoy to Switzerland in February 1945.[101] The vast majority of them were among the more than 18,000 people who were deported from Theresienstadt to Auschwitz-Birkenau in September and October 1944; some had already been deported before their names even appeared on the shipping lists.

Very few testimonies about parcels received by deportees from other countries have been located. Josef Magnus, who arrived from Westerbork in the Netherlands with his family on April 7, 1944, began to receive such help from Denmark in September 1944, according to a diary that his son, Simon Magnus, kept in the ghetto.[102] According to the shipping lists, fourteen parcels were sent to Josef Magnus between September 6, 1944, and March 14, 1945.[103] The packages are mentioned in the diary entries for the autumn of 1944, but the six sent in 1945 are not mentioned at all. Whether they were received cannot be determined.

Even though a system of signed receipts was in place, it was impossible to know who actually signed for the parcels. Most receipts were stamped and signed by employees at the ghetto post office, and therefore members of the Fund, who did not know about the autumn transports that decimated the population of the ghetto, continued to ship about two parcels per month to each person until mid-March 1945.[104] They could not monitor who was in the ghetto from abroad and who had been sent away. Even the names of people who had never been in Theresienstadt, but were believed by friends or relatives to be there, sometimes appeared on the lists. But it was important that the food continued to arrive, even though the senders were not always sure that it did. The food was without any doubt desperately needed in the ghetto.

Food in the Ghetto Economy

Food in Theresienstadt was distributed every day, but at least one if not two of the three daily servings consisted of only thin soup or ersatz "coffee." These provisions have been described as "too much to die from, too little to live on."[105] The question of how to obtain more food thus rapidly became a daily worry. Food represented not only nourishment but also hope for a future, and it was the most important currency in the ghetto. To receive parcels regularly was therefore of great value. Food could be traded, bartered, and used as a bribe or as charity. Hierarchy and privilege permeated prisoner society in Theresienstadt on several levels. On the one hand, some prisoners achieved a "prominent" status because of their previous merits; this primarily brought better housing conditions but not greater food rations.[106] On the other hand, having a good job in the ghetto conferred a high status on certain prisoners: cooks but also those with direct access to food, for example, were highly valued.[107] Therefore, when the parcels began to arrive regularly, the position of the Danes rose in the ghetto hierarchy. Once among the poorest, the Danish prisoners who had arrived without luggage now joined the ranks of the "wealthy."

Survivors' testimonies suggest that most of the parcels arrived fully intact. However, they were invariably searched for contraband such as cigarettes or medicine, neither of which was ever included in the parcels from the Fund or the Danish Red Cross. Occasionally items "disappeared" from the boxes before they were handed out, and in a few cases recipients had to sign for empty or almost empty parcels.[108] Many Danes also received a few private parcels from Sweden. These parcels were particularly sought after, for they sometimes contained rare and valuable foods such as citrus fruit or orange juice.[109]

How valuable were the shipments in the economy of the ghetto? What difference did they make for the people receiving them? We can follow the fluctuation of food prices in the ghetto in the diary of Salomon Katz. On May 9, 1944, he wrote about a trade he and his wife had made: "We sold some lard to get bread. We paid 15 Marks for a loaf of bread. We received 60 Marks for about a 1/4 kilo lard."[110] On June 6, 1944, Katz wrote: "One pays fantastic prices here. For example: 125g liver paté costs 15 Marks, or calculated in Danish money,

30 Crowns. A big box of sardines 40 Marks, oranges between 25–30 Marks. Lemons the same. Cigarettes between 3 and 5 Marks a piece. An expensive passion for a smoker."[111] A month later, Katz mentioned bread prices: 16 Marks a loaf.[112] The bread prices had increased by one Mark since May, but on August 18, 1944, bread prices had risen seriously due to shortages: "We have to save our bread, since there is no bread available at the moment, and it now costs up to 25 Marks." On October 8, ten days after a wave of transports to Auschwitz-Birkenau had started, Katz mentions the bread shortage again: "It is becoming harder and harder to get hold of bread. A 2-kilo loaf costs 25 Marks and you still cannot get it." Another Danish ghetto inmate, Elias Leiman, also mentioned the bread prices in a short testimony written upon his arrival in Sweden; during the period of transports, prices went up to 85 Marks for a two-kilo loaf but dropped again after the last transport to Auschwitz-Birkenau had left.[113]

Fresh fruits and vegetables cost astronomical amounts: On May 11, 1944, Katz described how a fellow Dane sold a lemon for him and his wife. The woman managed to sell it for 25 Marks, Katz commented: "This was a good rate, since the usual price is between 15 and 20 Marks."[114] They immediately used the money to buy extra bread. A few months later he described his daughter receiving a small tomato from her boyfriend's sister, who managed to keep a tiny garden in the ghetto. Such produce was usually only available if smuggled into the ghetto by prisoners from the agricultural work unit, and according to Katz's diary, even a tiny tomato cost between 3 and 5 Marks.[115] The food parcels made it possible for the Danes to buy bread even during periods where the prices were highest. Sources from the ghetto indicate they were hungry despite the parcels, thus suggesting how difficult conditions must have been for prisoners who did not receive these important supplements to their rations. Thanks to the food parcels—and, of course, the fact that the Danish prisoners were exempted from transports farther east—89 percent of the deportees from Denmark survived.

Conclusion

When Ruth Salm wrote to her foster parents on October 5, 1943, little would she know that her card, together with the other requests for food, would spur Danish citizens to participate in a major parcel scheme. The amount of food sent from Denmark to Theresienstadt was indisputably considerable. The Fund of 1944 alone shipped 7,500 parcels to the ghetto, and another 4,900 parcels were sent by the Danish Red Cross, each parcel weighing between four and five kilos. These became an important contribution to the food circulating in the ghetto, though it was never distributed equally among those in need.[116] Not all of this food was sent to ghetto inmates from Denmark; about 4,900 parcels from the Fund went to people deported from other countries.

The parcel scheme was for the most part paid for by the state, and even the parcels sent to prisoners from other countries were mostly financed through the Ministry of Social Affairs. However, a number of private contributors also supported the scheme financially.[117] A relatively small number of individuals made an enormous impact on the lives of those in need, beginning with the private initiative of Mrs. Pels but also encompassing the involvement and steadfast commitment of the volunteers of the Fund of 1944. People acting on behalf of the group pursued information about missing neighbors and family members, not only constructing name lists but also trying to uncover their stories and social networks: Where had they lived? Were they arrested alone, or had their entire family been deported? Did they have relatives in Denmark who could help? Friends or neighbors? Could someone apply for an export permit on their behalf? Many gaps remain in our knowledge of these activities, but we do know that a committed group of women and men volunteered to maintain lists, contact relatives and neighbors, and visit apartments to salvage clothing for deportees. Many more applied for export permits and lent their names for private parcel shipments. The parcels gave hope. They meant moral support. They meant being less hungry. And they made it possible to barter and exchange and thereby obtain other much-needed goods. No exact overview of how much food was shipped from Denmark to Theresienstadt can be reconstructed, for the numbers of individual private parcels are missing. Yet for those who received the food, every parcel or shared parcel made a vital difference.

Notes

1 Ruth Salm (1924–2008) was born in Brühl, Germany, in 1924. She immigrated to the United States after the war.

2 I have described this as well as the daily life of the ghetto inmates from Denmark in detail in Silvia Goldbaum Tarabini Fracapane, *The Jews of Denmark in the Holocaust: Life and Death in Theresienstadt Ghetto* (London: Routledge, 2021).

3 Card from Ruth Salm to Aage Davidsen, October 5, 1943, copy in the Danish National Archives (DNA), Archives of the Women's International League for Peace and Freedom (WILPF).

4 Sofie Lene Bak, *Da krigen var forbi. De danske jøders hjemkomst efter besættelsen* (Copenhagen: Gyldendal, 2012), 52.

5 Other shipments to Stutthof followed on November 20 and December 10. On December 10, shipments were also sent to non-Jewish men in Sachsenhausen and non-Jewish women in Ravensbrück who had arrived in these two camps at the same time as the sixteen Jews deported on November 23, 1943. No parcels were sent to the Jews in either camp. Furthermore, cod liver oil and cigarettes were sent to Stutthof on November 20, 1943; apples were sent on November 22; and vitamin preparations were sent to Sachsenhausen on December 12, 1943. All information here stems from a list attached to a letter to Landsforeningen af Besættelsestidens Politiske Fanger prepared by H. C. Hansen, Nov. 17, 1947, Archives of the Danish Red Cross at the DNA, file 74.

6 Hans Kirchhoff, *Et menneske uden pas er ikke noget menneske* (Odense: Syddansk Universitetsforlag, 2005), 234.

7 Jørgen Hæstrup, *Passage to Palestine* (Odense: Odense Universitetsforlag, 1983); Lone Rünitz, *Diskret ophold* (Odense: Syddansk Universitetsforlag, 2010).

8 While the policy of cooperation staved off persecution of the Danish Jews for some time, it also resulted in the expulsion and subsequent death of at least twenty Jewish refugees. See Vilhjálmur Örn Vilhjálmsson, *Medaljens bagside. Jødiske flygtningeskæbner i Danmark 1933–1945* (Copenhagen: Vandkunsten, 2005). Jakob Halvas Bjerre has demonstrated how the most "efficient" part of the German *Judenpolitik* in Denmark actually took place in the business sector: Jacob Halvas Bjerre, "Excluding the Jews: The Aryanization of Danish-German Trade and German Anti-Jewish Policy in Denmark 1937–1943" (PhD diss., Copenhagen Business School, 2018).

9 Claus Bundgård Christensen, Joachim Lund, Niels Wium Olesen, and Jakob Sørensen, *Danmark besat. Krig og hverdag 1940–45* (Copenhagen: Informations Forlag, 2005), 453–58.

10 Mogens Rostgaard Nissen, "Det danske landbrug i den tyske krigsøkonomi 1940–45," *Landbohistorisk Tidsskrift* 1 (2005): 73.

11 Sigurd Jensen, *Levevilkår under besættelsen* (Copenhagen: Gyldendal, 1971), 198; Joachim Lund, *Hitlers spisekammer—Danmark og den europæiske nyordning 1940–43* (Copenhagen: Gyldendal, 2005), 293: Dutch butter rations were 145 grams weekly. By contrast, Norwegian rations stood at 210 grams per week, and even in neutral Sweden, butter rations were 250 grams per week.

12 Christensen et al., *Danmark besat*, 352–54; Nissen, "Det danske landbrug," 84–85, 91.

13 Otto Schwarzbart, undated manuscript, 43, 47 (copy in my collection); author's interview with Otto Schwarzbart, June 1, 2008. See also the note dated January 14, 1944, DNA, UM 120D43/13a.

14 Căcilie Pels (née Cohn, 1882–1965), born in Hamburg. Liepmann (Ludwig) Pels (1874–1945), born in Emden. Both died in Copenhagen.

15 DNA, UDL 65751; Staatsarchiv Hamburg, Wiedergutmachung, 351–11 2583; 351–11 6058. I thank Christina Igla, who located the files in Hamburg for me.

16 DNA, UDL 65751.

17 Ibid.; census of 1940, accessible through www.sa.dk (accessed March 27, 2020).

18 Yad Vashem Archive (YVA), O.27/36–105, includes a large number of grateful letters from recipients of the parcels. See also the exhibition "Meine Liebe Frau Pels," www.yadvashem.org/yv/en/exhibitions/through-the-lens/pels.asp (accessed March 27, 2020).

19 Letter from Grete Metzon to Mrs. Pels, March 4, 1942, YVA, O.27/100. A few applications to the Administration of Goods Supply are preserved in the DNA, WILPF Archives.

20 Available material suggests that at least half of them received parcels in the ghetto. Other names of deportees from Hamburg also appear on lists of the Fund of 1944 (see below), some of whom might have received parcels from the Pels group until September 1943.

21 Dr. Nathan Max Nathan, 1879–1944, married to Dora (née Rieger, 1881–1944). The couple was deported from Theresienstadt to Auschwitz-Birkenau on October 23, 1944.

22 Letter from N. M. Nathan, dated June 27, 1941, YVA, O.27/43. The letter suggests that this was not the first parcel the Nathans had received.

23 Some addressees cover couples, families, or whole institutions, and thus more than the 200 individuals.

24 Dec. 21, 1941, YVA, O.27/37. Steffie Kunstadt (1892–1973), born in Vienna, widow of the cantor Heinrich Kunstadt (1890–1933). The letter is typewritten but contained a handwritten greeting for Mrs. Pels from Hildegard Cohen (1900–1942), who was the head of the Paulinenstift orphanage. On July 11, 1942, the children and staff were deported from Hamburg to Auschwitz-Birkenau, none of whom survived.

25 Sompolinsky, *De danske jøders redning under Holocaust*, YVA, O.27/13X (30), 2.

26 I have cross-checked names and addresses from the Pels archive in a range of sources: the Danish Jewish Genealogical Database, accessible

through the Danish Jewish Historical Society; the census of 1940; phone directories from the 1940s; and the database of naturalizations, 1776–1960, www.ddd.dda.dk/immibas/immibas2.asp (accessed March 27, 2020). Some of the names probably belonged to refugees who did not remain in Denmark after the war and were therefore difficult to locate.

27 Conversation with Arthur Arnheim, Jerusalem, Dec. 18, 2016; see also the aforementioned exhibition, "Meine Liebe Frau Pels."

28 Leni Yahil, *The Rescue of Danish Jewry: Test of a Democracy* (Philadelphia: Jewish Publication Society of America, 1969); Sofie Lene Bak, *Nothing to Speak Of: Wartime Experiences of the Danish Jews 1943–1945* (Copenhagen: Dansk Jødisk Museum, 2011).

29 Six men were brought to Sachsenhausen and ten women and children to Ravensbrück on the last transport that left Denmark on November 23, 1943. Four of the men and all of the women and children were brought to Theresienstadt in early 1944. Of the two remaining men, one survived and returned to Denmark in June 1945; the other was sent on to KZ Majdanek in December 1943, where he died shortly after arriving. Goldbaum Tarabini Fracapane, *Jews of Denmark*, 91–93.

30 Parcels were also sent without any coordination from relatives in Sweden.

31 Ellen Oppenhejm, pocket diary, December 16, 1943, private collection.

32 The inquiries can be followed in DNA, UM 120D43/13a. At times they received conflicting answers.

33 Note of October 26, 1944, DNA, UM 120D43/13a.

34 Letter from Socialtjenesten to Permanent Secretary Koch, November 4, 1943, DNA, Ministry of Social Affairs, office 2, journal no. 880/1943. For more on the work of Socialtjenesten, see Bak, *Da krigen var forbi*, 35–58.

35 Minutes from a meeting of November 11, 1943, DNA, UM 120D43/13a; cover letter, December 14, 1943, from H. H. Koch, Ministry of Social Affairs, to Nils Svenningsen, Ministry of Foreign Affairs, and correspondence lists, DNA, UM 120D43/13a.

36 Horst Wagner to Werner Best, November 5, 1943, reprinted in John T. Lauridsen, ed., *Werner Bests korrespondance med Auswärtiges Amt og andre tyske akter vedrørende besættelsen af Danmark 1942–1945* (Copenhagen: Museum Tusculanum, 2012), 4:453–54.

37 The available sources indicate that two visits took place at the same time. See Goldbaum Tarabini Fracapane, *Jews of Denmark*, 225–26. Besides comparing notes after the visit, the Danish delegates and the Swiss ICRC representative did not have a common agenda.

38 The reports of Frants Hvass and Eigil Juel Henningsen, both in DNA, private archive of Eigil Juel Henningsen, as well as the report of Rossel, later published in *Theresienstädter Studien und Dokumente* 3 (1996): 284–320, as Maurice Rossel, "Besuch im Ghetto," annotated by Vojtěch Blodig.

39 Schmul Sender Jonisch (1899–1944) was deported with Transport DX to Auschwitz-Birkenau on March 20, 1944.

40 Goldbaum Tarabini Fracapane, *Jews of Denmark*, 62–66. Referencing Yahil, *Rescue of Danish Jewry: Test of a Democracy*, 300, it is often stated that the protection of the Danes traces back to Best, who on November 2, 1943, had a meeting with Eichmann. Among other things, they discussed a future visit to Theresienstadt, and Best's report to the German Ministry of Foreign Affairs, November 3, 1943, includes: "All Jews deported from Denmark are to remain in Theresienstadt and to be visited there in the foreseeable future by representatives of the Danish central administration and the Danish Red Cross." Lauridsen, ed., *Werner Bests korrespondance med Auswärtiges Amt*, 444. Yahil in her rephrasing of this point added that they would "not be transferred to other camps (that is, Auschwitz)." There is no documentation about why their stay in Theresienstadt continued after the visit had taken place.

41 Sune Persson, *Escape from the Third Reich: Folke Bernadotte and the White Buses* (London: Frontline Books, 2009).

42 Richard Ege, "Pakker til Theresienstadt," *Jødisk Samfund* 22, no. 1 (1948): 11.

43 Ibid.

44 Richard Ege, "Hjælpearbejdet for danske jøder i Theresienstadt," *Samariten* 35, no. 9 (Oct. 1963): 201; letter from Richard Ege to Chief Rabbi Friediger, June 20, 1945, DNA, Archive of Dr. Friediger.

45 This can be followed through the various summaries and notes in DNA, UM 120D43/13a.

46 Letter, November 29, 1943, signed Ruth Bredsdorff for Rich. Ege, private collection; letter, December 10, 1943, signed H. Fuglsang-Damgaard, Rich. Ege, and P. Brandt Rehberg, DNA, Archive of Bishop Fuglsang-Damgaard.

47 On December 8, 59 parcels were shipped, and on December 22, 144 parcels. On January 20, 72 parcels went out, and on February 18, 118; see various documents in DNA, UM 120D43/13a.

48 Letter from Director Nils Svenningsen to Bishop Fuglsang-Damgaard, December 9, 1943, DNA, Archive of Bishop Fuglsang-Damgaard.

49 Note dated "Some time after October 2, 1943," DNA, Archive of Fritz Lerche.

50 Today this amounts to about €40,300 or $46,600. See correspondence between H. H. Bruun and Dr. Ege, from December 1943 and May/June 1946, in DNA, Archive of Bishop Fuglsang-Damgaard.

51 Salomon Katz, diary, January 25 and 30, 1944, private collection. Chief Rabbi Friediger mentioned that parcels arrived in December, but this could not be corroborated through any other source. See Max Friediger, *Theresienstadt* (Copenhagen: J. Fr. Clausen, 1946), 85.

52 Katz, diary, January 30, 1944. See also the list of what was suggested for inclusion in a parcel; DNA, Archive of Bishop Fuglsang-Damgaard.

53 Rachel Schlesinger (née Fingeret), Visual History Archive, USC Shoah Foundation (VHA), 1998, interview 45085–42.

54 See, e.g., letter from Benjamin Igre to the Bishop of Copenhagen, August 22, 1945, DNA, Archive of Bishop Fuglsang-Damgaard,

55 Leo Säbel (1924–2015) interview with the author, January 24, 2008. Säbel was born in Leizpig and came to Denmark through the Youth Aliyah. He was arrested in Copenhagen on the evening of October 1, 1943.

56 Note signed H. J. Hansen, December 3, 1943, DNA, UM 120D43/13a.

57 Copy of letter from Dr. Ege to chief medical officer Dr. J. Frandsen, January 8, 1944, DNA, Archive of Bishop Fuglsang-Damgaard.

58 Ralph Oppenhejm, diary, March 29, 1944, Danish Jewish Museum (JDK), 207A35/7.

59 Katz, diary, April 4, 1944.

60 Harold Blitzer, VHA, USC Shoah Foundation, 1996, interview 20609.

61 Two copies of the card index exist, one at JDK, 207A134/1/181, and the other in YVA, O.27/16. The latter seems to be an original copy of the former with only a few differences.

62 Besides them, a Mrs. L[. . .] and Mrs. K[. . .] are also mentioned, but I have not been able to identify them.

63 Notes in the card index, JDK, 207A134/1/181; YVA, file O.27/16.

64 No complete examination has been made about the return of the Theresienstadt survivors. Bak, *Da krigen var forbi*, does give a sense of the situation of all the returning Jews (people who had been in either Sweden or Theresienstadt). The testimonies from the Danish Theresienstadt survivors clearly indicate that many people were robbed by neighbors or guardians, Goldbaum Tarabini Fracapane, *Jews of Denmark*, 316–17.

65 The rate of intermarriage between Jews and Protestants was high, so many families included non-Jewish relatives who remained in Denmark after October 1943. A few Jews married to non-Jews also remained, but in most cases they were afraid that they risked deportation by remaining and therefore escaped to Sweden.

66 I have checked the names of the senders of parcels of February 21 and 23 (20 parcels in all), May 1 (40 parcels), and June 21 (40 parcels). The names were checked against the census of 1940, and out of the senders of these 100 parcels, I was able to identify 70. The architects, doctors, and clergymen were closely connected to the people behind the shipments, who were themselves doctors, clergymen, and other professionals. (Ruth Bredsdorff's husband was an architect.) Women's organizations had arranged for the Danish stay of the young refugees of the Youth Aliyah, of whom forty-three were deported to Theresienstadt, and were therefore eager to send parcels to "their" children. See lists in DNA, Fund of 1944.

67 Letter from Ruth Bredsdorff to Carla Sommer, June 30, 1944, Archives of the Museum of Danish Resistance 1940–1945 (AMDR), 30D-10844–47; another letter from Bredsdorff was sent to Keld Ehlers-Hansen on July 10, 1944, including a receipt card for a parcel sent to his fiancée in the ghetto. Mrs. Bredsdorff added that he was welcome to call her if he had not been present at the meeting a few days earlier, where Frants Hvass presented his impressions from the visit in the ghetto. Private collection.

68 Card from Richard Ege to Chief Rabbi Friediger, June 20, 1945, DNA, Archive of Dr Friediger.

69 Ege, "Hjælpearbejdet," 201.

70 Letter from Richard Ege to Chief Rabbi Friediger, June 20, 1945, DNA, Archive of Dr Friediger.

71 H. H. Koch in cooperation with Svend Hansen and Finn Nielsen, "Træk af Socialministeriets Arbejde under Besættelsen," in *Centraladministrationen 1848–1948* (Copenhagen: Nyt Nordisk Forlag, 1948), 67.

72 Goldbaum Tarabini Fracapane, *Jews of Denmark*, 125–28.

73 Hans Sode-Madsen, *De Hvide Busser 1941–45* (Copenhagen: Lindhardt og Ringhof, 2015), 122–23, includes a transcript of a document, supposedly a note of February 2–3, 1944, from the Ministry of Foreign Affairs, which refers to information from one of the returned prisoners. Unfortunately, I was unable to locate the original.

74 Phone message from the secretary of the Danish legation, January 19, 1944. Telegram, January 25, 1944, with the same message, both in DNA, UM 120D43/13a.

75 Note, January 22, 1944, signed H. J. Hansen, DNA, UM, 120D43/13a.
76 Note, January 26, 1944, signed Hvass, DNA, UM 120D43/13a.
77 Two letters from Richard Ege, dated January 25, 1944, and two letters from Ruth Bredsdorff, dated February 12, 1944, all in private collections. A letter from Ruth Bredsdorff similar to the two aforementioned documents, but dated February 14, 1944, is found in Randers City Archives, Hartogsohn family papers, A602.
78 Letter from Ruth Bredsdorff to Ellinor and Ingeborg Schultz, March 24, 1944, Royal Danish Library, Acc. 1971/125: Correspondence between Clara Schultz and her daughters from her stay in Theresienstadt 1944–45.
79 Ibid. This is confirmed by comparing the shipment lists of the Fund of 1944 with entries in diaries. Ellen Oppenhejm received her first parcel on April 5, 1944, which had been sent with the last shipment by ordinary post on March 2, 1944. Selfa Diamant, notebook, private: a parcel for her father arrived on April 3, 1944; it had been shipped by the Fund of 1944 on March 22.
80 Lists in DNA, Fund of 1944. By the end of May at least one parcel had been sent to 414 of the deportees from Denmark.
81 Author's interview with Klara Ruben Tixell, March 7, 2008; undated list, AMDR, 30D-10844.49, from August 1944 or later.
82 Comparing names of parcel recipients from the Pels group and the Fund of 1944, it is clear that a number of the Pels parcel recipients continued to receive parcels through the Fund when they began shipping to Danish ghetto inmates.
83 Various testimonies from Danish deportees given in Sweden in April 1945 to the World Jewish Congress, YVA, O.27/20.
84 Two deportees are named twice in the lists; two others were not in Theresienstadt but in Sachsenhausen. A baby born in the ghetto is on the list but had died before the first parcel for her arrived. The lists also include eleven people who in late 1943 were believed to be in Theresienstadt but who had actually arrived in Sweden.
85 Goldbaum Tarabini Fracapane, *Jews of Denmark*, 178–80; Yahil, *Rescue of Danish Jewry*, 295.
86 The numbers used here stem from H. G. Adler, *Theresienstadt 1941–1945: The Face of a Coerced Community* (New York: Cambridge University Press in association with the USHMM, 2017), 33–40.
87 Frants Hvass, Report, 12–13; DNA, Archive of E. Juel Henningsen.
88 The available sources do not make clear on which exact date the Danish Red Cross sent the first food parcels, but the earliest date that figures

in some of the real-time sources was during the first week of September; Salomon Katz, e.g., mentioned their arrival in his diary entry for September 5.

89 Undated list, AMDR, 30D-10844.49, from August 1944 or later.

90 Moritz Oppenhejm, notebook, January–April 1945, JDK, 207X27; Selfa Diamant, notebook.

91 Letter from the Danish Red Cross to the Ministry of Social Affairs, dated August 12, 1944, DNA, Ministry of Social Affairs, office 2, journal no. 880/1943 I.

92 Katz, diary, September 5, 1944.

93 Katz, diary, September 9, 1944.

94 Elias Leiman, Account, Jewish Museum Oslo (JMO) G00158. See also Ralph Oppenhejm, diary, December 14, 1944, JDK 207A35/7.

95 Ralph Oppenhejm, diary, January 14, 1945, JDK 207A35/7; Moritz Oppenhejm, notebook, January 13, 1945, JDK 0207X0027; František Beneš & Patricia Tošnerová, *Pošta v ghettu Terezín* (Prague: Profil, 1996), 224.

96 Katz, diary, January 21, 1945; Ralph Oppenhejm, diary, January 21, 1945, JDK 207A35/7; note signed Friediger, January 20, 1945. I wish to thank Klara Ruben Tixell and Arthur Arnheim, who both gave me a photocopy of the note.

97 Benjamin Murmelstein, "Meine Entsendung nach Theresienstadt . . . ," YVA, O.64/92, 58.

98 Ibid. See also Friediger, *Theresienstadt*, 89, who does not mention the disagreement with Murmelstein.

99 Katz, diary, March 31, 1945; Moritz Oppenhejm, notebook, March 31 and April 6, 1945, JDK 0207X0027.

100 On October 19, 1944, Fritz Lerche received through the Ministry of Foreign Affairs the names of Lieselotte Roeders (née Selinko), her husband Kurt, and their daughter Antoinette, note, in DNA, UM 120D43/13a. The sister of Lieselotte, the author Annemarie Selinko Kristiansen, was Danish by marriage and had lived in Denmark since 1938. She managed to get their names to the Fund of 1944 from Sweden. The Roeders had arrived in Theresienstadt on September 6, 1944, from the Netherlands, but were included in Transport Ev to Auschwitz-Birkenau on October 28, 1944. A first parcel for the family was sent from Copenhagen two days later.

101 About 1,200 Theresienstadt prisoners left for Switzerland on February 5, 1945, as a result of negotiations between former Swiss president

Jean-Marie Musy, who was acting on behalf of Jewish organizations, and Heinrich Himmler, who was willing to exchange Jewish prisoners for money. See H. G. Adler, *Theresienstadt 1941–1945*, 161–62; Yehuda Bauer, *Jews for Sale? Nazi-Jewish Negotiations, 1933–1945* (New Haven: Yale University Press, 1994), 225–31.

102 Diary of Simon Magnus, entries of September 1944; October 11, 1944; December 10, 1944. I am grateful to Anna Hájková for sharing these diary entries with me.

103 Lists in DNA, Fund of 1944.

104 Ibid. The last parcels were sent from Denmark on March 16, 1944.

105 Hermann Silberberg, in a letter written from the quarantine camp in Rosöga (Sweden) on April 24, 1945, nine days after his liberation; copy in my collection.

106 Goldbaum Tarabini Fracapane, *Jews of Denmark*, 88–91. In the spring of 1944, 3 percent of the Danish ghetto inmates had obtained the status of "prominent," while at the same time this was true for only 0.5 percent of the entire ghetto population.

107 For a broader analysis of the stratification and hierarchy in the ghetto, see Anna Hájková, *The Last Ghetto: An Everyday History of Theresienstadt* (Oxford: Oxford University Press, 2020), 59–99.

108 Ralph Oppenhejm, diary, June 29, 1944, JDK 207A35/7. Questionnaire (late 1940s) from Otto Schwarzbart, AMDR, 30C.

109 From March 1944 onward, it was possible to pay for parcels to Danish deportees in Theresienstadt through the Danish Office of Refugees in Stockholm, which organized shipments with a Swedish shipping company. Furthermore, beginning in July 1944, the Swedish Red Cross in cooperation with the Danish legation and the Committee of Support for the Jewish Deportees sent parcels to the deportees from Denmark in Theresienstadt. Folder with notes on the relief provided by the Refugee Office, Collections of the Jewish Community held by Royal Danish Library, MT Add 26; Per Møller & Knud Secher, *Danske Flygtninge i Sverige* (Copenhagen: Nordisk Forlag, 1945), 270; Torben L. Meyer, *Flugten over Øresund* (Copenhagen: Jespersen & Pio, 1945), 201. On the contents of the Swedish parcels, see Ellen Oppenhejm, diary notes; receipts for parcels sent by Julius to Irma Bamberger, AMDR, 30D-10801; Katz, diary, March 6, 1944.

110 Katz, diary, May 9, 1944.

111 Katz, diary, June 6, 1944.

112 Katz, diary, July 2, 1944. As a point of rough comparison, this meant 32 Danish crowns at the time, which amounted to about €92 or $114 in today's values.

113 Elias Leiman, Account, JMO, G00158.

114 Katz, diary, May 11, 1944.

115 Katz, diary, Aug. 19, 1944; the amount would be €16–27 or $19–31 in today's values.

116 Hájková, *Last Ghetto*, 108–17. Hájková argues convincingly that while food rations were not sufficient for a normal food intake, many more people could have survived had the food been divided up differently.

117 In December 1943, the Copenhagen branch of WILPF urged their members to contribute to the relief work for the Jewish deportees. Call signed by Ingeborg Rindung and Thyra Manicus-Hansen, DNA, UM 120D43/13a. In the correspondence between Ruth Bredsdorff and various friends or relatives of the deportees, a number of people mentioned that they wanted to support the initiative financially; they were encouraged to pay the sum they wished directly to the bank account of the Fund of 1944. Letter from Ruth Bredsdorff, May 31, 1944, private collection.

Acknowledgments

The editors wish to thank Gerald J. Steinacher, who offered many valuable suggestions for this project at its inception and has continued to provide welcome infusions of enthusiasm and wisdom along the way. We also thank the Holocaust Educational Foundation at Northwestern University, which gave the contributors an opportunity to discuss their research on this topic intensely in person at its 2018 Lessons and Legacies conference in St. Louis. We thank colleagues and staff at the School of Humanities and Languages, University of New South Wales in Sydney, and the United States Holocaust Memorial Museum in Washington, DC, for their vital support. We are immensely grateful to Annie Martin and the team at Wayne State University Press for their great skill and care in bringing this project into print. Anne Taylor served as a welcome and sensitive copyeditor for this volume. Finally, a number of friends have pushed us along, sharing their insights on this book at critical moments: Benton Arnovitz, Annette Becker, Steven Feldman, Annette Igra, Marion Kaplan, Lisa Peschel, Dan Stone, and particularly Jürgen Matthäus.

Suggested Further Reading

Adler, Eliyana R. *Survival on the Margins: Polish Jewish Refugees in the Wartime Soviet Union*. Cambridge, MA: Harvard University Press, 2020.

Adler, H. G. *Theresienstadt 1941–1945: The Face of a Coerced Community*. New York: Cambridge University Press in association with the USHMM, 2017.

Åmark, Klas. *Att bo granne med ondskan. Sveriges förhållande till nazismen, Nazityskland och Förintelsen*. Stockholm: Bonnier, 2011.

Ancel, Jean. *The History of the Holocaust in Romania*. Lincoln: University of Nebraska Press, 2011.

Bak, Sofie Lene. *Nothing to Speak of: Wartime Experiences of the Danish Jews, 1943–1945*. Copenhagen: Dansk Jødisk Museum, 2011.

Bańkowska, Aleksandra. "Jewish Social Welfare Institutions and Facilities in the General Government from 1939 to 1944: A Preliminary Study." *Studia z Dziejów Rosji i Europy Środkowo-Wschodniej* 53, no. 3 (2018): 129–67.

Bauer, Yehuda. *American Jewry and the Holocaust: The American Joint Distribution Committee, 1939–1945*. Detroit: Wayne State University Press, 1981.

Beaumont, Joan. "Starving for Democracy: Britain's Blockade of and Relief for Occupied Europe, 1939–1945." *War & Society* 8, no. 2 (1990): 57–82.

Beneš, František, and Patricia Tošnerová. *Posta v ghettu Terezin. Die Post im Ghetto Theresienstadt. Mail Service in the Ghetto Terezin. 1941–1945*. Prague: Profil, 1996.

Bernard, Jean-Jacques. *The Camp of Slow Death*. London: V. Gollancz, 1945.

Cohen, Raya. "The Lost Honour of Bystanders? The Case of Jewish Emissaries in Switzerland." In *"Bystanders" to the Holocaust: A Re-evaluation*, ed. David Cesarani and Paul A. Levine, 146–70. London: Frank Cass Publishers, 2002.

Collingham, E. M. *The Taste of War: World War II and the Battle for Food*. London: Allen Lane, 2011.

Dworzecki, Meir. "The International Red Cross and Its Policy vis-à-vis the Jews in Ghettos and Concentration Camps in Nazi-occupied Europe." In *Rescue*

Attempts during the Holocaust: Proceedings of the Second Yad Vashem International Historical Conference, ed. Yisrael Gutman and Efraim Zuroff, 71–107. Jerusalem: "Ahva" Cooperative Press, 1977.

Edele, Mark, and Wanda Warlik. "Saved by Stalin? Trajectories of Polish Jews in the Soviet Second World War." In *Shelter from the Holocaust: Rethinking Jewish Survival in the Soviet Union*, ed. Mark Edele, Sheila Fitzpatrick, and Atina Grossmann. Detroit: Wayne State University Press, 2017.

Eggers, Christian. *Unerwünschte Ausländer. Juden aus Deutschland und Mitteleuropa in französischen Internierungslagern 1940–1942*. Berlin: Metropol, 2002.

Engel, David. "Who Is a Collaborator? The Trials of Michał Weichert." In *The Jews in Poland*, ed. Sławomir Kapralski, 2:339–70. Kraków: Jagellonian University, 1999.

Engelking Barbara, and Jacek Leociak. *The Warsaw Ghetto: A Guide to the Perished City*. New Haven: Yale University Press, 2009.

Erbelding, Rebecca. *Rescue Board: The Untold Story of America's Efforts to Save the Jews of Europe*. New York: Doubleday, 2018.

Farré, Sébastien. *Colis de guerre: Secours alimentaire et organisations humanitaires (1914–1947)*. Rennes: Presses Universitaire de Rennes, 2014.

———. "The ICRC and the Detainees in Nazi Concentration Camps (1942–1945)." In *International Review of the Red Cross* 94 (winter 2012): 1381–408.

Favez, Jean-Claude. *The Red Cross and the Holocaust*. Cambridge: Cambridge University Press, 1999.

Forsythe, David P. *The Humanitarians: The International Committee of the Red Cross*. Cambridge: Cambridge University Press, 2005.

Fracapane, Silvia Goldbaum Tarabini. *The Jews of Denmark in the Holocaust: Life and Death in Theresienstadt Ghetto*. London: Routledge, 2021.

Garbarini, Alexandra, with Emil Kerenji, Jan Lambertz, and Avinoam Patt. *Jewish Responses to Persecution: Volume II, 1938–1940*. Lanham, MD: AltaMira Press in association with the USHMM, 2011.

Geissbühler, Simon, ed. *Romania and the Holocaust: Events, Context, Aftermath*. Stuttgart: Ibidem Verlag, 2016.

Grossmann, Atina. "Remapping Relief and Rescue: Flight, Displacement, and International Aid for Jewish Refugees during World War II." *New German Critique* 39, no. 3 (117) (2012): 61–79.

Grynberg, Anne. *Les camps de la honte. Les internés juifs des camps français 1939–1944*. Paris: La Découverte, 1991.

Hansson, Svante. *Flykt och överlevnad. Flyktingverksamhet i Mosaiska Församlingen i Stockholm 1933–1950*. Stockholm: Hillel, 2004.

Heuman, Johannes, and Pontus Rudberg, eds. *Early Holocaust Memory in Sweden: Archives, Testimonies and Reflections*. Cham: Palgrave Macmillan, 2021.

Hindley, Meredith. "Blockade before Bread: Allied Relief for Nazi Europe, 1939–1945." PhD diss., American University, 2007.

———. "Constructing Allied Humanitarian Policy." *Journal of Holocaust Education* 9, no. 2 (2000): 77–102.

Jockusch, Laura, and Gabriel N. Finder, eds. *Jewish Honor Courts: Revenge, Retribution, and Reconciliation in Europe and Israel after the Holocaust*. Detroit: Wayne State University Press, 2015.

Joly, Laurent. *Vichy dans la "Solution finale." Histoire du commissariat général aux questions juives (1941–1944)*. Paris: Grasset & Fasquelle, 2006.

Kaplan, Chaim A. *Scroll of Agony: The Warsaw Diary of Chaim A. Kaplan*. Bloomington: Indiana University Press, 1999.

Kassow, Samuel D. *Who Will Write Our History? Rediscovering a Hidden Archive from the Warsaw Ghetto*. Bloomington: Indiana University Press, 2007.

Láníček, Jan. *Arnošt Frischer and the Jewish Politics of Early 20th-Century Europe*. London: Bloomsbury, 2017.

Lazare, Lucien. *Rescue as Resistance: How Jewish Organizations Fought the Holocaust in France*. New York: Columbia University Press, 1996.

Le Crom, Jean-Pierre. *Au secours, Maréchal! L'instrumentalisation de l'humanitaire (1940–1944)*. Paris: Presses Universitaires de France, 2013.

Lomfors, Ingrid. *Blind fläck. Minne och glömska kring svenska Röda korsets hjälpinsats i Nazityskland 1945*. Stockholm: Atlantis 2005.

Matthäus, Jürgen. *Predicting the Holocaust: Jewish Organizations Report from Geneva on the Emergence of the "Final Solution," 1939–1942*. Lanham, MD: Rowman & Littlefield in association with the USHMM, 2019.

Matthäus, Jürgen, with Emil Kerenji, Jan Lambertz, and Leah Wolfson. *Jewish Responses to Persecution: Volume III, 1941–1942*. Lanham, MD: AltaMira Press in association with the USHMM, 2013.

Milgram, Avraham. *Portugal, Salazar and the Jews*. Jerusalem: Yad Vashem Publications, 2011.

Mitsel, Mikhail. "American Jewish Joint Distribution Committee Programs in the USSR, 1941–1948: A Complicated Partnership." In *The JDC at 100: A Century of Humanitarianism*, ed. Avinoam Patt, Atina Grossmann, Linda G. Levi, and Maud S. Mandel. Detroit: Wayne State University Press, 2019.

Morgenbrod, Birgitt, and Stephanie Merkenich. *Das Deutsche Rote Kreuz unter der NS-Diktatur 1933–1945*. Paderborn: Schöningh, 2008.

Mouré, Kenneth. "Food Rationing and the Black Market in France (1940–1944)." *French History* 24, no. 2 (2010).

Musiał, Bogdan. *Deutsche Zivilverwaltung und Judenverfolgung im Generalgouvernement. Eine Fallstudie zum Distrikt Lublin 1939–1944*. Wiesbaden: Harrassowitz, 1999.

Patt, Avinoam, Atina Grossmann, Linda G. Levi, and Maud S. Mandel, eds. *JDC at 100: A Century of Humanitarianism*. Detroit: Wayne State University Press, 2019.

Person, Katarzyna. "'I Sometimes Think That I Grew Up on a Different Planet': The Assimilated Jewish Community of the Warsaw Ghetto in the Letters of Wanda Lubelska and Hala Szwambaum." In *Who Is a Jew? Reflections on History, Religion, and Culture*, ed. Leonard Greenspoon, 257–66. Purdue: Purdue University Press, 2014.

Peschanski, Denis. *La France des camps—L'internement (1938–1946)*. Paris: Gallimard, 2002.

Picard, Jacques. *Die Schweiz und die Juden 1933–1945*. 2nd ed. Zurich: Chronos Verlag, 1994.

Poznanski, Renée. *Jews in France during World War II*. Waltham, MA: Brandeis University Press in association with the USHMM, 2001.

Poznanski, Renée, Denis Peschanski, and Benoît Pouvreau. *Drancy. Un Camp de France*. Paris: Fayard, 2015.

Rajsfus, Maurice. *Drancy. Un camp des concentration très ordinaire, 1941–1944*. Paris: Le Cherche Midi Èditeur, 1996.

Rayski, Adam. *The Choice of the Jews under Vichy: Between Submission and Resistance*. Notre Dame: University of Notre Dame Press in association with the USHMM, 2015.

Riegner, Gerhart M. *Never Despair: Sixty Years in the Service of the Jewish People and the Cause of Human Rights*. Chicago: Ivan R. Dee in association with the USHMM, 2006.

Rosen, Sarah. "Surviving in the Murafa Ghetto: A Case Study of One Ghetto in Transnistria." *Holocaust Studies: A Journal of Culture and History* 16, nos. 1–2 (2010): 157–76.

Rudberg, Pontus. *The Swedish Jews and the Holocaust*. New York: Routledge, 2017.

Sakowska, Ruta. "Łączność pocztowa warszawskiego getta." *Biuletyn Żydowskiego Instytutu Historycznego*, nos. 45–46 (1963): 94–109.

Segev, Zohar. *The World Jewish Congress during the Holocaust: Between Activism and Restraint*. Berlin: De Gruyter Oldenbourg, 2014.

Siperco, Andrei, ed. *Actiunea internationala de ajutorare a evreilor din Romania. Documente, 1943–1945*. Bucharest: Hasefer, 2003.

Steinacher, Gerald. *Humanitarians at War: The Red Cross in the Shadow of the Holocaust*. Oxford: Oxford University Press, 2017.

Sword, Keith. "The Welfare of Polish-Jewish Refugees in the USSR, 1941–43: Relief Supplies and Their Destination." In *Jews in Eastern Poland and the USSR, 1939–46*, ed. Norman Davies and Antony Polonsky. New York: St. Martin's Press, 1991.

Tibon, Gali. "Am I My Brother's Keeper? The Jewish Committees in the Ghettos of Moghilev Province and the Romanian Regime in Transnistria during the Holocaust, 1941–1944." *Dapim: Studies on the Holocaust* 30, no. 2 (2016): 93–116.

von Bueltzingsloewen, Isabelle. *"Morts d'inanition": Famine et exclusions en France sous l'Occupation*. Rennes: Presses Universitaires de Rennes, 2005.

Weinreb, Alice. *Modern Hungers: Food and Power in Twentieth-Century Germany*. Oxford: Oxford University Press, 2017.

Wieviorka, Annette, and Michel Laffitte. *À l'intérieur du camp de Drancy*. Paris: Perrin, 2012.

Yahil, Leni. *The Rescue of Danish Jewry: Test of a Democracy*. Philadelphia: Jewish Publication Society of America, 1969.

Zweig, Ronald W. "Feeding the Camps: Allied Blockade Policy and the Relief of Concentration Camps in Germany, 1944–1945." The *Historical Journal* 41, no. 3 (1998): 825–51.

Contributors

ELIYANA R. ADLER is associate professor of history and Jewish studies at Penn State University. Her most recent publication is *Survival on the Margins: Polish Jewish Refugees in the Wartime Soviet Union* (2020), and she is currently researching the history of East European Jewish memorial books.

LAURIE A. DRAKE recently completed her PhD in history from the University of Toronto. Her dissertation, "Feeding France's Outcasts: Rationing in Vichy's Internment Camps, 1940–1944," examined Vichy's role in creating the hunger crisis that unfolded in its internment camps.

REBECCA ERBELDING is a historian in Education Initiatives at the Levine Institute for Holocaust Education at the United States Holocaust Memorial Museum. She received her PhD in history from George Mason University and is the author of *Rescue Board: The Untold Story of America's Efforts to Save the Jews of Europe*, which won the 2018 JDC-Herbert Katzki National Jewish Book Award for Excellence in Writing Based on Archival Research.

SILVIA GOLDBAUM TARABINI FRACAPANE is a historian of modern Europe and an independent scholar. She has written extensively about Danish Jews during World War II, including her recent book *The Jews of Denmark in the Holocaust: Life and Death in Theresienstadt Ghetto* (2021).

STEFAN CRISTIAN IONESCU is currently a Theodore Zev and Alice R. Weiss-Holocaust Educational Foundation Visiting Associate Professor in Holocaust studies at Northwestern University. He is the author of recent articles in *Holocaust and Genocide Studies*, *Nationalities Papers*, the *Journal of Genocide Research*, *Holocaust Studies*, *Yad Vashem Studies*, and the *Journal of Romanian Studies*. His book *Jewish Resistance to Romanianization: 1940–1944* appeared in 2015.

Alicja Jarkowska is the author of a book on Jewish collaboration in occupied Kraków (2018) and the editor of two books in a series of document collections based on the Ringelblum Archive. She is a research fellow in the Department of Modern Polish History at Jagiellonian University and has published widely on the history of the Holocaust and the Jewish underground during World War II.

Jan Lambertz serves as an applied researcher at the Jack, Joseph and Morton Mandel Center for Advanced Holocaust Studies at the United States Holocaust Memorial Museum. She has published several studies of Jewish responses to persecution during the Nazi era and early postwar knowledge about the Holocaust. Her recent articles have appeared in *Medaon*, *German History*, and *Patterns of Prejudice*.

Jan Láníček is associate professor in modern European and Jewish history at the University of New South Wales in Sydney, Australia. His recent books include *Arnošt Frischer and the Jewish Politics of Early 20th-Century Europe* (2017), *The Jew in Czech and Slovak Imagination, 1938–89: Antisemitism, the Holocaust, and Zionism* (with Hana Kubátová, 2018), and *Czechs, Slovaks and the Jews, 1938–1948* (2013). He is currently completing a study of post-Holocaust reconciliation in Czechoslovakia and working on a project that analyzes responses to the Holocaust in Australia.

Anne Lepper is the representative of Yad Vashem's International School for Holocaust Studies in German-speaking countries. She also serves as a staff member of the Bildungswerk Stanisław Hantz and has organized several educational initiatives on the history of Nazi killing sites in Poland and other countries. She is a coeditor of *Fotos aus Sobibor. Die Niemann-Sammlung zu Holocaust und Nationalsozialismus* (2020) and has written widely about wartime Jewish aid networks.

Katarzyna Person received her PhD from the University of London and her *habilitacja* from the Polish Academy of Science. She works in the Jewish Historical Institute in Warsaw, where she leads the Ringelblum Archive publishing project. She has published on the Holocaust and its aftermath in occupied Poland. Her most recent book is *Warsaw Ghetto Police: The Jewish Order Service during the Nazi Occupation* (2021).

Pontus Rudberg is a historian and researcher in the fields of modern Jewish history and Holocaust studies at the Hugo Valentin Centre, Uppsala University, in Sweden. He is the author of *The Swedish Jews and the Holocaust* (2017) and coeditor of *Early Holocaust Memory in Sweden: Archives, Testimonies, Reflections* (2021). He also serves as a consultant to the Jewish Museum of Stockholm.

Gerald J. Steinacher is the James A. Rawley Professor of History at the University of Nebraska–Lincoln. His research focuses on twentieth-century European history, and he has published widely on the Holocaust, national socialism, and Italian fascism. His recent books include *Humanitarians at War: The Red Cross in the Shadow of the Holocaust* (2017) and *Nazis on the Run: How Hitler's Henchmen Fled Justice* (2011), which won a National Jewish Book Award from the Jewish Book Council.

Index

CPSIA information can be obtained
at www.ICGtesting.com
Printed in the USA
LVHW030236250522
719632LV00004B/80